Java

software solutions

for AP Computer Science

Java™

software solutions

for AP* Computer Science

JOHN LEWIS

WILLIAM LOFTUS

CARA COCKING

Addison
Wesley

Boston San Francisco New York
London Toronto Sydney Tokyo Singapore Madrid
Mexico City Munich Paris Cape Town Hong Kong Montreal

Executive Editor	Susan Hartman Sullivan
Assistant Editor	Elizabeth Paquin
Executive Marketing Manager	Michael Hirsch
Associate Managing Editor	Pat Mahtani
Project Management	Argosy Publishing
Copyeditor	Carol Noble
Proofreader	Kim Cofer
Composition and Art	Argosy Publishing
Interior and Cover Design	Joyce Cosentino Wells
Prepress and Manufacturing	Caroline Fell

Access the latest information about Addison-Wesley titles from our World Wide Web site: http://www.aw.com/cs

Library of Congress Cataloging-in-Publication Data

Lewis, John, Ph.D.

Java software solutions for AP computer science : foundations for program design / John Lewis, William Loftus, Cara Cocking.

p. cm.

ISBN 0-201-88259-0

1. Java (Computer program language) 2. Electronic data processing--Study and teaching (Secondary) I. Loftus, William. II. Cocking, Cara. III. Title.

QA76.73.J38L4885 2003

005.13'3—dc21   2002043863

ISBN 0-201-88259-0

45678910-QWT-0403

This book is dedicated to our families.

Sharon, Justin, and Kayla Lewis
—J.L.

Veena, Isaac, and Dévi Loftus
—W.L.

To my parents
—C.L.C.

Welcome to Java Software Solutions for AP* Computer Science. Specifically designed for beginning programmers, this Advanced Placement book matches the AP Computer Science topic outline and Java subset set forth by the College Board.

what's in this AP* book

This book has been specifically designed to meet the needs of today's AP students and faculty. Let's hit the highlights. Specifically:

- This book is designed for both the A and AB exam by identifying what material is required for each exam.

- We have developed and implemented a case study (called Bumper Cars) modeled after the one on the exam and broken up into chapter-specific sections in order to facilitate its use throughout the course.

- The discussion and examples fully embrace the Java 2 Version 1.4 Standard Edition and are backward-compatible with previous revisions.

- We utilize hundreds of example programs, fully implemented for students and faculty to experiment with.

- Graphics are covered in an optional section (called Graphics Track) at the end of each chapter. Building on the excitement of the web, the Graphics Track is intended to further inspire and engage students.

- The Self-Review Questions, Exercises, and Programming Projects have been specifically designed to adhere to various learning styles, including multiple choice, true/false, and short answer questions.

- The reference material in the appendices includes: Glossary, Unicode Character Set, Java Operators, and the AP Java Class Library.

- A robust supplements package accompanies this book and is outlined further in the preface.

- The full-color design aids learning by making it easier to distinguish between various elements in code and diagrams. Full-color screen shots make the discussions of graphical interfaces more insightful and realistic.

cornerstones of the text

This text is based on the following basic ideas that we believe make for a sound introductory text.

> **True object-orientation.** A text that really teaches a solid object-oriented approach must use what we call object-speak. That is, all processing should be discussed in object-oriented terms. That does not mean, however, that the first program a student sees must discuss the writing of multiple classes and methods. A student should learn to use objects before learning to write them. This text uses a natural progression that culminates in the ability to design real object-oriented solutions.

> **Sound programming practices.** Students should not be taught how to program; they should be taught how to write good software. There's a difference. Writing software is not a set of cookbook actions, and a good program is more than a collection of statements. This text integrates practices that serve as the foundation of good programming skills. These practices are used in all examples and are reinforced in the discussions. Students learn how to solve problems as well as how to implement solutions. We introduce and integrate basic software engineering techniques throughout the text.

> **Examples.** Students learn by example. This text is filled with fully implemented examples that demonstrate specific concepts. We have intertwined small, readily understandable examples with larger, more realistic ones. There is a balance between graphics and nongraphical programs and between applets and applications. Additional examples can be found on the book's Web site.

> **Graphics and GUIs.** Graphics can be a great motivator for students, and their use can serve as excellent examples of object-orientation. As such, we use them throughout the text in a well-defined set of sections that we call the Graphics Track. This coverage includes the use of event processing and graphical user interfaces (GUIs). Students learn to build GUIs in the appropriate way by using a natural progression of topics. The Graphics Track can be avoided entirely for those who do not choose to use graphics.

chapter breakdown

Chapter 1 (Computer Systems) introduces computer systems in general, including basic architecture and hardware, networking, programming, and language translation. Java is introduced in this chapter, and the basics of program development are discussed. This chapter contains broad introductory material that can be covered while students become familiar with their development environment.

Chapter 2 (Objects and Primitive Data) establishes the concept of objects and how they can be used. Many predefined classes from the Java standard library are explored and used, as well as the `Keyboard` class provided by the textbook authors. Primitive types, operators, and expressions are also explored.

Chapter 3 (Program Statements) covers most of the fundamental statements including conditionals and loops. Some additional operators are introduced at this point as well. Establishing key statements at this point allows the classes of the next chapter to be fully functional and realistic.

Chapter 4 (Writing Classes) explores issues related to writing classes and methods. Topics include instance data, visibility, scope, method parameters, and return types. Method overloading is covered as well. Some of the more involved topics are deferred to or revisited in Chapter 5. The key to Chapter 4 is the many fully implemented, realistic classes that are presented as examples of class design.

Chapter 5 (Enhancing Classes) covers additional issues related to class design and revisits topics that need further exploration. Object references are revisited and carefully explored, and their impact on parameter passing is discussed. Exceptions, interfaces, and their effect on design are also covered.

Chapter 6 (Arrays) contains extensive coverage of arrays and array processing. Topics include multidimensional arrays, searching, and sorting. The `ArrayList` class is explored as well.

Chapter 7 (Inheritance) covers class derivations and associated concepts such as class hierarchies, overriding, and polymorphism. Emphasis is put on the proper use of inheritance and its role in software design.

Chapter 8 (Recursion) covers the concept, implementation, and proper use of recursion. Several examples from various domains are used to demonstrate how recursive techniques make certain types of processing elegant. Recursive sorting algorithms are also covered.

Chapter 9 (Data Structures) introduces the idea of a collection and its underlying data structure. Abstraction is revisited in this context and the linked list, queue, and stack data structures are explored.

Chapter 10 (Data Structures II) further explores dynamic data structures, including trees and heaps. Sets and maps are also introduced and hashtables are revisited.

supplements

Students are welcome to visit *www.aw.com/APjava* for the following resources.

▸ **Source Code** to all program examples in the text.

The following supplements are available on-line for qualified instructors only. Please visit online *www.aw.com/APjava* or contact your representative for information. You can find your rep in the "rep locator" section at *www.phschool.com.*

▸ **Instructor's Manual (ISBN: 0-321-18076-3)**—includes Lesson Plans, Test Bank, Solutions, and Transparency Masters.

▸ **Solutions**—includes solutions to all exercises and programming projects.

▸ **Test Bank**—includes a wealth of free response, multiple choice, and true/false type questions.

▸ **Lab Manual**—lab exercises are designed to accompany the topic progression in the text.

▸ **PowerPoint Slides**—lecture notes to accompany the text.

▸ **Transparency Masters**—slides of the figures from the book.

acknowledgments

We are most grateful to the faculty and students from around the world who have provided their feedback on previous editions of this book. We are pleased to see the depth of the faculty's concern for their students and the students' thirst for knowledge. Your comments and questions are always welcome.

Susan Hartman Sullivan, Emily Genaway, and Elizabeth Paquin, our editors at Addison-Wesley, went above and beyond the call of duty to ensure that the book met the highest quality standards. Their support and enthusiasm are greatly appreciated. We are also grateful to Michael Hirsch and his assistant Lesly Hershman for making sure that instructors understand the pedagogical advantages of this text. The devotion that the Addison-Wesley folks show to their books is evident in the high-quality results.

The production team for this edition is a group of gifted and hard-working people—miracle workers all. Thanks go to Patty Mahtani, Joyce Wells (for the wonderful cover), Daniel Rausch, and Sally Boylan. The quality of the book is due largely to their personal attention, and it is greatly appreciated.

Special thanks go to Robert Burton of Brigham Young University, who served as a special and dedicated technical reviewer of the evolving content for the third edition. His insight was invaluable, as was his patience, professionalism, energy, speed, and thoroughness.

Special thanks also go to the following members of the AP community who offered valuable feedback during the development of this book:

Jenka Guevara	American School Foundation, Mexico City
Leigh Ann Sudol	Fox Lane High School/New York University, NY
Kathleen Weaver	Hillcrest High School, Dallas, TX
John E. Hanna	Teaneck High School, NJ
Brian G. Scarbeau	Lake Highland Preparatory School, FL
Frances Caruso Wolanczyk	Fieldston School, NY
Mark Hanington	Punahou School, Honolulu, HI
Rose M. Hoffman	Catholic Memorial High School, Waukesha, WI
Kathleen Larson	Kingston High School, Kingston, NY

The reviewers of previous editions of this text, as well as many other instructors and friends, have provided valuable feedback as well. They include Lewis Barnett, University of Richmond; Tom Bennet, Mississippi College; Gian Mario Besana, DePaul University; Hans-Peter Bischof, Rochester Institute of Technology; Robert Burton, Brigham Young University; James Cross, Auburn University; Eman El-Sheikh, University of West Florida; John Gauch, University of Kansas; Chris Haynes, Indiana University; Laurie Hendren, McGill University; Mike Higgs, Austin College; Karen Kluge, Dartmouth College; Jason Levy, University of Hawaii; Peter MacKenzie, McGill University; Blayne Mayfield, Oklahoma State University; Lawrence Osborne, Lamar University; Barry Pollack, City College of San Francisco; B. Ravikumar, University of Rhode Island; David Riley, University of Wisconsin (La Crosse); Jerry Ross, Lane Community College; Carolyn Schauble, Colorado State University; Arjit Sengupta, Georgia State University; Vijay Srinivasan, JavaSoft, Sun Microsystems, Inc.; Katherine St. John, Lehman College, CUNY; Ed Timmerman, University of Maryland, University College; Shengru Tu, University of New Orleans; Paul Tymann, Rochester Institute of Technology; John J. Wegis, JavaSoft, Sun Microsystems, Inc.; Linda Wilson, Dartmouth College; David Wittenberg, Brandeis University; Wang-Chan Wong, California State University (Dominguez Hills).

Thanks also go to our colleagues at Villanova University and Marquette University who have provided so much wonderful feedback. They include Bob Beck, Paul Gormley, Cathy Helwig, Dan Joyce, Najib Nadi, Beth Taddei, and Barbara Zimmerman; and John Simms and Marian Manyo.

Special thanks go to Pete DePasquale, currently working on his doctorate at Virginia Tech, for the original Java Class Library appendix. His interest in pedagogy is a joy to see. Pete will soon be a member of the faculty at some college or university; that school, and their students, will be lucky to have him.

Many other people have helped in various ways. They include Ken Arnold, Kevin Henry, John Loftus, Sammy Perugini, and Joshua Yanchar. Our apologies to anyone we may have forgotten.

The ACM Special Interest Group on Computer Science Education (SIGCSE) is a tremendous resource. Their conferences provide an opportunity for educators from all levels and all types of schools to share ideas and materials. If you are an educator in any area of computing and are not involved with SIGCSE, you're missing out.

Most importantly, we thank our families for their support and patience. They put up with more than they should have to during the busy process of writing, not to mention the other times.

feature walkthrough

Key Concepts. Throughout the text, the Key Concept boxes highlight fundamental ideas and important guidelines. These concepts are summarized at the end of each chapter.

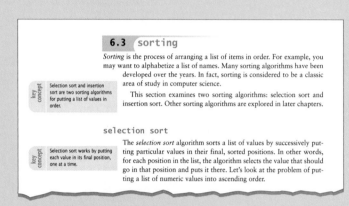

6.3 sorting

Sorting is the process of arranging a list of items in order. For example, you may want to alphabetize a list of names. Many sorting algorithms have been developed over the years. In fact, sorting is considered to be a classic area of study in computer science.

> **key concept**
> Selection sort and insertion sort are two sorting algorithms for putting a list of values in order.

This section examines two sorting algorithms: selection sort and insertion sort. Other sorting algorithms are explored in later chapters.

selection sort

> **key concept**
> Selection sort works by putting each value in its final position, one at a time.

The *selection sort* algorithm sorts a list of values by successively putting particular values in their final, sorted positions. In other words, for each position in the list, the algorithm selects the value that should go in that position and puts it there. Let's look at the problem of putting a list of numeric values into ascending order.

```
listing
 4.4

//********************************************************************
//  Banking.java        Author: Lewis/Loftus
//
//  Driver to exercise the use of multiple Account objects.
//********************************************************************

public class Banking
{
   //-----------------------------------------------------------------
   //  Creates some bank accounts and requests various services.
   //-----------------------------------------------------------------
   public static void main (String[] args)
   {
      Account acct1 = new Account ("Ted Murphy", 72354, 102.56);
      Account acct2 = new Account ("Jane Smith", 69713, 40.00);
      Account acct3 = new Account ("Edward Demsey", 93757, 759.32);

      acct1.deposit (25.85);

      double smithBalance = acct2.deposit (500.00);
      System.out.println ("Smith balance after deposit: " +
                          smithBalance);

      System.out.println ("Smith balance after withdrawal: " +
                          acct2.withdraw (430.75, 1.50));

      acct3.withdraw (800.00, 0.0);  // exceeds balance

      acct1.addInterest();
      acct2.addInterest();
      acct3.addInterest();

      System.out.println ();
      System.out.println (acct1);
      System.out.println (acct2);
      System.out.println (acct3);
   }
}
```

Listings. All programming examples are presented in clearly labeled listings, followed by the program output, a sample run, or screen shot display as appropriate. The code is colored to visually distinguish comments and reserved words.

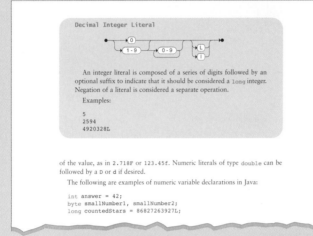

Decimal Integer Literal

An integer literal is composed of a series of digits followed by an optional suffix to indicate that it should be considered a `long` integer. Negation of a literal is considered a separate operation.

Examples:

```
5
2594
4920328L
```

of the value, as in `2.718F` or `123.45f`. Numeric literals of type `double` can be followed by a `D` or `d` if desired.

The following are examples of numeric variable declarations in Java:

```
int answer = 42;
byte smallNumber1, smallNumber2;
long countedStars = 86827263927L;
```

Syntax Diagrams. At appropriate points in the text, syntactic elements of the Java language are discussed in special highlighted sections with diagrams that clearly identify the valid forms for a statement or construct.

Graphics Track. All processing that involves graphics and graphical user interfaces is discussed in one or two sections at the end of each chapter that we collectively refer to as the Graphics Track. This material can be skipped without loss of continuity, or focused on specifically as desired. The material in any Graphics Track section relates to the main topics of the chapter in which it is found. Graphics Track sections are indicated by a patterned border on the edge of the page.

GRAPHICS TRACK

3.9 drawing using conditionals and loops

Conditionals and loops can help us create interesting graphics.

The program called `Bullseye`, shown in Listing 3.15, uses a loop to draw the rings of a target. The `Bullseye` program uses an `if` statement to alternate the colors between black and white. Each ring is drawn as a filled circle (an oval of equal width and length). Because we draw the circles on top of each other, the inner circles cover the inner part of the larger circles, so they look like rings. At the end, a final red circle is drawn for the bull's-eye.

Listing 3.16 shows the `Boxes` applet, in which several randomly sized rectangles are drawn in random locations. If the width of a rectangle is less than 5 pixels, the box is filled with the color yellow. If the height is less than 5 pixels, the box is filled with the color green. Otherwise, the box is drawn, unfilled, in white.

Case Study. The case study applies concepts from the text to the design and implementation of a large program (that of simulating the game of bumper cars). Broken up into chapter-specific sections, the case study can be used as an ongoing project throughout the course.

AP CASE STUDY

3.8 bumper cars case study: introduction

This section begins a case study that is spread over Chapters 3 through 8. In this case study we describe a solution to a programming problem. The problem is presented and the design and implementation of the solution are described in detail. Looking at case studies is a way for beginning programmers to learn.

Throughout the case study there will be questions and exercises. These give you a chance to stop and think about the issues that come up in large programming projects. Often there is more than one good solution to a problem, and the solutions chosen in this case study are not the only correct ones.

summary of key concepts

- Software requirements tell us *what* a program must do.
- A software design tells us *how* a program will fill its requirements.
- An algorithm is a step-by-step process for solving a problem, often written in pseudocode.
- Implementation should be the least creative of all development activities.
- The goal of testing is to find errors. We can never really be sure that all errors have been found.
- Conditionals and loops let us control the flow of execution through a method.
- An if statement lets a program choose whether to execute a particular statement.
- The compiler does not care about indentation. Indentation is important for human readers because it shows the relationship between one statement and another.
- An if-else statement lets a program do one thing if a condition is true and another thing if the condition is false.
- In a nested if statement, an else clause is matched to the closest unmatched if.
- Logical operators return a boolean value (true or false) and are often used for sophisticated conditions.
- The order of characters in Java is defined by the Unicode character set.
- The compareTo method determines the lexicographic order of strings, which is not necessarily alphabetical order.

Summary of Key Concepts. The Key Concepts presented throughout a chapter are summarized at the end of the chapter.

self-review questions

3.1   Name the four basic activities that are involved in a software development process.

3.2   What is an algorithm? What is pseudocode?

3.3   What is meant by the flow of control through a program?

3.4   What type of conditions are conditionals and loops based on?

3.5   What are the equality operators? The relational operators?

answers to self-review questions

3.1   The four basic activities in software development are requirements analysis (deciding what the program should do), design (deciding how to do it), implementation (writing the solution in source code), and testing (validating the implementation).

3.2   An algorithm is a step-by-step process that describes the solution to a problem. Every program can be described in algorithmic terms. An

Self-Review Questions and Answers. These short-answer questions review the fundamental ideas and terms established in the chapter. They are designed to allow students to assess their own basic grasp of the material. The answers to these questions can be found at the end of the problem sets.

Exercises. The multiple choice, true/false, and short answer exercises at the end of every chapter are designed to develop and test the students' knowledge of that chapter's material. These exercises generally do not require the use of a computer.

short answer

7.1   Draw an inheritance hierarchy containing classes that represent different types of clocks. Show the variables and method names for two of these classes.

7.2   Show another diagram for the hierarchy in Exercise 7.1. Explain why it may be better or worse than the original.

7.3   Draw a class hierarchy for types of teachers at a high school. Show what characteristics would be represented in the various classes of the hierarchy. Explain how polymorphism could play a role in assigning courses to each teacher.

7.4   Experiment with a simple is-a relationship between two classes. Put println statements in constructors of both the parent and child classes. Do not call the constructor of the parent in the child. What happens? Why? Change the child's constructor to call the constructor of the parent. Now what happens?

programming projects

8.1   Design and implement a recursive version of the PalindromeTester program from (Listing 3.X) Chapter 3.

8.2   Design and implement a program for finding the greatest common divisor of two positive numbers using Euclid's algorithm. The greatest common divisor is the largest number that divides both numbers without producing a remainder. An iterative version of this method was part of the Rational class presented in Chapter 4. In a class called DivisorCalc, define a static method called gcd that accepts two integers, num1 and num2. Create a driver to test your implementation. The recursive algorithm is defined as follows:

a. gcd (num1, num2) is num2 if num2 <= num1 and num2 divides num1

b. gcd (num1, num2) is gcd (num2, num1) if num1 < num2

c. gcd (num1, num2) is gcd (num2, num1%num2) otherwise

Programming Projects. These problems require the design and implementation of Java programs. They vary widely in level of difficulty.

contents

This book is about writing well-designed software. To understand software, we must first understand its role in a computer system. Hardware and software work together in a computer system to accomplish complex tasks. Furthermore, computer networks have changed how computers are used, and they now play a key role in even basic software development. This chapter explores a broad range of computing issues, laying the foundation for the study of software development.

chapter objectives

▶ Describe the relationship between hardware and software.

▶ Define various types of software and how they are used.

▶ Identify basic computer hardware and explain what it does.

▶ Explain how the hardware components execute programs and manage data.

▶ Describe how computers are connected together into networks to share information.

▶ Explain the importance of the Internet and the World Wide Web.

▶ Introduce the Java programming language.

▶ Describe the steps involved in program compilation and execution.

▶ Introduce graphics and their representations.

1.0   introduction

We begin our exploration of computer systems with an overview of computer processing, defining some basic terminology and showing how the key pieces of a computer system work together.

basic computer processing

A computer system is made up of hardware and software. The *hardware* components of a computer system are the physical pieces. They include chips, boxes, wires, keyboards, speakers, disks, cables, plugs, printers, mice, monitors, and so on. If you can physically touch it and it can be considered part of a computer system, then it is computer hardware.

> **key concept**
>
> A computer system consists of hardware and software that work together to help us solve problems.

The hardware components of a computer are useless without instructions to tell them what to do. A *program* is a series of instructions that the hardware executes one after another. *Software* includes programs and the data those programs use. Together hardware and software form a tool that we can use to solve problems.

The key hardware components in a computer system are:

- central processing unit (CPU)
- input/output (I/O) devices
- main memory
- secondary memory devices

Each of these hardware components is described in detail in the next section. For now, let's simply examine their basic roles. The *central processing unit* (CPU) is the device that executes the individual commands of a program. *Input/output* (I/O) *devices,* such as the keyboard, mouse, and monitor, allow a person to interact with the computer.

Programs and data are held in storage devices called memory, which fall into two categories: main memory and secondary memory. *Main memory* holds the software while it is being processed by the CPU. *Secondary memory* stores software more or less forever—until it is deliberately erased. The most important secondary memory device of a typical computer system is the hard disk, which is inside the main computer box. A floppy disk is like a hard disk, but it cannot store nearly as much information as a hard disk. Floppy disks are portable. That is, they can be removed or moved from computer to computer as needed. Other portable secondary memory devices include zip disks and compact discs (CDs).

Figure 1.1 shows how information moves among the basic hardware parts of a computer. Suppose you have a program you wish to run. The program is stored on some secondary memory device, such as a hard disk. When you tell the computer to execute your program, a copy of the program is brought in from secondary memory and stored in main memory. The CPU reads the program instructions from main memory. The CPU then executes the instructions one at a time until the program ends. The data that the instructions use, such as two numbers that will be added together, are also stored in main memory. They are either brought in from secondary memory or read from an input device such as the keyboard. During execution, the program may display information to an output device such as a monitor.

The process of executing a program is basic to the operation of a computer. All computer systems work in about the same way.

software categories

There are many types of software. At this point we will simply look at system programs and application programs.

The *operating system* is the main software of a computer. It does two things. First, it provides a *user interface* that allows the user to interact with the machine: to click on an icon, for example, or delete a file. Second, the operating system manages computer resources such as the CPU and main memory. It decides when programs can run, where they are loaded into memory, and how hardware devices communicate. It is the operating system's job to make the computer easy to use and to keep it running well.

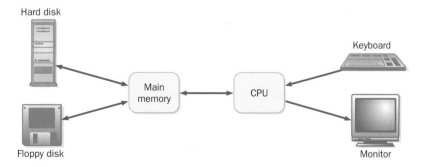

figure 1.1   A simplified view of a computer system

Several popular operating systems are in use today. Windows 98, Windows NT, Windows 2000, and Windows XP are versions of the operating system developed by Microsoft for personal computers. Versions of the Unix operating system are also quite popular, such as Linux. Mac OS is the operating system used on Apple computers.

An *application* is just about any software other than the operating system. Word processors, missile control systems, database managers, Web browsers, and games are all application programs. Each application program has its own user interface that allows the user to interact with that particular program.

The user interface for most modern operating systems and applications is a *graphical user interface* (GUI), which uses graphical screen elements. These elements include:

 ▸ *windows,* which are used to separate the screen into distinct work areas

 ▸ *icons,* which are small images that represent computer resources, such as a file

 ▸ *pull-down menus,* which give the user a list of options

 ▸ *scroll bars,* which let the user move up and down in a window

 ▸ *buttons,* which can be "pushed" with a mouse click

The mouse is the primary input device used with GUIs, so GUIs are sometimes called *point-and-click interfaces.* The screen shot in Figure 1.2 shows an example of a GUI.

The interface to an application or operating system is an important part of the software because it is the only part of the program the user directly interacts with. To the user, the interface *is* the program.

The focus of this book is high-quality application programs. We explore how to design and write software that will perform calculations, make decisions, and control graphics. We use the Java programming language throughout the text to demonstrate computing concepts.

> **key concept**
>
> As far as the user is concerned, the interface *is* the program.

digital computers

Two techniques are used to store and manage information: analog and digital. *Analog* information is continuous. For example, a thermometer is an analog device for measuring temperature. The mercury rises in a tube at the same time the temperature outside the tube rises. Another example of analog

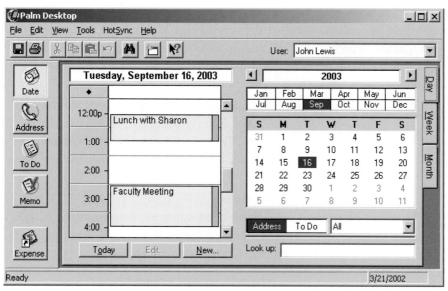

figure 1.2   An example of a graphical user interface (GUI) (Palm Desktop™
courtesy of 3COM Corporation)

information is the speed at which a car is going. As you press and release the
gas and brake pedals, the car's speed varies. Figure 1.3 graphically depicts a
car's speed as it varies over time.

Digital technology breaks information into pieces and shows those pieces
as numbers. The music on a compact disc is stored digitally, as a series of
numbers. Each number represents the voltage level of one specific instance
of the recording. Many of these measurements are taken in a short period

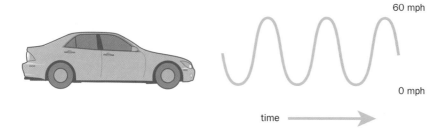

figure 1.3   A car's speed as it changes over time

of time, perhaps 40,000 measurements every second. The number of measurements per second is called the *sampling rate*. If samples are taken often enough, the separate voltage measurements can be used to create an analog signal that is "close enough" to the original. In most cases, the reproduction is good enough to satisfy the human ear.

Figure 1.4 shows the sampling of an analog signal. When analog information is converted to a digital format by breaking it into pieces, we say it has been *digitized*. Because the changes that occur in a signal between samples are lost, the sampling rate must be fast enough to make up the difference.

Sampling is only one way to digitize information. For example, a sentence can be stored on a computer as a series of numbers, where each number represents a single character in the sentence. Every letter, digit, and punctuation mark has been given a number. Even the space character gets a number. Consider the following sentence:

Hi, Heather.

The characters of the sentence are represented as a series of 12 numbers, as shown in Figure 1.5. When a character is repeated, such as the uppercase 'H', the same number is used. Note that the uppercase version of a letter is stored as a different number from the lowercase version, such as the 'H' and 'h' in the word Heather. They are considered different characters.

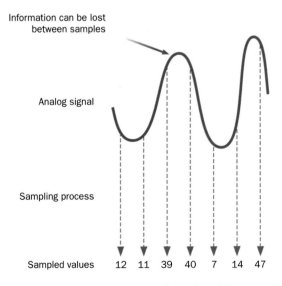

Information can be lost between samples

Analog signal

Sampling process

Sampled values   12 11 39 40 7 14 47

figure 1.4   Digitizing an analog signal by sampling

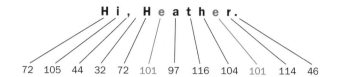

figure 1.5   Text is stored by mapping each character to a number

Modern computers are digital. Every kind of information, including text, images, numbers, audio, video, and even program instructions, is broken into pieces. Each piece is represented as a number. The information is stored by storing those numbers.

binary numbers

A digital computer stores information as numbers, but those numbers are not stored as *decimal* numbers. All information in a computer is stored and managed as *binary* numbers. Unlike the decimal system, which has 10 digits (0 through 9), the binary number system has only two digits (0 and 1). A single binary digit is called a *bit*.

All number systems work according to the same rules. The *base value* of a number system tells us how many digits we have to work with and what is the place value of each digit in a number. The decimal number system is base 10, whereas the binary number system is base 2.

Modern computers use binary numbers because the devices that store and move information are less expensive and more reliable if they have to represent only one of two possible values. Other than this, there is nothing special about the binary number system. Some computers use other number systems to store information, but they aren't as convenient.

Some computer memory devices, such as hard drives, are magnetic. Magnetic material can be polarized easily to one extreme or the other, but in-between levels are hard to tell apart. So magnetic devices can be used to represent binary values very well—a magnetized area represents a binary 1 and a demagnetized area represents a binary 0. Other computer memory devices are made up of tiny electrical circuits. These devices are easier to create and are less likely to fail if they have to switch between only two states. We're better off making millions of these simple devices than creating fewer, more complicated ones.

Binary values and digital electronic signals go hand in hand. They improve our ability to send information reliably along a wire. As we've seen, an analog signal has continuously varying voltage, but a digital signal is *discrete,* which means the voltage changes dramatically between one extreme (such as +5 volts) and the other (such as –5 volts). At any point, the voltage of a digital signal is considered to be either "high," which represents a binary 1, or "low," which represents a binary 0. Figure 1.6 compares these two types of signals.

As a signal moves down a wire, it gets weaker. That is, the voltage levels of the original signal change slightly. The trouble with an analog signal is that as it changes, it loses its original information. Since the information is directly analogous to the signal, any change in the signal changes the information. The changes in an analog signal cannot be recovered because the new, degraded signal is just as valid as the original. A digital signal degrades just as an analog signal does, but because the digital signal is originally at one of two extremes, it can be reinforced before any information is lost. The voltage may change slightly from its original value, but it still can be interpreted as either high or low.

The number of bits we use in any given situation determines how many items we can represent. A single bit has two possible values, 0 and 1, so it can represent two items or situations. If we want to represent the state of a lightbulb (off or on), one bit will suffice, because we can interpret 0 as the lightbulb being off and 1 as the lightbulb being on. If we want to represent more than two things, we need more than one bit.

Two bits, taken together, can represent four items because there are exactly four ways we can arrange two bits: 00, 01, 10, and 11. Suppose we want to represent the gear that a car is in (park, drive, reverse, or neutral). We would need only two bits, and could set up a mapping between the bits and the gears. For instance, we could say that 00 represents park, 01 represents drive, 10 represents reverse, and 11 represents neutral. (Remember that

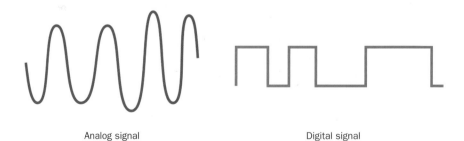

Analog signal   Digital signal

figure 1.6   An analog signal and a digital signal

'10' is not 'ten' but 'one-zero' and '11' is not 'eleven' but 'one-one.') In this case, it wouldn't matter if we switched that mapping around, though in some cases the relationships between the bit arrangements and what they represent is important.

Three bits can represent eight unique items, because there are eight arrangements of three bits. Similarly, four bits can represent 16 items, five bits can represent 32 items, and so on. Figure 1.7 shows the relationship between the number of bits used and the number of items they can represent. In general, N bits can represent 2^N unique items. For every bit added, the number of items that can be represented doubles.

> **key concept**
>
> There are exactly 2^N ways to arrange N bits. Therefore N bits can represent up to 2^N unique items.

We've seen how a sentence of text is stored on a computer as numeric values. Those numeric values are stored as binary numbers. Suppose we had character strings in a language with 256 characters and symbols. We would need to use eight bits to store each character because there are 256 unique ways of arranging eight bits (2^8 equals 256). Each arrangement of bits is a specific character.

Ultimately, representing information on a computer boils down to the number of items and how those items are mapped to binary values.

1 bit 2 items	2 bits 4 items	3 bits 8 items	4 bits 16 items	5 bits 32 items	
0	00	000	0000	00000	10000
1	01	001	0001	00001	10001
	10	010	0010	00010	10010
	11	011	0011	00011	10011
		100	0100	00100	10100
		101	0101	00101	10101
		110	0110	00110	10110
		111	0111	00111	10111
			1000	01000	11000
			1001	01001	11001
			1010	01010	11010
			1011	01011	11011
			1100	01100	11100
			1101	01101	11101
			1110	01110	11110
			1111	01111	11111

figure 1.7   The number of bits used determines the number of items that can be represented

1.1 hardware components

Let's look at the hardware components of a computer system in more detail. Consider the computer described in Figure 1.8. What does it all mean? Can the system run the software you want it to? How does it compare to other systems? These terms are explained in this section.

computer architecture

The architecture of a house describes its structure. Similarly, we use the term *computer architecture* to describe how the hardware components of a computer are put together. Figure 1.9 shows the basic architecture of a computer system. Information travels between components across a group of wires called a *bus*.

The CPU and the main memory make up the core of a computer. As we mentioned earlier, main memory stores programs and data that are being used, and the CPU executes program instructions one at a time.

> **key concept**
>
> The core of a computer is made up of the CPU and the main memory. Main memory is used to store programs and data. The CPU executes a program's instructions one at a time.

Suppose we have a program that figures out the average of a list of numbers. The program and the numbers must be in main memory while the program runs. The CPU reads one program instruction from main memory and executes it. When it needs data, such as a number in the list, the CPU reads that information as well. This process repeats until the program ends. The answer is stored in main memory to await further processing or in long-term storage in secondary memory.

Almost all devices in a computer system other than the CPU and main memory are called *peripherals*. Peripherals operate at the periphery, or outer

- 950 MHz Intel Pentium 4 processor
- 512 MB RAM
- 30 GB Hard Disk
- CD-RW 24x/10x/40x
- 17" Video Display with 1280 x 1024 resolution
- 56 Kb/s modem

figure 1.8   The hardware specification of a particular computer

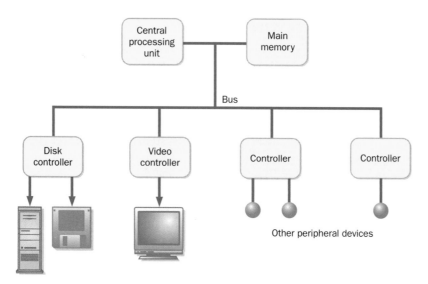

figure 1.9   Basic computer architecture

edges, of the system (although they may be in the same box). Users don't interact directly with the CPU or main memory. Instead users interact with the peripherals: the monitor, keyboard, disk drives, and so on. The CPU and main memory would not be useful without peripheral devices.

Controllers are devices that send information back and forth from the CPU and main memory to the peripherals. Every device has its own way of formatting and sending data, and part of the controller's job is to handle this. Furthermore, the controller often sends information back and forth, so the CPU can focus on other activities.

Input/output (I/O) devices and secondary memory devices are one kind of peripherals. Another kind of peripherals are *data transfer devices,* which allow information to be sent and received between computers. The computer described in Figure 1.8 has a data transfer device called a *modem,* which lets information be sent across a telephone line. The modem in the example can send data at a maximum rate of 56 *kilobits* (Kb) per second, or approximately 56,000 *bits per second* (bps).

Secondary memory devices and data transfer devices can be thought of as I/O devices because they represent a source of information (input) and a place to send information (output). For our discussion, however, we define I/O devices as devices that let the user interact with the computer.

input/output devices

Let's look at some I/O devices in more detail. The most common input devices are the keyboard and the mouse. Others include:

> *bar code readers,* such as the ones used at a grocery store checkout

> *joysticks,* often used for games and advanced graphical applications

> *microphones,* used by voice recognition systems that interpret simple voice commands

> *virtual reality devices,* such as gloves that interpret the movement of the user's hand

> *scanners,* which convert text, photographs, and graphics into machine-readable form

Monitors and printers are the most common output devices. Others include:

> *plotters,* which move pens across large sheets of paper (or vice versa)

> *speakers,* for audio output

> *goggles,* for virtual reality display

Some devices can handle both input and output. A touch screen system can detect the user touching the screen at a particular place. Software can then use the screen to display text and graphics in response to the user's touch. Touch screens are particularly useful in situations where the interface to the machine must be simple, such as at an information booth.

The computer described in Figure 1.8 includes a monitor with a 17-inch diagonal display area. A picture is created by breaking it up into small pieces called *pixels,* a term that stands for "picture elements." The monitor can display a grid of 1280 by 1024 pixels. The last section of this chapter explores the representation of graphics in more detail.

main memory and secondary memory

Main memory is made up of a series of small, connected *memory locations,* as shown in Figure 1.10. Each memory location has a unique number called an *address.*

When data is stored in a memory location, it overwrites and destroys any information that was stored at that location. However, data is read from a memory location without affecting it.

On many computers, each memory location consists of eight bits, or one *byte,* of information. If we need to store a value that cannot be

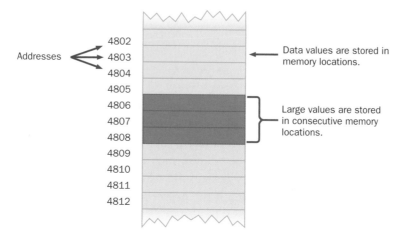

figure 1.10 Memory locations

represented in a single byte, such as a large number, then multiple, consecutive bytes are used to store the data.

The *storage capacity* of a device such as main memory is the total number of bytes it can hold. Devices can store thousands or millions of bytes, so you should become familiar with larger units of measure. Because computer memory is based on the binary number system, all units of storage are powers of two. A *kilobyte* (KB) is 1,024, or 2^{10}, bytes. Some larger units of storage are a *megabyte* (MB), a *gigabyte* (GB), and a *terabyte* (TB), as listed in Figure 1.11. It's usually easier to think about these numbers if we round them off. For example, most computer users think of a kilobyte as approximately one thousand bytes, a megabyte as approximately one million bytes, and so forth.

> **key concept**
>
> Data *written* to a memory location overwrites and destroys any information that was stored at that location. Data *read* from a memory location leaves the value in memory alone.

Unit	Symbol	Number of Bytes
byte		$2^0 = 1$
kilobyte	KB	$2^{10} = 1024$
megabyte	MB	$2^{20} = 1,048,576$
gigabyte	GB	$2^{30} = 1,073,741,824$
terabyte	TB	$2^{40} = 1,099,511,627,776$

figure 1.11 Units of binary storage

Many personal computers have 128, 256, or 512 megabytes of main memory, or RAM, such as the system described in Figure 1.8. (We discuss RAM in more detail later in the chapter.) A large main memory allows large programs, or several programs, to run because they don't have to get information from secondary memory as often.

Main memory is usually *volatile,* meaning that the information stored in it will be lost if its electric power supply is turned off. When you are working on a computer, you should often save your work onto a secondary memory device such as a disk in case the power is lost. Secondary memory devices are usually *nonvolatile,* meaning the information is saved even if the power supply is turned off.

The most common secondary storage devices are hard disks and floppy disks. A high-density floppy disk can store 1.44 MB of information. The storage capacities of hard drives vary, but on personal computers, the hard drive can usually store between 10 GB and 40 GB, such as in the system described in Figure 1.8.

A disk is a magnetic medium on which bits are represented as magnetized particles. A read/write head passes over the spinning disk, reading or writing information. A hard disk drive might actually have several disks in a column with several read/write heads, such as the one shown in Figure 1.12.

To get a feel for how much information these devices can store, all the information in this book, including pictures and formatting, requires about 6 MB of storage.

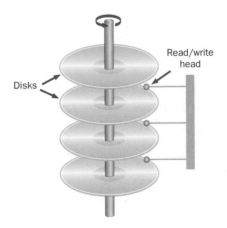

Read/write head

Disks

figure 1.12   A hard disk drive with multiple disks and read/write heads

Magnetic tapes are also used as secondary storage but are slower than disks because of the way information is accessed. A disk is a *direct access device* since the read/write head can move, in general, directly to the information needed. The terms *direct access* and *random access* are often confused. However, information on a tape can be accessed only after first getting past the intervening data. A tape must be rewound or fast-forwarded to get to the right place, the same way you have to fast-forward through a cassette tape to get to the song you want to hear. A tape is therefore considered a *sequential access device*. Tapes are usually used only to store information when it is no longer used very often, or to provide a backup copy of the information on a disk.

Two other terms are used to describe memory devices: *random access memory* (RAM) and *read-only memory* (ROM). It's important to understand these terms because they are used often, and their names can be misleading. RAM and main memory are basically the same thing. The term RAM seems to mean something it shouldn't. Both RAM and ROM are direct (or random) access devices. RAM should probably be called read-write memory, since data can be both written to it and read from it. Information stored on ROM, on the other hand, cannot be changed (as the term "read-only" implies). ROM chips are often embedded into the main circuit board of a computer and used to provide the instructions needed when the computer is initially turned on.

A *CD-ROM* is a portable secondary memory device. CD stands for compact disc. It is called ROM because information is stored permanently when the CD is created and cannot be changed. Like a musical CD, a CD-ROM stores information in binary format. When the CD is created, a microscopic pit is pressed into the disc to represent a binary 1, and the disc is left smooth to represent a binary 0. The bits are read by shining a low-intensity laser beam onto the spinning disc. The laser beam reflects strongly from a smooth area on the disc but weakly from a pitted area. A sensor determines whether each bit is a 1 or a 0. A typical CD-ROM can store about 650 MB.

> **key concept**
> The surface of a CD has both smooth areas and small pits. A pit represents a binary 1 and a smooth area represents a binary 0.

There are many kinds of CD technology today. It is now common for a home computer to come with a *CD-Recordable* (CD-R) drive. A CD-R can be used to create a CD for music or for general computer storage. Once created, you can use a CD-R disc in a standard CD player, but you can't change the information on a CD-R disc once it has been "burned." Music CDs that you buy in a store are pressed from a mold, whereas CD-Rs are burned with a laser.

A *CD-Rewritable* (CD-RW) disc can be erased and reused. It can be reused because the pits and flat surfaces of a normal CD are made on a CD-RW by coating the surface of the disc with a material that, when heated to one temperature becomes nonreflective and when heated to a different temperature becomes reflective. The CD-RW media doesn't work in all players, but CD-Rewritable drives can create both CD-R and CD-RW discs.

CDs started as a popular format for music; they later came to be used as a general computer storage device. Similarly, the *DVD* format was first created for video and is now making headway as a general format for computer data. DVD once stood for digital video disc or digital versatile disc. A DVD has a tighter format (more bits per square inch) than a CD so it can store much more information. It is likely that DVD-ROMs will replace CD-ROMs completely because a DVD drive can read a CD-ROM. There are currently six different formats for recordable DVDs.

The speed of a CD drive is expressed in multiples of x, which represents a data transfer speed of 153,600 bytes of data per second. The CD-RW drive described in Figure 1.8 has 24x/10x/40x maximum speed, which means it can write data onto CD-R discs at 24x, it can write data onto CD-RW discs at 10x, and it reads data from a disc at 40x.

How much a device can store changes as technology improves. A general rule in the computer industry is that storage capacity doubles every 18 months. However, this progress eventually will slow down as storage capacities approach absolute physical limits.

the central processing unit

The central processing unit (CPU) uses main memory to perform all the basic processing in a computer. The CPU reads and executes instructions, one after another, in a continuous cycle. The CPU is made up of three important components, as shown in Figure 1.13. The *control unit* handles the processing steps, the *registers* are small amounts of storage space in the CPU itself, and the *arithmetic/logic unit* does calculations and makes decisions.

The control unit transfers data and instructions between main memory and the registers in the CPU. It also controls the circuitry in the arithmetic/logic unit.

In most CPUs, some registers have special purposes. For example, the *instruction register* holds the current instruction being executed. The *program counter* holds the address of the next instruction to be executed. In

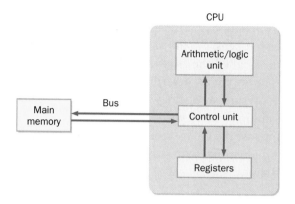

figure 1.13   CPU components and main memory

addition to these and other special-purpose registers, the CPU also contains a set of general-purpose registers.

The idea of storing both program instructions and data together in main memory is called the *von Neumann architecture* of computer design, named after John von Neumann, who first advanced this programming concept in 1945. These computers continually follow the *fetch-decode-execute* cycle depicted in Figure 1.14. An instruction is fetched from main memory and put into the instruction register. The program counter increases to get ready for the next cycle. Then the instruction is decoded electronically to determine which operation to carry out. Finally, the control unit turns on the correct circuitry to carry out the instruction, which may load a data value into a register or add two values together, for example.

> The von Neumann architecture and the fetch-decode-execute cycle form the foundation of computer processing.
>
> **key concept**

The CPU is on a chip called a *microprocessor,* a part of the main circuit board of the computer. This board also contains ROM chips and communication sockets to which device controllers, such as the controller that manages the video display, can be connected.

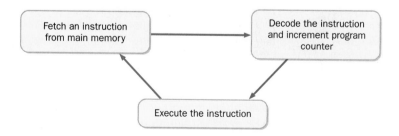

figure 1.14   The fetch-decode-execute cycle

Another part of the main circuit board is the *system clock*. The clock sends out an electronic pulse at regular intervals, so that everything going on in the CPU happens on the same schedule. The rate at which the pulses occur is called the *clock speed*, and it varies depending on the processor. The computer described in Figure 1.8 includes a Pentium 4 processor that runs at a clock speed of 950 megahertz (MHz), or about 950 million pulses per second. The speed of the system clock tells you about how fast the CPU executes instructions. The speed of processors is constantly increasing with advances in technology, approximately doubling every 18 months.

> **key concept**
> The speed of the system clock indicates how fast the CPU executes instructions.

1.2   networks

A single computer can do a lot, but connecting several computers together into networks can dramatically increase how much they can do and make it easier to share information. A *network* is two or more computers connected together so they can exchange information. Using networks is how commercial computers operate today. New technologies are emerging every day to improve networks.

Figure 1.15 shows a simple computer network. One of the devices on the network is a printer. Any computer connected to the network can print a document on that printer. One of the computers on the network is a *file server*, which does nothing but store programs and data that are needed by many network users. A file server usually has a large amount of secondary memory. When a network has a file server, each individual computer doesn't need its own copy of a program.

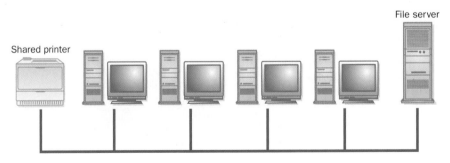

figure 1.15   A simple computer network

network connections

If two computers are directly connected, they can communicate in basically the same way that information moves across wires inside a single machine. When two computers are close to each other, this is called a *point-to-point connection*. If point-to-point connections are used, every computer is directly connected by a wire to every other computer in the network. But if the computers are far apart, having a separate wire for each connection won't work because every time a new computer is added to the network, a new wire will have to be installed for each computer already in the network. Furthermore, a single computer can handle only a small number of direct connections.

> **key concept**
> A network is two or more computers connected together so they can exchange information.

Figure 1.16 shows multiple point-to-point connections. Consider the number of wires that would be needed if two or three additional computers were added to the network.

Look at the diagrams in Figure 1.15 and Figure 1.16. All of the computers in Figure 1.15 share a single communication line. Each computer on the network has its own *network address*. These addresses are like the addresses in main memory except that they identify individual computers on a network instead of individual memory locations inside a single computer. A message from one computer to another needs the network address of the computer receiving the message.

Sharing a communication line is less expensive and makes adding new computers to the network easier. However, a shared line also means delays. The computers on the network cannot use the communication line at the same time. They have to take turns, which means they have to wait when the line is busy.

> **key concept**
> Sharing a communication line creates delays, but it is cost effective and simplifies adding new computers to the network.

One way to improve network delays is to divide large messages into small pieces, called *packets,* and then send the individual packets across the network mixed up with pieces of other messages sent by other users. The packets are collected at the destination and reassembled into the original message.

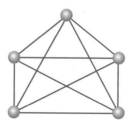

figure 1.16   Point-to-point connections

This is like a group of people using a conveyor belt to move a set of boxes from one place to another. If only one person were allowed to use the conveyor belt at a time, and that person had a lot of boxes to move, everyone else would have to wait a long time before they could use it. By taking turns, each person can put one box on at a time, and they all can get their work done. It's not as fast as having a conveyor belt of your own, but it's not as slow as having to wait until everyone else is finished.

local-area networks and wide-area networks

A *local-area network* (LAN) is designed to span short distances and connect a small number of computers. Usually a LAN connects the machines in only one building or in a single room. LANs are convenient to install and manage and are highly reliable. As computers became smaller, LANs became an inexpensive way to share information throughout an organization. However, having a LAN is like having a telephone system that allows you to call only the people in your own town. We need to be able to share information across longer distances.

> **key concept**
>
> A local-area network (LAN) is an inexpensive way to share information and resources throughout an organization.

A *wide-area network* (WAN) connects two or more LANs, often across long distances. Usually one computer on each LAN handles the communication across a WAN. This means the other computers in a LAN don't need to know the details of long-distance communication. Figure 1.17 shows several LANs connected into a WAN. The LANs connected by a WAN are often

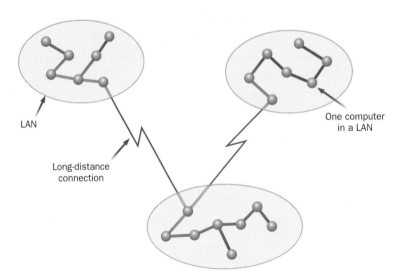

LAN

One computer
in a LAN

Long-distance
connection

figure 1.17   LANs connected into a WAN

owned by different companies or organizations, and might even be located in different countries.

Because of networks, computing resources can now be shared among many users, and computer-based communication across the entire world is now possible. In fact, the use of networks is now so common that some computers can't work on their own.

the Internet

Throughout the 1970s, a U.S. government organization called the Advanced Research Projects Agency (ARPA) funded several projects to explore network technology. One result of these efforts was the ARPANET, a WAN that eventually became known as the Internet. The *Internet* is a network of networks. The term "Internet" comes from the word *internetworking*—connecting many smaller networks together.

> **key concept**
> The Internet is a wide-area network (WAN) that spans the globe.

From the mid 1980s through today, the Internet has grown incredibly. In 1983, there were fewer than 600 computers connected to the Internet. By the year 2000, that number had reached over 10 million. As more and more computers connect to the Internet, keeping up with the larger number of users and heavier traffic has been difficult. New technologies have replaced the ARPANET several times over, each time providing more capacity and faster processing.

A *protocol* is a set of rules about how two things communicate. The software that controls the movement of messages across the Internet must follow a set of protocols called TCP/IP (pronounced by spelling out the letters, T-C-P-I-P). TCP stands for *Transmission Control Protocol*, and IP stands for *Internet Protocol*. The IP software defines how information is formatted and transferred. The TCP software handles problems such as pieces of information arriving out of order or information getting lost, which can happen if too much information arrives at one location at the same time.

> **key concept**
> TCP/IP is the set of software protocols, or rules, that govern the movement of messages across the Internet.

Every computer connected to the Internet has an *IP address* that identifies it among all other computers on the Internet. An example of an IP address is 204.192.116.2. Fortunately, the users of the Internet rarely have to deal with IP addresses. The Internet lets each computer be given a name. Like IP addresses, the names must be unique. The Internet name of a computer is often called its *Internet address*. Two examples of Internet addresses are spencer.mcps.org and kant.gestalt-llc.com.

The first part of an Internet address is the local name of a specific computer. The rest of the address is the *domain name*. The domain name tells you

key concept

Every computer connected to the Internet has an IP address that uniquely identifies it.

about the organization to which the computer belongs. For example, mcps.org is the domain name for the network of computers in the Montgomery County public school system, and spencer might be the name of a particular computer in the network. Because the domain names are unique, many organizations can have a computer named spencer without confusion. Individual schools might be assigned *subdomains* that are added to the basic domain name. For example, the chs.mcps.org subdomain is devoted to Christiansburg High School.

The last part of each domain name, called a *top-level domain* (TLD), usually indicates the type of organization to which the computer belongs. The TLD edu indicates an educational institution. The TLD com refers to a commercial business. For example, gestalt-llc.com refers to Gestalt, LLC, a company specializing in software technologies. Another common TLD is org, used by nonprofit organizations. Many computers, especially those outside of the United States, use a TLD that tells the country of origin, such as uk for the United Kingdom. Recently, some new top-level domain names have been created, such as biz, info, and name.

When an Internet address is referenced, it gets translated to its corresponding IP address, which is used from that point on. The software that does this translation is called the *Domain Name System* (DNS). Each organization connected to the Internet operates a *domain server* that maintains a list of all computers at that organization and their IP addresses. It works like telephone directory assistance in that you give the name, and the domain server gives back a number. If the local domain server does not have the IP address for the name, it contacts another domain server that does.

The Internet has revolutionized computer processing. At first, interconnected computers were used to send electronic mail. Today the Internet connects us through the World Wide Web.

the World Wide Web

The Internet lets us share information. The *World Wide Web* (also known as WWW or simply the Web) makes sharing information easy, with the click of a mouse.

The Web is based on the ideas of hypertext and hypermedia. The term *hypertext* was first used in 1965 to describe a way to organize information. In fact, that idea was around as early as the 1940s. Researchers on the Manhattan Project, who were developing the first atomic bomb, envisioned such an approach. The idea is that documents can be linked at logical points so that the reader can jump from one document to

key concept

The World Wide Web is software that makes sharing information across a network easy.

another. When graphics, sound, animations, and video are mixed in, we call this *hypermedia*.

A *browser* is a software tool that loads and formats Web documents for viewing. *Mosaic*, the first graphical interface browser for the Web, was released in 1993. The designer of a Web document defines *links* to other Web information that might be anywhere on the Internet. Some of the people who developed Mosaic went on to found the Netscape Communications Corp. and create the popular Netscape Navigator browser, which is shown in Figure 1.18. Microsoft's Internet Explorer is another popular browser.

A computer dedicated to providing access to Web documents is called a *Web server*. Browsers load and interpret documents provided by a Web server. Many such documents are formatted using the *HyperText Markup Language* (HTML). Java programs can be embedded in HTML documents and executed through Web browsers. We explore this relationship in more detail in Chapter 2.

> **key concept**
>
> A browser is a software tool that loads and formats Web documents for viewing. These documents are often written using the HyperText Markup Language (HTML).

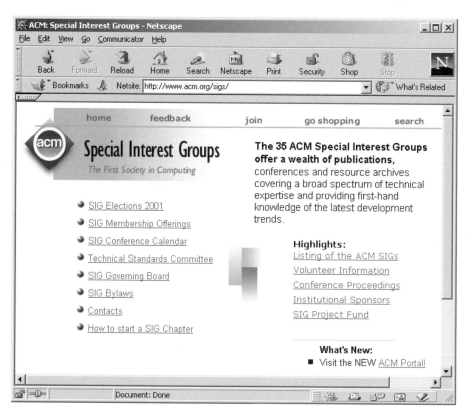

figure 1.18   Netscape Navigator browsing an HTML document
(used with permission of ACM)

Uniform Resource Locators

Every Web document has a *Uniform Resource Locator* (URL). A URL uniquely specifies documents and other information for a Web browser. An example URL is:

> http://www.yahoo.com

A URL contains several pieces of information. The first piece is a protocol, which determines the way the browser should communicate. The second piece is the Internet address of the machine on which the document is stored. The third piece of information is the file name. If no file name is given, as is the case with the Yahoo URL, the Web server often provides a default page (such as index.html).

Let's look at another example URL:

> http://www.gestalt-llc.com/vision.html

In this URL, the protocol is http, which stands for *HyperText Transfer Protocol*. The machine referenced is www (a typical reference to a Web server), found at domain gestalt-llc.com. Finally, vision.html is a file to be transferred to the browser for viewing. Many other forms for URLs exist, but this form is the most common.

the Internet vs. the World Wide Web

The terms *Internet* and *World Wide Web* do not mean the same thing. There are important differences between the two. The Internet is a network of computers all over the world. The Web is a set of software applications that lets us use the Internet to view and exchange information. The Web is not a network. Although the Web is used effectively with the Internet, it is not bound to it. The Web can be used on a LAN that is not connected to any other network or even on a single machine to display HTML documents.

1.3 programming

The Java programming language allows software to be easily exchanged and executed via the Web. The rest of this book shows you how to create programs using Java. This section discusses the purpose of programming in general and introduces the Java programming language.

problem solving

The purpose of writing a program is to solve a problem. Problem solving, in general, consists of multiple steps:

1. Understanding the problem.

2. Breaking the problem into manageable pieces.

3. Designing a solution.

4. Considering alternatives to the solution and refining the solution.

5. Implementing the solution.

6. Testing the solution and fixing any problems.

> **key concept**
> The purpose of writing a program is to solve a problem.

Although this approach applies to any kind of problem solving, it works particularly well when developing software.

The first step, understanding the problem, may sound obvious, but skipping this step can cause us all kinds of problems. If we try to solve a problem we don't completely understand, we often end up solving the wrong problem.

After we understand the problem, we then break the problem into manageable pieces and design a solution. These steps go hand in hand. A solution to any problem is almost never one big activity. Instead, it is a series of small tasks that work together to perform a larger task. When developing software, we don't write one big program. We design separate pieces that are responsible for parts of the solution, then we put all the parts together.

Our first idea for a solution may not be the best one. We must consider all the possible solutions. The earlier we consider alternatives, the easier it is to modify our approach.

> **key concept**
> The first solution we design to solve a problem may not be the best one.

Next we take the design and put it in a usable form. This stage is where we actually write the program. Too often programming is thought of as writing code. But in most cases, this is one of the last and easiest steps. The act of designing the program should be more interesting and creative than just turning the design into a particular programming language.

Finally, we test our solution to find any mistakes so that we can fix them. Testing makes sure the program correctly represents the design, which in turn provides a solution to the problem.

Throughout this text we explore programming techniques that let us elegantly design and implement solutions to problems. Although we will often go into detail, we should not forget that programming is just a tool to help us solve problems.

the Java programming language

A program is written in a particular *programming language* that uses specific words and symbols to express the problem solution. A programming language defines a set of rules that determine exactly how a programmer can combine the words and symbols of the language into *programming statements,* which are the instructions that are carried out when the program is executed.

There are many programming languages. We use the Java language in this book to demonstrate programming concepts and techniques. Although our main goal is to learn these software development concepts, an important side-effect will be to learn the development of Java programs.

Java was developed in the early 1990s by James Gosling at Sun Microsystems. Java was introduced to the public in 1995 and has gained tremendous popularity since.

One reason Java got attention was because it was the first programming language created for the Web, but it also has important features that make it a useful general-purpose programming language.

> **key concept**
>
> This book focuses on the principles of object-oriented programming.

Java is an *object-oriented programming language.* Objects are the basic pieces that make up a program. Other programming languages, such as C++, let a programmer use objects but don't reinforce that approach, which can lead to confusing program designs.

Most importantly, Java is a good language to use to learn programming concepts. It doesn't get bogged down in unnecessary issues as some other languages do. Using Java, we can focus on important issues and not on less important details.

The Java language has a library of extra software that we can use when developing programs. This library lets us create graphics, communicate over networks, and interact with databases, among many other features. Although we won't be able to cover all aspects of the libraries, we will explore many of them.

Java is used all over the world. It is one of the fastest growing programming technologies of all time. So not only is it a good language in which to learn programming concepts, it is also a practical language that will serve you well in the future.

a Java program

Let's look at a simple but complete Java program. The program in Listing 1.1 prints two sentences to the screen. This program prints a quote by Abraham Lincoln. The output is shown below the program listing.

All Java applications have a similar basic structure. Despite its small size and simple purpose, this program contains several important features. Let's examine its pieces.

The first few lines of the program are comments, which start with the // symbols and continue to the end of the line. Comments don't affect what the program does but are included to help someone reading the code understand what the program does. Programmers should include comments throughout a program to clearly identify the purpose of the program and describe any special processing. Any written comments or documents, including a user's guide and technical references, are called *documentation*. Comments included in a program are called *inline documentation*.

> **key concept**
>
> Comments do not affect a program's processing; instead, they help someone reading the code understand what the program does.

listing 1.1

```
//********************************************************************
//  Lincoln.java        Author: Lewis/Loftus/Cocking
//
//  Demonstrates the basic structure of a Java application.
//********************************************************************

public class Lincoln
{
   //-----------------------------------------------------------------
   //  Prints a presidential quote.
   //-----------------------------------------------------------------
   public static void main (String[] args)
   {
      System.out.println ("A quote by Abraham Lincoln:");

      System.out.println ("Whatever you are, be a good one.");
   }
}
```

output

```
A quote by Abraham Lincoln:
Whatever you are, be a good one.
```

The rest of the program in Listing 1.1 is a *class definition*. This class is called `Lincoln`, though we could have named it just about anything we wished. The class definition runs from the first opening brace (`{`) to the final closing brace (`}`) on the last line of the program. All Java programs are defined using class definitions.

Inside the class definition are some more comments describing the purpose of the `main` method, which is defined directly below the comments. A *method* is a group of programming statements that are given a name. In this case, the name of the method is `main` and it contains only two programming statements. Like a class definition, a method is also enclosed in braces.

All Java applications have a `main` method, which is where processing begins. Each programming statement in the `main` method is executed, one at a time in order, until the end of the method is reached. Then the program ends, or *terminates*. The `main` method definition in a Java program is always preceded by the words `public`, `static`, and `void`, which we examine later in the text. The use of `String` and `args` does not come into play in this particular program. We describe these later also.

> **key concept**
>
> In a Java application, processing begins with the `main` method. The `main` method must always be defined using the words `public`, `static`, and `void`.

The two lines of code in the `main` method invoke another method called `println` (pronounced "print line"). We *invoke*, or *call*, a method when we want it to execute. The `println` method prints the specified characters to the screen. The characters to be printed are represented as a *character string*, enclosed in double quote characters (`"`). When the program is executed, it calls the `println` method to print the first statement, calls it again to print the second statement, and then, because that is the last line in the program, the program terminates.

The code executed when the `println` method is invoked is not defined in this program. The `println` method is part of the `System.out` object, which we explore in more detail in Chapter 2.

comments

Let's look at comments in more detail. Comments are the only language feature that let programmers tell a person reading the code what they are thinking. Comments should tell the reader what the programmer wants the program to do. A program is often used for many years, and often many changes are made to it over time. Even the original programmer may not remember the details of a particular program when, at some point in the future, changes are needed. Furthermore, the original programmer is not always available to make the changes, and someone completely unfamiliar with the program will need to understand it. Good documentation is therefore very important.

As far as the Java programming language is concerned, comments can be written using any content whatsoever. Comments are ignored by the computer; they do not affect how the program executes.

The comments in the `Lincoln` program represent one of two types of comments allowed in Java. The comments in `Lincoln` take the following form:

```
// This is a comment.
```

This type of comment begins with a double slash (`//`) and continues to the end of the line. You cannot have any characters between the two slashes. The computer ignores any text after the double slash and to the end of the line. A comment can follow code on the same line to document that particular line, as in the following example:

```
System.out.println ("Monthly Report"); // always use this title
```

The second form a Java comment may have is:

```
/*  This is another comment.  */
```

This comment type does not use the end of a line to indicate the end of the comment. Anything between the first slash-asterisk (`/*`) and the second asterisk-slash (`*/`) is part of the comment, including the invisible *newline* character that represents the end of a line. Therefore, this type of comment can extend over multiple lines. No space can be between the slash and the asterisk.

The two basic comment types can be used to create different documentation styles, such as:

```
// This is a comment on a single line.

//----------------------------------------------------------
// Some comments such as those above methods or classes
// deserve to be blocked off to focus special
// attention on a particular aspect of your code.  Note
// that each of these lines is technically a separate
// comment.
//----------------------------------------------------------

/*
   This is one comment
   that spans several lines.
*/
```

Programmers often concentrate so much on writing code that they focus too little on documentation. You should develop good commenting practices and make them a habit. Comments should be well written, often in complete sentences. They should not tell the reader things that are obvious or confusing. The following examples are *not* good comments:

```
System.out.println ("hello");   // prints hello
System.out.println ("test");    // change this later
```

The first comment tells the obvious purpose of the line and does not add any new information to the statement. It is better to have no comment than a useless one. The second comment is confusing. What should be changed later? When is later? Why should it be changed?

It is considered good programming style to use comments in a consistent way throughout an entire program.

identifiers and reserved words

The various words used when writing programs are called *identifiers*. The identifiers in the Lincoln program are class, Lincoln, public, static, void, main, String, args, System, out, and println. These fall into three categories:

- words that we make up (Lincoln and args)
- words that another programmer chose (String, System, out, println, and main)
- words that are reserved for special purposes in the language (class, public, static, and void)

While writing the program in Listing 1.1, we simply chose to name the class Lincoln, but we could have used one of many other names. For example, we could have called it Quote, or Abe, or GoodOne. The identifier args (which is short for arguments) is often used in the way we use it in Lincoln, but we could have used just about any identifier in its place.

The identifiers String, System, out, and println were chosen by other programmers. These words are not part of the Java language. They are part of a huge library of predefined code, a set of classes and methods that someone has already written for us. The authors of that code chose the identifiers—we're just using them. We discuss this library of predefined code in more detail in Chapter 2.

Reserved words are identifiers that have a special meaning in a programming language and can only be used in predefined ways. In the Lincoln program, the reserved words used are `class`, `public`, `static`, and `void`. Throughout this book, we show Java reserved words in blue type. Figure 1.19 lists all of the Java reserved words in alphabetical order. The words marked with an asterisk are reserved for possible future use in later versions of the language but right now have no meaning in Java. A reserved word cannot be used for any other purpose, such as naming a class or method.

An identifier that we make up for use in a program can be any combination of letters, digits, the underscore character (_), and the dollar sign ($), but it cannot begin with a number. Identifiers may be of any length. Therefore `total`, `label7`, `nextStockItem`, `NUM_BOXES`, and `$amount` are all valid identifiers, but `4th_word` and `coin#value` are not valid.

Both uppercase and lowercase letters can be used in an identifier, and the difference is important. Java is *case sensitive,* which means that two identifier names that differ only in the case of their letters are considered to be different identifiers. Therefore `total`, `Total`, `ToTaL`, and `TOTAL` are all different identifiers. As you can imagine, it is not a good idea to use identifiers that differ only in their case because they can be easily confused.

Although the Java language doesn't require it, using the same case format for each kind of identifier makes your identifiers easier to understand. For example, we use *title case* (uppercase for the first letter of each word) for class names. That is a Java convention, although it does not technically have to be followed. Throughout the text, we

> **key concept**
>
> Java is case sensitive. The uppercase and lowercase versions of a letter are distinct. You should use the same case convention for different types of identifiers.

abstract	do	implements	protected	throws
boolean	double	import	public	transient
break	else	instanceof	return	true
byte	extends	int	short	try
case	false	interface	static	void
catch	final	long	strictfp	volatile
char	finally	native	super	while
class	float	new	switch	
const*	for	null	synchronized	
continue	goto*	package	this	
default	if	private	throw	

figure 1.19   Java reserved words

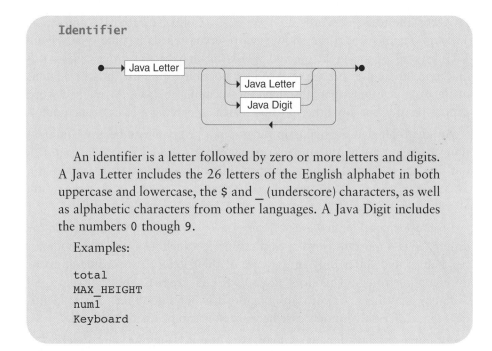

Identifier

An identifier is a letter followed by zero or more letters and digits. A Java Letter includes the 26 letters of the English alphabet in both uppercase and lowercase, the $ and _ (underscore) characters, as well as alphabetic characters from other languages. A Java Digit includes the numbers 0 though 9.

Examples:

```
total
MAX_HEIGHT
num1
Keyboard
```

describe the preferred case style for each type of identifier as we introduce them.

An identifier can be as long as you like, but you should choose your names carefully. They should be descriptive but not wordy. Don't use meaningless names such as a or x. An exception to this rule can be made if the short name is actually descriptive, such as using x and y to represent (*x, y*) coordinates on a graph. Likewise, you should not use unnecessarily long names, such as the identifier theCurrentItemBeingProcessed. The name currentItem would serve just as well.

> **key concept**
> Identifier names should be descriptive and readable.

As you might imagine, wordy identifiers are much less common than the names that are not descriptive. You should always be careful when abbreviating words. You might think curStVal is a good name to represent the current stock value, but another person trying to understand the code may have trouble figuring out what you meant. It might not even be clear to you two months after writing it.

A *name* in Java is a series of identifiers separated by the dot (period) character. The name System.out is the way we designate the object through which we invoked the println method. Names appear quite regularly in Java programs.

white space

All Java programs use *white space* to separate the words and symbols used in a program. White space consists of blanks, tabs, and newline characters. The phrase *white space* refers to the fact that, on a white sheet of paper with black printing, the space between the words and symbols is white. A programmer uses white space to emphasize parts of the code and make a program easier to read.

> **key concept**
> White space can make a program easier to read and understand.

Except when it's used to separate words, the computer ignores white space. It does not affect the execution of a program. This fact gives programmers a great deal of flexibility in how they format a program. The lines of a program should be divided in logical places and certain lines should be indented and aligned so that the program's structure is clear.

Because white space is ignored, we can write a program in many different ways. For example, we could put as many words as possible on each line. The code in Listing 1.2, the `Lincoln2` program, is formatted quite differently from Listing 1.1, `Lincoln`, but prints the same message.

Taking white space to the other extreme, we could write almost every word and symbol on a different line, such as `Lincoln3`, shown in Listing 1.3.

All three versions of `Lincoln` are technically valid and will execute in the same way, but they are different from a reader's point of view. Listings 1.2 and 1.3 show poor style and make the program hard to understand. You should use a set of style guidelines that increase the readability of your code.

> **key concept**
> You should always follow a set of guidelines that establish the way you format and document your programs.

listing
1.2

```java
//********************************************************************
//  Lincoln2.java       Author: Lewis/Loftus/Cocking
//
//  Demonstrates a poorly formatted, though valid, program.
//********************************************************************

public class Lincoln2{public static void main(String[]args){
System.out.println("A quote by Abraham Lincoln:");
System.out.println("Whatever you are, be a good one.");}}
```

output

```
A quote by Abraham Lincoln:
Whatever you are, be a good one.
```

listing
1.3

```
//****************************************************************
//  Lincoln3.java        Author: Lewis/Loftus/Cocking
//
//  Demonstrates another valid program that is poorly formatted.
//****************************************************************

        public          class
     Lincoln3
   {
                   public
   static
        void
  main
        (
String
          []
     args                       )
   {
   System.out.println        (
"A quote by Abraham Lincoln:"              )
   ;        System.out.println
            (
       "Whatever you are, be a good one."
        )
   ;
}
          }
```

output

```
A quote by Abraham Lincoln:
Whatever you are, be a good one.
```

1.4 programming languages

Suppose you are giving travel directions to a friend. You might explain those directions in any one of several languages, such as English, French, or Italian. The directions are the same no matter which language you use, but the way you express the directions is different. Furthermore, your friend must be able to understand the language you use in order to follow the directions.

Similarly, you can write a program in one of many programming languages, such as Java, Ada, C, C++, Pascal, and Smalltalk. The purpose of the program is the same no matter which language you use, but the particular statements used to express the instructions, and the overall organization of those instructions, vary with each language. Furthermore, a computer must be able to understand the instructions in order to carry them out.

This section explores types of programming languages and describes the special programs used to prepare and execute them.

programming language levels

There are four groups of programming languages. These groups basically reflect the historical development of computer languages:

- machine language
- assembly language
- high-level languages
- fourth-generation languages

In order for a program to run on a computer, it must be in that computer's *machine language*. Each type of CPU has its own language. For that reason, we can't run a program written for a Sun Workstation, with its Sparc processor, on an IBM PC, with its Intel processor.

Each machine language instruction can do only a simple task. For example, a single machine language instruction might copy a value into a register or compare a value to zero. It might take four separate machine language instructions to add two numbers together and to store the result. However, a computer can do millions of these instructions in a second, and therefore many simple commands can be quickly executed to accomplish complex tasks.

> **key concept**
>
> All programs must be translated to a particular CPU's machine language in order to be executed.

Machine language code is expressed as a series of binary digits and is extremely difficult for humans to read and write. Originally, programs were entered into the computer using switches or some similarly tedious method. These techniques were time consuming and error prone.

Next came *assembly language*, which replaced binary digits with *mnemonics*, short English-like words that represent commands or data. It is much easier for programmers to deal with words than with binary digits. However, an assembly language program cannot be executed directly on a computer. It must first be translated into machine language.

Generally, each assembly language instruction equals a machine language instruction. Therefore, like machine language, each assembly language instruction does only one simple operation. Although assembly language is better than machine code from a programmer's point of view, it is still tedious to use. Both assembly language and machine language are considered *low-level languages.*

Today, most programmers use a *high-level language* to write software. A high-level language uses English-like phrases, so it is easier for programmers to read and write. A single high-level language programming statement can accomplish the equivalent of many—perhaps hundreds—of machine language instructions. The term *high-level* means the programming statements are like natural language. Java is a high-level language, as are Ada, C, C++, and Smalltalk.

Figure 1.20 shows the same expressions written in a high-level language, assembly language, and machine language. The expressions add two numbers together.

The high-level language expression in Figure 1.20 is readable for programmers. It is like an algebraic expression. The same assembly language code is longer and somewhat less readable. The machine language is basically unreadable and much longer. In fact, only a small portion of the binary machine code to add two numbers together is shown in Figure 1.20. The complete machine language code for this particular expression is over 400 bits long.

High-level language code must be translated into machine language before it can be executed. A high-level language means programmers don't need to know the machine language for the processor on which they are working.

Some programming languages operate at an even higher level than high-level languages. They might be used for automatic report generation or interaction with a database. These languages are called *fourth-generation languages,* or simply 4GLs, because they followed

High-Level Language	Assembly Language	Machine Language
a + b	ld [%fp-20], %o0	. . .
	ld [%fp-24], %o1	1101 0000 0000 0111
	add %o0, %o1, %o0	1011 1111 1110 1000
		1101 0010 0000 0111
		1011 1111 1110 1000
		1001 0000 0000 0000
		. . .

figure 1.20   The same expression in a high-level language, assembly language, and machine language

the first three generations of computer programming: machine, assembly, and high-level.

compilers and interpreters

Several special-purpose programs are needed to help with the process of developing new programs. They are sometimes called *software tools* because they are used to build programs. Examples of basic software tools include an editor, a compiler, and an interpreter.

You use an *editor* as you type a program into a computer and store it in a file. There are many different editors with many different features. You should get to know the editor you will use regularly so you can enter and change your programs quickly.

Each time you need to make a change to the code of your program, you open it in an editor. Figure 1.21 shows a very basic view of the program development process. After editing and saving your program, you try to translate it from high-level code into a form that can be executed. That translation may result in errors, in which case you return to the editor to make changes to the code to fix the problems. Once the translation works, you can execute the program and see the results. If the results are not what you want, you again return to the editor to make changes.

The translation of source code into (ultimately) machine language for a particular type of CPU can occur in many ways. A *compiler* is a program that translates code in one language to code in another language. The original code is called *source code,* and the language into which it is translated is called the *target language.* For many compilers, the source code is translated directly into a particular machine language. In that case, the translation process occurs once, and the resulting program can be run whenever needed.

An *interpreter* is like a compiler but with an important difference. An interpreter does the translation and execution in short bursts. A small part

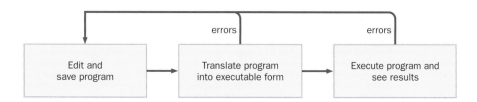

figure 1.21   Editing and running a program

of the source code, such as one statement, is translated and executed. Then another statement is translated and executed, and so on. One advantage of this technique is that it eliminates the need for a separate compilation phase. However, the program generally runs more slowly because the translation process occurs during each execution.

The process often used to translate and execute Java programs combines the use of a compiler and an interpreter. This process is pictured in Figure 1.22. The Java compiler translates Java source code into Java *bytecode*, which is a low-level form something like machine language code. The Java interpreter reads Java bytecode and executes it on a specific machine. Another compiler could translate the bytecode into a particular machine language for execution on that machine.

The difference between Java bytecode and true machine language code is that Java bytecode is not tied to any particular processor type. This makes Java *architecture neutral*, and therefore will work on many types of machines. The only restriction is that there must be a Java interpreter or a bytecode compiler for each processor type on which the Java bytecode is to be executed.

Since the compilation process translates the high-level Java source code into a low-level representation, the interpretation process works better than

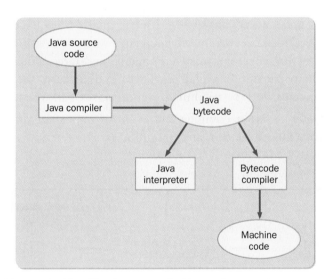

figure 1.22   The Java translation and execution process

interpreting high-level code directly. Executing a program by interpreting its bytecode is still slower than executing machine code directly, but it is fast enough for most applications. Note that Java bytecode could be compiled into machine code.

The Java compiler and interpreter are part of the Java *Software Development Kit* (SDK), which is sometimes referred to simply as the *Java Development Kit* (JDK). This kit also contains several other software tools that may be useful to a programmer. The JDK can be downloaded for free from the Sun Microsystem Web site (java.sun.com) or from this book's Web site. Note that the standard JDK tools are executed on the command line. That is, they are not graphical programs with menus and buttons but rather are used by typing commands in a command window.

> **key concept**
>
> Java is architecture neutral because Java bytecode is not associated with any particular machine.

Other programs, called *Integrated Development Environments* (IDEs), support the development of Java programs. IDEs combine an editor, compiler, and other Java support tools. Which tools you will use to develop your programs depend on your environment.

syntax and semantics

Each programming language has its own unique *syntax*. The syntax rules of a language dictate exactly how the vocabulary elements of the language can be combined to form statements. These rules must be followed in order to create a program. We've already discussed several Java syntax rules (for instance, the fact that an identifier cannot begin with a number is a syntax rule). The fact that braces are used to begin and end classes and methods is also a syntax rule. During compilation, all syntax rules are checked. If a program is not syntactically correct, the compiler will issue error messages and will not produce bytecode.

The *semantics* of a statement in a programming language define what will happen when that statement is executed. The semantics of a program are usually very well defined. That is, there is one and only one interpretation for each statement. On the other hand, the language that people use, such as English or French, can often have two or more different meanings. For example, consider the following sentence:

> Time flies like an arrow.

Most people would take this sentence to mean that time moves quickly in the same way that an arrow moves quickly. However, if *time* is a verb (as in "run the 50-yard dash and I'll time you") and the word *flies* is a noun (the plural of fly), the meaning changes completely. A computer would have a hard time determining which meaning is correct. Moreover, this statement could describe the preferences of an unusual insect known as a "time fly," which might be found near an archery range. After all, as Groucho Marx pointed out, fruit flies like a banana.

The point is that English allows multiple valid meanings, but a computer language can't. If a programming language instruction could have two different meanings, a computer would not be able to tell which one to follow.

errors

Several different kinds of problems can occur in software, particularly during program development. The term *computer error* is often misused. From a user's point of view, anything that goes wrong is often called a computer error. For example, suppose you charged a $23 item to your credit card, but when you received the bill, the item was listed at $230. After you have the problem fixed, the credit card company apologizes for the "computer error." Did the computer arbitrarily add a zero to the end of the number, or did it perhaps multiply the value by 10? Of course not. A computer does what we tell it to do and uses the data we give it. If our programs or data are wrong, then we can't expect the results to be correct. We call this "garbage in, garbage out."

You will encounter three kinds of errors as you develop programs:

- compile-time error
- runtime error
- logical error

The compiler checks to make sure you are using the correct syntax. If the syntax is wrong the compiler will produce a *syntax error.* The compiler also tries to find other problems, such as the use of incompatible types of data. The syntax might be technically correct, but you are still attempting to do something that the language doesn't semantically allow. Any error identified by the compiler is called a *compile-time error.* If a compile-time error occurs, an executable version of the program is not created.

The second kind of problem occurs during program execution. It is called a *runtime error,* and it causes the program to terminate abnormally or "crash." For example, if we try to divide by zero, the program will crash. The system simply stops processing your program. The best programs are *robust;* that is, they avoid as many runtime errors as possible. For example, the program code could guard against the possibility of dividing by zero and handle the situation appropriately if it arises. In Java, many runtime errors are represented as *exceptions* that can be caught and dealt with. We discuss exceptions in Chapter 5.

The third kind of software problem is a *logical error*. In this case, the software compiles and executes without complaint, but it produces the wrong results. For example, a logical error occurs when a value is calculated incorrectly, such as adding two numbers when they should have been multiplied. A programmer must test the program thoroughly, comparing the expected results to those that actually occur. When defects are found, they must be traced back to the source of the problem in the code and corrected. Finding and correcting defects in a program is called *debugging*. Logical errors can show up in many ways, and the cause might be hard to find.

language evolution

As computer technology evolves, so must the languages we use to program them. The Java programming language has changed since its creation. This text uses the most recent Java technology. Specifically, this book uses the *Java 2 Platform,* which simply refers to the most advanced collection of Java language features, software libraries, and tools. Several important changes have been made since the previous version. The Java 2 Platform is organized into three major groups:

- ▸ Java 2 Platform, Standard Edition (J2SE)
- ▸ Java 2 Platform, Enterprise Edition (J2EE)
- ▸ Java 2 Platform, Micro Edition (J2ME)

This book focuses on the Standard Edition.

As we discussed earlier in this chapter, the Java Development Kit (JDK) is the set of software tools provided by Sun Microsystems that can be used for creating Java software. These tools include a compiler and an interpreter. The most recent version of the JDK (at the time of this printing), which goes with the latest version of the Standard Edition of the Java 2 Platform, is JDK 1.4. You might use the JDK to develop your programs, or you might use some other development environment.

1.5 graphics

Graphics play an important role in computer systems. In this book we explore graphics and discuss how they are created and used. In fact, the last one or two sections of each chapter are devoted to graphics topics. (These sections can be skipped without losing continuity through the rest of the text.) In this section, we explore representing a picture in a computer and displaying it on a screen.

A picture, like all other information stored on a computer, must be digitized by breaking the information into pieces and representing those pieces as numbers. In the case of pictures, we break the picture into *pixels* (picture elements), as we mentioned earlier in this chapter. A pixel is a very small piece of the picture. The complete picture is stored by storing the color of each pixel.

> **key concept**
>
> The pixels of a black-and-white picture can be represented using a single bit each, 0 for white and 1 for black.

A black-and-white picture can be stored by representing each pixel using a single bit. If the bit is zero, that pixel is white; if the bit is 1, it is black. The more pixels used to represent a picture, the more realistic it looks. Figure 1.23 shows a black-and-white picture that has been stored digitally and an enlargement of part of that picture, which shows the pixels.

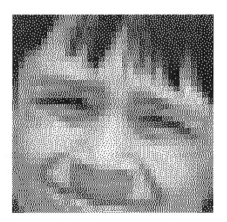

figure 1.23   A digitized picture with a small portion magnified

coordinate systems

When drawn, each pixel of a picture is mapped to a pixel on the screen. Each computer system and programming language defines a coordinate system like a coordinate system on a street map, so that we can find particular pixels.

The Java programming language has a relatively simple coordinate system. Figure 1.24 shows the Java coordinate system.

Each point in the Java coordinate system is represented using an (x, y) pair of values. The top-left corner of any Java drawing area has coordinates (0, 0). The x-axis coordinates get larger as you move to the right, and the y-axis coordinates get larger as you move down.

A Java program does not have to be graphical in nature. However, if it is, each graphical component in the program has its own coordinate system, with the origin (0, 0) in the top-left corner. This makes it easy to manage graphical elements.

representing color

Color pictures are divided into pixels, just as black-and-white pictures are. However, because each pixel can be one of many colors, it is not enough to represent each pixel using only one bit. There are many ways to represent the color of a pixel. This section explores one popular technique.

> **key concept**
>
> The pixels of a color picture can be represented using three numbers, collectively called the RGB value, which represent the relative contributions of three primary colors: red, green, and blue.

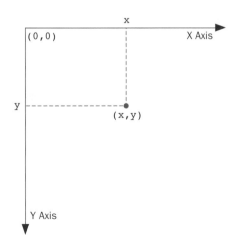

figure 1.24   The Java coordinate system

Every color can be represented as a mix of three *primary colors:* red, green, and blue. In Java, as in many other computer languages, colors are specified by three numbers called an *RGB value.* RGB stands for Red-Green-Blue. Each number represents the contribution of a primary color. Using one byte (8 bits) to store each of the three numbers, the numbers can range from 0 to 255. How much of each primary color determines the overall color. For example, high values of red and green combined with a low level of blue results in a shade of yellow.

In the graphics sections of other chapters we explore the use of color and how to control it in a Java program.

summary of
key concepts

summary of key concepts

▸ A computer system consists of hardware and software that work together to help us solve problems.

▸ To execute a program, the computer first copies the program from secondary memory to main memory. The CPU then reads the program instructions from main memory, executing them one at a time until the program ends.

▸ The operating system provides a user interface and manages computer resources.

▸ As far as the user is concerned, the interface *is* the program.

▸ Digital computers store information by breaking it into pieces and representing each piece as a number.

▸ Binary values are used to store all information in a computer because binary-based devices are inexpensive and reliable.

▸ There are exactly 2^N ways of arranging N bits. Therefore N bits can represent up to 2^N unique items.

▸ The core of a computer is made up of the CPU and the main memory. Main memory is used to store programs and data. The CPU executes a program's instructions one at a time.

▸ An address is a unique number assigned to each memory location. It is used when storing and retrieving data from memory.

▸ Data *written* to a memory location overwrites and destroys any information that was stored at that location. Data *read* from a memory location leaves information in memory alone.

▸ The information in main memory is stored only as long as electric power is supplied. The information in secondary memory is stored until it is deliberately deleted.

▸ The surface of a CD has both smooth areas and small pits. A pit represents a binary 1 and a smooth area represents a binary 0.

▸ A rewritable CD imitates the pits and smooth areas of a regular CD using a coating that can be made nonreflective or reflective as needed.

▸ The von Neumann architecture and the fetch-decode-execute cycle are the foundation of computer processing.

▸ The speed of the system clock tells us how fast the CPU executes instructions.

- A network is two or more computers connected together so they can exchange information.

- Sharing a communication line creates delays, but it is inexpensive and makes adding new computers to the network easier.

- A local-area network (LAN) is an inexpensive way to share information and resources throughout an organization.

- The Internet is a wide-area network (WAN) that spans the globe.

- TCP/IP is the set of software protocols, or rules, for moving messages across the Internet.

- Every computer connected to the Internet has a unique IP address.

- The World Wide Web is software that makes sharing information across a network easy.

- A browser is a software tool that loads and formats Web documents for viewing. These documents are often written in HyperText Markup Language (HTML).

- A URL is the unique name of a Web document that a browser needs to find and display it.

- The purpose of writing a program is to solve a problem.

- The first solution to a problem may not be the best one.

- Java is an object-oriented programming language.

- Comments help the people who read code understand what the programmer had in mind.

- Comments should be clear and helpful.

- In a Java application, processing begins with the `main` method. The `main` method must always be defined using the words `public`, `static`, and `void`.

- Java is case sensitive. The uppercase and lowercase versions of a letter are distinct. You should use the same case convention for different types of identifiers.

- Identifier names should be descriptive and readable.

- White space can make a program easier to read and understand.

- You should always follow a set of guidelines that establish the way you format and document your programs.

- All programs must be translated to a particular CPU's machine language in order to be executed.

‣ Working with high-level languages lets the programmer ignore the machine language.

‣ A Java compiler translates Java source code into Java bytecode. A Java interpreter translates and executes the bytecode.

‣ Java is architecture neutral because Java bytecode doesn't have to run on any particular hardware platform.

‣ The syntax rules of a programming language dictate the form of a program. The semantics dictate the meaning of the program statements.

‣ A computer follows our instructions exactly. The programmer is responsible for the accuracy and reliability of a program.

‣ A Java program must be syntactically correct or the compiler will not produce bytecode.

‣ The pixels of a black-and-white picture can be represented using a single bit each, 0 for white and 1 for black.

‣ The pixels of a color picture can be represented using three numbers, called the RGB value, for the three primary colors: red, green, and blue.

self-review questions

1.1   What is hardware? What is software?

1.2   What are the two jobs of an operating system?

1.3   What happens to information when it is stored digitally?

1.4   How many items can be represented with the following?

    a. 2 bits

    b. 4 bits

    c. 5 bits

    d. 7 bits

1.5   How many bits are there in each of the following?

    a. 8 bytes

    b. 2 KB

    c. 4 MB

1.6   What are the two main hardware components in a computer? How do they work with each other?

1.7   What is a memory address?

1.8   What does volatile mean? Which memory devices are volatile and which are nonvolatile?

1.9   What is a file server?

1.10 What is the total number of communication lines needed for a fully connected point-to-point network of five computers? Six computers?

1.11 Where does the word "Internet" come from?

1.12 Explain the parts of the following URLs:

   a. chs.mcps.org/Faculty/math.htm

   b. java.sun.com/products/index.html

1.13 What is the difference between a high-level language and machine language?

1.14 What is Java bytecode?

1.15 What is white space? Does it change program execution?

1.16 Which of the following are not valid Java identifiers? Why?

   a. `RESULT`

   b. `result`

   c. `12345`

   d. `x12345y`

   e. `black&white`

   f. `answer_7`

1.17 What do we mean by the syntax and semantics of a programming language?

1.18 How can a black-and-white picture be represented using 1s and 0s?

multiple choice

1.1 If a picture was made up of 64 possible colors, how many bits would be needed to store each pixel of the picture?

a. 4

b. 5

c. 6

d. 7

e. 8

1.2 How many bits are there in 12 KB?

a. 12,000

b. 98,304

c. 8192

d. 9600

e. 12,288

1.3 Which of the following is equivalent to $2^{20} \times 2^2$ bits?

a. 2 KB

b. 4 KB

c. 2 MB

d. 4 MB

e. 4 GB

1.4 How many different items can be represented with 11 bits?

a. 11

b. 22

c. 121

d. 1100

e. 2048

1.5 Which of the following is an example of an analog device?

a. mercury thermometer

b. computer

c. music CD

d. digital alarm clock

e. vending machine

1.6   Which of the following is *not* a valid Java identifier?

a. `Factorial`

b. `anExtremelyLongIdentifierIfYouAskMe`

c. `2ndLevel`

d. `level2`

e. `highest$`

1.7   Which of the following *is* a valid Java identifier?

a. `14andCounting`

b. `max_value`

c. `123`

d. `%taxRate`

e. `hook&ladder`

1.8   Which of the following pairs of variables are different from each other?

a. `Total` and `total`

b. `case` and `CASE`

c. `codeTwo` and `code2`

d. `oneMore` and `one_More`

e. all of the above

true/false

1.1   The identifiers `Maximum` and `maximum` are considered the same in Java.

1.2   ROM means random access device.

1.3   Computers continually follow the fetch-decode-execute cycle.

1.4   A network is two or more computers connected together so they can exchange information.

1.5   The first step in problem solving is to start implementing the solution.

1.6   Web pages are usually formatted using the HyperText Markup Language (HTML).

1.7   Identifiers in Java may contain any characters you can find on your keyboard.

1.8   Java is an object-oriented programming language.

1.9   The term *white space* refers to characters that are not part of the alphabet or numbers, such as the symbols %, &, and @.

1.10 Java is an assembly language.

short answer

1.1   Describe the hardware parts of your personal computer or of a computer in your school lab. Include the processor type and speed, storage capacities of main and secondary memory, and types of I/O devices.

1.2   Why do we use the binary number system to store information on a computer?

1.3   If a language uses 240 letters and symbols, how many bits would be needed to store each character of a document? Why?

1.4   Explain the difference between random access memory (RAM) and read-only memory (ROM).

1.5   Explain the differences between a local-area network (LAN) and a wide-area network (WAN). How do they work with each other?

1.6   What is the total number of communication lines needed for a fully connected point-to-point network of eight computers? Nine computers? Ten computers? What is a general formula for determining this result?

1.7   Give examples of the two types of Java comments and explain the differences between them.

1.8   Why are the following valid Java identifiers not considered good identifiers?

   a. q

   b. totVal

   c. theNextValueInTheList

1.9   Identify each of the following situations as a compile-time error, runtime error, or logical error.

a. multiplying two numbers when you meant to add them

b. dividing by zero

c. forgetting a semicolon at the end of a programming statement

d. spelling a word wrong in the output

e. producing inaccurate results

f. typing a { when you should have typed a (

1.10 How many bits are needed to store a color picture that is 400 pixels wide and 250 pixels high? Assume color is represented using the RGB technique described in this chapter.

programming projects

1.1   Enter, compile, and run the following application:

```java
public class Test
{
    public static void main (String[] args)
    {
        System.out.println ("An Emergency Broadcast");
    }
}
```

1.2   Introduce the following errors, one at a time, to the program from the Programming Project 1.1. Record any error messages that the compiler produces. Fix the previous error each time before you introduce a new one. If no error messages are produced, explain why. Try to predict what will happen before you make each change.

a. change Test to test

b. change Emergency to emergency

c. remove the first quotation mark in the string

d. remove the last quotation mark in the string

e. change main to man

f. change println to bogus

g. remove the semicolon at the end of the println statement

h. remove the last brace in the program

1.3   Write an application that prints, on separate lines, your name, your birthday, your hobbies, your favorite book, and your favorite movie. Label each piece of information in the output.

1.4   Write an application that prints the phrase `Knowledge is power`:

a. on one line

b. on three lines, one word per line, with the words centered relative to each other

c. inside a box made up of the characters = and |

1.5   Write an application that prints the following diamond shape. Don't print any unneeded characters. (That is, don't make any character string longer than it has to be.)

```
    *
   ***
  *****
 *******
*********
 *******
  *****
   ***
    *
```

1.6   Write an application that displays your initials in large block letters. Make each large letter out of the corresponding regular character. For example:

```
JJJJJJJJJJJJJJ    AAAAAAAAA    LLLL
JJJJJJJJJJJJJJ    AAAAAAAAAAA   LLLL
         JJJJ     AAA     AAA   LLLL
         JJJJ     AAA     AAA   LLLL
         JJJJ     AAAAAAAAAAA   LLLL
J        JJJJ     AAAAAAAAAAA   LLLL
JJ       JJJJ     AAA     AAA   LLLL
 JJJJJJJJJJJ      AAA     AAA   LLLLLLLLLLLLL
  JJJJJJJJJ       AAA     AAA   LLLLLLLLLLLLLL
```

answers to self-review questions

1.1   The hardware of a computer system is its physical parts such as a circuit board, monitor, or keyboard. Computer software are the programs that are executed by the hardware and the data that those programs use. In order to be useful, hardware requires software and software requires hardware.

1.2 The operating system provides a user interface and coordinates the use of resources such as main memory and the CPU.

1.3 The information is broken into pieces, and those pieces are represented as numbers.

1.4 In general, N bits can represent 2^N unique items. Therefore:

a. 2 bits can represent 4 items because $2^2 = 4$.

b. 4 bits can represent 16 items because $2^4 = 16$.

c. 5 bits can represent 32 items because $2^5 = 32$.

d. 7 bits can represent 128 items because $2^7 = 128$.

1.5 There are eight bits in a byte. Therefore:

a. 8 bytes = 8 * 8 bits = 64 bits

b. 2 KB = 2 * 1,024 bytes = 2,048 bytes = 2,048 * 8 bits = 16,384 bits

c. 4 MB = 4 * 1,048,576 bytes = 4,194,304 bytes = 4,194,304 * 8 bits = 33,554,432 bits

1.6 The two main hardware components are main memory and the CPU. Main memory holds the currently active programs and data. The CPU retrieves individual program instructions from main memory, one at a time, and executes them.

1.7 A memory address is a number that identifies a particular memory location in which a value is stored.

1.8 Main memory is volatile, which means the information that is stored in it will be lost if the power supply to the computer is turned off. Secondary memory devices are nonvolatile; therefore the information that is stored on them is retained even if the power goes off.

1.9 A file server is a network computer that is dedicated to storing and providing programs and data that are needed by many network users.

1.10 Counting the number of unique connections in Figure 1.16, there are 10 communication lines needed to fully connect a point-to-point network of five computers. Adding a sixth computer to the network will require that it be connected to the original five, bringing the total to 15 communication lines.

1.11 The word *Internet* comes from the word *internetworking*, a concept related to wide-area networks (WANs). An internetwork connects one network to another. The Internet is a WAN.

1.12 Breaking down the parts of each URL:

   a. `chs` is the name of the computer within the `mcps.org` domain, which represents Montgomery County public schools in Virginia. The `org` top-level domain indicates that it is an organization. This URL is requesting a file called `math.htm` from within a subdirectory called `Faculty`.

   b. `java` is the name of a computer (Web server) at the `sun.com` domain, which represents Sun Microsystems, Inc. The `com` top-level domain indicates that it is a commercial business. This URL is requesting a file called `index.html` from within a subdirectory called `products`.

1.13 High-level languages let a programmer write program instructions in English-like terms that are relatively easy to read and use. However, in order to execute, a program must be translated into machine language, which is a series of bits that are basically unreadable by humans. A high-level language program must be translated into machine language before it can be run.

1.14 Java bytecode is low-level Java source code. The Java compiler translates the source code into bytecode, which can then be executed using the Java interpreter. The bytecode might travel across the Web before being executed by a Java interpreter that is part of a Web browser.

1.15 White space is the spaces, tabs, and newline characters that separate words and symbols in a program. The compiler ignores extra white space, so it doesn't affect execution. However, white space can make a program readable to humans.

1.16 All of the identifiers shown are valid except `12345` (since an identifier cannot begin with a number) and `black&white` (since an identifier cannot contain the character `&`). The identifiers `RESULT` and `result` are both valid, but should not be used together in a program because they differ only by case. The underscore character (as in `answer_7`) is a valid part of an identifier.

1.17 Syntax rules define how the symbols and words of a programming language can be put together. Semantics determine what will happen when that instruction is executed.

1.18 A black-and-white picture can be drawn using a series of dots, called pixels. Pixels with a value of 0 are displayed in white and pixels with a value of 1 are displayed in black. A realistic black-and-white photo can be produced on a computer screen using thousands of pixels.

This chapter explores the key elements that we use in a program: objects and primitive data. We learn to create and use objects, which is basic to writing any program in an object-oriented language such as Java. We use objects to work with character strings, get information from the user, do difficult calculations, and format output. In the Graphics Track of this chapter, we explore the relationship between Java and the Web, and delve into Java's abilities to work with color and draw shapes.

chapter objectives

▹ Define the difference between primitive data and objects.

▹ Declare and use variables.

▹ Perform mathematical computations.

▹ Create objects and use them.

▹ Explore the difference between a Java application and a Java applet.

▹ Create graphical programs that draw shapes.

2.0   an introduction to objects

As we stated in Chapter 1, Java is an object-oriented language. An *object* is a basic part of a Java program. This book focuses on developing software by defining objects that interact with us and with each other.

In addition to objects, a Java program also manages primitive data. *Primitive data* include common values such as numbers and characters. An object usually represents something more complicated, such as a bank account. An object often contains primitive values and is in part defined by them. For example, an object that represents a bank account might contain the account balance, which is stored as a primitive numeric value.

A *data type* defines a set of values and operations—what we can do with those values. We perform operations on primitive types using *operators* that are built into the programming language. For example, the addition operator + is used to add two numbers together. We discuss Java's primitive data types and their operators later in this chapter.

An object is defined by a *class,* which is like the data type of the object. The operations that can be performed on the object are defined by the methods in the class. As we discussed in Chapter 1, a method is a collection of programming statements that is given a name so that we can use the method when we need it.

Once a class has been defined, objects can be created from that class. For example, once we define a class to represent the idea of a bank account, we can create objects that represent individual bank accounts. Each bank account object would keep track of its own balance. This is an example of *encapsulation*, meaning that each object protects and manages its own information. The methods defined in the bank account class would let us perform operations on individual bank account objects. For instance, we might withdraw money from a particular account. We can think of these operations as services that the object performs. Invoking a method is like sending a message to the object, asking that the service be performed.

Classes can be created from other classes using *inheritance*. That is, the definition of one class can be based on another class that already exists. Inheritance is a form of software *reuse*. We are taking advantage of the ways some kinds of classes are alike. One class can be used to create several new classes. These classes can then be used to create even more classes. This creates a family of classes, where characteristics defined in one class are inherited by its children, which in turn pass them on to their children, and so on. For example, we might create a family of classes for different types of bank accounts. Common characteristics are defined in high-level classes, and specific differences are defined in child, or *derived classes*.

Classes, objects, encapsulation, and inheritance are the ideas that make up the world of object-oriented software. They are shown in Figure 2.1.

This chapter focuses on how to use objects and primitive data. In Chapter 4 we define our own objects by writing our own classes and methods. In Chapter 7, we explore inheritance.

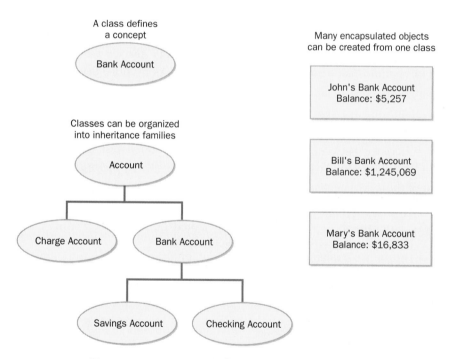

figure 2.1   Aspects of object-oriented software

2.1   using objects

In the `Lincoln` program in Chapter 1 (Listing 1.1), we invoked a method through an object as follows:

```
System.out.println ("Whatever you are, be a good one.");
```

The `System.out` object represents an output device or file, which by default is the monitor screen. The object's name is `out` and it is stored in the `System` class. We explore that relationship in more detail later in the text.

The `println` method is a service that the `System.out` object performs for us. Whenever we ask it to, the object will print a string of characters to the screen. We can say that we send the `println` message to the `System.out` object to ask that some text be printed.

Each piece of data that we send to a method is called a *parameter*. In this case, the `println` method takes only one parameter: the string of characters to be printed.

The `System.out` object also provides another service we can use: the `print` method. Let's look at both of these services in more detail.

the print and println methods

The difference between `print` and `println` is small but important. The `println` method prints the information sent to it, then moves to the beginning of the next line. The `print` method is like `println`, but does not go to the next line when completed.

The program shown in Listing 2.1 is called `Countdown`, and it invokes both the `print` and `println` methods.

Carefully compare the output of the `Countdown` program to the program code. Note that the word `Liftoff` is printed on the same line as the first few words, even though it is printed using the `println` method. Remember that the `println` method moves to the beginning of the next line *after* the information passed to it is printed.

Often it is helpful to use graphics to show objects and their interaction. Figure 2.2 shows part of what happens in the `Countdown` program. The `Countdown` class, with its `main` method, is shown invoking the `println` method of the `System.out` object.

We mentioned in the previous section that invoking a method is like sending a message. The diagram in Figure 2.2 shows the method name—the message—on the arrow. We could also have shown the information that makes up the rest of the message: the parameters to the methods.

listing
    2.1

```
//********************************************************************
//  Countdown.java          Author: Lewis/Loftus/Cocking
//
//  Demonstrates the difference between print and println.
//********************************************************************

public class Countdown
{
   //-----------------------------------------------------------------
   //  Prints two lines of output representing a rocket countdown.
   //-----------------------------------------------------------------
   public static void main (String[] args)
   {
      System.out.print ("Three... ");
      System.out.print ("Two... ");
      System.out.print ("One... ");
      System.out.print ("Zero... ");

      System.out.println ("Liftoff!"); // appears on first output line
      System.out.println ("Houston, we have a problem.");
   }
}
```

output

```
Three . . . Two . . . One . . . Zero . . . Liftoff!
Houston, we have a problem.
```

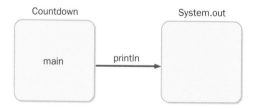

figure 2.2   Sending a message

As we explore objects and classes in more detail in this book, we will use these types of diagrams to explain object-oriented programs. The more complex our programs get, the more helpful such diagrams become.

abstraction

An object is an *abstraction*, meaning that the details of how it works don't matter to the user of the object. We don't really need to know how the `println` method prints characters to the screen as long as we can count on it to do its job.

Sometimes it is important to hide or ignore certain details. People can manage around seven (plus or minus two) pieces of information in short-term memory. Beyond that, we start to lose track of some of the pieces. However, if we group pieces of information together, we can manage those pieces as one "chunk" in our minds. We don't deal with all of the details in the chunk, just the chunk itself. This way, we can deal with large quantities of information by organizing them into chunks. An object organizes information and lets us hide the details inside. An object is therefore a wonderful abstraction.

We use abstractions every day. Think about a car for a moment. You don't need to know how a four-cycle combustion engine works in order to drive a car. You just need to know some basic operations: how to turn it on, how to put it in gear, how to make it move with the pedals and steering wheel, and how to stop it. These operations define the way a person interacts with the car. They mask the details of what is happening inside the car that allow it to function. When you're driving a car, you're not usually thinking about the spark plugs igniting the gasoline that drives the piston that turns the crankshaft that turns the axle that turns the wheels. If you had to worry about all of these details, you'd probably never be able to operate something as complicated as a car.

> **key concept**
>
> An abstraction hides details. A good abstraction hides the right details at the right time so that we can manage complexity.

At one time, all cars had manual transmissions. The driver had to understand and deal with the details of changing gears with the stick shift. When automatic transmissions were developed, the driver no longer had to worry about shifting gears. Those details were hidden by raising the *level of abstraction*.

Of course, someone has to deal with the details. The car manufacturer has to know the details in order to design and build the car in the first place. A car mechanic relies on the fact that most people don't have the expertise or tools necessary to fix a car when it breaks.

Thus, the level of abstraction must be appropriate for each situation. Some people prefer to drive a manual transmission car. A race car driver, for instance, needs to control the shifting manually for optimum performance.

Likewise, someone has to create the code for the objects we use. Soon we will define our own objects, but for now, we can use objects that have been defined for us already. Abstraction makes that possible.

2.2 string literals

A character string is an object in Java, defined by the class `String`. Because strings are such an important part of computer programming, Java provides something called a *string literal*, which appears inside double quotation marks, as we've seen in previous examples. We explore the `String` class and its methods in more detail later in this chapter. For now, let's explore two other useful details about strings: concatenation and escape sequences.

string concatenation

The program called `Facts` shown in Listing 2.2 contains several `println` statements. The first one prints a sentence that is somewhat long and will not fit on one line of the program. A character string in double quotation marks cannot be split between two lines of code. One way to get around this problem is to use the *string concatenation* operator, the plus sign (+). String concatenation adds one string to another. The string concatenation operation in the first `println` statement results in one large string that is passed to the method and printed.

Note that we don't have to pass any information to the `println` method, as shown in the second line of the `Facts` program. This call does not print characters that you can see, but it does move to the next line of output. In this case, the call to `println` passing in no parameters makes it "print" a blank line.

The rest of the calls to `println` in the `Facts` program demonstrate another interesting thing about string concatenation: Strings can be concatenated with numbers. Note that the numbers in those lines are not enclosed in double quotes and are therefore not character strings. In these cases, the number is automatically converted to a string, and then the two strings are concatenated.

listing
    2.2

```
//********************************************************************
//  Facts.java          Author: Lewis/Loftus/Cocking
//
//  Demonstrates the use of the string concatenation operator and the
//  automatic conversion of an integer to a string.
//********************************************************************

public class Facts
{
    //-----------------------------------------------------------------
    //  Prints various facts.
    //-----------------------------------------------------------------
    public static void main (String[] args)
    {
        // Strings can be concatenated into one long string
        System.out.println ("We present the following facts for your "
                            + "extracurricular edification:");

        System.out.println ();

        // A string can contain numeric digits
        System.out.println ("Letters in the Hawaiian alphabet: 12");

        // A numeric value can be concatenated to a string
        System.out.println ("Dialing code for Antarctica: " + 672);

        System.out.println ("Year in which Leonardo da Vinci invented "
                            + "the parachute: " + 1515);

        System.out.println ("Speed of ketchup: " + 40 + " km per year");
    }
}
```

output

```
We present the following facts for your extracurricular edification:

Letters in the Hawaiian alphabet: 12
Dialing code for Antarctica: 672
Year in which Leonardo da Vinci invented the parachute: 1515
Speed of ketchup: 40 km per year
```

Because we are printing particular values, we simply could have included the numeric value as part of the string literal, such as:

```
"Speed of ketchup: 40 km per year"
```

Digits are characters and can be included in strings as needed. We separate them in the `Facts` program to demonstrate how to concatenate a string and a number. This technique will be useful in upcoming examples.

As we've mentioned, the + operator is also used for arithmetic. Therefore, what the + operator does depends on the types of data on which it operates. If either or both of the operands of the + operator are strings, then string concatenation is performed.

The `Addition` program shown in Listing 2.3 shows the distinction between string concatenation and arithmetic addition. The `Addition` program uses the + operator four times. In the first call to `println`, both + operations perform string concatenation. This is because the operators execute left to right. The first operator concatenates the string with the first number (24), creating a larger string. Then that string is concatenated with the second number (45), creating an even larger string, which gets printed.

In the second call to `println`, parentheses are used to group the + operation with the two numbers. This forces that operation to happen first.

listing
2.3

```java
//********************************************************************
//  Addition.java        Author: Lewis/Loftus/Cocking
//
//  Demonstrates the difference between the addition and string
//  concatenation operators.
//********************************************************************

public class Addition
{
    //-----------------------------------------------------------------
    //  Concatenates and adds two numbers and prints the results.
    //-----------------------------------------------------------------
    public static void main (String[] args)
    {
        System.out.println ("24 and 45 concatenated: " + 24 + 45);

        System.out.println ("24 and 45 added: " + (24 + 45));
    }
}
```

output

```
24 and 45 concatenated: 2445
24 and 45 added: 69
```

Because both operands are numbers, the numbers are added together, producing the result 69. That number is then concatenated with the string, producing a larger string that gets printed.

We revisit this type of situation later in this chapter when we learn the rules that define the order in which operators get evaluated.

escape sequences

Because the double quotation mark (") is used in the Java language to indicate the beginning and end of a string, we need a special way to print a quotation mark. If we simply put it in a string ("""), the compiler gets confused because it thinks the second quotation character is the end of the string and doesn't know what to do with the third one. This results in a compile-time error.

To overcome this problem, Java defines several *escape sequences* to represent special characters. An escape sequence begins with the backslash character (\), and indicates that the character or characters that follow should be interpreted in a special way. Figure 2.3 lists the Java escape sequences.

The program in Listing 2.4, called Roses, prints some text resembling a poem. It uses only one println statement to do so, despite the fact that the poem is several lines long. Note the escape sequences used throughout the string. The \n escape sequence forces the output to a new line, and the \t escape sequence represents a tab character. The \" escape sequence ensures that the quotation mark is treated as part of the string, not the end of it, so it can be printed as part of the output.

Escape Sequence	Meaning
\n	newline
\"	double quote
\\	backslash
\b	backspace
\t	tab
\r	carriage return
\'	single quote

AP→ (rows 1, 2, 3)

figure 2.3   Java escape sequences

```
listing
  2.4

//***********************************************************
//  Roses.java          Author: Lewis/Loftus/Cocking
//
//  Demonstrates the use of escape sequences.
//***********************************************************

public class Roses
{
   //-----------------------------------------------------------
   //  Prints a poem (of sorts) on multiple lines.
   //-----------------------------------------------------------
   public static void main (String[] args)
   {
      System.out.println ("Roses are red,\n\tViolets are blue,\n" +
         "Sugar is sweet,\n\tBut I have \"commitment issues\",\n\t" +
         "So I'd rather just be friends\n\tAt this point in our " +
         "relationship.");
   }
}
```

output

```
Roses are red,
        Violets are blue,
Sugar is sweet,
        But I have "commitment issues",
        So I'd rather just be friends
        At this point in our relationship.
```

2.3 variables and assignment

Most of the information in a program is represented by variables. Let's look at how we declare and use them in a program.

variables

A *variable* is a name for a location in memory used to hold a data value. A variable declaration tells the compiler to reserve a portion of main memory space large enough to hold the value. It also tells the compiler what name to call the location.

> **key concept**
> A variable is a name for a memory location used to hold a value.

Consider the program PianoKeys, shown in Listing 2.5. The first line of the main method is the declaration of a variable named keys that holds a number, or an integer (int), value. The declaration also gives keys an ini-

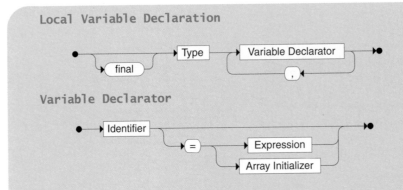

Local Variable Declaration

Variable Declarator

A variable declaration is a Type followed by a list of variables. Each variable can be given a value computed from the Expression. If the `final` modifier comes before the declaration, the variables are declared as named constants whose values cannot be changed.

Examples:

```
int total;
double num1, num2 = 4.356, num3;
char letter = 'A', digit = '7';
final int MAX = 45;
```

listing
2.5

```
//********************************************************************
//  PianoKeys.java        Author: Lewis/Loftus/Cocking
//
//  Demonstrates the declaration, initialization, and use of an
//  integer variable.
//********************************************************************

public class PianoKeys
{
   //-----------------------------------------------------------------
   //  Prints the number of keys on a piano.
   //-----------------------------------------------------------------
   public static void main (String[] args)
   {
      int keys = 88;

      System.out.println ("A piano has " + keys + " keys.");
   }
}
```

output

```
A piano has 88 keys.
```

tial value of 88. If you don't give an initial value for a variable, the value is undefined. Most Java compilers give errors or warnings if you try to use a variable before you've given it a value.

In the `PianoKeys` program, the string passed to the `println` method is formed from three pieces. The first and third are string literals, and the second is the variable `keys`. When the program gets to the variable it uses the currently stored value. Because the value of `keys` is an integer, it is automatically converted to a string so it can be concatenated with the first string. Then the concatenated string is passed to `println` and printed.

Note that a variable declaration can have many variables of the same type on one line. Each variable on the line can be declared with or without an initializing value. For example, the following declaration declares two variables, `weight` and `total`, and gives `total` a beginning value of 0.

```
int weight, total = 0:
```

the assignment statement

Let's look at a program that changes the value of a variable. Listing 2.6 shows a program called `Geometry`. This program first declares an integer variable called `sides` and initializes it to 7. It then prints out the current value of `sides`.

The next line in `main` changes the value stored in the variable `sides`:

```
sides = 10;
```

This is called an *assignment statement* because it gives or *assigns* a value to a variable. When the statement is executed, the expression on the right-hand side of the assignment operator (=) is evaluated, and the result is stored in

---

Basic Assignment

The basic assignment statement uses the assignment operator (=) to store the result of the Expression in the Identifier, usually a variable.

Examples:

```
total = 57;
count = count + 1;
value = (min / 2) * lastValue;
```

```
//********************************************************************
//  Geometry.java        Author: Lewis/Loftus/Cocking
//
//  Demonstrates the use of an assignment statement to change the
//  value stored in a variable.
//********************************************************************

public class Geometry
{
    //-----------------------------------------------------------------
    //  Prints the number of sides of several geometric shapes.
    //-----------------------------------------------------------------
    public static void main (String[] args)
    {
        int sides = 7;   // declaration with initialization
        System.out.println ("A heptagon has " + sides + " sides.");

        sides = 10;   // assignment statement
        System.out.println ("A decagon has " + sides + " sides.");

        sides = 12;
        System.out.println ("A dodecagon has " + sides + " sides.");
    }
}
```

output

```
A heptagon has 7 sides.
A decagon has 10 sides.
A dodecagon has 12 sides.
```

the memory location indicated by the variable on the left-hand side. In this example, the expression is simply a number, 10. We discuss expressions that are more involved than this in the next section.

A variable can store only one value of its declared type. A new value overwrites the old one. In this case, when the value 10 is assigned to sides, the original value 7 is overwritten and lost forever. However, when a reference is made to a variable, such as when it is printed, the value of the variable is not changed.

> **key concept**
>
> A variable can store only one value of its declared type.

The Java language is *strongly typed*, meaning that we can't assign a value to a variable that is inconsistent with its declared type. Trying to combine incompatible types will cause an error when you attempt to compile the program. Therefore, the expression on the right-hand side of an assignment statement must have the same type as the variable on the left-hand side.

> **key concept**
>
> Java is a strongly typed language. Each variable has a declared type and we cannot assign a value of one type to a variable of another type.

constants

Sometimes we use data that never changes—it is constant throughout a program. For instance, we might write a program that deals with a theater that can hold no more than 427 people. It is often helpful to give a constant value a name, such as `MAX_OCCUPANCY`, instead of using a literal value, such as `427`, throughout the code. Literal values such as `427` are sometimes referred to as "magic" numbers because their meaning in a program is mystifying.

Constants are identifiers and are like variables except that they always have the same value. In Java, if you write reserved word `final` before a declaration, the identifier is made a constant. Uppercase letters are used for constant names to help us tell them apart from regular variables, and words are separated by the underscore character. For example, the constant describing the maximum occupancy of a theater could be:

```java
final int MAX_OCCUPANCY = 427;
```

The compiler will give you an error message if you try to change the value of a constant once it has been given its initial value. This is another good reason to use them. Constants prevent accidental coding errors because the only place you can change their value is in the initial assignment.

> **key concept**
>
> Constants are like variables, but they have the same value throughout the program.

There is a third good reason to use constants. If a constant is used throughout a program and its value needs to be changed, then you only have to change it in one place. For example, if the capacity of the theater changes (because of a renovation) from 427 to 535, then you have to change only one declaration, and all uses of `MAX_OCCUPANCY` automatically reflect the change. If you had used the literal `427` throughout the code, you would have had to find and change each use. If you were to miss one or two, problems would surely arise.

2.4   primitive data types

There are eight primitive data types in Java: four kinds of integers, two kinds of floating point numbers, a character data type, and a boolean data type.

Everything else is represented using objects. Of the eight primitive types, three are a part of the AP subset. We look at these three (`int`, `double`, and `boolean`) plus a fourth (`char`), in more detail. A discussion of the other primitive types can be found on the Web site.

integers and floating points

Java has two basic kinds of numeric values: integers, which have no fractional part, and floating points, which do. The primitive type `int` is an integer data type and `double` is a floating point data type. The numeric types are *signed*, meaning that both positive and negative values can be stored in them.

> **key concept**
>
> Java has two kinds of numeric values: integers and floating point. The primitive type `int` is an integer data type and the type `double` is a floating point data type.

The `int` data type can be used to represent numbers in the range –2,147,483,648 to 2,147,483,647. The `double` data type can represent numbers from approximately –1.7E+308 to 1.7E+308 with 15 significant digits.

A *literal* is a specific data value used in a program. The numbers used in programs such as `Facts` (Listing 2.2) and `Addition` (Listing 2.3) and `PianoKeys` (Listing 2.5) are all *integer literals*. Java assumes all integer literals are of type `int`. Likewise, Java assumes that all *floating point literals* are of type `double`. The following are examples of numeric variable declarations in Java:

```
int answer = 42;
int number1, number2;
double delta = 453.523311903;
```

The specific numbers used, `42` and `453.523311903`, are literals.

booleans

A boolean value, defined in Java using the reserved word `boolean`, has only two values: `true` and `false`. A boolean variable usually tells us whether a condition is true, but it can also represent any situation that has two states, such as a lightbulb being on or off.

A boolean value cannot be changed to any other data type, nor can any other data type be changed to a boolean value. The words `true` and `false` are called *boolean literals* and cannot be used for anything else.

Here are some examples of boolean variable declarations in Java:

```
boolean flag = true;
boolean tooHigh, tooSmall, tooRough;
boolean done = false;
```

characters

Characters are another type of data. Note, however, that they are not part of the AP subset. Individual characters can be treated as separate data items, or, as we've seen in several example programs, they can be combined to form character strings.

A *character literal* is expressed in a Java program with single quotes, such as `'b'` or `'J'` or `';'`. Remember that *string literals* come in double quotation marks, and that the `String` type is not a primitive data type in Java, it is a class name. We discuss the `String` class in detail later in this chapter.

Note the difference between a digit as a character (or part of a string) and a digit as a number (or part of a larger number). The number `602` is a numeric value that can be used in an arithmetic calculation. But in the string `"602 Greenbriar Court"` the 6, 0, and 2 are characters, just like the rest of the characters that make up the string.

The characters are defined by a *character set*, which is just a list of characters in a particular order. Each programming language has its own particular character set. Several character sets have been proposed, but only a few have been used regularly over the years. The *ASCII character set* is a popular choice. ASCII stands for the American Standard Code for Information Interchange. The basic ASCII set uses seven bits per character, which leaves enough room to support 128 different characters, including:

- uppercase letters, such as `'A'`, `'B'`, and `'C'`
- lowercase letters, such as `'a'`, `'b'`, and `'c'`
- punctuation, such as the period (`'.'`), semicolon (`';'`), and comma (`','`)
- the digits `'0'` through `'9'`
- the space character, `' '`
- special symbols, such as the ampersand (`'&'`), vertical bar (`'|'`), and backslash (`'\'`)
- control characters, such as the carriage return, null, and end-of-text marks

The *control characters* are sometimes called nonprinting or invisible characters because they do not have a symbol that represents them. Yet they can be stored and used in the same way as any other character. Many control characters have special meanings to certain software applications.

As computers became more popular all over the world, users needed character sets that included other language alphabets. ASCII was changed to use eight bits per character, and the number of characters in the set doubled to 256. The new ASCII has many characters not used in English.

But even with 256 characters, the ASCII character set can't represent all the world's alphabets, especially the Asian alphabets, which have many thousands of characters, called ideograms. So the developers of the Java programming language chose the *Unicode character set,* which uses 16 bits per character, supporting 65,536 unique characters. The characters and symbols from many languages are included in the Unicode definition. ASCII is a subset of the Unicode character set. Appendix B discusses the Unicode character set in more detail.

In Java, the data type char represents a single character. The following are some examples of character variable declarations in Java:

```
char topGrade = 'A';
char symbol1, symbol2, symbol3;
char terminator = ';', separator = ' ';
```

2.5   arithmetic expressions

An *expression* is a combination of operators and operands, like a mathematical expression. Expressions usually do a calculation such as addition or division. The answer does not have to be a number, but it often is. The operands might be literals, constants, variables, or other sources of data. The way expressions are used is basic to programming.

> **key concept**
> Expressions are combinations of one or more operands and the operators used to perform a calculation.

For now we will focus on mathematical expressions. The usual arithmetic operations include addition (+), subtraction (–), multiplication (*), and division (/). Java also has another arithmetic operation: the *remainder operator* (%).The remainder operator returns the remainder after dividing the second operand into the first. For example, 17%4 equals 1 because 17 divided by 4 equals 4 with one remaining. The remainder operator returns the 1. The sign of the result is the sign of the numerator. So because 17 and 4 are both positive, the remainder is positive. Likewise, –20%3 equals –2, and 10%–5 equals 0.

As you might expect, if either or both operands to any numeric operator are floating point values, the result is a floating point value. However, the division operator produces results that are somewhat more complicated. If both operands are integers, the / operator performs *integer division,* meaning that any fractional part of the result is discarded. If one or the other or both operands are floating point values, the / operator performs *floating point division,* and the fractional part of the result is kept. For example, in the expression 10/4 both 10 and 4 are integers so integer division is performed. 4 goes into 10 2.5 times but the fractional part (the .5) is discarded, so the answer is 2, an integer. On the other hand, the results of 10.0/4 and 10/4.0 and 10.0/4.0 are all 2.5, because in these cases floating point division is peformed.

operator precedence

Operators can be combined to create more complicated expressions. For example, consider the following assignment statement:

```
result = 14 + 8 / 2;
```

The entire right-hand side of the assignment is solved, and then the answer is stored in the variable. But what is the answer? It is 11 if the addition is done first, or it is 18 if the division is done first. The order makes a big difference. In this case, the division is done before the addition, so the answer is 18. You should note that in this and other examples we have used literal values rather than variables to keep the expression simple. The order of operation is the same no matter what the operands are.

All expressions are solved according to an *operator precedence hierarchy,* the rules that govern the order in which operations are done. In the case of arithmetic operators, multiplication, division, and the remainder operator are all performed before addition and subtraction. Otherwise arithmetic operators are done left to right. Therefore we say the arithmetic operators have a *left-to-right association.*

> **key concept**
>
> Java follows a set of rules that govern the order in which operators will be evaluated in an expression. These rules are called an operator precedence hierarchy.

You can change the order, however, by using parentheses. For instance, if we really wanted the addition to be performed first, we could write the expression as follows:

```
result = (14 + 8) / 2;
```

Any expression in parentheses is done first. In complicated expressions, it is a good idea to use parentheses even when it is not strictly necessary.

Parentheses can be placed one inside another, and the innermost expressions are done first. Consider the following expression:

```
result = 3 * ((18 − 4) / 2);
```

In this example, the result is 21. First, the subtraction is done, because it is inside the inner parentheses. Then, even though multiplication and division usually would be done left to right, the division is done next because of the outer parentheses. Finally, the multiplication is done.

After the arithmetic operations are complete, the answer is stored in the variable on the left-hand side of the assignment operator (=), in this case the variable `result`.

Figure 2.4 shows a table with the order of the arithmetic operators, parentheses, and the assignment operator. Appendix C includes a full precedence table showing all Java operators.

A *unary operator* has only one operand, while a *binary operator* has two. The + and − arithmetic operators can be either unary or binary. The binary versions are for addition and subtraction, and the unary versions show positive and negative numbers. For example, −1 has a unary negation operator.

For an expression to be syntactically correct, the number of left parentheses must match the number of right parentheses and they must be properly nested inside one another. The following examples are *not* valid expressions:

```
result = ((19 + 8) % 3) − 4);   // not valid
result = (19 (+ 8 %) 3 − 4);    // not valid
```

The program in Listing 2.7, called `TempConverter`, converts Celsius to Fahrenheit. Note that the operands to the division operation are double to ensure that the fractional part of the number is kept. The precedence rules dictate that the multiplication happens before the addition, which is what we want.

Precedence Level	Operator	Operation	Associates
1	+	unary plus	R to L
	−	unary minus	
2	*	multiplication	L to R
	/	division	
	%	remainder	
3	+	addition	L to R
	−	subtraction	
	+	string concatenation	
4	=	assignment	R to L

figure 2.4   Precedence among some of the Java operators

listing 2.7

```java
//********************************************************************
//  TempConverter.java        Author: Lewis/Loftus/Cocking
//
//  Demonstrates the use of primitive data types and arithmetic
//  expressions.
//********************************************************************

public class TempConverter
{
   //-----------------------------------------------------------------
   //  Computes the Fahrenheit equivalent of a specific Celsius
   //  value using the formula F = (9/5)C + 32.
   //-----------------------------------------------------------------
   public static void main (String[] args)
   {
      final int BASE = 32;
      final double CONVERSION_FACTOR = 9.0 / 5.0;

      int celsiusTemp = 24;   // value to convert
      double fahrenheitTemp;

      fahrenheitTemp = celsiusTemp * CONVERSION_FACTOR + BASE;

      System.out.println ("Celsius Temperature: " + celsiusTemp);
      System.out.println ("Fahrenheit Equivalent: " + fahrenheitTemp);
   }
}
```

output

```
Celsius Temperature: 24
Fahrenheit Equivalent: 75.2
```

data conversion

Because Java is a strongly typed language, each data value is associated with a particular type. It is sometimes helpful or necessary to convert a data value of one type to another type, but we must be careful that we don't lose important information in the process. For example, suppose a double variable that holds the number 23.45 is converted to an int value. Because an int cannot store the fractional part of a number, some information would be lost in the conversion, and the number represented in the int would not keep its original value.

A conversion between one primitive type and another falls into one of two categories: widening conversions and narrowing conversions. *Widening conversions* are the safest because they usually do not lose information. Converting from an `int` to a `double` is a widening conversion.

Narrowing conversions are more likely to lose information than widening conversions are. Therefore, in general, they should be avoided. Converting from a `double` to an `int` is a narrowing conversion.

Note that `boolean` values are not mentioned in either widening or narrowing conversions. A `boolean` value (true or false) cannot be converted to any other primitive type and vice versa.

In Java, conversions can occur in three ways:

▸ assignment conversion

▸ arithmetic promotion

▸ casting

Assignment conversion happens when a value of one type is assigned to a variable of another type and the value is converted to the new type. Only widening conversions can be done this way. For example, if `money` is a `double` variable and `dollars` is an `int` variable, then the following assignment statement automatically converts the value in `dollars` to a `double`:

```
money = dollars;
```

So if `dollars` contains the value 25, after the assignment, `money` contains the value 25.0. However, if we try to go the other way around and assign `money` to `dollars`, the compiler will send us an error message telling us that we are trying to do a narrowing conversion that could lose information. If we really want to do this assignment, we have to do something called *casting*, which we'll get to in a minute.

Arithmetic promotion happens automatically when certain arithmetic operators need to change their operands in order to perform the operation. For example, when a floating point value called `sum` is divided by an integer value called `count`, the value of `count` becomes a floating point value automatically, before the division takes place, producing a floating point result:

```
result = sum / count;
```

Casting is the most general form of conversion in Java. If a conversion can be done at all in a Java program, it can be done using a cast. A cast is a type name in parentheses, placed in front of the value to be converted. For example, to convert `money` to an integer value, we could put a cast in front of it:

```
dollars = (int) money;
```

The cast returns the value in `money`, cutting off any fractional part. If `money` contained the value `84.69`, then after the assignment, `dollars` would contain the value `84`. Note, however, that the cast does not change the value in `money`. After the assignment operation is complete, `money` still contains the value `84.69`.

We can use casting to round a floating point number to the nearest integer. Since casting to an `int` cuts off the fractional part of a number, we can add 0.5 to a positive floating point value, cast it to an `int`, and get the effect of rounding the value. If `number` is a `double` variable with a positive value, then the expression `(int)(number+0.5)` is the nearest integer. For example, if `number` is 7.4, then (7.4 + 0.5) equals 7.9 so the `int` cast rounds `number` down to 7. If `number` is 7.5, then (7.5 + 0.5) equals 8.0 and `number` is rounded up to 8. Likewise, if `number` has a negative value, then `(int)(number−0.5)` is the nearest integer.

Casts are also helpful where we need to treat a value as another type. For example, if we want to divide the integer value `total` by the integer value `count` and get a floating point, we could do it as follows:

```
result = (double) total / count;
```

First, the cast operator returns a floating point version of the value in `total`. This operation does not change the value in `total`. Then, `count` is treated as a floating point value by arithmetic promotion. Now the division operator will do floating point division. If the cast had not been included, the operation would have done integer division and cut the fraction off before assigning it to `result`. Also note that because the cast operator has a higher precedence than the division operator, the cast operates on the value of `total`, not on the result of the division.

2.6 creating objects

A variable can hold either a primitive value or a *reference to an object*. Like variables that hold primitive types, a variable that holds an object reference must be declared. A class is used to define an object, and the class name can be thought of as the type of an object. The declarations of object references are structured like the declarations of primitive variables.

For example, this declaration creates a reference to a `String` object:

```
String name;
```

This is like the declaration of an integer: the type is followed by the variable name we want to use. However, no string object actually exists yet. To create an object, we use the new operator:

```
name = new String ("James Gosling");
```

Creating an object using the new operator is called *instantiation*. An object is called an *instance* of a particular class. After the new operator creates the object, a *constructor* helps set it up. A constructor has the same name as the class and is like a method. In this example, the parameter to the constructor is a string literal ("James Gosling"), which spells out the characters that the string object will hold.

We can declare the object reference variable and create the object itself in one step by initializing the variable in the declaration, just as we do with primitive types:

```
String name = new String ("James Gosling");
```

After an object has been instantiated, we use the *dot operator* to get its methods. We've used the dot operator many times in previous programs, such as in calls to System.out.println. The dot operator is added right after the object reference and is followed by the method being invoked. For example, to invoke the length method defined in the String class, we use the dot operator on the name reference variable:

```
count = name.length()
```

The length method does not take any parameters, but we need the parentheses to show that length is a method. Some methods produce a value that is *returned*. The length method will return the length of the string (the number of characters it contains). In this example, the returned value is assigned to the variable count. For the string "James Gosling", the length method returns 13 (this includes the space between the first and last names). Some methods do not return a value.

An object reference variable (such as name) stores the address where the object is stored in memory. We learn more about object references, instantiation, and constructors in later chapters.

the String class

Let's look at the String class in more detail. Strings in Java are objects represented by the String class. Figure 2.5 lists some of the more useful methods of the String class. The method headers indicate the type of information that must be passed to the method. The type shown in front of

```
String (String str)
    Constructor: creates a new string object with the same characters as str.

char charAt (int index)
    Returns the character at the specified index.
```

AP→
```
int compareTo (String str)
    Returns a number indicating whether this string comes before (a negative
    return value), is equal to (a zero return value), or comes after (a positive
    return value), the string str.
```

```
String concat (String str)
    Returns a new string made up of this string added to (concatenated with) str.
```

AP→
```
boolean equals (String str)
    Returns true if this string contains the same characters as str (including upper
    or lowercase) and false if it does not.
```

```
boolean equalsIgnoreCase (String str)
    Returns true if this string contains the same characters as str (ignoring upper
    and lowercase) and false if it does not.
```

AP→
```
int indexOf (String str)

    Returns the position of the first character in the first occurrence of str in this
    string.
```

AP→
```
int length ()
    Returns the number of characters in this string.
```

```
String replace (char oldChar, char newChar)
    Returns a new string that is identical with this string except that every
    oldChar is replaced by newChar.
```

AP→
```
String substring (int offset, int endIndex)
    Returns a new string that is a subset of this string starting at index offset
    and ending with the character at position endIndex-1.
```

AP→
```
String substring (int offset)
    Returns a new string that starts at index offset and extends to the end
    of the string.
```

```
String toLowerCase ()
    Returns a new string that is the same as this string except all uppercase
    letters are changed to lowercase.
```

```
String toUpperCase ()
    Returns a new string that is the same as this string except all lowercase
```

figure 2.5   Some methods of the String class

the method name is called the *return type* of the method. This is the type of
information that will be returned, if anything. A return type of void means
that the method does not return a value. The returned value can be used in
the calling method as needed.

Once a `String` object is created, its value cannot be lengthened or shortened, nor can any of its characters change. Thus we say that a `String` object is *immutable*. We can, however, create new `String` objects that have the new version of the original string's value.

Notice that some of the `String` methods refer to the *index* of a particular character. The index is a character's position in the string. The index of the first character in a string is zero, the index of the next character is one, and so on. Therefore in the string `"Hello"`, the index of the character `'H'` is zero, `'e'` is one, and so on.

Several `String` methods are used in the program called `String-Mutation`, shown in Listing 2.8.

Figure 2.6 shows the `String` objects that are created in Listing 2.8, the `StringMutation` program. Compare this diagram to the program code and the output. Keep in mind this program creates five separate `String` objects using various methods of the `String` class.

Even though they are not primitive types, strings are so basic and so often used that Java defines string literals in double quotation marks, as we've seen in various examples. This is a shortcut notation. Whenever a string literal appears, a `String` object is created. Therefore the following declaration is valid:

```
String name = "James Gosling";
```

That is, for `String` objects, we don't need the `new` operator and the call to the constructor. In most cases, we will use this simplified syntax.

wrapper classes

All of the primitive types in Java have *wrapper classes*. These are classes that let you create objects representing primitive data. The `Integer` class wraps (represents) an `int` and the `Double` class wraps (represents) a `double`. We can create `Integer` and `Double` objects from primitive data by passing an `int` or `double` value to the constructor of `Integer` or `Double`, respectively. For example, the following declaration creates an `Integer` object representing the integer `45`:

```
Integer number = new Integer (45);
```

Like strings, `Integer` and `Double` objects are immutable. Once an `Integer` or `Double` object is created, its value cannot be changed. Figures 2.7 and 2.8 list the methods on the `Integer` and `Double` classes that are part of the AP subset.

listing
 2.8

```java
//*************************************************************************
//  StringMutation.java          Author: Lewis/Loftus/Cocking
//
//  Demonstrates the use of the String class and its methods.
//*************************************************************************

public class StringMutation
{
   //----------------------------------------------------------------
   //  Prints a string and various mutations of it.
   //----------------------------------------------------------------
   public static void main (String[] args)
   {
      String phrase = new String ("Change is inevitable");
      String mutation1, mutation2, mutation3, mutation4;

      System.out.println ("Original string: \"" + phrase + "\"");
      System.out.println ("Length of string: " + phrase.length());

      mutation1 = phrase.concat (", except from vending machines.");
      mutation2 = mutation1.toUpperCase();
      mutation3 = mutation2.replace ('E', 'X');
      mutation4 = mutation3.substring (3, 30);

      // Print each mutated string
      System.out.println ("Mutation #1: " + mutation1);
      System.out.println ("Mutation #2: " + mutation2);
      System.out.println ("Mutation #3: " + mutation3);
      System.out.println ("Mutation #4: " + mutation4);

      System.out.println ("Mutated length: " + mutation4.length());
   }
}
```

output

```
Original string: "Change is inevitable"
Length of string: 20
Mutation #1: Change is inevitable, except from vending machines.
Mutation #2: CHANGE IS INEVITABLE, EXCEPT FROM VENDING MACHINES.
Mutation #3: CHANGX IS INXVITABLX, XXCXPT FROM VXNDING MACHINXS.
Mutation #4: NGX IS INXVITABLX, XXCXPT F
Mutated length: 27
```

phrase

"Change is inevitable"

mutation1

"Change is inevitable, except from vending machines."

mutation2

"CHANGE IS INEVITABLE, EXCEPT FROM VENDING MACHINES"

mutation3

"CHANGX IS INXVITABLX, XXCXPT FROM VXNDING MACHINXS"

mutation4

"NGX IS INXVITABLX, XXCXPT F"

figure 2.6   The String objects created in the StringMutation program

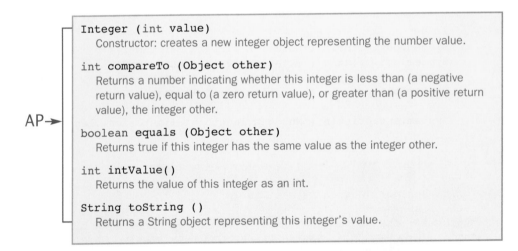

AP→

Integer (int value)
   Constructor: creates a new integer object representing the number value.

int compareTo (Object other)
   Returns a number indicating whether this integer is less than (a negative return value), equal to (a zero return value), or greater than (a positive return value), the integer other.

boolean equals (Object other)
   Returns true if this integer has the same value as the integer other.

int intValue()
   Returns the value of this integer as an int.

String toString ()
   Returns a String object representing this integer's value.

figure 2.7   Some methods of the Integer class

```
Double (double value)
   Constructor: creates a new double object representing the number value.

int compareTo(Object other)
   Returns a number indicating whether this double is less than (a negative
   return value), equal to (a zero return value), or greater than (a positive return
   value), the double other.

int doubleValue()
   Returns the value of this double as a double.

boolean equals(Object other)
   Returns true if this double has the same value as the double other.

String toString ()
   Returns a String object representing this double's value.
```

AP→

figure 2.8   Some methods of the Double class

2.7 class libraries and packages

A *class library* is a set of classes that supports the development of programs.
A compiler often comes with a class library. You can also get class libraries
separately through third-party vendors. The classes in a class library have
methods that are often valuable to a programmer because of their special
functions. In fact, programmers often depend on the methods in a class
library and begin to think of them as part of the language, even though technically, they are not in the language definition.

The String class, for instance, is not part of the Java language. It
is part of the Java *standard class library*. The classes that make up the
library were created by employees at Sun Microsystems, the people
who created the Java language.

> **key concept**
>
> The Java standard class library
> is a useful set of classes that
> anyone can use when writing
> Java programs.

The class library is made up of several sets of related classes, which are
sometimes called Java APIs, or *Application Programmer Interfaces*. For
example, we may refer to the Java Database API when we're talking about
the set of classes that help us write programs that interact with a database.
Another example of an API is the Java Swing API, which is a set of classes

used in a graphical user interface (GUI). Sometimes the entire standard library is referred to as the Java API.

The classes of the Java standard class library are also grouped into *packages*, which, like the APIs, let us group related classes by one name. Each class is part of a particular package. The `String` class, for example, is part of the `java.lang` package. The `System` class is part of the `java.lang` package as well. Figure 2.9 shows how the library is organized into packages.

The package organization is more fundamental and language based than the API names. The groups of classes that make up a given API might cross packages. We mostly refer to classes in terms of their package organization in this text.

Figure 2.10 describes some of the packages that are part of the Java standard class library. These packages are available on any type of computer system that supports Java software development. Many of these packages are very sophisticated and are not used in the development of basic programs.

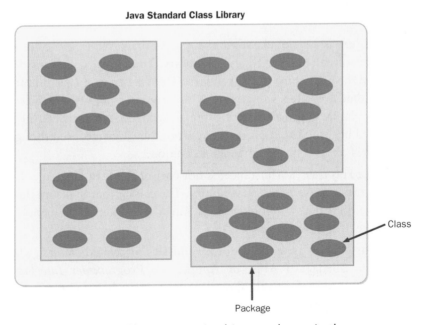

figure 2.9   Classes organized into packages in the Java standard class library

Package	Provides support to
java.applet	Create programs (applets) that are easily transported across the Web.
java.awt	Draw graphics and create graphical user interfaces; AWT stands for Abstract Windowing Toolkit.
java.beans	Define software components that can be easily combined into applications.
java.io	Perform many kinds of input and output functions.
java.lang	General support; it is automatically imported into all Java programs.
java.math	Perform calculations.
java.net	Communicate across a network.
java.rmi	Create programs that can be distributed across many computers; RMI stands for Remote Method Invocation.
java.security	Enforce security restrictions.
java.sql	Interact with databases; SQL stands for Structured Query Language.
java.text	Format text for output.
java.util	General utilities.
javax.swing	Create graphical user interfaces that extend the AWT capabilities.
javax.xml.parsers	Process XML documents; XML stands for eXtensible Markup Language.

figure 2.10   Some packages in the Java standard class library

Many classes of the Java standard class library are discussed throughout this book. The classes that are part of the AP subset are found in the java.lang and java.util packages. Appendix D serves as a general reference for all of the Java classes in the AP subset.

the import declaration

We can use the classes of the package java.lang when we write a program. To use classes from any other package, however, we must either *fully qualify* the reference, or use an *import declaration*.

When you want to use a class from a class library in a program, you could use its fully qualified name, including the package name, every time it is referenced. For example, every time you want to refer to the Random class that is defined in the java.util package, you can write java.util.Random.

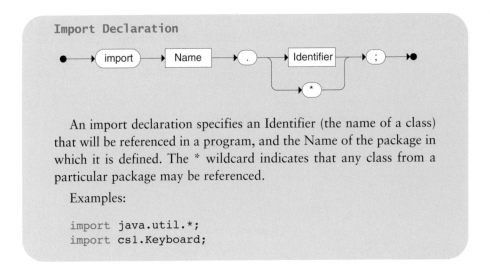

Import Declaration

An import declaration specifies an Identifier (the name of a class) that will be referenced in a program, and the Name of the package in which it is defined. The * wildcard indicates that any class from a particular package may be referenced.

Examples:

```
import java.util.*;
import cs1.Keyboard;
```

However, typing the whole package and class name every time it is needed quickly gets tiring. An import declaration makes this easier.

The import declaration identifies the packages and classes that will be used in a program so that the fully qualified name is not necessary with each reference. The following is an example of an import declaration:

```
import java.util.Random;
```

This declaration says that the Random class of the java.util package may be used in the program. Once you make this import declaration you only need to use the simple name Random when referring to that class in the program.

Another form of the import declaration uses an asterisk (*) to indicate that any class in the package might be used in the program. For example, the following declaration lets you use all classes in the java.util package in the program without having to type in the package name:

```
import java.util.*;
```

Once a class is imported, it is as if its code has been brought into the program. The code is not actually moved, but that is the effect.

The classes of the java.lang package are automatically imported because they are like basic extensions to the language. Therefore, any class in the java.lang package, such as String, can be used without an explicit import statement. It's as if all programs automatically contain the following statement:

```
import java.lang.*;
```

the Random class

You will often need random numbers when you are writing software. Games often use a random number to represent the roll of a die or the shuffle of a deck of cards. A flight simulator may use random numbers to decide how often a simulated flight has engine trouble. A program designed to help high school students prepare for the SATs may use random numbers to choose the next question to ask.

The Random class uses a *pseudorandom number generator.* A random number generator picks a number at random out of a range of values. A program that does this is called *pseudorandom*, because a program can't really pick a number randomly. A pseudorandom number generator might do a series of complicated calculations, starting with an initial *seed value,* and produce a number. Though they are technically not random (because they are calculated), the numbers produced by a pseudorandom number generator usually seem to be random, at least random enough for most situations. Figure 2.11 lists the methods of the Random class that are part of the AP subset.

The nextInt method is called with a single integer value as a parameter. If we pass a value, say N, to nextInt, the method returns a value from 0 to N–1. For example, if we pass in 100, we'll get a return value that is greater than or equal to 0 and less than or equal to 99.

Note that the value that we pass to the nextInt method is also the number of possible values we can get in return. We can shift the range by adding or subtracting the proper amount. To get a random number in the range 1 to 6, we can call nextInt(6) to get a value from 0 to 5, and then add 1.

AP→

Random ()
    Constructor: creates a new pseudorandom number generator.

double nextDouble ()
    Returns a random number between 0.0 (inclusive) and 1.0 (exclusive).

int nextInt (int num)
    Returns a random number in the range 0 to num-1.

figure 2.11   Some methods of the Random class

The nextDouble method of the Random class returns a double value that is greater than or equal to 0.0 and less than 1.0. If we want, we can use multiplication to scale the result, cast it into an int value to cut off the fractional part, then shift the range as we do with integers.

The program shown in Listing 2.9 produces several random numbers.

listing
   2.9

```
//********************************************************************
//   RandomNumbers.java        Author: Lewis/Loftus/Cocking
//
//   Demonstrates the import statement, and the creation of pseudo-
//   random numbers using the Random class.
//********************************************************************

import java.util.Random;

public class RandomNumbers
{
    //----------------------------------------------------------------
    //   Generates random numbers in various ranges.
    //----------------------------------------------------------------
    public static void main (String[] args)
    {
        Random generator = new Random();
        int num1;
        double num2;

        num1 = generator.nextInt(10);
        System.out.println ("From 0 to 9: " + num1);

        num1 = generator.nextInt(10) + 1;
        System.out.println ("From 1 to 10: " + num1);

        num1 = generator.nextInt(15) + 20;
        System.out.println ("From 20 to 34: " + num1);

        num1 = generator.nextInt(20) - 10;
        System.out.println ("From -10 to 9: " + num1);

        num2 = generator.nextDouble();
        System.out.println ("A random double [between 0-1]: " + num2);

        num2 = generator.nextDouble() * 6;   // 0.0 to 5.999999
        num1 = (int) num2 + 1;
        System.out.println ("From 1 to 6: " + num1);
    }
}
```

listing
   2.9   continued

output

```
From 0 to 9: 6
From 1 to 10: 4
From 20 to 34: 30
From -10 to 9: -4
A random double [between 0-1]: 0.052495003
From 1 to 6: 6
```

2.8 invoking class methods

Some methods can be invoked through their class name, without having to instantiate an object of the class first. These are called *class methods* or *static methods*. Let's look at some examples.

the Math class

The Math class lets us do a large number of basic mathematical functions. The Math class is part of the Java standard class library and is defined in the java.lang package. Figure 2.12 lists several of its methods.

The reserved word static indicates that the method can be invoked through the name of the class. For example, a call to Math.abs(total) will return the absolute value of the number stored in total. A call to Math.pow(7, 4) will return 7 raised to the fourth power. Note that you can pass integer values to a method that accepts a double parameter. This is a form of assignment conversion, which we discussed earlier in this chapter.

We'll make use of some Math methods in examples after we look at the Keyboard class.

the Keyboard class

The Keyboard class contains methods that help us get data that the user types on the keyboard. The methods of the Keyboard class are static and are therefore invoked through the Keyboard class name.

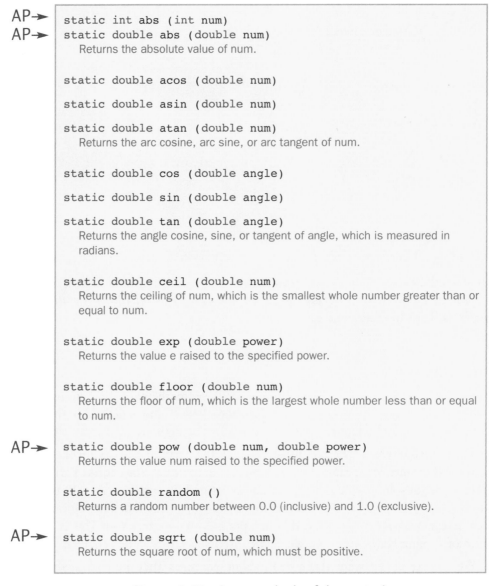

AP→
AP→

```
static int abs (int num)
static double abs (double num)
   Returns the absolute value of num.

static double acos (double num)

static double asin (double num)

static double atan (double num)
   Returns the arc cosine, arc sine, or arc tangent of num.

static double cos (double angle)

static double sin (double angle)

static double tan (double angle)
   Returns the angle cosine, sine, or tangent of angle, which is measured in
   radians.

static double ceil (double num)
   Returns the ceiling of num, which is the smallest whole number greater than or
   equal to num.

static double exp (double power)
   Returns the value e raised to the specified power.

static double floor (double num)
   Returns the floor of num, which is the largest whole number less than or equal
   to num.

static double pow (double num, double power)
   Returns the value num raised to the specified power.

static double random ()
   Returns a random number between 0.0 (inclusive) and 1.0 (exclusive).

static double sqrt (double num)
   Returns the square root of num, which must be positive.
```

AP→

AP→

figure 2.12   Some methods of the Math class

One very important characteristic of the Keyboard class must be made clear: the Keyboard class is *not* part of the Java standard class library, nor is it part of the AP subset. It has been written by the authors of this book to help you read user input. It is defined as part of a package called cs1 (that's cs-one, not cs-el). Because it is not part of the Java

key concept

The Keyboard class is not part of the Java standard library. It is therefore not available on all Java development platforms.

standard class library, it will not be found on generic Java development environments. You may have to configure your environment so that it knows where to find the Keyboard class.

Reading input from the user in Java can get somewhat involved. The Keyboard class lets you ignore those details for now. We explore these issues later in the book, at which point we fully explain the details currently hidden by the Keyboard class.

For now we will use the Keyboard class for the services it provides, just as we do any other class. In that sense, the Keyboard class is a good example of object abstraction. We rely on classes and objects for the services they provide. It doesn't matter if they are part of a library, if a third party writes them, or if we write them ourselves. We use and interact with them in the same way. Figure 2.13 lists the input methods of the Keyboard class.

Let's look at some examples that use the Keyboard class. The program shown in Listing 2.10, called Echo, simply reads a string that is typed by the user and echoes it back to the screen.

The Quadratic program, shown in Listing 2.11, uses the Keyboard and Math classes. Recall that a quadratic equation has the following general form:

$ax^2 + bx + c$

```
static boolean readBoolean ()

static byte readByte ()

static char readChar ()

static double readDouble ()

static float readFloat ()

static int readInt ()

static long readLong ()

static short readShort ()

static String readString ()
   Returns a value of the indicated type obtained from user keyboard input.
```

figure 2.13 Some methods of the Keyboard class

listing
   2.10

```
//********************************************************************
//  Echo.java        Author: Lewis/Loftus/Cocking
//
//  Demonstrates the use of the readString method of the Keyboard
//  class.
//********************************************************************

import cs1.Keyboard;

public class Echo
{
   //-----------------------------------------------------------------
   //  Reads a character string from the user and prints it.
   //-----------------------------------------------------------------
   public static void main (String[] args)
   {
      String message;

      System.out.println ("Enter a line of text:");

      message = Keyboard.readString();

      System.out.println ("You entered: \"" + message + "\"");
   }
}
```

output

```
Enter a line of text:
Set your laser printer on stun!
You entered: "Set your laser printer on stun!"
```

The Quadratic program reads values that represent the coefficients in a quadratic equation (a, b, and c), and then evaluates the quadratic formula to determine the roots of the equation. The quadratic formula is:

$$\text{roots} = \frac{-b \pm \sqrt{b^2 - 4ac}}{2a}$$

listing
   2.11

```java
//********************************************************************
//  Quadratic.java        Author: Lewis/Loftus/Cocking
//
//  Demonstrates a calculation based on user input.
//********************************************************************

import cs1.Keyboard;

public class Quadratic
{
    //----------------------------------------------------------------
    //  Determines the roots of a quadratic equation.
    //----------------------------------------------------------------
    public static void main (String[] args)
    {
        int a, b, c;   // ax^2 + bx + c

        System.out.print ("Enter the coefficient of x squared: ");
        a = Keyboard.readInt();

        System.out.print ("Enter the coefficient of x: ");
        b = Keyboard.readInt();

        System.out.print ("Enter the constant: ");
        c = Keyboard.readInt();

        // Use the quadratic formula to compute the roots.
        // Assumes a positive discriminant.

        double discriminant = Math.pow(b, 2) - (4 * a * c);
        double root1 = ((-1 * b) + Math.sqrt(discriminant)) / (2 * a);
        double root2 = ((-1 * b) - Math.sqrt(discriminant)) / (2 * a);

        System.out.println ("Root #1: " + root1);
        System.out.println ("Root #2: " + root2);
    }
}
```

output

```
Enter the coefficient of x squared: 3
Enter the coefficient of x: 8
Enter the constant: 4
Root #1: -0.6666666666666666
Root #2: -2.0
```

2.9 formatting output

The `NumberFormat` class and the `DecimalFormat` class are used to format information so that it looks right when printed or displayed. They are both part of the Java standard class library and are defined in the `java.text` package. These classes are not part of the AP subset.

the NumberFormat class

The `NumberFormat` class lets you format numbers. You don't instantiate a `NumberFormat` object using the `new` operator. Instead, you ask for an object from one of the methods that you can invoke through the class itself. We haven't covered the reasons for this yet, but we will explain them later. Figure 2.14 lists some of the methods of the `NumberFormat` class.

Two of the methods in the `NumberFormat` class, `getCurrency-Instance` and `getPercentInstance`, return an object that is used to format numbers. The `getCurrencyInstance` method returns a formatter for money values. The `getPercentInstance` method returns an object that formats a percentage. The `format` method is called through a formatter object and returns a `String` that contains the formatted number.

The `Price` program shown in Listing 2.12 uses both types of formatters. It reads in a sales transaction and computes the final price, including tax.

```
String format (double number)
    Returns a string containing the specified number formatted according to
    this object's pattern.

static NumberFormat getCurrencyInstance()
    Returns a NumberFormat object that represents a currency format for the
    current locale.

static NumberFormat getPercentInstance()
    Returns a NumberFormat object that represents a percentage format for
    the current locale.
```

figure 2.14   Some methods of the `NumberFormat` class

```
listing
   2.12
```

```
//****************************************************************
//   Price.java         Author: Lewis/Loftus/Cocking
//
//   Demonstrates the use of various Keyboard and NumberFormat
//   methods.
//****************************************************************

import cs1.Keyboard;
import java.text.NumberFormat;

public class Price
{
   //-----------------------------------------------------------------
   //  Calculates the final price of a purchased item using values
   //  entered by the user.
   //-----------------------------------------------------------------
   public static void main (String[] args)
   {
      final double TAX_RATE = 0.06;  // 6% sales tax

      int quantity;
      double subtotal, tax, totalCost, unitPrice;

      System.out.print ("Enter the quantity: ");
      quantity = Keyboard.readInt();

      System.out.print ("Enter the unit price: ");
      unitPrice = Keyboard.readDouble();

      subtotal = quantity * unitPrice;
      tax = subtotal * TAX_RATE;
      totalCost = subtotal + tax;

      // Print output with appropriate formatting
      NumberFormat money = NumberFormat.getCurrencyInstance();
      NumberFormat percent = NumberFormat.getPercentInstance();

      System.out.println ("Subtotal: " + money.format(subtotal));
      System.out.println ("Tax: " + money.format(tax) + " at "
                          + percent.format(TAX_RATE));
      System.out.println ("Total: " + money.format(totalCost));
   }
}
```

listing
    2.12   continued

output

```
Enter the quantity: 5
Enter the unit price: 3.87
Subtotal: $19.35
Tax: $1.16 at 6%
Total: $20.51
```

the DecimalFormat class

Unlike the NumberFormat class, the DecimalFormat class is instantiated in the usual way using the new operator. Its constructor takes a string that represents the formatting pattern. We can then use the format method to format a particular value. Later on, if we want to change the formatting pattern, we can call the applyPattern method. Figure 2.15 describes these methods.

The pattern defined by the string that is passed to the DecimalFormat constructor gets pretty complicated. Different symbols are used to represent different formatting guidelines. The pattern defined by the string "0.###", for example, tells us that at least one digit should be printed to the left of the decimal point and should be a zero if that part of the number is zero. It also indicates that the value to the right of the decimal point should be rounded to three digits. This pattern is used in the CircleStats program shown in Listing 2.13, which reads the radius of a circle from the user and computes its area and circumference. The final zero, such as in 78.540, is not printed.

DecimalFormat (String pattern)
    Constructor: creates a new DecimalFormat object with the specified pattern.

void applyPattern (String pattern)
    Applies the specified pattern to this DecimalFormat object.

String format (double number)
    Returns a string containing the specified number formatted according to the current pattern.

---

figure 2.15   Some methods of the DecimalFormat class

listing
   2.13

```java
//************************************************************************
//  CircleStats.java        Author: Lewis/Loftus/Cocking
//
//  Demonstrates the formatting of decimal values using the
//  DecimalFormat class.
//************************************************************************

import cs1.Keyboard;
import java.text.DecimalFormat;

public class CircleStats
{
   //--------------------------------------------------------------------
   //  Calculates the area and circumference of a circle given its
   //  radius.
   //--------------------------------------------------------------------
   public static void main (String[] args)
   {
      int radius;
      double area, circumference;

      System.out.print ("Enter the circle's radius: ");
      radius = Keyboard.readInt();

      area = Math.PI * Math.pow(radius, 2);
      circumference = 2 * Math.PI * radius;

      // Round the output to three decimal places
      DecimalFormat fmt = new DecimalFormat ("0.###");

      System.out.println ("The circle's area: " + fmt.format(area));
      System.out.println ("The circle's circumference: "
                          + fmt.format(circumference));
   }
}
```

output

```
Enter the circle's radius: 5
The circle's area: 78.54
The circle's circumference: 31.416
```

2.10 an introduction to applets

There are two kinds of Java programs: Java applets and Java applications. A Java *applet* is a Java program that is embedded in an HTML document, transported across a network, and executed using a Web browser. A Java *application* is a stand-alone program that can be executed using the Java interpreter. All programs shown so far in this book have been Java applications.

The Web lets users send and receive different types of media, such as text, graphics, and sound, using a point-and-click interface that is extremely convenient and easy to use. A Java applet was the first kind of executable program that could be retrieved using Web software. Java applets are just another type of media that can be exchanged across the Web.

Though Java applets are meant to be transported across a network, they don't have to be. They can be viewed locally using a Web browser. For that matter, they don't even have to be executed through a Web browser at all. A tool in Sun's Java Software Development Kit called appletviewer can be used to interpret and execute an applet. We use appletviewer to display most of the applets in the book. However, usually the point of making a Java applet is to provide a link to it on a Web page so it can be retrieved and executed by Web users anywhere in the world.

Java bytecode (not Java source code) is linked to an HTML document and sent across the Web. A version of the Java interpreter that is part of a Web browser executes the applet once it reaches its destination. A Java applet must be compiled into bytecode format before it can be used with the Web.

There are some important differences between a Java applet and a Java application. Because the Web browser that executes an applet is already running, applets can be thought of as a part of a larger program. That means they do not have a `main` method where execution starts. For example, the `paint` method in an applet is automatically invoked by the applet. Consider the program in Listing 2.14, in which the `paint` method is used to draw a few shapes and write a quotation by Albert Einstein to the screen.

The two import statements at the beginning of the program tell which packages are used in the program. In this example, we need the `Applet` class, which is part of the `java.applet` package, and the graphics capabilities defined in the `java.awt` package.

A class that defines an applet extends the `Applet` class, as shown in the header line of the class declaration. This makes use of the object-oriented concept of inheritance, which we explore in more detail in Chapter 7. Applet classes must also be declared as `public`.

listing
   2.14

```java
//***********************************************************************
//   Einstein.java        Author: Lewis/Loftus/Cocking
//
//   Demonstrates a basic applet.
//***********************************************************************

import java.applet.Applet;
import java.awt.*;

public class Einstein extends Applet
{
    //-------------------------------------------------------------
    //  Draws a quotation by Albert Einstein among some shapes.
    //-------------------------------------------------------------
    public void paint (Graphics page)
    {
        page.drawRect (50, 50, 40, 40);     // square
        page.drawRect (60, 80, 225, 30);    // rectangle
        page.drawOval (75, 65, 20, 20);     // circle
        page.drawLine (35, 60, 100, 120);   // line

        page.drawString ("Out of clutter, find simplicity.", 110, 70);
        page.drawString ("-- Albert Einstein", 130, 100);
    }
}
```

display

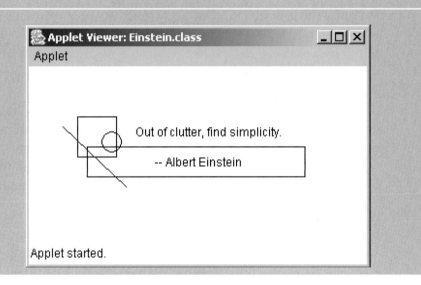

The `paint` method is one of several special applet methods. It is invoked automatically whenever the graphic elements of the applet need to be "painted" to the screen, such as when the applet is first run or when another window that was covering it is moved.

Note that the `paint` method accepts a `Graphics` object as a parameter. A `Graphics` object defines a particular *graphics context*, a part of the screen we can use. The graphics context passed into an applet's `paint` method represents the entire applet window. Each graphics context has its own coordinate system. In later examples, we will have multiple components, each with its own graphics context.

A `Graphics` object lets us draw shapes using methods such as `drawRect`, `drawOval`, `drawLine`, and `drawString`. The parameters passed to the drawing methods list the coordinates and sizes of the shapes to be drawn. We explore these and other methods that draw shapes in the next section.

executing applets using the Web

In order for the applet to travel over the Web and be executed by a browser, it must be referenced in a HyperText Markup Language (HTML) document. An HTML document contains *tags* that spell out formatting instructions and identify the special types of media that are to be included in a document. A Java program is considered a specific media type, just as text, graphics, and sound are. An HTML tag is enclosed in angle brackets:

```
<applet code="Einstein.class" width=350 height=175>
</applet>
```

This tag says that the bytecode stored in the file `Einstein.class` should travel over the network and be executed on the machine that wants to view this particular HTML document. The applet tag also states the width and height of the applet in pixels.

Note that the applet tag refers to the bytecode file of the `Einstein` applet, not to the source code file. Before an applet can travel over the Web, it must be compiled into its bytecode format. Then, as shown in Figure 2.16, the document can be loaded using a Web browser, which will automatically interpret and execute the applet.

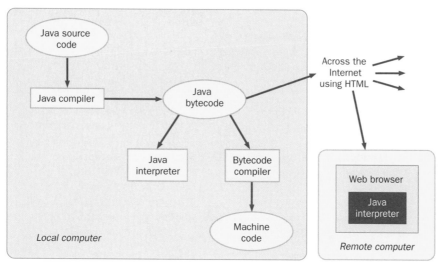

figure 2.16   The Java translation and execution process, including applets

2.11 drawing shapes

The Java standard class library provides many classes that let us use graphics. The Graphics class is the basic tool for presenting and using graphics.

the Graphics class

The Graphics class is defined in the java.awt package. Its methods let us draw shapes, including lines, rectangles, and ovals. Figure 2.17 lists some of the drawing methods of the Graphics class. Note that these methods also let us draw circles and squares, which are types of ovals and rectangles. We discuss more drawing methods of the Graphics class later in this book.

The methods of the Graphics class let us fill, or color in, a shape if we want to. An unfilled shape is only an outline and is transparent (you can see any underlying graphics). A filled shape is solid and covers any underlying graphics.

> Most shapes can be drawn filled (opaque) or unfilled (as an outline).

key concept

All of these methods rely on the Java coordinate system, which we discussed in Chapter 1. Recall that point (0,0) is in the upper-left corner, such that x values get larger as we move to the right, and y values get larger as we move down. Any shapes drawn at coordinates that are outside the visible area will not be seen.

```
void drawArc (int x, int y, int width, int height, int
startAngle, int arcAngle)
     Paints part of an oval in the rectangle defined by x, y, width, and
     height. The oval starts at startAngle and continues for a distance
     defined by arcAngle.

void drawLine (int x1, int y1, int x2, int y2)
     Paints a line from point (x1, y1) to point (x2, y2).

void drawOval (int x, int y, int width, int height)
     Paints an oval in the rectangle with an upper left corner of (x, y) and
     dimensions width and height.

void drawRect (int x, int y, int width, int height)
     Paints a rectangle with upper left corner (x, y) and dimensions width and
     height.

void drawString (String str, int x, int y)
     Paints the character string str at point (x, y), extending to the right.

void fillArc (int x, int y, int width, int height,
int startAngle, int arcAngle)

void fillOval (int x, int y, int width, int height)

void fillRect (int x, int  y, int width, int height)
     Draws a shape and fills it with the current foreground color.

Color getColor ()
     Returns this graphics context's foreground color.

void setColor (Color color)
     Sets this graphics context's foreground color to the specified color.
```

figure 2.17   Some methods of the Graphics class

> **key concept**
> A bounding rectangle defines the position and size of curved shapes such as ovals.

Many of the Graphics drawing methods are self-explanatory, but some require a little more discussion. Note, for instance, that the drawOval method draws an oval inside an imaginary rectangle, called the *bounding rectangle*. Shapes with curves such as ovals are often drawn inside a rectangle as a way of giving their perimeters. Figure 2.18 shows a bounding rectangle for an oval.

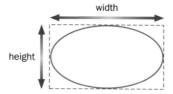

figure 2.18   An oval and its bounding rectangle

An arc is a segment of an oval. To draw an arc, we describe the oval and the part of the oval we're interested in. The starting point of the arc is the *start angle* and the ending point is the *arc angle*. The arc angle does not say where the arc ends, but rather its range. The start angle and the arc angle are measured in degrees. The beginning of the start angle is an imaginary horizontal line passing through the center of the oval and can be referred to as 0°; as shown in Figure 2.19.

> An arc is a segment of an oval; the segment begins at a start angle and extends for a distance specified by the arc angle.
>
> **key concept**

the Color class

In Java, a programmer uses the `Color` class, which is part of the `java.awt` package, to define and manage colors. Each object of the `Color` class represents a single color. The class provides a basic set of predefined colors. Figure 2.20 lists the colors of the `Color` class.

> A `Color` class contains several common colors.
>
> **key concept**

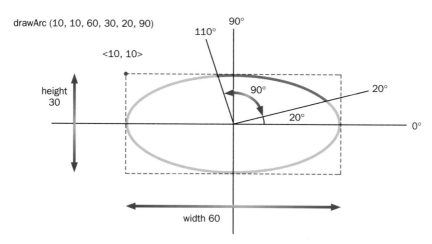

figure 2.19   An arc defined by an oval, a start angle, and an arc angle

Color	Object	RGB Value
black	Color.black	0, 0, 0
blue	Color.blue	0, 0, 255
cyan	Color.cyan	0, 255, 255
gray	Color.gray	128, 128, 128
dark gray	Color.darkGray	64, 64, 64
light gray	Color.lightGray	192, 192, 192
green	Color.green	0, 255, 0
magenta	Color.magenta	255, 0, 255
orange	Color.orange	255, 200, 0
pink	Color.pink	255, 175, 175
red	Color.red	255, 0, 0
white	Color.white	255, 255, 255
yellow	Color.yellow	255, 255, 0

figure 2.20   Predefined colors in the Color class

The Color class also contains methods you can use to define and manage many other colors. Recall from Chapter 1 that you can create colors using the RGB technique by mixing the primary colors: red, green, and blue.

Every graphics context has a current *foreground color* that is used whenever shapes or strings are drawn. Every surface that can be drawn on has a *background color.* The foreground color is set using the setColor method of the Graphics class, and the background color is set using the setBackground method of the component on which we are drawing, such as the applet.

Listing 2.15 shows an applet called Snowman. It uses drawing and color methods to draw a snowman. Look at the code carefully to see how each shape is drawn to create the picture.

Note that the snowman is based on two constant values called MID and TOP, which define the midpoint of the snowman (left to right) and the top of the snowman's head. The entire snowman is drawn relative to these values. Using constants like these makes it easier to create the snowman and to make changes later. For example, to shift the snowman to the right or left in our picture, we only have to change one constant declaration.

listing
    2.15

```
//************************************************************************
//   Snowman.java        Author: Lewis/Loftus/Cocking
//
//   Demonstrates basic drawing methods and the use of color.
//************************************************************************

import java.applet.Applet;
import java.awt.*;

public class Snowman extends Applet
{
    //-----------------------------------------------------------------
    //   Draws a snowman.
    //-----------------------------------------------------------------
    public void paint (Graphics page)
    {
        final int MID = 150;
        final int TOP = 50;

        setBackground (Color.cyan);

        page.setColor (Color.blue);
        page.fillRect (0, 175, 300, 50);   // ground

        page.setColor (Color.yellow);
        page.fillOval (-40, -40, 80, 80);   // sun

        page.setColor (Color.white);
        page.fillOval (MID-20, TOP, 40, 40);        // head
        page.fillOval (MID-35, TOP+35, 70, 50);   // upper torso
        page.fillOval (MID-50, TOP+80, 100, 60);   // lower torso

        page.setColor (Color.black);
        page.fillOval (MID-10, TOP+10, 5, 5);    // left eye
        page.fillOval (MID+5, TOP+10, 5, 5);     // right eye

        page.drawArc (MID-10, TOP+20, 20, 10, 190, 160);   // smile

        page.drawLine (MID-25, TOP+60, MID-50, TOP+40);  // left arm
        page.drawLine (MID+25, TOP+60, MID+55, TOP+60);  // right arm

        page.drawLine (MID-20, TOP+5, MID+20, TOP+5);  // brim of hat
        page.fillRect (MID-15, TOP-20, 30, 25);         // top of hat
    }
}
```

listing
     2.15   continued

display

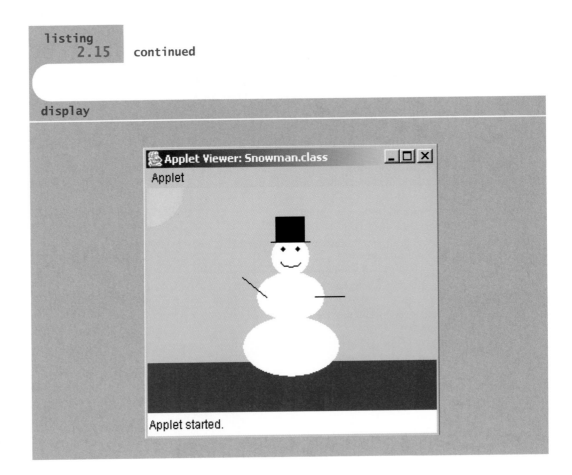

summary of key concepts

- The information we manage in a Java program is either primitive data or objects.

- An abstraction hides details. A good abstraction hides the right details at the right time.

- A variable is a name for a memory location used to hold a value of a particular data type.

- A variable can store only one value of its declared type.

- Java is a strongly typed language. Each variable has a specific type, and we cannot assign a value of one type to a variable of another type.

- Constants are like variables, but they hold one particular value.

- Java has two kinds of numeric values: integers and floating point. The primitive type `int` is an integer data type and `double` is a floating point data type.

- Many programming statements involve expressions. Expressions are combinations of one or more operands and the operators used to perform a calculation.

- Java has rules that govern the order in which operators will be evaluated in an expression.

- Avoid narrowing conversions because they can lose information.

- The `new` operator returns a reference to a newly created object.

- The Java standard class library is a useful set of classes that anyone can use when writing Java programs.

- A package is a Java language element used to group related classes under a common name.

- The `Keyboard` class is not part of the Java standard library. It is not available on all Java development platforms.

- Applets are Java programs that can travel across a network and be executed using a Web browser. Java applications are stand-alone programs that can be executed using the Java interpreter.

- Most shapes can be drawn filled in or left unfilled.

- A bounding rectangle is often used to define the position and size of curved shapes such as ovals.

▶ An arc is a segment of an oval; the segment begins at a specific start angle and extends for a distance specified by the arc angle.

▶ The Color class contains several common predefined colors.

self-review questions

2.1   What are the primary concepts that support object-oriented programming?

2.2   Why is an object an example of abstraction?

2.3   What is primitive data? How are primitive data types different from objects?

2.4   What is a string literal?

2.5   What is the difference between the print and println methods?

2.6   What is a parameter?

2.7   What is an escape sequence? Give some examples.

2.8   What is a variable declaration?

2.9   How many values can be stored in an integer variable?

2.10 What is a character set?

2.11 What is operator precedence?

2.12 What is the result of 19%5 when evaluated in a Java expression? Explain.

2.13 What is the result of 13/4 when evaluated in a Java expression? Explain.

2.14 Why are widening conversions safer than narrowing conversions?

2.15 What does the new operator do?

2.16 What is a Java package?

2.17 Why doesn't the `String` class have to be imported into our programs?

2.18 What is a class method (also called a static method)?

2.19 What is the difference between a Java application and a Java applet?

multiple choice

2.1   What will be printed by the following statement?

```
System.out.println("Use a \"\\\"");
```

a. `Use a \"\\\"`

b. `"Use a "\""`

c. `Use a "\"`

d. `Use a \"\""`

e. `Use a "\\"`

2.2   Which keyword is used to declare a constant?

a. `int`

b. `double`

c. `MAX`

d. `constant`

e. `final`

2.3   The expression `"number" + 6 + 4 * 5` produces which of the following string literals?

a. `"number645"`

b. `"number105"`

c. `"number50"`

d. `"number620"`

e. `"number26"`

2.4   Which of the following is a character literal?

    a. b

    b. 'b'

    c. "b"

    d. 2

    e. 2.0

2.5   What is the result of the operation 30 % 4?

    a. 2

    b. 3

    c. 4

    d. 7

    e. 7.5

2.6   The expression 1 / 4 is equal to which of the following?

    a. 1.0 / 4.0

    b. (double)2 / 8

    c. 0.25

    d. (int)1.0 / 4.0

    e. 1 / (int)4.0

2.7   Which of the following instantiates a String object?

    a. String word;

    b. word = new String("the");

    c. word.length();

    d. word = name;

    e. String word = name;

2.8   Assuming g is an instance of the Random class, which statement
       will generate a random number between 10 and 100 inclusive?

    a. num = g.nextInt(101);

    b. num = 10 + g.nextInt(101);

    c. num = 10 + g.nextInt(91);

    d. num = 10 + g.nextInt(90);

    e. num = g.nextInt(110) − 10;

2.9 Which statement would we use to create an object from a class called Thing?

a. Thing something;

b. Thing something = Thing();

c. Thing something = new Thing;

d. Thing something = new Thing();

e. new Thing() = something;

2.10 Suppose we have a variable something that is a reference to a Thing object. How would we call the method doIt on our Thing object?

a. doIt()

b. something.doIt()

c. doIt(something)

d. something/doIt

e. something(doIt)

true/false

2.1 An object is an abstraction, meaning that the user doesn't need to know the details of how it works.

2.2 A string literal appears inside single quotation marks.

2.3 In order to include a double quotation mark (") or a backslash (\) in a string literal, we must use an escape sequence.

2.4 The operators *, /, and % have precedence over + and −.

2.5 Widening conversions can happen automatically, such as in the expression 1 + 2.5 where 1 is converted to a double.

2.6 In the declaration int num = 2.4; the 2.4 will automatically be converted to an int and num will get the value 2.

2.7 In Java, Integer is a class, whereas int is a primitive type.

2.8 Assuming generator is an object of the Random class, the call generator.nextInt(8) will generate a random number between 0 and 7 inclusive.

short answer

2.1   Explain the following programming statement in terms of objects and the services they provide:

```
System.out.println ("I gotta be me!");
```

2.2   What output is produced by the following code fragment? Explain.

```
System.out.print ("Here we go!");
System.out.println ("12345");
System.out.print ("Test this if you are not sure.");
System.out.print ("Another.");
System.out.println ();
System.out.println ("All done.");
```

2.3   What is wrong with the following program statement? How can it be fixed?

```
System.out.println ("To be or not to be, that
is the question.");
```

2.4   What output is produced by the following statement? Explain.

```
System.out.println ("50 plus 25 is " + 50 + 25);
```

2.5   What is the output produced by the following statement? Explain.

```
System.out.println ("He thrusts his fists\n\tagainst" +
" the post\nand still insists\n\the sees the \"ghost\"");
```

2.6   Given the following declarations, what result is stored in each of the listed assignment statements?

```
int iResult, num1 = 25, num2 = 40, num3 = 17, num4 = 5;
double fResult, val1 = 17.0, val2 = 12.78;
```

Example: iResult = num2%num1;

The result that gets stored is 15 because 40%25 equals 15 (25 goes into 40 once, with remainder 15).

a. `iResult = num1 / num4;`

b. `fResult = num1 / num4;`

c. `iResult = num3 / num4;`

d. `fResult = num3 / num4;`

e. `fResult = val1 / num4;`

f. `fResult = val1 / val2;`

g. `iResult = num1 / num2;`

h. `fResult = (double) num1 / num2;`

i. `fResult = num1 / (double) num2;`

j. `fResult = (double) (num1 / num2);`

k. `iResult = (int) (val1 / num4);`

l. `fResult = (int) (val1 / num4);`

m. `fResult = (int) ((double) num1 / num2);`

n. `iResult = num3 % num4;`

o. `iResult = num2 % num3;`

p. `iResult = num3 % num2;`

q. `iResult = num2 % num4;`

2.7   For each of the following expressions, indicate the order in which the operators will be evaluated by writing a number beneath each operator.

Example: `a + b * c - d`

```
          2   1   3
```

a. `a - b - c - d`

b. `a - b + c - d`

c. `a + b / c / d`

d. `a + b / c * d`

e. `a / b * c * d`

f. `a % b / c * d`

g. `a % b % c % d`

h. `a - (b - c) - d`

i. `(a - (b - c)) - d`

j. a − ((b − c) − d)

k. a % (b % c) * d * e

l. a + (b − c) * d − e

m. (a + b) * c + d * e

n. (a + b) * (c / d) % e

2.8   What output is produced by the following code fragment?

```
String m1, m2, m3;
m1 = "Quest for the Holy Grail";
m2 = m1.toLowerCase();
m3 = m1 + " " + m2;
System.out.println (m3.replace('h', 'z'));
```

2.9   Write an assignment statement that computes the square root of the sum of num1 and num2 and assigns the result to num3.

2.10   Write a single statement that computes and prints the absolute value of total.

2.11   Assuming that a Random object called generator has been created, what is the range of the result of each of the following expressions?

a. generator.nextInt(20)

b. generator.nextInt(8) + 1

c. generator.nextInt(45) + 10

d. generator.nextInt(100) − 50

2.12   Write code to declare and instantiate an object of the Random class (call the object reference variable rand). Then write a list of expressions using the nextInt method that generates random numbers in the following ranges, including the endpoints.

a. 0 to 10

b. 0 to 500

c. 1 to 10

d. 1 to 500

e. 25 to 50

f. −10 to 15

programming projects

2.1 Create a new version of the `Lincoln` application from Chapter 1 with quotation marks around the quotation.

2.2 Write an application that reads three numbers and prints their average.

2.3 Write an application that reads two floating point numbers and prints their sum, difference, and product.

2.4 Create a revised version of the `TempConverter` application to convert from Fahrenheit to Celsius. Read the Fahrenheit temperature from the user.

2.5 Write an application that converts miles to kilometers. (One mile equals 1.60935 kilometers.) Read the miles value from the user as a floating point value.

2.6 Write an application that reads values representing a time in hours, minutes, and seconds. Then print the same time in seconds. (For example, 1 hour, 28 minutes, and 42 seconds is equal to 5322 seconds.)

2.7 Create a new version of Programming Project 2.6 that works in reverse. That is, read a value representing a number of seconds, then print the same amount of time in hours, minutes, and seconds. (For example, 9999 seconds is equal to 2 hours, 46 minutes, and 39 seconds.)

2.8 Write an application that reads the (x, y) coordinates for two points. Compute the distance between the two points using the following formula:

$$\text{Distance} = \sqrt{(x_2 - x_1)^2 + (y_2 - y_1)^2}$$

2.9 Write an application that reads the radius of a sphere and prints its volume and surface area. Use the following formulas. Print the output to four decimal places. r represents the radius.

$$\text{Volume} = \tfrac{4}{3}\pi r^3$$

$$\text{Surface area} = 4\pi r^2$$

2.10 Write an application that reads the lengths of the sides of a triangle from the user. Compute the area of the triangle using Heron's formula (below), in which s is half of the perimeter of the triangle, and a, b, and c are the lengths of the three sides. Print the area to three decimal places.

$$\text{Area} = \sqrt{s(s - a)(s - b)(s - c)}$$

2.11 Write an application that computes the number of miles per gallon (mpg) of gas for a trip. The total amount of gas used should be a floating point number. Also accept two numbers representing the odometer readings at the start and end of the trip.

2.12 Write an application that determines the value of the coins in a jar and prints the total in dollars and cents. Read integer values that represent the number of quarters, dimes, nickels, and pennies. Use a currency formatter to print the output.

2.13 Write an application that creates and prints a random phone number of the form XXX–XXX–XXXX. Include the dashes in the output. Do not let the first three digits contain an 8 or 9 (but don't be more restrictive than that), and make sure that the second set of three digits is not greater than 742. *Hint:* Think through the easiest way to construct the phone number. Each digit does not have to be determined separately.

2.14 Create a revised version of the Snowman applet (Listing 2.15) with the following modifications:

  ‣ Add two red buttons to the upper torso.

  ‣ Make the snowman frown instead of smile.

  ‣ Move the sun to the upper-right corner of the picture.

  ‣ Display your name in the upper-left corner of the picture.

  ‣ Shift the entire snowman 20 pixels to the right.

2.15 Write an applet that draws a smiling face. Give the face a nose, ears, a mouth, and eyes with pupils.

answers to self-review questions

2.1 The main elements that support object-oriented programming are objects, classes, encapsulation, and inheritance. An object is defined by a class, which contains methods that define the operations on those objects (the services that they perform). Objects store and manage their own data. Inheritance is a technique in which one class can be created from another.

2.2 An object is abstract because the details of the object are hidden from, and largely unimportant to, the user of the object. Hidden details help us manage the complexity of software.

2.3 Primitive data are basic values such as numbers or characters. Objects are more complex and usually contain primitive data that help define them.

2.4 A string literal is a sequence of characters that appear in double quotation marks.

2.5 Both the `print` and `println` methods of the `System.out` object write a string of characters to the computer screen. The difference is that, after printing the characters, the `println` does a carriage return so that whatever's printed next appears on the next line. The `print` method lets new output appear on the same line.

2.6 A parameter is data that is passed into a method. The method usually uses that data. For example, the parameter to the `println` method is the string of characters to be printed. As another example, the two numeric parameters to the `Math.pow` method are the operands to the power function that is computed and returned.

2.7 An escape sequence is a series of characters that begins with the backslash (\). The characters that follow should be treated in some special way. Examples: \n represents the newline character and \" represents the quotation character (as opposed to using it to terminate a string).

2.8 A variable declaration gives the name of a variable and the type of data that it can contain. A declaration may also have an initialization, which gives the variable an initial value.

2.9 An integer variable can store only one value at a time. When a new value is assigned to it, the old one is overwritten and lost.

2.10 A character set is a list of characters in a particular order. A character set defines the valid characters that a particular type of computer or programming language will recognize. Java uses the Unicode character set.

2.11 Operator precedence is the set of rules that dictates the order in which operators are evaluated in an expression.

2.12 The result of `19%5` in a Java expression is 4. The remainder operator `%` returns the remainder after dividing the second operand into the first. Five goes into 19 three times, with 4 left over.

2.13 The result of 13/4 in a Java expression is 3 (not 3.25). The result is an integer because both operands are integers. Therefore the / operator performs integer division, and the fractional part of the result is cut off.

2.14 A widening conversion does not cause information to be lost. Information is more likely to be lost in a narrowing conversion, which is why narrowing conversions are considered to be less safe than widening ones.

2.15 The new operator creates a new instance (an object) of a class. The constructor of the class helps set up the newly created object.

2.16 A Java package is a set of classes that have something in common. The Java standard class library is a group of packages that support common programming tasks.

2.17 The String class is part of the java.lang package, which is automatically imported into any Java program. Therefore, no separate import declaration is needed.

2.18 A class or static method can be invoked through the name of the class that contains it, such as Math.abs. If a method is not static, it can be executed only through an instance (an object) of the class.

2.19 A Java applet is a Java program that can be executed using a Web browser. Usually, the bytecode form of the Java applet is pulled across the Internet from another computer. A Java application is a Java program that can stand on its own. It does not need a Web browser in order to execute.

program statements

All programming languages have statements that help you perform basic operations. These statements handle all programmed activity. This chapter looks at several of these programming statements as well as some additional operators. It begins by exploring the basic steps that a programmer takes when developing software. These activities are the basis of high-quality software development and a disciplined development process. Finally, we use some of the statements we have learned to produce graphical output.

chapter objectives

- ▶ Discuss basic program development steps.

- ▶ Define the flow of control through a program.

- ▶ Learn to use `if` statements.

- ▶ Define expressions that let us make complex decisions.

- ▶ Learn to use `while` and `for` statements.

- ▶ Use conditionals and loops to draw graphics.

3.0 program development

Creating software involves much more than just writing code. As you learn about programming language statements you you should develop good programming habits. This section introduces some of the basic programming steps in developing software.

Software development involves four basic *development activities*:

▶ establishing the requirements

▶ creating a design

▶ implementing the code

▶ testing the implementation

It would be nice if these activities always happened in this order, but they almost never do. Instead, they often overlap. Let's discuss each development stage briefly.

Software requirements are the things that a program must accomplish. They are the tasks that a program should do, not how it should do them. You may recall from Chapter 1 that programming is really about solving a problem. Requirements are the clear expression of that problem. Until we know what problem we are trying to solve, we can't solve it.

> **key concept**
>
> Software requirements specify *what* a program must accomplish.

The person or group who wants a software product developed (the *client*) will usually give you a set of requirements. However, these requirements are often incomplete, ambiguous, or even contradictory. You must work with the client until you both agree on what the system will do.

Requirements often have to do with user interfaces such as output format, screen layouts, and graphics. These are the things that make the program useful for the end user. Requirements may also apply constraints to your program, such as how fast a task must be performed. They may also impose restrictions such as deadlines.

A *software design* describes *how* a program will meet the requirements. The design spells out the classes and objects needed in a program and how they work with each other. A detailed design might even list the steps that parts of the code will follow.

> **key concept**
>
> A software design spells out *how* a program will accomplish its requirements.

A civil engineer would never consider building a bridge without designing it first. The design of software is just as important. Many software problems are the result of poor or sloppy design. You need to consider all the different ways of meeting the requirements, not jump on the first idea. Often, the first attempt at a design is not the best solution. Luckily, changes are easy to make during the design stage.

One basic design issue is defining the *algorithms* to be used in the program. An algorithm is a step-by-step process for solving a problem. A recipe is like an algorithm. Travel directions are like an algorithm. Every program uses one or more algorithms. Every software developer should spend time thinking about the algorithms before writing any code.

An algorithm is often written in *pseudocode,* which is a mixture of code statements and English phrases sort of like a rough draft of an essay. Pseudocode helps you decide how the code will operate without getting bogged down in the details of a particular programming language.

> **key concept**
> An algorithm is a step-by-step process for solving a problem, often expressed in pseudocode.

When you develop an algorithm, you should study all of the requirements involved with that part of the problem. This ensures that the algorithm takes into account all aspects of the problem. You should be willing to revise many times before you're done.

Implementation is the process of writing the source code, in a particular programming language. Too many programmers focus on implementation, when actually it should be the least creative part of development. The important decisions should be made when the requirements are established and the design is created.

Testing a program includes running it many times with different inputs and carefully studying the results. Testing might also include hand-tracing program code, in which you mentally play the role of the computer to see where the program logic might fail.

> **key concept**
> Implementation should be the least creative of all development activities.

The goal of testing is to find errors. By finding errors and fixing them, we improve the quality of our program. It's likely that later on someone else will find errors that remained hidden during development, when the cost of fixing that error is much higher. Taking the time to uncover problems as early as possible is always worth the effort.

Running a program and getting the correct results only means that the program works for the data you put in. The more times you test, with different input, the more confident you will feel. But you can never really be sure that you've caught all the errors. There could always be an error you didn't find. Because of that, it is important to thoroughly test a program with many different kinds of input. When one problem is fixed, you should run your tests over again to make sure that when you fixed the problem you didn't create a new problem. This technique is called *regression testing.*

> **key concept**
> The goal of testing is to find errors. We can never really be sure that all errors have been found.

3.1   control flow

The order in which statements are executed is called the *flow of control*. Most of the time, a running program starts at the first programming statement and moves down one statement at a time until the program is complete. A Java application begins with the first line of the `main` method and proceeds step by step until it gets to the end of the `main` method.

Invoking a method changes the flow of control. When a method is called, control jumps to the code for that method. When the method finishes, control returns to the place where the method was called and processing continues from there. In our examples so far, we've invoked methods in classes and objects using the Java libraries, and we haven't been concerned about the code that defines those methods. We discuss how to write our own classes and methods in Chapter 4.

> **key concept**
>
> Conditionals and loops let us control the flow of execution through a method.

Within a given method, we can changes the flow of control through the code by using certain types of programming statements. Statements that control the flow of execution through a method fall into two categories: conditionals and loops.

A *conditional statement* is sometimes called a *selection statement* because it lets us choose which statement will be executed next. The conditional statements in Java that we will study are the `if` statement and the `if-else` statement. These statements let us decide which statement to execute next. Each decision is based on a *boolean expression* (also called a *condition*), which says whether something is true or false. The result of the expression determines which statement is executed next.

For example, the cost of life insurance might depend on whether the insured person is a smoker. If the person smokes, we calculate the cost using one particular formula; if not, we calculate it using another. The role of a conditional statement is to evaluate a boolean condition (whether the person smokes) and then to execute the proper calculation accordingly.

A *loop, or repetition statement,* lets us execute the same statement over and over again. Like a conditional, a loop is based on a boolean expression that determines how many times the statement is executed.

For example, suppose we wanted to calculate the grade point average of every student in a class. The calculation is the same for each student; it is just performed on different data. We would set up a loop that repeats the calculation for each student until there are no more students to process.

Java has three types of loop statements:

▸ the `while` statement

▸ the `do` statement

▸ the `for` statement

Each type of loop statement has unique characteristics. We will study the `while` and `for` statements in this book. Information on the `do` statement (which is not in the AP subset) can be found on the Web site.

Conditionals and loops control the flow through a method and are needed in many situations. This chapter explores conditional and loop statements as well as some additional operators.

3.2 the if statement

The *if statement* is a conditional statement found in many programming languages, including Java. The following is an example of an `if` statement:

```
if (total > amount)
    total = total + (amount + 1);
```

An `if` statement consists of the reserved word `if` followed by a boolean expression, or condition, followed by a statement. The condition is enclosed in parentheses and must be either true or false. If the condition is true, the statement is executed and processing continues with the next statement. If the condition is false, the statement is skipped and processing continues immediately with the next statement. In this example, if the value in `total` is greater than the value in `amount`, the assignment statement is executed; otherwise, the assignment statement is skipped. Figure 3.1 shows how this works.

> **key concept**
> An `if` statement lets a program choose whether to execute a particular statement.

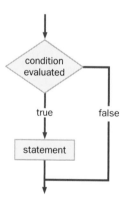

figure 3.1 The logic of an `if` statement

Note that the assignment statement in this example is indented under the header line of the `if` statement. This tells us that the assignment statement is part of the `if` statement; it means that the `if` statement controls whether the assignment statement will be executed. This indentation is extremely important for the people who read the code.

<table>
<tr><td>**key concept**</td><td>Indentation is important for human readability. It shows the relationship between one statement and another.</td></tr>
</table>

The example in Listing 3.1 reads the age of the user and then decides which sentence to print, based on the age that is entered.

listing 3.1

```
//********************************************************************
//   Age.java        Author: Lewis/Loftus/Cocking
//
//   Demonstrates the use of an if statement.
//********************************************************************

import cs1.Keyboard;

public class Age
{
   //-----------------------------------------------------------------
   //   Reads the user's age and prints comments accordingly.
   //-----------------------------------------------------------------
   public static void main (String[] args)
   {
      final int MINOR = 21;

      System.out.print ("Enter your age: ");
      int age = Keyboard.readInt();

      System.out.println ("You entered: " + age);

      if (age < MINOR)
         System.out.println ("Youth is a wonderful thing. Enjoy.");

      System.out.println ("Age is a state of mind.");
   }
}
```

output

```
Enter your age: 35
You entered: 35
Age is a state of mind.
```

The `Age` program in Listing 3.1 echoes (reads back) the age value that is entered in all cases. If the age is less than the value of the constant `MINOR`, the statement about youth is printed. If the age is equal to or greater than the value of `MINOR`, the `println` statement is skipped. In either case, the final sentence about age being a state of mind is printed.

equality and relational operators

Boolean expressions evaluate to either true or false. Java has several operators that produce a true or false result. The `==` and `!=` operators are called *equality operators*; they test if two values are equal (`==`) or not equal (`!=`). Note that the equality operator is two equal signs side by side and should not be mistaken for the assignment operator that uses only one equal sign.

The following `if` statement prints a sentence only if the variables `total` and `sum` contain the same value:

```
if (total == sum)
    System.out.println ("total equals sum");
```

Likewise, the following `if` statement prints a sentence only if the variables `total` and `sum` do *not* contain the same value:

```
if (total != sum)
    System.out.println ("total does NOT equal sum");
```

In the `Age` program in Listing 3.1 we used the `<` operator to decide whether one value was less than another. The less than operator is one of several *relational operators* that let us decide the relationships between values. Figure 3.2 lists the Java equality and relational operators.

Operator	Meaning
==	equal to
!=	not equal to
<	less than
<=	less than or equal to
>	greater than
>=	greater than or equal to

figure 3.2   Java equality and relational operators

The equality and relational operators have precedence lower than the arithmetic operators. This means that arithmetic operations are evaluated first, followed by equality and relational operations. As always, parentheses can be used to specify the order of evaluation.

Let's look at a few more examples of basic `if` statements.

```
if (size >= MAX)
    size = 0;
```

This `if` statement causes the variable `size` to be set to zero if its current value is greater than or equal to the value in the constant `MAX`.

The condition of the following `if` statement first adds three values together, then compares the result to the value stored in `numBooks`.

```
if (numBooks < stackCount + inventoryCount + duplicateCount)
    reorder = true;
```

If `numBooks` is less than the other three values combined, the boolean variable `reorder` is set to `true`. The addition operations are performed before the less than operator because the arithmetic operators have a higher precedence than the relational operators.

The following `if` statement compares the value returned from a call to `nextInt` to the calculated result of dividing the constant `HIGH` by 5. The odds of this code picking a winner are 1 in 5.

```
if (generator.nextInt(HIGH) < HIGH / 5)
    System.out.println ("You are a randomly selected winner!");
```

the if-else statement

Sometimes we want to do one thing if a condition is true and another thing if that condition is false. We can add an *else clause* to an `if` statement, making it an *if-else statement*, to handle this kind of situation. The following is an example of an `if-else` statement:

```
if (height <= MAX)
    adjustment = 0;
else
    adjustment = MAX - height;
```

If the condition is true, the first assignment statement is executed; if the condition is false, the second statement is executed. Only one or the other will be executed because a boolean condition will evaluate to either true or false. Note that we indented to show that the statements are part of the if statement.

The Wages program shown in Listing 3.2 uses an if-else statement to compute the payment for an employee.

In the Wages program, if an employee works over 40 hours in a week, the payment amount includes the overtime hours. An if-else statement is used to determine whether the number of hours entered by the user is greater than 40. If it is, the extra hours are paid at a rate one and a half times the normal rate. If there are no overtime hours, the total payment is based simply on the number of hours worked and the standard rate.

Let's look at another example of an if-else statement:

```
if (roster.getSize() == FULL)
    roster.expand();
else
    roster.addName (name);
```

This example uses an object called roster. Even without knowing what roster is, we can see that it has at least three methods: getSize, expand, and addName. The condition of the if statement calls getSize and compares the result to the constant FULL. If the condition is true, the expand method is invoked (apparently to expand the size of the roster). If the roster is not yet full, the variable name is passed as a parameter to the addName method.

If Statement

An if statement tests the boolean Expression. If it is true, the program executes the first Statement. The optional else clause shows the Statement that should be executed if the Expression is false.

Examples:

```
if (total < 7)
    System.out.println ("Total is less than 7.");

if (firstCh != 'a')
    count++;
else
    count = count / 2;
```

listing
    3.2

```
//***************************************************************
//  Wages.java        Author: Lewis/Loftus/Cocking
//
//  Demonstrates the use of an if-else statement.
//***************************************************************

import java.text.NumberFormat;
import cs1.Keyboard;

public class Wages
{
   //----------------------------------------------------------------
   //  Reads the number of hours worked and calculates wages.
   //----------------------------------------------------------------
   public static void main (String[] args)
   {
      final double RATE = 8.25;  // regular pay rate
      final int STANDARD = 40;   // standard hours in a work week

      double pay = 0.0;

      System.out.print ("Enter the number of hours worked: ");
      int hours = Keyboard.readInt();

      System.out.println ();

      // Pay overtime at "time and a half"
      if (hours > STANDARD)
         pay = STANDARD * RATE + (hours-STANDARD) * (RATE * 1.5);
      else
         pay = hours * RATE;

      NumberFormat fmt = NumberFormat.getCurrencyInstance();
      System.out.println ("Gross earnings: " + fmt.format(pay));
   }
}
```

output

```
Enter the number of hours worked: 46

Gross earnings: $404.25
```

using block statements

We may want to do more than one thing as the result of evaluating a boolean condition. In Java, we can replace any single statement with a *block statement*. A block statement is a collection of statements enclosed in braces. We've already seen these braces used with the `main` method and a class definition. The program called `Guessing`, shown in Listing 3.3, uses an `if-else` statement with the statement of the `else` clause in a block statement.

If the user's guess equals the answer, the sentences "You got it! Good guessing" are printed. If the guess doesn't match two statements are printed, one that says that the guess is wrong and one that prints the actual answer. A programming project at the end of this chapter expands this into the Hi-Lo game.

Note that if we didn't use the block braces, the sentence stating that the guess is incorrect would be printed if the guess was wrong, but the sentence revealing the correct answer would be printed in all cases. That is, only the first statement would be considered part of the `else` clause.

Remember that indentation is only for people reading the code. Statements that are not blocked properly can cause the programmer to misunderstand how the code will execute. For example, the following code is misleading:

```
if (depth > 36.238)
   delta = 100;
else
   System.out.println ("WARNING: Delta is being reset to ZERO");
   delta = 0;  // not part of the else clause!
```

The indentation (not to mention the logic of the code) seems to mean that the variable `delta` is reset only when `depth` is less than `36.238`. However, without using a block, the assignment statement that resets `delta` to zero is not governed by the `if-else` statement at all. It is executed in either case, which is clearly not what is intended.

listing
    3.3

```
//********************************************************************
//  Guessing.java        Author: Lewis/Loftus/Cocking
//
//  Demonstrates the use of a block statement in an if-else.
//********************************************************************

import cs1.Keyboard;
import java.util.Random;

public class Guessing
{
   //-----------------------------------------------------------------
   //  Plays a simple guessing game with the user.
   //-----------------------------------------------------------------
   public static void main (String[] args)
   {
      final int MAX = 10;
      int answer, guess;

      Random generator = new Random();
      answer = generator.nextInt(MAX) + 1;

      System.out.print ("I'm thinking of a number between 1 and "
                        + MAX + ". Guess what it is: ");
      guess = Keyboard.readInt();

      if (guess == answer)
         System.out.println ("You got it! Good guessing!");
      else
      {
         System.out.println ("That is not correct, sorry.");
         System.out.println ("The number was " + answer);
      }
   }
}
```

output

```
I'm thinking of a number between 1 and 10. Guess what it is: 7
That is not correct, sorry.
The number was 4
```

A block statement can be used anywhere a single statement is called for in Java syntax. For example, the `if` part of an `if-else` statement could be a block, or the `else` portion could be a block (as we saw in the `Guessing` program), or both parts could be block statements. For example:

```
if (boxes != warehouse.getCount())
{
   System.out.println ("Inventory and warehouse do NOT match.");
   System.out.println ("Beginning inventory process again!");
   boxes = 0;
}
else
{
   System.out.println ("Inventory and warehouse MATCH.");
   warehouse.ship();
}
```

In this `if-else` statement, the value of `boxes` is compared to a value that we got by calling the `getCount` method of the `warehouse` object (whatever that is). If they do not match exactly, two `println` statements and an assignment statement are executed. If they do match, a different message is printed and the `ship` method of `warehouse` is invoked.

nested if statements

The statement executed as the result of an `if` statement could be another `if` statement. This situation is called a *nested if*. It lets us make another decision after getting the results of a previous decision. The program in Listing 3.4, called `MinOfThree`, uses nested `if` statements to find the smallest of three integer values entered by the user.

Carefully trace the logic of the `MinOfThree` program, using different sets of numbers, with the smallest number in a different position each time, to see how the program chooses the lowest value.

An important situation arises with nested `if` statements. It may seem that an `else` clause after a nested `if` could apply to either `if` statement. For example:

```
if (code == 'R')
   if (height <= 20)
      System.out.println ("Situation Normal");
   else
      System.out.println ("Bravo!");
```

listing
   3.4

```
//************************************************************************
//  MinOfThree.java        Author: Lewis/Loftus/Cocking
//
//  Demonstrates the use of nested if statements.
//************************************************************************

import cs1.Keyboard;

public class MinOfThree
{
   //-----------------------------------------------------------------
   //  Reads three integers from the user and determines the smallest
   //  value.
   //-----------------------------------------------------------------
   public static void main (String[] args)
   {
      int num1, num2, num3, min = 0;

      System.out.println ("Enter three integers: ");
      num1 = Keyboard.readInt();
      num2 = Keyboard.readInt();
      num3 = Keyboard.readInt();

      if (num1 < num2)
         if (num1 < num3)
            min = num1;
         else
            min = num3;
      else
         if (num2 < num3)
            min = num2;
         else
            min = num3;

      System.out.println ("Minimum value: " + min);
   }
}
```

output

```
Enter three integers:
45    22    69
Minimum value: 22
```

Is the `else` clause matched to the inner `if` statement or the outer `if` statement? The indentation in this example seems to mean that it is part of the inner `if` statement, and that is correct. An `else` clause is always matched to the closest unmatched `if` that came before it. However, if we're not careful, we can easily mismatch it in our mind and imply our intentions, but not reality, by misaligned indentation. This is another reason why accurate, consistent indentation is so important.

Braces can be used to show which `if` statement belongs with which `else` clause. For example, if our example had been written so that the string `"Bravo!"` is printed if `code` is not equal to `'R'`, we could force that relationship (and properly indent) as follows:

> **key concept**
>
> In a nested `if` statement, an `else` clause is matched to the closest unmatched `if`.

```java
if (code == 'R')
{
   if (height <= 20)
      System.out.println ("Situation Normal");
}
else
   System.out.println ("Bravo!");
```

By using the block statement in the first `if` statement, we establish that the `else` clause belongs to it.

3.3   boolean expressions revisited

Let's look at a few more uses of boolean expressions.

logical operators

In addition to the equality and relational operators, Java has three *logical operators* that produce boolean results. They also take boolean operands. Figure 3.3 lists and describes the logical operators.

Operator	Description	Example	Result
!	logical NOT	! a	true if a is false and false if a is true
&&	logical AND	a && b	true if a and b are both true and false otherwise
||	logical OR	a || b	true if a or b or both are true and false otherwise

figure 3.3   Java logical operators

The ! operator is used to perform the *logical NOT* operation, which is also called the *logical complement*. The logical complement of a boolean value gives its opposite value. That is, if a boolean variable called found has the value false, then !found is true. Likewise, if found is true, then !found is false. The logical NOT operation does not change the value stored in found.

A logical operation can be described by a *truth table* that lists all the combinations of values for the variables involved in an expression. Because the logical NOT operator is unary, there are only two possible values for its one operand, true or false. Figure 3.4 shows a truth table that describes the ! operator.

The && operator performs a *logical AND* operation. The result is true if both operands are true, but false otherwise. Since it is a binary operator and each operand has two possible values, there are four combinations to consider.

The result of the *logical OR* operator (||) is true if one or the other or both operands are true, but false otherwise. It is also a binary operator. Figure 3.5 is a truth table that shows both the && and || operators.

The logical NOT has the highest precedence of the three logical operators, followed by logical AND, then logical OR.

Logical operators are often used as part of a condition for a selection or repetition statement. For example, consider the following if statement:

```
if (!done && (count > MAX))
    System.out.println ("Completed.");
```

Under what conditions would the println statement be executed? The value of the boolean variable done is either true or false, and the NOT operator reverses that value. The value of count is either greater than MAX or it isn't. The truth table in Figure 3.6 shows all of the possibilities.

a	!a
false	true
true	false

figure 3.4   Truth table describing the logical NOT operator

a	b	a && b	a || b
false	false	false	false
false	true	false	true
true	false	false	true
true	true	true	true

figure 3.5   Truth table describing the logical AND and OR operators

An important characteristic of the && and || operators is that they are "short-circuited." That is, if their left operand is enough to decide the boolean result of the operation, the right operand is not evaluated. This situation can occur with both operators but for different reasons. If the left operand of the && operator is false, then the result of the operation will be false no matter what the value of the right operand is. Likewise, if the left operand of the || is true, then the result of the operation is true no matter what the value of the right operand is.

> Logical operators return a boolean value and are often used to build sophisticated conditions.
>
> key concept

This can be very useful. For example, the condition in the following if statement will not try to divide by zero if the left operand is false. If count has the value zero, the left side of the && operation is false; so the whole expression is false and the right side is not evaluated.

```
if (count != 0 && total/count > MAX)
    System.out.println ("Testing.");
```

Be careful when you use these programming language characteristics. Not all programming languages work the same way. As we have mentioned several times, you should always make it clear to the reader exactly how the logic of your program works.

done	count > MAX	!done	!done && (count > MAX)
false	false	true	false
false	true	true	true
true	false	false	false
true	true	false	false

figure 3.6   A truth table for a specific condition

comparing characters and strings

We know what it means when we say that one *number* is less than another, but what does it mean to say one *character* is less than another? As we discussed in Chapter 2, characters in Java are based on the Unicode character set, which orders all possible characters that can be used. Because the character `'a'` comes before the character `'b'` in the character set, we can say that `'a'` is less than `'b'`.

We can use the equality and relational operators on character data. For example, if two character variables, `ch1` and `ch2`, hold the values of two characters, we might determine their order in the Unicode character set with an `if` statement as follows:

```
if (ch1 > ch2)
    System.out.println (ch1 + " is greater than " + ch2);
else
    System.out.println (ch1 + " is NOT greater than " + ch2);
```

> **key concept**
>
> The order of characters in Java is defined by the Unicode character set.

In the Unicode character set all lowercase alphabetic characters (`'a'` through `'z'`) are in alphabetical order. The same is true of uppercase alphabetic characters (`'A'` through `'Z'`) and digits (`'0'` through `'9'`). The digits come before the uppercase alphabetic characters, which come before the lowercase alphabetic characters. Before, after, and in between these groups are other characters. (See the chart in Appendix B.)

This makes it easy to sort characters and strings of characters. If you have a list of names, for instance, you can put them in alphabetical order based on the relationships in the character set.

However, you should not use the equality or relational operators to compare `String` objects. The `String` class has a method called `equals` that returns a `boolean` value that is true if the two strings contain exactly the same characters, and false if they do not. For example:

```
if (name1.equals(name2))
    System.out.println ("The names are the same.");
else
    System.out.println ("The names are not the same.");
```

Assuming that `name1` and `name2` are `String` objects, this condition determines whether the characters they contain are exactly the same. Because both objects were created from the `String` class, they both respond to the `equals` message. Therefore we could have written the condition as `name2.equals(name1)` and gotten the same result.

We could test the condition (`name1 == name2`), but that actually tests to see whether both reference variables refer to the same `String` object.

That is, the == operator tests whether both reference variables contain the same address. That's different than testing to see whether two different String objects contain the same characters. We discuss this in more detail later in the book.

To determine the relative ordering of two strings, use the compareTo method of the String class. The compareTo method is more flexible than the equals method. Instead of returning a boolean value, the compareTo method returns a number. The return value is negative if the first String object (name1) is less than the second string (name2). The return value is zero if the two strings contain the same characters. The return value is positive if the first String object is greater than the second string. For example:

```
int result = name1.compareTo(name2);
if (result < 0)
   System.out.println (name1 + " comes before " + name2);
else
   if (result == 0)
      System.out.println ("The names are equal.");
   else
      System.out.println (name1 + " follows " + name2);
```

Keep in mind that comparing characters and strings is based on the Unicode character set (see Appendix B). This is called a *lexicographic ordering*. If all alphabetic characters are in the same case (upper or lower), the lexicographic ordering will be alphabetic. However, when comparing two strings, such as "able" and "Baker", the compareTo method will conclude that "Baker" comes first because all of the uppercase letters come before all of the lowercase letters in the Unicode character set. A string that is the prefix of another, longer string is considered to precede the longer string. For example, when comparing two strings such as "horse" and "horsefly", the compareTo method will conclude that "horse" comes first.

> **key concept**
>
> The compareTo method determines lexicographic order, which does not correspond exactly to alphabetical order.

comparing floating point values

Another interesting situation occurs when floating point data is compared. Specifically, you should rarely use the equality operator (==) when comparing floating point values. Two floating point values are equal, according to the == operator, only if all the binary digits of their underlying representations match. If the compared values are the results of computation, they may not be exactly equal. For example, 5.349 is not equal to 5.3490001.

A better way to check for floating point equality is to get the absolute value of the difference between the two values and compare the result to some tolerance level. For example, we may choose a tolerance level of `0.00001`. If the two floating point values are so close that their difference is less than the tolerance, then we may consider them equal. For example, two floating point values, `f1` and `f2`, could be compared as follows:

```
if (Math.abs(f1 - f2) < TOLERANCE)
    System.out.println ("Essentially equal.");
```

The value of the constant `TOLERANCE` should be appropriate for the situation.

3.4   more operators

Let's look at a few more Java operators to give us even more ways to express our program commands. Some of these operators are commonly used in loop processing.

increment and decrement operators

The *increment operator* (++) adds 1 to any integer or floating point value. The two plus signs cannot be separated by white space. The *decrement operator* (--) is similar except that it subtracts 1 from the value. The increment and decrement operators are both unary operators because they operate on only one operand. The following statement causes the value of `count` to be increased by one, or *incremented*.

```
count++;
```

The result is stored back in the variable `count`. Therefore this statement is the same as the following statement:

```
count = count + 1;
```

assignment operators

Several *assignment operators* in Java combine a basic operation with assignment. For example, the += operator can be used as follows:

```
total += 5;
```

This does the thing as the following statement:

```
total = total + 5;
```

The right-hand side of the assignment operator can be a full expression. The expression on the right-hand side of the operator is evaluated, then that result is added to the current value of the variable on the left-hand side, and that value is stored in the variable. So the following statement:

```
total += (sum - 12) / count;
```

is the same as:

```
total = total + ((sum - 12) / count);
```

Many similar Java assignment operators are listed in Figure 3.7.

All of the assignment operators evaluate the expression on the right-hand side first, then use the result as the right operand of the other operation. So the following statement:

```
result *= count1 + count2;
```

is the same as:

```
result = result * (count1 + count2);
```

Likewise, the following statement:

```
result %= (highest - 40) / 2;
```

is the same as:

```
result = result % ((highest - 40) / 2);
```

Operator	Description	Example	Equivalent Expression
=	assignment	x = y	x = y
+=	addition, then assignment	x += y	x = x + y
+=	string concatenation, then assignment	x += y	x = x + y
-=	subtraction, then assignment	x -= y	x = x - y
*=	multiplication, then assignment	x *= y	x = x * y
/=	division, then assignment	x /= y	x = x / y
%=	remainder, then assignment	x %= y	x = x % y

figure 3.7   Java assignment operators

Some assignment operators have special functions depending on the types of the operands, just as regular operators do. For example, if the operands to the += operator are strings, then the assignment operator performs string concatenation.

3.5 the while statement

As we discussed earlier in this chapter, a repetition statement (or loop) lets us execute a statement as many times as we need to. A while *statement* is a loop that evaluates a boolean condition—just like an if statement does—and executes a statement (called the *body* of the loop) if the condition is true.

However, unlike the if statement, after the body is executed, the condition is evaluated again. If it is still true, the body is executed again. This repeats until the condition becomes false; then processing continues with the statement after the body of the while loop. Figure 3.8 shows this processing.

The Counter program shown in Listing 3.5 simply prints the values from 1 to 5. Each turn through the loop prints one value, then increases the counter by one. A constant called LIMIT holds the maximum value that count is allowed to reach. The condition of the while loop, (count <= LIMIT), means that the loop will keep going as long as count is less than or equal to LIMIT. Once count reaches the limit, the condition is false an the loop quits.

Note that the body of the while loop is a block containing two statements. Because the value of count is increased by one each time, we are guaranteed that count will eventually reach the value of LIMIT.

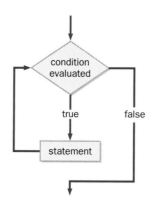

figure 3.8 The logic of a while loop

```java
//********************************************************************
//  Counter.java        Author: Lewis/Loftus/Cocking
//
//  Demonstrates the use of a while loop.
//********************************************************************

public class Counter
{
   //-----------------------------------------------------------------
   //  Prints integer values from 1 to a specific limit.
   //-----------------------------------------------------------------
   public static void main (String[] args)
   {
      final int LIMIT = 5;
      int count = 1;

      while (count <= LIMIT)
      {
         System.out.println (count);
         count = count + 1;
      }

      System.out.println ("Done");
   }
}
```

output

```
1
2
3
4
5
Done
```

Let's look at another program that uses a `while` loop. The `Average` program shown in Listing 3.6 reads integer values from the user, adds them up, and computes their average.

We don't know how many values the user may enter, so we need to have a way to show that the user is done. In this program, we pick zero to be a *sentinel value*, which is a value that shows the end of the input the way a sentinel stands guard at the gate of a fort or perimeter of an army's camp. The `while` loop continues to process input values until the user enters zero. This assumes that zero is not one of the valid numbers that should contribute to

```java
//********************************************************************
//  Average.java        Author: Lewis/Loftus/Cocking
//
//  Demonstrates the use of a while loop, a sentinel value, and a
//  running sum.
//********************************************************************

import java.text.DecimalFormat;
import cs1.Keyboard;

public class Average
{
   //-----------------------------------------------------------------
   //  Computes the average of a set of values entered by the user.
   //  The running sum is printed as the numbers are entered.
   //-----------------------------------------------------------------
   public static void main (String[] args)
   {
      int sum = 0, value, count = 0;
      double average;

      System.out.print ("Enter an integer (0 to quit): ");
      value = Keyboard.readInt();

      while (value != 0)  // sentinel value of 0 to terminate loop
      {
         count++;

         sum += value;
         System.out.println ("The sum so far is " + sum);

         System.out.print ("Enter an integer (0 to quit): ");
         value = Keyboard.readInt();
      }

      System.out.println ();
      System.out.println ("Number of values entered: " + count);

      average = (double)sum / count;

      DecimalFormat fmt = new DecimalFormat ("0.###");
```

listing
3.6   continued

```
    System.out.println ("The average is " + fmt.format(average));
  }
}
```

output

```
Enter an integer (0 to quit): 25
The sum so far is 25
Enter an integer (0 to quit): 164
The sum so far is 189
Enter an integer (0 to quit): -14
The sum so far is 175
Enter an integer (0 to quit): 84
The sum so far is 259
Enter an integer (0 to quit): 12
The sum so far is 271
Enter an integer (0 to quit): -35
The sum so far is 236
Enter an integer (0 to quit): 0
Number of values entered: 6
The average is 39.333
```

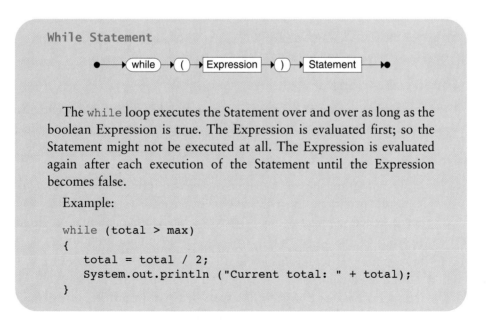

While Statement

The `while` loop executes the Statement over and over as long as the boolean Expression is true. The Expression is evaluated first; so the Statement might not be executed at all. The Expression is evaluated again after each execution of the Statement until the Expression becomes false.

Example:

```
while (total > max)
{
   total = total / 2;
   System.out.println ("Current total: " + total);
}
```

the average. A sentinel value must always be outside the normal range of values entered.

Note that in the Average program in Listing 3.6, a variable called sum is used to keep a *running sum*, which means it is the total of the values entered so far. The variable sum starts at zero, and each value read is added to and stored back into sum.

We also have to count the number of values that are entered so that after the loop finishes we can divide by the right number to get the average. Note that the sentinel value is not counted. But what if the user immediately enters the sentinel value before entering any valid values? The value of count in this case will still be zero and the computation of the average will result in a runtime error. Fixing this problem is left as a programming project.

Let's look at another program that uses a while loop. The WinPercentage program shown in Listing 3.7 computes the winning percentage of a sports team based on the number of games won.

We use a while loop in the WinPercentage program to *validate the input,* meaning we guarantee that the user enters a value that we consider to be valid. In this example, that means that the number of games won must be greater than or equal to zero and less than or equal to the total number of games played. The while loop keeps executing, repeatedly asking the user for valid input, until the entered number is indeed valid.

Validating input data, avoiding errors such as dividing by zero, and performing other actions that guarantee proper processing are important design steps. We generally want our programs to be *robust,* which means that they handle errors—even user errors—well.

infinite loops

The programmer must make sure that the condition of a loop will eventually become false. If it doesn't, the loop will keep going forever, or at least until the program is interrupted. This situation, called an *infinite loop,* is a common mistake.

The program shown in Listing 3.8 has an infinite loop. If you execute this program, you will have to interrupt it to make it stop. On most systems, pressing the Control-C keyboard combination (hold down the Control key and press C) stops a running program.

In the Forever program in Listing 3.8, the starting value of count is 1 and it is subtracted from, or decremented, in the loop body. The while loop will continue as long as count is less than or equal to 25. Because count gets smaller with each iteration, the condition will always be true.

listing
   3.7

```java
//********************************************************************
//  WinPercentage.java        Author: Lewis/Loftus/Cocking
//
//  Demonstrates the use of a while loop for input validation.
//********************************************************************

import java.text.NumberFormat;
import cs1.Keyboard;

public class WinPercentage
{
   //-----------------------------------------------------------------
   //  Computes the percentage of games won by a team.
   //-----------------------------------------------------------------
   public static void main (String[] args)
   {
      final int NUM_GAMES = 12;
      int won;
      double ratio;

      System.out.print ("Enter the number of games won (0 to "
                        + NUM_GAMES + "): ");
      won = Keyboard.readInt();

      while (won < 0 || won > NUM_GAMES)
      {
         System.out.print ("Invalid input. Please reenter: ");
         won = Keyboard.readInt();
      }

      ratio = (double)won / NUM_GAMES;

      NumberFormat fmt = NumberFormat.getPercentInstance();

      System.out.println ();
      System.out.println ("Winning percentage: " + fmt.format(ratio));
   }
}
```

output

```
Enter the number of games won (0 to 12): -5
Invalid input. Please reenter: 13
Invalid input. Please reenter: 7

Winning percentage: 58%
```

listing
3.8

```java
//********************************************************************
//  Forever.java        Author: Lewis/Loftus/Cocking
//
//  Demonstrates an INFINITE LOOP.  WARNING!!
//********************************************************************

public class Forever
{
    //-----------------------------------------------------------------
    //  Prints ever-decreasing integers in an INFINITE LOOP!
    //-----------------------------------------------------------------
    public static void main (String[] args)
    {
        int count = 1;

        while (count <= 25)
        {
            System.out.println (count);
            count = count - 1;
        }

        System.out.println ("Done");   // this statement is never reached
    }
}
```

output

```
1
0
-1
-2
-3
-4
-5
-6
-7
-8
-9
and so on until interrupted
```

Let's look at some other examples of infinite loops:

```java
int count = 1;
while (count != 50)
    count += 2;
```

In this code fragment, the variable `count` begins at 1 and moves in a positive direction. However, note that it is increased by 2 each time. This loop will never terminate because `count` will never equal 50. It begins at 1 and then changes to 3, then 5, and so on. Eventually it reaches 49, then changes to 51, then 53, and continues forever.

Now consider the following situation:

```
double num = 1.0;
while (num != 0.0)
    num = num − 0.1;
```

Once again, the value of the loop control variable seems to be moving in the right direction. And, in fact, it seems like `num` will eventually take on the value `0.0`. However, this loop is infinite (at least on most systems) because `num` will never have a value *exactly* equal to `0.0`. This situation is like the one we discussed earlier in this chapter when we compared floating point values in the condition of an `if` statement. Because of the way the values are represented in binary, tiny differences make comparing floating point values (for equality) a problem.

nested loops

The body of a loop can contain another loop. This situation is called a *nested loop*. Keep in mind that each time the outer loop executes once, the inner loop executes completely. Consider the following code fragment. How many times does the string `"Here again"` get printed?

```
int count1, count2;
count1 = 1;
while (count1 <= 10)
{
    count2 = 1;
    while (count2 <= 50)
    {
        System.out.println ("Here again");
        count2++;
    }
    count1++;
}
```

The `println` statement is inside the inner loop. The outer loop executes 10 times, as `count1` iterates between 1 and 10. The inner loop executes 50 times, as `count2` iterates between 1 and 50. Each time the outer loop executes, the inner loop executes completely. So the `println` statement is executed 500 times.

As with any loop, we must study the conditions of the loops and the initializations of variables. Let's consider some small changes to this code. What if the condition of the outer loop were (`count1 < 10`) instead of (`count1 <= 10`)? How would that change the total number of lines printed? Well, the outer loop would execute 9 times instead of 10, so the `println` statement would be executed 450 times. What if the outer loop were left as it was originally defined, but `count2` were initialized to 10 instead of 1 before the inner loop? The inner loop would then execute 40 times instead of 50, so the total number of lines printed would be 400.

Let's look at another example of a nested loop. A *palindrome* is a string of characters that reads the same forward or backward. For example, the following strings are palindromes:

- radar
- drab bard
- ab cde xxxx edc ba
- kayak
- deified
- able was I ere I saw elba

Note that some palindromes have an even number of characters, whereas others have an odd number of characters. The `PalindromeTester` program shown in Listing 3.9 tests to see whether a string is a palindrome. Users may test as many strings as they want.

The code for `PalindromeTester` contains two loops, one inside the other. The outer loop controls how many strings are tested, and the inner loop scans through each string, character by character, until it determines whether the string is a palindrome.

The variables `left` and `right` store the indexes of two characters. At first they indicate the characters on either end of the string. Each execution of the inner loop compares the two characters indicated by `left` and `right`. We fall out of the inner loop when either the characters don't match, meaning the string is not a palindrome, or when the value of `left` becomes equal to or greater than the value of `right`, which means the entire string has been tested and it is a palindrome.

listing
    3.9

```java
//********************************************************************
//  PalindromeTester.java       Author: Lewis/Loftus/Cocking
//
//  Demonstrates the use of nested while loops.
//********************************************************************

import cs1.Keyboard;

public class PalindromeTester
{
   //-----------------------------------------------------------------
   //  Tests strings to see if they are palindromes.
   //-----------------------------------------------------------------
   public static void main (String[] args)
   {
      String str, another = "y";
      int left, right;

      while (another.equalsIgnoreCase("y")) // allows y or Y
      {
         System.out.println ("Enter a potential palindrome:");
         str = Keyboard.readString();

         left = 0;
         right = str.length() - 1;

         while (str.charAt(left) == str.charAt(right) && left < right)
         {
            left++;
            right--;
         }

         System.out.println();

         if (left < right)
            System.out.println ("That string is NOT a palindrome.");
         else
            System.out.println ("That string IS a palindrome.");

         System.out.println();
         System.out.print ("Test another palindrome (y/n)? ");
         another = Keyboard.readString();
      }
   }
}
```

listing
    3.9   continued

output

```
Enter a potential palindrome:
radar

That string IS a palindrome.

Test another palindrome (y/n)? y
Enter a potential palindrome:
able was I ere I saw elba

That string IS a palindrome.

Test another palindrome (y/n)? y
Enter a potential palindrome:
abcddcba

That string IS a palindrome.

Test another palindrome (y/n)? y
Enter a potential palindrome:
abracadabra

That string is NOT a palindrome.

Test another palindrome (y/n)? n
```

Note that the following phrases would not be considered palindromes by the current version of the program:

- A man, a plan, a canal, Panama.
- Dennis and Edna sinned.
- Rise to vote, sir.
- Doom an evil deed, liven a mood.
- Go hang a salami; I'm a lasagna hog.

These strings fail our rules for a palindrome because of the spaces, punctuation marks, and changes in uppercase and lowercase. However, if these were removed or ignored, these strings read the same forward and backward. Consider how the program could be changed to handle these situations. These changes are left as a programming project at the end of the chapter.

the StringTokenizer class

Let's look at another useful class from the Java standard class library. The types of problems this class helps us solve are repetitious, so the solutions almost always involve loops. Note that the StringTokenizer class is not in the AP subset.

To the Java compiler, a string is just a series of characters, but often we want to use just part of a string. Taking data out of a string so we can work with it is a common programming activity. The individual parts of the string are called *tokens*, so taking them out is called *tokenizing* the string. The characters used to separate one token from another are called *delimiters*.

For example, we may want to separate a sentence such as the following into individual words:

```
"The quick brown fox jumped over the lazy dog"
```

In this case, each word is a token and the space character is the delimiter. As another example, we may want to separate the elements of a URL such as:

```
"www.csc.villanova.edu/academics/courses"
```

The delimiters in this case are the period (.) and the slash (/). In yet another situation we may want to get individual data values from a string, such as:

```
"75.43 190.49 69.58 140.77"
```

The delimiter in this case is once again the space character. A second step in processing this data is to change the token strings into numeric values. This kind of processing is done by the code in the Keyboard class. When we invoke a Keyboard method such as readDouble or readInt, the data is first read as a string, then tokenized, and finally changed into numeric form. If there are several values on one line, the Keyboard class keeps track of them, and takes them out and uses them as needed.

The `StringTokenizer` class, which is part of the `java.util` package in the Java standard class library, is used to separate a string into tokens. The default delimiters used by the `StringTokenizer` class are the space, tab, carriage return, and newline characters. Figure 3.9 lists some methods of the `StringTokenizer` class. Note that the second constructor in the list gives us a way to pick another set of delimiters for separating tokens. Once the `StringTokenizer` object is created, a call to the `nextToken` method returns the next token from the string. The `hasMoreTokens` method, which returns a `boolean` value, is often used in the condition of a loop to determine whether more tokens are left to process in the string.

The `CountWords` program shown in Listing 3.10 uses the `StringTokenizer` class and a nested `while` loop to analyze several lines of text. The user types in lines of text, ending with a line that contains only the word `"DONE"`. The outer loop processes one line of text at a time. The inner loop extracts and processes the tokens in the current line. The program counts the number of words and the number of characters in the words. After the sentinel value `"DONE"` (which is not counted) is entered, the results are displayed.

Note that the punctuation characters in the strings are included with the tokenized words because the program uses only the default delimiters of the `StringTokenizer` class. Changing this program so it will ignore punctuation is left as a programming project.

```
StringTokenizer (String str)
   Constructor: creates a new StringTokenizer object to parse the specified string
   str based on white space.

StringTokenizer (String str, String delimiters)
   Constructor: creates a new StringTokenizer object to parse the specified string
   str based on the specified set of delimiters.

int countTokens ()
   Returns the number of tokens still left to be processed in the string.

boolean hasMoreTokens ()
   Returns true if there are tokens still left to be processed in the string.

String nextToken ()
   Returns the next token in the string.
```

figure 3.9   Some methods of the `StringTokenizer` class

listing
   3.10

```java
//********************************************************************
//  CountWords.java        Author: Lewis/Loftus/Cocking
//
//  Demonstrates the use of the StringTokenizer class and nested
//  loops.
//********************************************************************

import cs1.Keyboard;
import java.util.StringTokenizer;

public class CountWords
{
   //-----------------------------------------------------------------
   //  Reads several lines of text, counting the number of words
   //  and the number of non-space characters.
   //-----------------------------------------------------------------
   public static void main (String[] args)
   {
      int wordCount = 0, characterCount = 0;
      String line, word;
      StringTokenizer tokenizer;

      System.out.println ("Please enter text (type DONE to quit):");

      line = Keyboard.readString();
      while (!line.equals("DONE"))
      {
         tokenizer = new StringTokenizer (line);
         while (tokenizer.hasMoreTokens())
         {
            word = tokenizer.nextToken();
            wordCount++;
            characterCount += word.length();
         }
         line = Keyboard.readString();
      }

      System.out.println ("Number of words: " + wordCount);
      System.out.println ("Number of characters: " + characterCount);
   }
}
```

listing
   3.10   continued

output

```
Please enter text (type DONE to quit):
Mary had a little lamb; its fleece was white as snow.
And everywhere that Mary went, the fleece shed all
over and made quite a mess. Little lambs do not make
good house pets.
DONE
Number of words: 34
Number of characters: 141
```

3.6   the for statement

The while statement is good to use when you don't know how many times you want to execute the loop body. The *for statement* is a repetition statement that works well when you *do* know exactly how many times you want to execute the loop.

The Counter2 program shown in Listing 3.11 once again prints the numbers 1 through 5, except this time we use a for loop to do it.

The header of a for loop has three parts, separated by semicolons. Before the loop begins, the first part of the header, called the *initialization*, is executed. The second part of the header is the boolean condition. If the condition is true, the body of the loop is executed, followed by the third part of the header, which is called the *increment*. Note that the initialization part is executed only once, but the increment part is executed each time. Figure 3.10 shows this processing.

A for loop can be a bit tricky to read until you get used to it. The execution of the code doesn't follow a "top to bottom, left to right" reading. The increment code executes after the body of the loop, even though it is in the header.

Note how the three parts of the for loop header match the parts of the original Counter program that uses a while loop. The initialization part of the for loop header declares the variable count as well as gives it a beginning value. We don't have to declare a variable there, but it is common practice when the variable is not needed outside the loop. Because count is declared in the for loop header, it exists only inside the loop body and can't be referenced elsewhere. The loop control variable is set up, checked, and

listing
   3.11

```java
//************************************************************************
//   Counter2.java        Author: Lewis/Loftus/Cocking
//
//   Demonstrates the use of a for loop.
//************************************************************************

public class Counter2
{
   //-----------------------------------------------------------------
   //   Prints integer values from 1 to a specific limit.
   //-----------------------------------------------------------------
   public static void main (String[] args)
   {
      final int LIMIT = 5;

      for (int count=1; count <= LIMIT; count++)
         System.out.println (count);

      System.out.println ("Done");
   }
}
```

output

```
1
2
3
4
5
Done
```

changed by the actions in the loop header. It can be referenced inside the loop body, but it should not be changed except by the actions defined in the loop header.

The increment part of the for loop header, in spite of its name, could decrement a value rather than increment it. For example, the following loop prints the integer values from 100 down to 1:

```java
for (int num = 100; num > 0; num--)
   System.out.println (num);
```

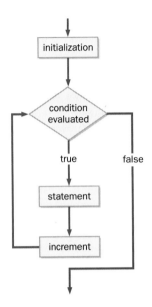

figure 3.10   The logic of a `for` loop

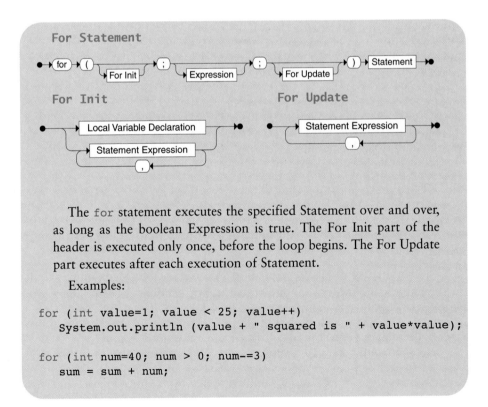

The `for` statement executes the specified Statement over and over, as long as the boolean Expression is true. The For Init part of the header is executed only once, before the loop begins. The For Update part executes after each execution of Statement.

Examples:

```
for (int value=1; value < 25; value++)
   System.out.println (value + " squared is " + value*value);

for (int num=40; num > 0; num-=3)
   sum = sum + num;
```

In fact, the increment part of the for loop can do any calculation, not just a simple increment or decrement. Look at the program in Listing 3.12, which prints multiples of a particular value up to a limit.

listing
   3.12

```java
//********************************************************************
//  Multiples.java        Author: Lewis/Loftus/Cocking
//
//  Demonstrates the use of a for loop.
//********************************************************************

import cs1.Keyboard;

public class Multiples
{
   //-----------------------------------------------------------------
   //  Prints multiples of a user-specified number up to a user-
   //  specified limit.
   //-----------------------------------------------------------------
   public static void main (String[] args)
   {
      final int PER_LINE = 5;
      int value, limit, mult, count = 0;

      System.out.print ("Enter a positive value: ");
      value = Keyboard.readInt();

      System.out.print ("Enter an upper limit: ");
      limit = Keyboard.readInt();

      System.out.println ();
      System.out.println ("The multiples of " + value + " between " +
                     value + " and " + limit + " (inclusive) are:");

      for (mult = value; mult <= limit; mult += value)
      {
         System.out.print (mult + "\t");

         // Print a specific number of values per line of output
         count++;
         if (count % PER_LINE == 0)
            System.out.println();
      }
   }
}
```

listing
     3.12   continued

output

```
Enter a positive value: 7
Enter an upper limit: 400

The multiples of 7 between 7 and 400 (inclusive) are:
7          14         21         28         35
42         49         56         63         70
77         84         91         98         105
112        119        126        133        140
147        154        161        168        175
182        189        196        203        210
217        224        231        238        245
252        259        266        273        280
287        294        301        308        315
322        329        336        343        350
357        364        371        378        385
392        399
```

The increment part of the for loop adds the value entered by the user. The number of values printed per line is controlled by counting the values printed and then moving to the next line whenever count is evenly divisible by the PER_LINE constant.

The Stars program in Listing 3.13 shows the use of nested for loops. The output is a triangle made of asterisks. The outer loop executes exactly 10 times, each time printing one line of asterisks. The inner loop has a different number of iterations depending on the line value controlled by the outer loop. Each time it executes, the inner loop prints one star on the current line. Variations on this triangle program are included in the projects at the end of the chapter.

comparing loops

The while and for loop statements are about the same: any loop written using one type of loop statement can be written using the other loop type. Which type of statement we use depends on the situation.

A for loop is like a while loop in that the condition is evaluated before the loop body is executed. Figure 3.11 shows the general structure of for and while loops.

listing
3.13

```java
//***************************************************************
//   Stars.java          Author: Lewis/Loftus/Cocking
//
//   Demonstrates the use of nested for loops.
//***************************************************************

public class Stars
{
   //------------------------------------------------------------
   //  Prints a triangle shape using asterisk (star) characters.
   //------------------------------------------------------------
   public static void main (String[] args)
   {
      final int MAX_ROWS = 10;

      for (int row = 1; row <= MAX_ROWS; row++)
      {
         for (int star = 1; star <= row; star++)
            System.out.print ("*");

         System.out.println();
      }
   }
}
```

output

```
*
**
***
****
*****
******
*******
********
*********
**********
```

We generally use a `for` loop when we know how many times we want to go through a loop. Most of the time it is easier to put the code that sets up and controls the loop in the `for` loop header.

```
for (initialization; condition; increment)     initialization;
    statement;                                  while (condition)
                                                {
                                                    statement;
                                                    increment;
                                                }
```

figure 3.11   The general structure of equivalent `for` and `while` loops

3.7   program development revisited

Now let's apply what we know to program development. Suppose a teacher wants a program that will analyze exam scores. The requirements are first given as follows. The program will:

- accept a series of test scores as input
- compute the average test score
- determine the highest and lowest test scores
- display the average, highest, and lowest test scores

Our first task is to look at the requirements. The requirements raise questions that need to be answered before we can design a solution. Understanding the requirements often means talking with the client. The client may very well have a clear idea of what the program should do, but this list of requirements does not provide enough detail.

For example, how many test scores should be processed? Will this program handle only one class size or should it handle different size classes? Is the input stored in a data file or will it be entered by the teacher, using the keyboard? What degree of accuracy does the teacher expect: two decimal places? Three? None? Should the output be in any particular format?

Let's assume we know that the program needs to handle a different number of test scores each time it is run and that the input will be entered by the teacher. The teacher wants the average presented to two decimal places, but lets us (the developer) pick the format.

Now let's consider some design questions. Because there is no limit to the number of grades that can be entered, how should the user indicate that there are no more grades? We can address this several ways. The program could ask the user, after each grade is entered, if there are more grades to process. Or the program could begin by asking the user for the total number of grades that will be entered, then read exactly that many grades. Or, when prompted for a grade, the teacher could enter a sentinel value to say that there are no more grades to be entered.

The first option requires a lot more input from the user, which is too awkward. The second option means the user must know exactly how many grades to enter and better not make any mistakes. The third option is reasonable, but before we can pick a sentinel value to end the input, we must ask more questions. What is the range of valid grades? What would be a good sentinel value? Talking with the client again, we learn that a student cannot get a negative grade, so we can use –1 as a sentinel value.

Let's sketch out an algorithm for this program. The pseudocode for a program that reads in a list of grades and computes their average might look like this:

```
prompt for and read the first grade.
while (grade does not equal -1)
{
    increment count.
    sum = sum + grade;
    prompt for and read another grade.
}
average = sum / count;
print average
```

This algorithm only calculates the average grade. Now we must change the algorithm to compute the highest and lowest grade. Further, the algorithm does not deal well with the unusual case of entering –1 for the first grade. We can use two variables, max and min, to keep track of the highest and lowest scores. The new pseudocode looks like this:

```
prompt for and read the first grade.
max = min = grade;
while (grade does not equal -1)
{
    increment count.
    sum = sum + grade;
    if (grade > max)
        max = grade;
    if (grade < min)
        min = grade;
    prompt for and read another grade.
}
if (count is not zero)
{
    average = sum / count;
    print average, highest, and lowest grades
}
```

Having planned out an algorithm for the program, we can start implementing it. Consider the solution to this problem shown in Listing 3.14.

listing
   3.14

```
//***********************************************************************
//   ExamGrades.java        Author: Lewis/Loftus/Cocking
//
//   Demonstrates the use of various control structures.
//***********************************************************************

import java.text.DecimalFormat;
import cs1.Keyboard;

public class ExamGrades
{
    //-------------------------------------------------------------------
    //   Computes the average, minimum, and maximum of a set of exam
    //   scores entered by the user.
    //-------------------------------------------------------------------
    public static void main (String[] args)
    {
        int grade, count = 0, sum = 0, max, min;
        double average;

        //   Get the first grade and give max and min that initial value
        System.out.print ("Enter the first grade (-1 to quit): ");
        grade = Keyboard.readInt();

        max = min = grade;

        //   Read and process the rest of the grades
        while (grade >= 0)
        {
            count++;
            sum += grade;

            if (grade > max)
                max = grade;
            else
                if (grade < min)
                    min = grade;

            System.out.print ("Enter the next grade (-1 to quit): ");
            grade = Keyboard.readInt ();
        }
```

listing
   3.14   continued

```
    // Produce the final results
    if (count == 0)
        System.out.println ("No valid grades were entered.");
    else
    {
        DecimalFormat fmt = new DecimalFormat ("0.##");
        average = (double)sum / count;
        System.out.println();
        System.out.println ("Total number of students: " + count);
        System.out.println ("Average grade: " + fmt.format(average));
        System.out.println ("Highest grade: " + max);
        System.out.println ("Lowest grade: " + min);
    }
  }
}
```

output

```
Enter the first grade (-1 to quit): 89
Enter the next grade (-1 to quit): 95
Enter the next grade (-1 to quit): 82
Enter the next grade (-1 to quit): 70
Enter the next grade (-1 to quit): 98
Enter the next grade (-1 to quit): 85
Enter the next grade (-1 to quit): 81
Enter the next grade (-1 to quit): 73
Enter the next grade (-1 to quit): 69
Enter the next grade (-1 to quit): 77
Enter the next grade (-1 to quit): 84
Enter the next grade (-1 to quit): 82
Enter the next grade (-1 to quit): -1

Total number of students: 12
Average grade: 82.08
Highest grade: 98
Lowest grade: 69
```

Let's look at how this program does what the teacher wanted. After the variable declarations in the main method, we ask the user to enter the first grade. Prompts should tell the user about any special input requirements. In this case, we tell the user that entering –1 will indicate the end of the input.

The variables max and min are set to the first value entered. This is done using *chained assignments*. An assignment statement returns a value and can be used as an expression. The value returned by an assignment statement is the value that gets assigned. Therefore, the value of grade is first assigned to min, then that value is assigned to max. If no larger or smaller grade is ever entered, the values of max and min will not change.

The while loop condition says that the loop body will be executed as long as the grade being processed is greater than or equal to zero. Therefore, any negative value will indicate the end of the input, even though the prompt tells the user that only –1 will end the input. This change is a slight variation on the original design and makes sure that no negative values will be counted as grades.

We use a nested if structure to decide if the new grade should be the highest or lowest grade. It cannot be both, so using an else clause is slightly more efficient. There is no need to ask whether the grade is a minimum if we already know it is a maximum.

If at least one positive grade was entered, then count is not equal to zero after the loop, and the else part of the if statement is executed. The average is computed by dividing the sum of the grades by the number of grades. Note that the if statement keeps us from trying to divide by zero in situations where no valid grades are entered. As we've mentioned before, we want to design robust programs that handle unexpected or wrong input without causing a runtime error. The solution for this problem is robust up to a point because it processes any numeric input without a problem, but it will fail if a nonnumeric value (like a string) is entered at the grade prompt.

3.8 bumper cars case study: introduction

This section begins a case study that is spread over Chapters 3 through 8. In this case study we describe a solution to a programming problem. The problem is presented and the design and implementation of the solution are described in detail. Looking at case studies is a way for beginning programmers to learn.

Throughout the case study there will be questions and exercises. These give you a chance to stop and think about the issues that come up in large programming projects. Often there is more than one good solution to a problem, and the solutions chosen in this case study are not the only correct ones.

AP CASE STUDY

We encourage you to think about other solutions to the problems and issues that come up.

The programming problem in this case study is a simulation. Simulations are often created to help us understand the real system they represent. When new ideas need to be tested, it is less expensive to try them out in a simulation than to use the real system. The results may not be as accurate as results from real system tests, but they are often close enough to be worthwhile.

We use the Java programming language in this case study. Object-oriented languages like Java are good for writing simulations because we can design program objects that act like the real-world objects in the system, and use interactions (method calls) between the objects to model the interactions of the objects in the real world.

requirements

The first step in solving any programming problem is setting the requirements. The programming problem in this case study is to write a simulation of bumper cars. A company that makes bumper cars for amusement parks has asked us to write a simulation that will help them gather information on the cars and allow them to test ideas inexpensively. In bumper cars, people drive specially designed cars in an arena with walls on all sides. Much of the fun of the game for people is bumping their cars into each other and into walls. The company is mostly interested in how many times a car bumps into obstacles (other cars or walls) during a given period. This gives them an idea of how long the cars will last, because the bumps are the major source of wear and tear on the car.

We have been given the following information:

1. Different people drive the bumper cars differently, so the design should allow for different driving patterns.

2. Once a round of bumper cars begins, no cars are allowed to enter or leave the arena until the round is over.

3. The cars can go forward and can turn; they cannot go in reverse.

4. A bump should be counted whenever a car bumps into a wall or into another car.

5. The number of cars in the simulation, the size of the arena, and the length of time the simulation runs varies from one run of the simulation to the next.

6. Where the bumper cars start in the arena is not set. That is, the cars are not placed in any particular spot, they are just left wherever they happen to be.

7. There are no cars without drivers in the arena while the bumper cars game is going on. Likewise, there are no drivers without cars.

8. After the simulation is done, the number of bumps that each car received, and the average number of bumps per car, should be output.

Once we have all the requirements, we must create a design. We need to know about classes, objects, and their interactions before we can design a solution, so we'll save that for the next chapter.

exercises

1. What is the trade-off between making a simulation more versus less realistic?

2. Think of another real-world system that can be simulated. What could we learn from the simulation?

3. In addition to what the company has already told us, what other information about bumper cars might we need to know?

3.9 drawing using conditionals and loops

Conditionals and loops can help us create interesting graphics.

The program called `Bullseye`, shown in Listing 3.15, uses a loop to draw the rings of a target. The `Bullseye` program uses an `if` statement to alternate the colors between black and white. Each ring is drawn as a filled circle (an oval of equal width and length). Because we draw the circles on top of each other, the inner circles cover the inner part of the larger circles, so they look like rings. At the end, a final red circle is drawn for the bull's-eye.

Listing 3.16 shows the `Boxes` applet, in which several randomly sized rectangles are drawn in random locations. If the width of a rectangle is less than 5 pixels, the box is filled with the color yellow. If the height is less than 5 pixels, the box is filled with the color green. Otherwise, the box is drawn, unfilled, in white.

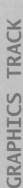
GRAPHICS TRACK

**listing
3.15**

```java
//********************************************************************
//  Bullseye.java         Author: Lewis/Loftus/Cocking
//
//  Demonstrates the use of conditionals and loops to guide drawing.
//********************************************************************

import java.applet.Applet;
import java.awt.*;

public class Bullseye extends Applet
{
   //-----------------------------------------------------------------
   //  Paints a bullseye target.
   //-----------------------------------------------------------------
   public void paint (Graphics page)
   {
      final int MAX_WIDTH = 300, NUM_RINGS = 5, RING_WIDTH = 25;
      int x = 0, y = 0, diameter;

      setBackground (Color.cyan);

      diameter = MAX_WIDTH;
      page.setColor (Color.white);

      for (int count = 0; count < NUM_RINGS; count++)
      {
         if (page.getColor() == Color.black)  // alternate colors
            page.setColor (Color.white);
         else
            page.setColor (Color.black);

         page.fillOval (x, y, diameter, diameter);

         diameter -= (2 * RING_WIDTH);
         x += RING_WIDTH;
         y += RING_WIDTH;
      }

      // Draw the red bullseye in the center
      page.setColor (Color.red);
      page.fillOval (x, y, diameter, diameter);
   }
}
```

listing
    3.15   continued

display

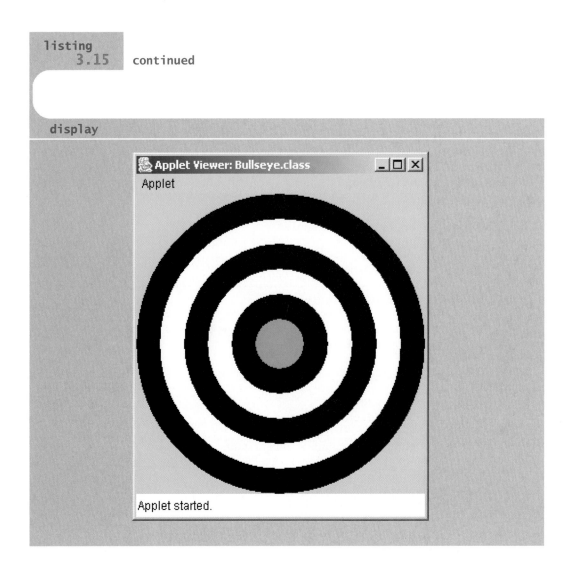

Note that in the Boxes program, the color is decided before each rectangle is drawn. In the BarHeights applet, shown in Listing 3.17, we handle the situation differently. The goal of BarHeights is to draw 10 vertical bars of random heights, coloring the tallest bar in red and the shortest bar in yellow.

In the BarHeights program, we don't know if the bar we are about to draw is either the tallest or the shortest because we haven't created them all yet. Therefore we keep track of the position of both the tallest and shortest bars as they are drawn. After all the bars are drawn, the program goes back and redraws these two bars in the right color.

**listing
3.16**

```java
//********************************************************************
//  Boxes.java         Author: Lewis/Loftus/Cocking
//
//  Demonstrates the use of conditionals and loops to guide drawing.
//********************************************************************

import java.applet.Applet;
import java.awt.*;
import java.util.Random;

public class Boxes extends Applet
{
   //-----------------------------------------------------------------
   //  Paints boxes of random width and height in a random location.
   //  Narrow or short boxes are highlighted with a fill color.
   //-----------------------------------------------------------------
   public void paint(Graphics page)
   {
      final int NUM_BOXES = 50, THICKNESS = 5, MAX_SIDE = 50;
      final int MAX_X = 350, MAX_Y = 250;
      int x, y, width, height;

      setBackground (Color.black);
      Random generator = new Random();

      for (int count = 0; count < NUM_BOXES; count++)
      {
         x = generator.nextInt (MAX_X) + 1;
         y = generator.nextInt (MAX_Y) + 1;

         width = generator.nextInt (MAX_SIDE) + 1;
         height = generator.nextInt (MAX_SIDE) + 1;

         if (width <= THICKNESS)  // check for narrow box
         {
            page.setColor (Color.yellow);
            page.fillRect (x, y, width, height);
         }
         else
```

listing
3.16   continued

```
if (height <= THICKNESS)  // check for short box
{
   page.setColor (Color.green);
   page.fillRect (x, y, width, height);
}
else
{
   page.setColor (Color.white);
   page.drawRect (x, y, width, height);
}
         }
      }
}
```

display

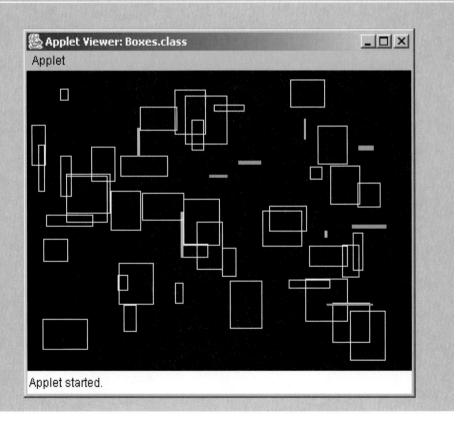

```
//***********************************************************************
//  BarHeights.java        Author: Lewis/Loftus/Cocking
//
//  Demonstrates the use of conditionals and loops to guide drawing.
//***********************************************************************

import java.applet.Applet;
import java.awt.*;
import java.util.Random;

public class BarHeights extends Applet
{
   //-----------------------------------------------------------------
   //  Paints bars of varying heights, tracking the tallest and
   //  shortest bars, which are redrawn in color at the end.
   //-----------------------------------------------------------------
   public void paint (Graphics page)
   {
      final int NUM_BARS = 10, WIDTH = 30, MAX_HEIGHT = 300, GAP =9;
      int tallX = 0, tallest = 0, shortX = 0, shortest = MAX_HEIGHT;
      int x, height;

      Random generator = new Random();
      setBackground (Color.black);

      page.setColor (Color.blue);
      x = GAP;

      for (int count = 0; count < NUM_BARS; count++)
      {
         height = generator.nextInt(MAX_HEIGHT) + 1;
         page.fillRect (x, MAX_HEIGHT-height, WIDTH, height);

         // Keep track of the tallest and shortest bars
         if (height > tallest)
         {
            tallX = x;
            tallest = height;
         }

         if (height < shortest)
         {
            shortX = x;
            shortest = height;
         }
```

listing
    3.17   continued

```
        x = x + WIDTH + GAP;
    }

    // Redraw the tallest bar in red
    page.setColor (Color.red);
    page.fillRect (tallX, MAX_HEIGHT-tallest, WIDTH, tallest);

    // Redraw the shortest bar in yellow
    page.setColor (Color.yellow);
    page.fillRect (shortX, MAX_HEIGHT-shortest, WIDTH, shortest);
  }
}
```

display

summary of key concepts

- Software requirements tell us *what* a program must do.

- A software design tells us *how* a program will fill its requirements.

- An algorithm is a step-by-step process for solving a problem, often written in pseudocode.

- Implementation should be the least creative of all development activities.

- The goal of testing is to find errors. We can never really be sure that all errors have been found.

- Conditionals and loops let us control the flow of execution through a method.

- An `if` statement lets a program choose whether to execute a particular statement.

- The compiler does not care about indentation. Indentation is important for human readers because it shows the relationship between one statement and another.

- An `if-else` statement lets a program do one thing if a condition is true and another thing if the condition is false.

- In a nested `if` statement, an `else` clause is matched to the closest unmatched `if`.

- Logical operators return a boolean value (true or false) and are often used for sophisticated conditions.

- The order of characters in Java is defined by the Unicode character set.

- The `compareTo` method determines the lexicographic order of strings, which is not necessarily alphabetical order.

- A `while` statement lets a program execute the same statement over and over.

- We must design our programs carefully to avoid infinite loops. The body of the loop must eventually make the loop condition false.

- A `for` statement is usually used when a loop will be executed a set number of times.

self-review questions

3.1   Name the four basic activities that are involved in a software development process.

3.2   What is an algorithm? What is pseudocode?

3.3   What is meant by the flow of control through a program?

3.4   What type of conditions are conditionals and loops based on?

3.5   What are the equality operators? The relational operators?

3.6   What is a nested `if` statement? A nested loop?

3.7   How do block statements help us construct conditionals and loops?

3.8   What is a truth table?

3.9   How do we compare strings for equality?

3.10   Why must we be careful when comparing floating point values for equality?

3.11   What is an assignment operator?

3.12   What is an infinite loop? Specifically, what causes it?

3.13   When would we use a `for` loop instead of a `while` loop?

multiple choice

3.1   Which of the following statements increase the value of x by 1?

I.   x++;

II.   x = x + 1;

III. x += 1;

a. I only

b. II only

c. I and III

d. II and III

e. I, II, and III

3.2 What will be printed by the following code segment?

```
boolean flag = true;
int x = -1;
if (flag && (x > 0))
   System.out.println("yes");
else if (x == 0)
   System.out.println("maybe");
else if (!flag)
   System.out.println("sometimes");
else
   System.out.println("no");
```

a. yes

b. maybe

c. sometimes

d. no

e. There will be an error because you can't mix integers and booleans in the same expression.

3.3. The expression !f || g is the same as which of the following?

a. f || !g

b. !(f || g)

c. !(f && g)

d. !(!f && !g)

e. !(f && !g)

3.4 In the following code, what value should go in the blank so that there will be exactly six lines of output?

```
for (int x = 0; x < _____; x = x + 2)
   System.out.println("-");
```

a. 5

b. 6

c. 10

d. 11

e. 13

3.5   What will be the largest value printed by the following code?

```
for (int x=5; x > 0; x--)
    for (int y=0; y < 8; y++)
        System.out.println(x*y);
```

a. 5

b. 8

c. 35

d. 40

e. 64

3.6   Assume x is an integer and has been initialized to some value.
Consider the code

```
for (int a = 1; a < 20; a++)
    if (x < 0)
        x = a;
```

Which statement will have the same effect on the value of x?

a. `if (x < 0)   x = 1;`

b. `if (x < 20)   x = 19;`

c. `if (x < 0)   x = 19;`

d. `if (x < 20)   x = 20;`

e. `x = 1;`

3.7   Assume num and max are integer variables. Consider the code

```
while (num < max)
    num++;
```

Which values of num and max will cause the body of the loop to
be executed exactly once?

a. `num = 1, max = 1;`

b. `num = 1, max = 2;`

c. `num = 2, max = 2;`

d. `num = 2, max = 1;`

e. `num = 1, max = 3;`

3.8   Which `for` loop is equivalent to this `while` loop?

```
int y = 5;
while (y >= 0)
{
    System.out.println(y);
    y--;
}
```

a. `for (int y = 0; y < 5; y++)`

   `System.out.println(y);`

b. `for (int y = 5; y > 0; y--)`

   `System.out.println(y);`

c. `for (int y = 5; y >= 0; y--)`

   `System.out.println(y);`

d. `for (int y = 0; y > 5; y++)`

   `System.out.println(y);`

e. `for (int y = 0; y > 5; y--)`

   `System.out.println(y);`

3.9   Which expression tests to make sure the grade is between 0 and 100 inclusive?

a. `(grade <= 100) || (graph <= 0)`

b. `(grade <= 100) || (graph >= 0)`

c. `(grade < 101) || (graph > -1)`

d. `(grade <= 100) && (graph >= 0)`

e. `(grade >= 100) && (graph <= 0)`

3.10 Which values of x, y, a, or b will cause the `if` statement to be short-circuited?

```
if ((x > y) && (a || b))
    statement;
```

a. `x = 1, y = 1`

b. `x = 5, y = 1`

c. `x = 2, y = 1, a = true, b = false`

d. `a = false, b = true`

e. `a = false, b = false`

true/false

3.1   An `if` statement may be used to make a decision in a program.

3.2   The expression `x > 0` is the same as the expression `0 <= x`.

3.3   The operators `+=`, `*=`, `-=`, and `/=` may only be used with integers.

3.4   The expression `a || b` is the same as `a && !b`.

3.5   If the expression `a && !b` evaluates to true, then the expression `a || b` will evaluate to true.

3.6   The expression `a || b` will be short-circuited if `a` is false.

3.7   Any loop written using a `for` statement can be written using a `while` statement.

3.8   An algorithm is a step-by-step process for solving a problem.

3.9   Once an initial design is created, it should never be revised.

short answer

3.1   What happens in the `MinOfThree` program if two or more of the values are equal? If exactly two of the values are equal, does it matter whether the equal values are lower or higher than the third?

3.2   What is wrong with the following code fragment? Rewrite it so that it produces correct output.

```
if (total == MAX)
   if (total < sum)
      System.out.println ("total == MAX and is < sum.");
else
   System.out.println ("total is not equal to MAX");
```

3.3   What is wrong with the following code fragment? Will this code compile if it is part of a valid program? Explain.

```
if (length = MIN_LENGTH)
   System.out.println ("The length is minimal.");
```

3.4   What output is produced by the following code fragment?

```
int num = 87, max = 25;
if (num >= max*2)
    System.out.println ("apple");
    System.out.println ("orange");
System.out.println ("pear");
```

3.5 What output is produced by the following code fragment?

```
int limit = 100, num1 = 15, num2 = 40;
if (limit <= limit)
{
    if (num1 == num2)
        System.out.println ("lemon");
    System.out.println ("lime");
}
System.out.println ("grape");
```

3.6 Put the following list of strings in lexicographic order as if determined by the compareTo method of the String class. Consult the Unicode chart in Appendix B.

```
"fred"
"Ethel"
"?-?-?-?"
"{([])}"
"Lucy"
"ricky"
"book"
"******"
"12345"
"          "
"HEPHALUMP"
"bookkeeper"
"6789"
";+<?"
"^^^^^^^^^^"
"hephalump"
```

3.7 What output is produced by the following code fragment?

```
int num = 1, max = 20;
while (num < max)
{
    if (num%2 == 0)
        System.out.println (num);
    num++;
}
```

3.8   What output is produced by the following code fragment?

```
for (int num = 0; num <= 200; num += 2)
    System.out.println (num);
```

3.9   What output is produced by the following code fragment?

```
for (int val = 200; val >= 0; val -= 1)
    if (val % 4 != 0)
        System.out.println (val);
```

3.10 Transform the following while loop into a for loop (make sure it produces the same output).

```
int num = 1;
while (num < 20)
{
    num++;
    System.out.println (num);
}
```

3.11 What is wrong with the following code fragment? What are three ways it could be changed to remove the flaw?

```
count = 50;
while (count >= 0)
{
    System.out.println (count);
    count = count + 1;
}
```

3.12 Write a while loop that makes sure the user enters a positive integer value.

3.13 Write a code fragment that reads and prints integer values entered by a user until a particular sentinel value (stored in SENTINEL) is entered. Do not print the sentinel value.

3.14 Write a for loop to print the odd numbers from 1 to 99 (inclusive).

3.15 Write a for loop to print the multiples of 3 from 300 down to 3.

3.16 Write a code fragment that reads 10 integer values from the user and prints the highest value entered.

3.17 Write a code fragment that determines and prints the number of times the character 'a' appears in a String object called name.

3.18 Write a code fragment that prints the characters stored in a `String` object called `str` backward.

3.19 Write a code fragment that prints every other character in a `String` object called `word` starting with the first character.

programming projects

3.1 Create a new version of the `Average` program (Listing 3.6) that prevents a runtime error when the user immediately enters the sentinel value (without entering any valid values).

3.2 Design and implement an application that reads an integer value representing a year input by the user. The purpose of the program is to determine if the year is a leap year (and therefore has 29 days in February) in the Gregorian calendar. A year is a leap year if it is divisible by 4, unless it is also divisible by 100 but not 400. For example, the year 2003 is not a leap year, but 2004 is. The year 1900 is not a leap year because it is divisible by 100, but the year 2000 is a leap year because even though it is divisible by 100, it is also divisible by 400. Produce an error message for any input value less than 1582 (the year the Gregorian calendar was adopted).

3.3 Change the solution to the Programming Project 3.2 so that the user can enter more than one year. Let the user end the program by entering a sentinel value. Validate each input value to make sure it is greater than or equal to 1582.

3.4 Design and implement an application that reads an integer value and prints the sum of all even integers between 2 and the input value, inclusive. Print an error message if the input value is less than 2. Prompt the user accordingly.

3.5 Design and implement an application that reads a string from the user and prints it one character per line.

3.6 Design and implement an application that determines and prints the number of odd, even, and zero digits in an integer value read from the keyboard.

3.7 Design and implement an application that produces a multiplication table, showing the results of multiplying the integers 1 through 12 by themselves.

3.8 Change the `CountWords` program (Listing 3.10) so that it does not include punctuation characters in its character count. *Hint*:

You must change the set of delimiters used by the
`StringTokenizer` class.

3.9   Create a new version of the `Counter` program (Listing 3.5) such
that the `println` statement comes after the counter increment
in the body of the loop. Make sure the program still produces
the same output.

3.10 Design and implement an application that prints the first few
verses of the traveling song "One Hundred Bottles of Beer." Use
a loop so that each iteration prints one verse. Read the number
of verses to print from the user. Validate the input. The following are the first two verses of the song:

>   100 bottles of beer on the wall
>
>   100 bottles of beer
>
>   If one of those bottles should happen to fall
>
>   99 bottles of beer on the wall
>
>   99 bottles of beer on the wall
>
>   99 bottles of beer
>
>   If one of those bottles should happen to fall
>
>   98 bottles of beer on the wall

3.11 Design and implement an application that plays the Hi-Lo guessing game with numbers (Listing 3.3). The program should pick a
random number between 1 and 100 (inclusive), then keep asking
the user to guess the number. On each guess, report to the user
that he or she is correct or that the guess is high or low. Keep
accepting guesses until the user guesses correctly or quits. Use a
sentinel value to determine whether the user wants to quit.
Count the number of guesses and report that value when the
user guesses correctly. At the end of each game (by quitting or a
correct guess), ask whether the user wants to play again. Keep
playing games until the user chooses to stop.

3.12 Create a new version of the `PalindromeTester` program
(Listing 3.9) so that the spaces, punctuation, and changes in
uppercase and lowercase are not considered when determining
whether a string is a palindrome. *Hint*: You can handle this in
several ways. Think carefully about your design.

3.13 Create new versions of the Stars program (Listing 3.13) to print the following patterns. Create a separate program to produce each pattern. *Hint:* Parts b, c, and d require several loops, some of which print a specific number of spaces.

```
a. **********    b.            *    c. **********    d.          *
   *********                  **       *********              ***
   ********                  ***       ********              *****
   *******                  ****       *******             *******
   ******                  *****       ******            *********
   *****                  ******       *****            *********
   ****                  *******       ****            *******
   ***                  ********       ***            *****
   **                  *********       **            ***
   *                  **********       *            *
```

3.14 Design and implement an application that reads a string from the user, then determines and prints how many of each lowercase vowel (a, e, i, o, and u) appear in the entire string. Have a separate counter for each vowel. Also count and print the number of consonants, spaces, and punctuation marks.

3.15 Design and implement an application that plays the rock-paper-scissors game against the computer. When played between two people, each person picks one of three options (usually shown by a hand gesture) at the same time, and a winner is determined. In the game, rock beats scissors, scissors beats paper, and paper beats rock. The program should randomly choose one of the three options (without revealing it), then ask for the user's selection. At that point, the program reveals both choices and prints a statement indicating that the user won, that the computer won, or that it was a tie. Keep playing until the user chooses to stop, then print the number of user wins, losses, and ties.

3.16 Design and implement an application that simulates a simple slot machine in which three numbers between 0 and 9 are randomly selected and printed side by side. Print a statement saying all three of the numbers are the same, or any two of the numbers are the same, when this happens. Keep playing until the user chooses to stop.

3.17 Design and implement an applet that draws the side view of stair steps from the lower left to the upper right.

3.18 Design and implement an applet that draws 100 circles of random color and random diameter in random locations. Make sure that in each case the whole circle appears in the visible area of the applet.

answers to self-review questions

3.1   The four basic activities in software development are requirements analysis (deciding what the program should do), design (deciding how to do it), implementation (writing the code), and testing (validating the implementation).

3.2   An algorithm is a step-by-step process that describes the solution to a problem. Every program can be described in algorithmic terms. An algorithm is often written in pseudocode, a loose combination of English and code-like terms used to capture the basic processing steps.

3.3   The flow of control through a program determines the program statements that will be executed when the program is run.

3.4   Each conditional and loop is based on a boolean condition that evaluates to either true or false.

3.5   The equality operators are equal (==) and not equal (!=). The relational operators are less than (<), less than or equal to (<=), greater than (>), and greater than or equal to (>=).

3.6   A nested if is an if statement inside an if or else clause. A nested if lets the programmer make a series of decisions. A nested loop is a loop within a loop.

3.7   A block statement groups several statements together. We use them to define the body of an if statement or loop when we want to do several things based on the boolean condition.

3.8   A truth table shows all possible results of a boolean expression, given all possible combinations of variables and conditions.

3.9   We compare strings for equality using the equals method of the String class, which returns a boolean result. The compareTo method of the String class can also be used to compare strings. It returns a positive, 0, or negative integer result depending on the relationship between the two strings.

3.10 Because they are stored internally as binary numbers, comparing floating point values for exact equality will be true only if they are the same bit-by-bit. It's better to use a reasonable tolerance value and consider the difference between the two values.

3.11 An assignment operator combines an operation with assignment. For example, the += operator performs an addition, then stores the value back into the variable on the right-hand side.

3.12 An infinite loop is a repetition statement that never ends. The body of the loop never causes the condition to become false.

3.13 A `for` loop is usually used when we know, or can calculate, how many times we want to iterate through the loop body. We use a `while` loop when we don't know how many times the loop should execute.

In Chapters 2 and 3 we used objects and classes for the services they provide. We also explored several basic programming statements. We are now ready to design more complex software by creating our own classes to define objects that perform whatever services we define. This chapter explores the details of class definitions, including the structure and semantics of methods and the scope and encapsulation of data.

chapter objectives

▌ Define classes that act like blueprints for new objects, made of variables and methods.

▌ Explain encapsulation and Java modifiers.

▌ Explore the details of method declarations.

▌ Review method invocation and parameter passing.

▌ Explain and use method overloading.

▌ Learn to divide complicated methods into simpler, supporting methods.

▌ Describe relationships between objects.

▌ Create graphics-based objects.

4.0 objects revisited

In Chapters 2 and 3 we created objects from classes in the Java standard class library. We didn't need to know the details of how the classes did their jobs; we simply trusted them to do so. That is one of the advantages of abstraction. Now we are ready to write our own classes.

First, let's review the concept of an object and explore it in more detail. Think about objects in the world around you. How would you describe them? Let's use a ball as an example. A ball has a diameter, color, and elasticity. We say the properties that describe an object, called *attributes*, define the object's *state of being*. We also describe a ball by what it does, such as the fact that it can be thrown, bounced, or rolled. These are the object's *behavior*.

All objects have a state and a set of behaviors. So do software objects. The values of an object's variables describe the object's state, and the methods define the object's behaviors.

> **key concept**
>
> Each object has a state and a set of behaviors. The values of an object's variables define its state and the methods define its behaviors.

Consider a computer game that uses a ball. The ball could be represented as an object. It could have variables to store its size and location, and methods that draw it on the screen and calculate how it moves when thrown, bounced, or rolled. The variables and methods defined in the ball object are the state and behavior of the ball in the computerized ball game.

Each object has its own state. Each ball object has a particular location, for instance, which is different from the location of all other balls. Behaviors, though, tend to apply to all objects of a particular type. For instance, any ball can be thrown, bounced, or rolled. The act of rolling a ball is generally the same for all balls.

The state of an object and that object's behaviors work together. How high a ball bounces depends on its elasticity. A basketball will bounce higher than, say, a golf ball. The action is the same, but the result depends on that particular object's state. An object's behavior often changes its state. For example, when a ball is rolled, its location changes.

Any object can be described in terms of its state and behavior. Let's take another example. In software that is used to manage a school, a student could be represented as an object. The collection of all such objects represents the entire student body at the school. Each student has a state. That is, each student object would contain the variables that store information about a particular student, such as name, address, courses taken, grades, and grade point average. A student object also has behaviors. For example, the class of the student object may contain a method to add a new course.

Although software objects often represent physical things, like balls and students, they don't have to. For example, an error message can be an object, with its state being the text of the message and behaviors, including printing the error message. A common mistake made by new programmers is to limit the possibilities to physical things.

classes

An object is defined by a class. A class is the model, pattern, or blueprint from which an object is created. Consider the blueprint created by an architect when designing a house. The blueprint defines the important characteristics of the house—its walls, windows, doors, electrical outlets, and so on. Once the blueprint is created, several houses can be built using it, as shown in Figure 4.1.

The houses built from the blueprint are different. They are in different locations, they have different addresses, contain different furniture, and different people live in them. Yet in many ways they are the "same" house. The layout of the rooms, number of windows and doors, and so on are the same in each. To create a different house, we would need a different blueprint.

A class is a blueprint of an object. However, a class is not an object any more than a blueprint is a house. In general, no space to store data values is reserved in a class. To create space to store data values, we must instantiate

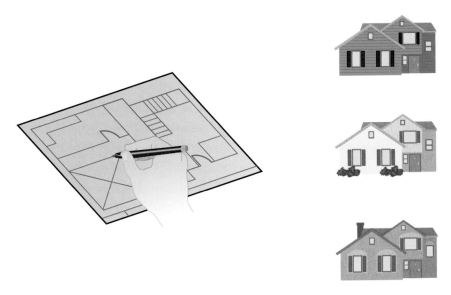

figure 4.1   A house blueprint and three houses created from it

one or more objects from the class. (We discuss the exception to this rule in the next chapter.) Each object is an instance of a class. Each object has space for its own data, which is why each object can have its own state.

4.1   anatomy of a class

A class contains the declarations of the data that will be stored in each instantiated object and the declarations of the methods that can be invoked using an object. These are called the *members* of the class, as shown in Figure 4.2.

Consider the CountFlips program shown in Listing 4.1. It uses an object that represents a coin that can be flipped to get a random "heads" or "tails." The CountFlips program simulates the flipping of a coin 1,000 times to see how often it comes up heads or tails. The myCoin object is instantiated from a class called Coin.

Listing 4.2 shows the Coin class used by the CountFlips program. A class, and therefore any object created from it, is made up of data values (variables and constants) and methods. In the Coin class, we have two integer constants, HEADS and TAILS, and one integer variable, face. The rest of the Coin class is made up of the Coin constructor and three regular methods: flip, isHeads, and toString.

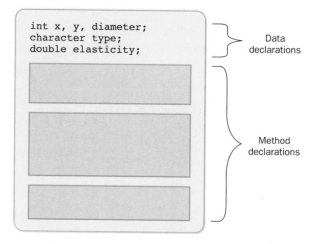

figure 4.2   The members of a class: data and method declarations

listing
  4.1

```
//***********************************************************************
//  CountFlips.java        Author: Lewis/Loftus/Cocking
//
//  Demonstrates the use of a programmer-defined class.
//***********************************************************************

public class CountFlips
{
   //------------------------------------------------------------------
   //  Flips a coin multiple times and counts the number of heads
   //  and tails that result.
   //------------------------------------------------------------------
   public static void main (String[] args)
   {
      final int NUM_FLIPS = 1000;
      int heads = 0, tails = 0;

      Coin myCoin = new Coin();   // instantiate the Coin object

      for (int count=1; count <= NUM_FLIPS; count++)
      {
         myCoin.flip();

         if (myCoin.isHeads())
            heads++;
         else
            tails++;
      }

      System.out.println ("The number flips: " + NUM_FLIPS);
      System.out.println ("The number of heads: " + heads);
      System.out.println ("The number of tails: " + tails);
   }
}
```

output

```
The number flips: 1000
The number of heads: 486
The number of tails: 514
```

listing
  4.2

```java
//********************************************************************
//  Coin.java          Author: Lewis/Loftus/Cocking
//
//  Represents a coin with two sides that can be flipped.
//********************************************************************

import java.util.Random;

public class Coin
{
   private final int HEADS = 0;
   private final int TAILS = 1;

   private int face;

   //------------------------------------------------------------
   //  Sets up the coin by flipping it initially.
   //------------------------------------------------------------
   public Coin ()
   {
      flip();
   }

   //------------------------------------------------------------
   //  Flips the coin by randomly choosing a face value.
   //------------------------------------------------------------
   public void flip ()
   {
      face = (int) (Math.random() * 2);
   }

   //------------------------------------------------------------
   //  Returns true if the current face of the coin is heads.
   //------------------------------------------------------------
   public boolean isHeads ()
   {
      return (face == HEADS);
   }

   //------------------------------------------------------------
   //  Returns the current face of the coin as a string.
   //------------------------------------------------------------
   public String toString()
   {
      String faceName;
```

listing
4.2   continued

```
    if (face == HEADS)
        faceName = "Heads";
    else
        faceName = "Tails";

    return faceName;
  }
}
```

Remember from Chapter 2 that constructors are special methods that have the same name as the class. The `Coin` constructor gets called when the `new` operator is used to create a new instance of the `Coin` class. The rest of the methods in the `Coin` class define the various services provided by `Coin` objects.

Note that a header block of documentation is used to explain the purpose of each method in the class. This practice is not only important for anyone trying to understand the software, it also separates the code so that it's easy to see where one method ends and the next begins. The definitions of these methods have many parts, and we'll look at them in later sections of this chapter.

Figure 4.3 lists the services defined in the `Coin` class. The `Coin` class looks like other classes that we've used in previous examples. The only important difference is that the `Coin` class is not part of the Java standard class library. We wrote it ourselves.

```
Coin ()
   Constructor: sets up a new Coin object with a random initial face.

void flip ()
   Flips the coin.

boolean isHeads ()
   Returns true if the current face of the coin shows heads.

String toString ()
   Returns a string describing the current face of the coin.
```

figure 4.3   Some methods of the `Coin` class

For most of the examples in this book, we store each class in its own file. Java lets you put several classes in one file. If a file contains several classes, only one of those classes can be declared using the reserved word `public`. Also, the name of the public class must match the name of the file. For instance, class `Coin` is stored in a file called `Coin.java`.

instance data

The scope of a variable, which determines where it can be referenced, depends on where it is declared.

In the `Coin` class, the constants `HEADS` and `TAILS`, and the variable `face` are declared inside the class, but not inside any method. The location at which a variable is declared defines its *scope*, which is the area in a program where that variable can be referenced. Because they are declared at the class level (not within a method), these variables and constants can be referenced in any method of the class.

Attributes such as the variable `face` are also called *instance data* because memory space is created for each instance of the class that is created. Each `Coin` object, for example, has its own `face` variable with its own data space. Therefore at any point in time, two `Coin` objects can have their own states: one can be showing heads and the other can be showing tails, for example.

The program `FlipRace` shown in Listing 4.3 declares two `Coin` objects. They are used in a race to see which coin will flip first to three heads in a row.

The output of the `FlipRace` program shows the results of each coin flip on each turn. The object reference variables, `coin1` and `coin2`, are used in the `println` statement. When an object is used as an operand of the string concatenation operator (+), that object's `toString` method is automatically called to get a string representation of the object. The `toString` method is also called if an object is sent to a `print` or `println` method by itself. If no `toString` method is defined for a class, a default version returns a string that contains the name of the class, together with other information. It is usually a good idea to define a specific `toString` method for a class.

We have now used the `Coin` class to create objects in two separate programs (`CountFlips` and `FlipRace`). This is no different from using the `String` class in whatever program we need it. When designing a class, it is always good to try to give the class behaviors that can be used in other programs, not just the program you are creating at the moment.

Java automatically initializes any variables declared at the class level. For example, all variables of numeric types such as `int` and `double` are initialized to zero. However, it is good practice to initialize variables explicitly (usually in a constructor) so that anyone reading the code will clearly understand what you are doing.

listing
    4.3

```java
//********************************************************************
//  FlipRace.java       Author: Lewis/Loftus/Cocking
//
//  Demonstrates the existence of separate data space in multiple
//  instantiations of a programmer-defined class.
//********************************************************************

public class FlipRace
{
   //----------------------------------------------------------------
   //  Flips two coins until one of them comes up heads three times
   //  in a row.
   //----------------------------------------------------------------
   public static void main (String[] args)
   {
      final int GOAL = 3;
      int count1 = 0, count2 = 0;

      // Create two separate coin objects
      Coin coin1 = new Coin();
      Coin coin2 = new Coin();

      while (count1 < GOAL && count2 < GOAL)
      {
         coin1.flip();
         coin2.flip();

         // Print the flip results (uses Coin's toString method)
         System.out.print ("Coin 1: " + coin1);
         System.out.println ("   Coin 2: " + coin2);

         // Increment or reset the counters
         if (coin1.isHeads())
            count1++;
         else
            count1 = 0;
         if (coin2.isHeads())
            count2++;
         else
            count2 = 0;
      }

      // Determine the winner
      if (count1 < GOAL)
         System.out.println ("Coin 2 Wins!");
      else
         if (count2 < GOAL)
            System.out.println ("Coin 1 Wins!");
```

listing
    4.3   continued

```
        else
            System.out.println ("It's a TIE!");
    }
}
```

output

```
Coin 1: Heads    Coin 2: Tails
Coin 1: Heads    Coin 2: Tails
Coin 1: Tails    Coin 2: Heads
Coin 1: Tails    Coin 2: Heads
Coin 1: Heads    Coin 2: Tails
Coin 1: Tails    Coin 2: Heads
Coin 1: Heads    Coin 2: Tails
Coin 1: Heads    Coin 2: Heads
Coin 1: Heads    Coin 2: Tails
Coin 1 Wins!
```

encapsulation and visibility modifiers

We can think about an object in one of two ways, depending on what we are trying to do. First, when we are designing and implementing an object, we need to think about how an object works. That is, we have to design the class—we have to define the variables that will be held in the object and write the methods that make the object useful.

However, when we are designing a solution to a larger problem, we have to think about how the objects in the program work with each other. At that level, we have to think only about the services that an object provides, not the details of how those services are provided. As we discussed in Chapter 2, an object provides a level of abstraction that lets us focus on the big picture when we need to.

This abstraction works only if we are careful to respect its boundaries. An object should be *self-governing*, which means that the variables contained in an object should be changed only within the object. Only the methods within an object should have access to the variables in that object. For example, the methods of the Coin class should be the only methods that can change the value of the face variable. We should make it difficult or impossible for code outside of a class to "reach in" and change the value of a variable that is declared inside the class.

In Chapter 2 we mentioned that the *object-oriented* term for this is *encapsulation*. An object should be encapsulated from the rest of the system. It should work with other parts of a program only through the object's own methods. These methods define the *interface* between that object and the program that uses it.

Figure 4.4 shows how encapsulation works. The code that uses an object, called the *client* of an object, should not be able to get to variables directly. The client should interact with the object's methods, and those methods then interact with the data encapsulated in the object. For example, the `main` method in the `CountFlips` program calls the `flip` and `isHeads` methods of the `myCoin` object. The `main` method should not (and in fact cannot) get to the `face` variable directly.

In Java, we create object encapsulation using *modifiers*. A modifier is a Java reserved word that names special characteristics of a programming language construct. We've already seen one modifier, `final`, which we use to declare a constant. Java has several modifiers that can be used in different ways. Some modifiers can be used together. We discuss various Java modifiers at appropriate points throughout this book.

Some Java modifiers are called *visibility modifiers*. They control whether client code can "see" what's "inside" an object. The reserved words `public` and `private` are visibility modifiers that can be applied to the variables and methods of a class. If a member of a class has *public visibility*, it can be "seen" (read and perhaps changed) from outside the object. If a member of a class has *private visibility*, it can be used anywhere inside but not outside the class definition.

Public variables let code outside the class reach in and read or change the value of the data. Therefore instance data should be defined with private visibility. Data that is declared as `private` can be read or changed only by the

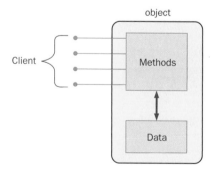

figure 4.4   A client interacting with the methods of an object

methods of the class, which makes the objects created from that class self-governing. Whether a method has public or private visibility depends on the purpose of that method. Methods that provide services to the client of the class must have public visibility so that they can be invoked by the client. These methods are sometimes called *service methods*. A `private` method cannot be invoked from outside the class. The only purpose of a `private` method is to help the other methods of the class do their job. Therefore they are sometimes called *support methods*. We discuss an example that makes use of several support methods later in this chapter.

The table in Figure 4.5 summarizes the effects of public and private visibility on both variables and methods.

Note that a client can still read or change `private` data by invoking service methods that change the data. For example, although the `main` method of the `FlipRace` class cannot directly get to the `face` variable, it can invoke the `flip` service method, which sets the value of `face`. A class must provide service methods for valid client operations. The code of those methods must be carefully designed to allow only appropriate access and valid changes.

Giving constants public visibility is generally considered acceptable because, although their values can be accessed directly, they cannot be changed. That is because constants are declared using the `final` modifier. Keep in mind that encapsulation means that data values should not be able to be *changed* directly by another part of the code. Because constants, by definition, cannot be changed, they don't need to be protected. If we had thought it important to provide external access to the values of the constants `HEADS` and `TAILS` in the `Coin` class, we could have declared them with public visibility.

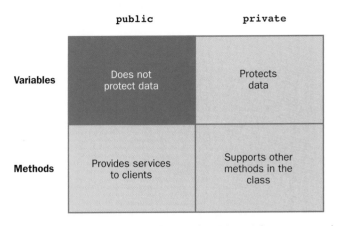

figure 4.5   The effects of public and private visibility

4.2 anatomy of a method

We've seen that a class is made up of data declarations and method declarations. Let's look at method declarations in more detail.

As we stated in Chapter 1, a method is a group of programming language statements that is given a name. Every method in a Java program is part of a particular class. A *method declaration* defines the code that is executed when the method is invoked.

When a method is called, the statements of that method are executed. When that method is done, control returns to the location where the call was made and execution continues. A method that is called might be part of the same object (defined in the same class) as the method that called it, or it might be part of a different object. If the called method is part of the same object, only the method name is needed to call it. If it is part of a different object, it is invoked through that object's name, as we've seen many times. Figure 4.6 shows what this process looks like.

We've defined the `main` method of a program many times in our examples. The `main` method follows the same syntax as all methods. The header of a method includes the type of the return value, the method name, and a list of parameters that the method accepts. The statements that make up the body of the method are defined in a block inside braces.

Let's look at another example. The `Banking` class shown in Listing 4.4 contains a `main` method that creates and then calls methods on a few `Account` objects. The `Banking` program doesn't really do anything useful except show how to interact with `Account` objects. Such programs are often

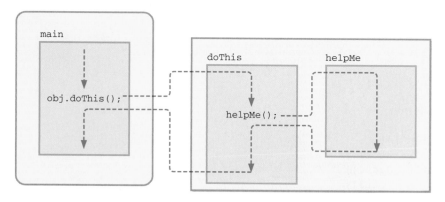

figure 4.6 The flow of control following method invocations

called *driver programs* because all they do is drive other, more interesting parts of a program. They are often used for testing.

The Account class represents a basic bank account and is shown in Listing 4.5. Its data values include the account number, the balance, and the name of the account's owner. The interest rate is stored as a constant.

listing 4.4

```java
//********************************************************************
//  Banking.java       Author: Lewis/Loftus/Cocking
//
//  Driver to exercise the use of multiple Account objects.
//********************************************************************

public class Banking
{
   //-----------------------------------------------------------------
   //  Creates some bank accounts and requests various services.
   //-----------------------------------------------------------------
   public static void main (String[] args)
   {
      Account acct1 = new Account ("Ted Murphy", 72354, 102.56);
      Account acct2 = new Account ("Anita Gomez", 69713, 40.00);
      Account acct3 = new Account ("Sanchit Reddy", 93757, 759.32);

      acct1.deposit (25.85);

      double gomezBalance = acct2.deposit (500.00);
      System.out.println ("Gomez balance after deposit: " +
                          gomezBalance);

      System.out.println ("Gomez balance after withdrawal: " +
                          acct2.withdraw (430.75, 1.50));

      acct3.withdraw (800.00, 0.0);   // exceeds balance

      acct1.addInterest();
      acct2.addInterest();
      acct3.addInterest();

      System.out.println ();
      System.out.println (acct1);
      System.out.println (acct2);
      System.out.println (acct3);
   }
}
```

listing
   4.4   continued

output

```
Gomez balance after deposit: 540.0
Gomez balance after withdrawal: 107.75

Error: Insufficient funds.
Account: 93757
Requested: $800.00
Available: $759.32

72354    Ted Murphy      $132.90
69713    Anita Gomez     $111.52
93757    Sanchit Reddy   $785.90
```

Method Declaration

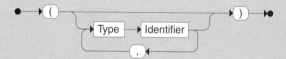

Parameters

A method is defined by optional modifiers, followed by a return Type, followed by an Identifier that determines the method name, followed by a list of Parameters, followed by the Method Body. The return Type indicates the type of value that will be returned by the method, which may be void. The Method Body is a block of statements that executes when the method is called.

Example:

```java
public void instructions (int count)
{
    System.out.println ("Follow all instructions.");
    System.out.println ("Use no more than " + count +
                        " turns.");
}
```

listing
   4.5

```java
//********************************************************************
//   Account.java         Author: Lewis/Loftus/Cocking
//
//   Represents a bank account with basic services such as deposit
//   and withdraw.
//********************************************************************

import java.text.NumberFormat;

public class Account
{
   private NumberFormat fmt = NumberFormat.getCurrencyInstance();

   private final double RATE = 0.035;  // interest rate of 3.5%

   private int acctNumber;
   private double balance;
   private String name;

   //-----------------------------------------------------------------
   //   Sets up the account by defining its owner, account number,
   //   and initial balance.
   //-----------------------------------------------------------------
   public Account (String owner, int account, double initial)
   {
      name = owner;
      acctNumber = account;
      balance = initial;
   }

   //-----------------------------------------------------------------
   //   Validates the transaction, then deposits the specified amount
   //   into the account. Returns the new balance.
   //-----------------------------------------------------------------
   public double deposit (double amount)
   {
      if (amount < 0)  // deposit value is negative
      {
         System.out.println ();
         System.out.println ("Error: Deposit amount is invalid.");
         System.out.println (acctNumber + "   " + fmt.format(amount));
      }
      else
         balance = balance + amount;

      return balance;
   }
```

listing
    4.5   continued

```java
//------------------------------------------------------------------
//  Validates the transaction, then withdraws the specified amount
//  from the account. Returns the new balance.
//------------------------------------------------------------------
public double withdraw (double amount, double fee)
{
    amount += fee;

    if (amount < 0)  // withdraw value is negative
    {
        System.out.println ();
        System.out.println ("Error: Withdraw amount is invalid.");
        System.out.println ("Account: " + acctNumber);
        System.out.println ("Requested: " + fmt.format(amount));
    }
    else
        if (amount > balance)  // withdraw value exceeds balance
        {
            System.out.println ();
            System.out.println ("Error: Insufficient funds.");
            System.out.println ("Account: " + acctNumber);
            System.out.println ("Requested: " + fmt.format(amount));
            System.out.println ("Available: " + fmt.format(balance));
        }
        else
            balance = balance - amount;

    return balance;
}


//------------------------------------------------------------------
//  Adds interest to the account and returns the new balance.
//------------------------------------------------------------------
public double addInterest ()
{
    balance += (balance * RATE);
    return balance;
}


//------------------------------------------------------------------
//  Returns the current balance of the account.
//------------------------------------------------------------------
public double getBalance ()
{
    return balance;
}
```

listing
    4.5   continued

```
//------------------------------------------------------------------
//   Returns the account number.
//------------------------------------------------------------------
public int getAccountNumber ()
{
    return acctNumber;
}


//------------------------------------------------------------------
//   Returns a one-line description of the account as a string.
//------------------------------------------------------------------
public String toString ()
{
    return (acctNumber + "\t" + name + "\t" + fmt.format(balance));
}
}
```

The methods of the `Account` class do things like make deposits and withdrawals. The program also makes sure that the data are valid, such as preventing the withdrawal of a negative amount. We explore the methods of the `Account` class in detail in the following sections.

the return statement

The return type in the method header can be a primitive type, class name, or the reserved word `void`. When a method does not return any value, `void` is used as the return type, as is always done with the `main` method.

> **key concept**
>
> A return value must match the return type in the method header.

A method that returns a value must have a *return statement*. After a `return` statement is executed, control is immediately returned to the statement in the calling method, and processing continues there. A `return` statement is the reserved word `return` followed by an expression that dictates the value to be returned. The expression must match the return type in the method header.

For example, the `return` statement in a method that returns a `double` could look like this:

```
return sum/2.0;
```

If the variable `sum` had the value 14 when the `return` statement was reached, then the value returned would be 7.0.

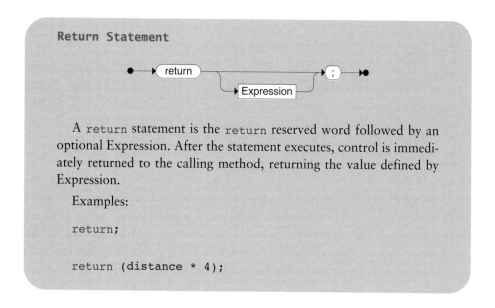

Return Statement

A `return` statement is the `return` reserved word followed by an optional Expression. After the statement executes, control is immediately returned to the calling method, returning the value defined by Expression.

Examples:

```
return;
```

```
return (distance * 4);
```

A method that does not return a value does not usually need a `return` statement because it automatically returns to the calling method when it is done. A method with a `void` return type may, however, have a `return` statement without an expression.

It is usually not good practice to use more than one `return` statement in a method. In general, the `return` statement should be the last line of the method body.

Many of the methods of the `Account` class in Listing 4.5 return a `double` that represents the balance of the account. Constructors do not have a return type at all (not even `void`), so they cannot have a `return` statement. We discuss constructors in more detail in a later section.

Note that a return value can be ignored. In the `main` method of the `Banking` class, sometimes the value that is returned by a method is used in some way, and sometimes the value returned is simply ignored.

parameters

Remember from Chapter 2 that a parameter is a value that is passed into a method when it is invoked. The *parameter list* in the header of a method lists the types of the values that are passed and their names.

The parameters in the header of the method declaration are called *formal parameters*. The values passed into a method are called *actual parameters*.

The parameter list is always in parentheses after the method name. If there are no parameters, the parentheses are empty.

The formal parameters are identifiers that act as variables inside the method. Their initial values come from the actual parameters in the invocation. When a method is called, the value in each actual parameter is copied and stored in the matching formal parameter. Actual parameters can be literals, variables, or full expressions. If an expression is used as an actual parameter, it is fully evaluated before the method call and the result is passed as the parameter.

The parameter lists in the invocation and the method declaration must match up. That is, the value of the first actual parameter is copied into the first formal parameter, the second actual parameter into the second formal parameter, and so on, as shown in Figure 4.7. The types of the actual parameters must match the types of the formal parameters.

The `deposit` method of the `Account` class in Listing 4.5, for example, takes one formal parameter called `amount`, of type `double`, representing the amount to be deposited into the account. Each time the method is invoked in the `main` method of the `Banking` class, one literal value of type `double` is passed as an actual parameter. For example, in the first call to `deposit`, the actual parameter is `25.85`. When the program is running and the statement `acct1.deposit(25.85)` is invoked, control transfers to the `deposit` method and the parameter `amount` takes on the value `25.85`. In the case of the `withdraw` method, two parameters of type `double` are expected. The types and number of parameters must match or you will get an error message.

Constructors can also take parameters, as we discuss in the next section. We discuss parameter passing in more detail in Chapter 5.

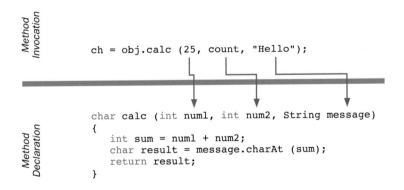

figure 4.7   Passing parameters from the method invocation to the declaration

constructors

As we stated in Chapter 2, a constructor is like a method that is called when an object is instantiated. When we define a class, we usually define a constructor to help us set up the class. In particular, we often use a constructor to initialize the variables associated with each object.

A constructor is different from a regular method in two ways. First, the name of a constructor is the same name as the class. Therefore the name of the constructor in the `Coin` class is `Coin`, and the name of the constructor of the `Account` class is `Account`. Second, a constructor cannot return a value and does not have a return type specified in the method header. A constructor cannot be called like other methods. It is called only when an object is first created.

A common mistake made by programmers is to put a `void` return type on a constructor. As far as the compiler is concerned, putting any return type on a constructor, even `void`, turns it into a regular method that happens to have the same name as the class. That means it cannot be invoked as a constructor. This leads to error messages that are sometimes difficult to figure out.

> **key concept**
> A constructor cannot have any return type, even `void`.

A constructor is generally used to initialize the newly instantiated object. For instance, the constructor of the `Coin` class calls the `flip` method to determine the initial face value of the coin. The constructor of the `Account` class sets the values of the instance variables to the values passed in as parameters to the constructor.

We don't have to define a constructor for every class. Each class has a *default constructor* that takes no parameters and is used if we don't provide our own. This default constructor generally has no effect on the newly created object.

local data

As we described earlier in this chapter, the scope of a variable (or constant) is the part of a program where a valid reference to that variable can be made. A variable can be declared inside a method, making it *local data* as opposed to instance data. Recall that instance data is declared in a class but not inside any particular method. Local data has scope limited to only the method where it is declared. The `faceName` variable declared in the `toString` method of the `Coin` class is local data. Any reference to `faceName` in any other method of the `Coin` class would cause an error message. A local variable simply does not exist outside of the

> **key concept**
> A variable declared in a method is local to that method and cannot be used outside of it.

method in which it is declared. Instance data, declared at the class level, has a scope of the entire class; any method of the class can refer to it.

Because local data and instance data have different levels of scope, it's possible to declare a local variable inside a method using the same name as an instance variable declared at the class level. In the method that name will reference the local version of the variable. This naming practice could confuse anyone reading the code, so it should be avoided.

The formal parameter names in a method header serve as local data for that method. They don't exist until the method is called, and they stop existing when the method ends. For example, although `amount` is the name of the formal parameter in both the `deposit` and `withdraw` method of the `Account` class, each is a separate piece of local data that doesn't exist until the method is invoked.

4.3 method overloading

When a method is invoked, control transfers to the code that defines the method. After the method finishes, control returns to the location of the call, and processing continues.

Often the method name is enough to indicate which method is being called by a specific invocation. But in Java, as in other object-oriented languages, you can use the same method name with different parameter lists for several methods. This is called *method overloading*. It is useful when you need to perform similar operations on different types of data.

The compiler must still be able to match up each invocation with a specific method declaration. If the method name for two or more methods is the same, then additional information is used to tell which version is being invoked. In Java, a method name can be used for several methods as long as the number of parameters, the types of those parameters, and/or the order of the types of parameters is different. A method's name along with the number, type, and order of its parameters is called the method's *signature*. The compiler uses the complete method signature to *bind* a method invocation to its definition.

> **key concept**
>
> You can tell the versions of an overloaded method apart by their signature, which is the number, type, and order of the parameters.

The compiler must be able to examine a method invocation, including the parameter list, to determine which method is being called. If you try to create two method names with the same signature, you will get an error message.

Note that the return type of a method is not part of the method signature. So two overloaded methods cannot differ only by their return type. This is because the value returned by a method can be ignored and the compiler would not be able to tell which version of an overloaded method was being referenced.

The `println` method is an example of a method that is overloaded several times, each accepting a single type. The following is a list of some of its signatures:

- `println (String s)`
- `println (int i)`
- `println (double d)`
- `println (char c)`
- `println (boolean b)`

The following two lines of code actually call different methods that have the same name:

```
System.out.println ("The total number of students is: ");
System.out.println (count);
```

The first line calls the `println` that accepts a string. The second line calls the version that accepts an integer.

We often use a `println` statement that prints several types, such as:

```
System.out.println ("The total number of students is: " +
                    count);
```

In this case, the plus sign is the string concatenation operator. First, the value in the variable `count` is converted to a string representation, then the two strings are concatenated into one longer string, and finally the definition of `println` that accepts a single string is called.

Constructors are a good candidates for overloading. Several versions of a constructor give us several ways to set up an object. For example, the `SnakeEyes` program shown in Listing 4.6 instantiates two `Die` objects and initializes them using different constructors.

The purpose of the program is to roll the dice and count the number of times both dice show a 1 on the same throw (snake eyes). In this case, however, one die has 6 sides and the other has 20 sides. Each `Die` object is initialized using different constructors of the `Die` class. Listing 4.7 shows the `Die` class.

Both `Die` constructors have the same name, but one takes no parameters and the other takes an integer as a parameter. The compiler can examine the invocation and determine which version of the method is intended.

**listing
    4.6**

```java
//********************************************************************
//  SnakeEyes.java         Author: Lewis/Loftus/Cocking
//
//  Demonstrates the use of a class with overloaded constructors.
//********************************************************************

public class SnakeEyes
{
   //-----------------------------------------------------------------
   //  Creates two die objects, then rolls both dice a set number of
   //  times, counting the number of snake eyes that occur.
   //-----------------------------------------------------------------
   public static void main (String[] args)
   {
      final int ROLLS = 500;
      int snakeEyes = 0, num1, num2;

      Die die1 = new Die();     // creates a six-sided die
      Die die2 = new Die(20);   // creates a twenty-sided die

      for (int roll = 1; roll <= ROLLS; roll++)
      {
         num1 = die1.roll();
         num2 = die2.roll();

         if (num1 == 1 && num2 == 1)   // check for snake eyes
            snakeEyes++;
      }

      System.out.println ("Number of rolls: " + ROLLS);
      System.out.println ("Number of snake eyes: " + snakeEyes);
      System.out.println ("Ratio: " + (double)snakeEyes/ROLLS);
   }
}
```

output

```
Number of rolls: 500
Number of snake eyes: 6
Ratio: 0.012
```

listing
4.7

```java
//********************************************************************
//  Die.java         Author: Lewis/Loftus/Cocking
//
//  Represents one die (singular of dice) with faces showing values
//  between 1 and the number of faces on the die.
//********************************************************************

import java.util.Random;
public class Die
{
   private final int MIN_FACES = 4;

   private static Random generator = new Random();
   private int numFaces;   // number of sides on the die
   private int faceValue;  // current value showing on the die

   //-----------------------------------------------------------------
   //  Defaults to a six-sided die. Initial face value is 1.
   //-----------------------------------------------------------------
   public Die ()
   {
      numFaces = 6;
      faceValue = 1;
   }

   //-----------------------------------------------------------------
   //  Explicitly sets the size of the die. Defaults to a size of
   //  six if the parameter is invalid.  Initial face value is 1.
   //-----------------------------------------------------------------
   public Die (int faces)
   {
      if (faces < MIN_FACES)
         numFaces = 6;
      else
         numFaces = faces;

      faceValue = 1;
   }

   //-----------------------------------------------------------------
   //  Rolls the die and returns the result.
   //-----------------------------------------------------------------
   public int roll ()
   {
      faceValue = generator.nextInt(numFaces) + 1;
```

listing
   4.7   continued

```
    return faceValue;
  }

//------------------------------------------------------------
// Returns the current die value.
//------------------------------------------------------------
public int getFaceValue ()
{
    return faceValue;
  }
}
```

4.4 method decomposition

Sometimes we want to do something so complicated we need more than one method. One thing we can do is to break a method into several simpler methods to create a more understandable design. As an example, let's examine a program that translates English sentences into Pig Latin.

Pig Latin is a made-up language in which each word of a sentence is changed by moving the first letter of the word to the end and adding "ay." For example, the word *happy* would be written and pronounced *appyhay* and the word *birthday* would become *irthdaybay*. Words that begin with vowels simply have a "yay" added on the end, turning the word *enough* into *enoughyay*. Pairs of letters, called blends, such as "ch" and "st" are moved to the end together, so *grapefruit* becomes *apefruitgray*.

The `PigLatin` program shown in Listing 4.8 reads one or more sentences, translating each into Pig Latin.

The real workhorse behind the `PigLatin` program is the `PigLatinTranslator` class, shown in Listing 4.9. An object of type `PigLatinTranslator` provides a method called `translate`, which accepts a string and translates it into Pig Latin. Note that the `PigLatinTranslator` class does not contain a constructor because none is needed.

**listing
    4.8**

```java
//********************************************************************
//  PigLatin.java        Author: Lewis/Loftus/Cocking
//
//  Driver to exercise the PigLatinTranslator class.
//********************************************************************

import cs1.Keyboard;

public class PigLatin
{
    //-----------------------------------------------------------------
    //  Reads sentences and translates them into Pig Latin.
    //-----------------------------------------------------------------
    public static void main (String[] args)
    {
        String sentence, result, another = "y";;
        PigLatinTranslator translator = new PigLatinTranslator();

        while (another.equalsIgnoreCase("y"))
        {
            System.out.println ();
            System.out.println ("Enter a sentence (no punctuation):");
            sentence = Keyboard.readString();

            System.out.println ();
            result = translator.translate (sentence);
            System.out.println ("That sentence in Pig Latin is:");
            System.out.println (result);

            System.out.println ();
            System.out.print ("Translate another sentence (y/n)? ");
            another = Keyboard.readString();
        }
    }
}
```

listing
    4.8   continued

output

```
Enter a sentence (no punctuation):
Do you speak Pig Latin

That sentence in Pig Latin is:
oday ouyay eakspay igpay atinlay

Translate another sentence (y/n)? y

Enter a sentence (no punctuation):
Play it again Sam

That sentence in Pig Latin is:
ayplay ityay againyay amsay

Translate another sentence (y/n)? n
```

listing
    4.9

```java
//********************************************************************
//   PigLatinTranslator.java        Author: Lewis/Loftus/Cocking
//
//   Represents a translation system from English to Pig Latin.
//   Demonstrates method decomposition and the use of StringTokenizer.
//********************************************************************

import java.util.StringTokenizer;

public class PigLatinTranslator
{
    //----------------------------------------------------------------
    //   Translates a sentence of words into Pig Latin.
    //----------------------------------------------------------------
    public String translate (String sentence)
    {
        String result = "";

        sentence = sentence.toLowerCase();
        StringTokenizer tokenizer = new StringTokenizer (sentence);
```

listing
4.9   continued

```java
      while (tokenizer.hasMoreTokens())
      {
         result += translateWord (tokenizer.nextToken());
         result += " ";
      }

      return result;
   }

   //-----------------------------------------------------------------
   //  Translates one word into Pig Latin. If the word begins with a
   //  vowel, the suffix "yay" is appended to the word.  Otherwise,
   //  the first letter or two are moved to the end of the word,
   //  and "ay" is appended.
   //-----------------------------------------------------------------
   private String translateWord (String word)
   {
      String result = "";

      if (beginsWithVowel(word))
         result = word + "yay";
      else
         if (beginsWithBlend(word))
            result = word.substring(2) + word.substring(0,2) + "ay";
         else
            result = word.substring(1) + word.charAt(0) + "ay";

      return result;
   }

   //-----------------------------------------------------------------
   //  Determines if the specified word begins with a vowel.
   //-----------------------------------------------------------------
   private boolean beginsWithVowel (String word)
   {
      String vowels = "aeiou";

      char letter = word.charAt(0);

      return (vowels.indexOf(letter) != -1);
   }
```

listing
    4.9   continued

```
//------------------------------------------------------------
//  Determines if the specified word begins with a particular
//  two-character consonant blend.
//------------------------------------------------------------
private boolean beginsWithBlend (String word)
{
    return ( word.startsWith ("bl") || word.startsWith ("sc") ||
             word.startsWith ("br") || word.startsWith ("sh") ||
             word.startsWith ("ch") || word.startsWith ("sk") ||
             word.startsWith ("cl") || word.startsWith ("sl") ||
             word.startsWith ("cr") || word.startsWith ("sn") ||
             word.startsWith ("dr") || word.startsWith ("sm") ||
             word.startsWith ("dw") || word.startsWith ("sp") ||
             word.startsWith ("fl") || word.startsWith ("sq") ||
             word.startsWith ("fr") || word.startsWith ("st") ||
             word.startsWith ("gl") || word.startsWith ("sw") ||
             word.startsWith ("gr") || word.startsWith ("th") ||
             word.startsWith ("kl") || word.startsWith ("tr") ||
             word.startsWith ("ph") || word.startsWith ("tw") ||
             word.startsWith ("pl") || word.startsWith ("wh") ||
             word.startsWith ("pr") || word.startsWith ("wr") );
}
}
```

Translating an entire sentence into Pig Latin is not easy. One big method would be very long and difficult to follow. A better solution is to break the translate method into simpler methods and use several other support methods to help.

The translate method uses a StringTokenizer object to separate the string into words. Recall that the StringTokenizer class (discussed in Chapter 3) separates a string into smaller elements called tokens. In this case, the tokens are separated by space characters so we can use the default white space delimiters like we did in our word count program in Chapter 3. The PigLatin program assumes that no punctuation is included in the input.

The translate method passes each word to the private support method translateWord. Even the job of translating one word is complicated, so the translateWord method uses two other private methods, beginsWithVowel and beginsWithBlend.

The beginsWithVowel method returns a boolean value that tells translateWord whether the word begins with a vowel. Instead of checking each vowel separately, the code for this method declares a string of all the vowels, and then invokes the `String` method `indexOf` to see whether the first character of the word is in the vowel string. If the character cannot be found, the `indexOf` method returns a value of −1.

The `beginsWithBlend` method also returns a `boolean` value. The body of the method has one large expression that makes several calls to the `startsWith` method of the `String` class. If any of these calls returns true, because the word begins with a blend, then the `beginsWithBlend` method returns true as well.

Note that the `translateWord`, `beginsWithVowel`, and `beginsWithBlend` methods are all declared with private visibility. They do not deal directly with clients outside the class. Instead, they only help the `translate` method do its job. Because they have private visibility, they cannot be called from outside this class. If the `main` method of the `PigLatin` class attempted to call the `translateWord` method, for instance, the compiler would issue an error message.

Whenever a method becomes large or complicated, we should consider breaking it into simpler methods to create a more understandable class design. First, however, we must consider how other classes and objects can be defined to create better overall system design. In an object-oriented design, breaking up methods must happen after objects have been broken up.

> **key concept**
>
> A complicated method can be broken into several simpler methods and helped by support methods.

4.5   object relationships

Classes, and their objects, can have particular types of relationships, or associations, to each other. This section looks at associations between objects of the same class. We then explore aggregation, in which one object is made up of other objects, creating a "has-a" relationship.

Inheritance, which we introduced in Chapter 2, is another important relationship between classes. It creates a generalization, or an "is-a" relationship, between classes. We examine inheritance in Chapter 7.

association

Two classes have a general association if they are "aware" of each other. Objects of those classes may use each other. This is sometimes called a *use relationship*.

An association can be described in general terms, such as the fact that an `Author` object writes a `Book` object. Because association relationships are so general, they are very useful. We introduce uses of general associations throughout the book.

association between objects of the same class

Some associations occur between two objects of the same class. That is, a method of one object takes as a parameter another object of the same class. The operation performed often involves the internal data of both objects.

The concat method of the String class is an example of this. The method is executed through one String object and gets another String object as a parameter. For example:

```
str3 = str1.concat(str2);
```

The String object executing the method (str1) attaches its characters to those of the String passed as a parameter (str2). A new String object is returned as a result (and stored as str3).

The RationalNumbers program shown in Listing 4.10 works like this. Recall that a rational number is a value that can be represented as a fraction, such as 2/2 (which equals 1), or 35/5 (which equals 7), or 1/2. The

listing
4.10

```
//********************************************************************
//  RationalNumbers.java       Author: Lewis/Loftus/Cocking
//
//  Driver to exercise the use of multiple Rational objects.
//********************************************************************

public class RationalNumbers
{
   //-----------------------------------------------------------------
   //  Creates some rational number objects and performs various
   //  operations on them.
   //-----------------------------------------------------------------
   public static void main (String[] args)
   {
      Rational r1 = new Rational (6, 8);
      Rational r2 = new Rational (1, 3);
      Rational r3, r4, r5, r6, r7;

      System.out.println ("First rational number: " + r1);
      System.out.println ("Second rational number: " + r2);
```

listing
    4.10   continued

```
        if (r1.equals(r2))
            System.out.println ("r1 and r2 are equal.");
        else
            System.out.println ("r1 and r2 are NOT equal.");

        r3 = r1.reciprocal();
        System.out.println ("The reciprocal of r1 is: " + r3);

        r4 = r1.add(r2);
        r5 = r1.subtract(r2);
        r6 = r1.multiply(r2);
        r7 = r1.divide(r2);

        System.out.println ("r1 + r2: " + r4);
        System.out.println ("r1 - r2: " + r5);
        System.out.println ("r1 * r2: " + r6);
        System.out.println ("r1 / r2: " + r7);
    }
}
```

output

```
First rational number: 3/4
Second rational number: 1/3
r1 and r2 are NOT equal.
The reciprocal of r1 is: 4/3
r1 + r2: 13/12
r1 - r2: 5/12
r1 * r2: 1/4
r1 / r2: 9/4
```

RationalNumbers program creates two objects representing rational numbers and then does things to them to produce new rational numbers.

The Rational class is shown in Listing 4.11. Each object of type Rational represents one rational number. The Rational class contains operations on rational numbers, such as addition and subtraction.

The methods of the Rational class, such as add, subtract, multiply, and divide, use the Rational object that is executing the method as the first (left) operand and the Rational object passed as a parameter as the second (right) operand.

Note that some of the methods in the Rational class are private because we don't want them executed directly from outside a Rational object. They are there only to support the other services of the object.

listing
     4.11

```java
//********************************************************************
//  Rational.java        Author: Lewis/Loftus/Cocking
//
//  Represents one rational number with a numerator and denominator.
//********************************************************************

public class Rational
{
   private int numerator, denominator;

   //-----------------------------------------------------------------
   //  Sets up the rational number by ensuring a nonzero denominator
   //  and making only the numerator signed.
   //-----------------------------------------------------------------
   public Rational (int numer, int denom)
   {
      if (denom == 0)
         denom = 1;

      // Make the numerator "store" the sign
      if (denom < 0)
      {
         numer = numer * -1;
         denom = denom * -1;
      }

      numerator = numer;
      denominator = denom;

      reduce();
   }

   //-----------------------------------------------------------------
   //  Returns the numerator of this rational number.
   //-----------------------------------------------------------------
   public int getNumerator ()
   {
      return numerator;
   }

   //-----------------------------------------------------------------
   //  Returns the denominator of this rational number.
   //-----------------------------------------------------------------
   public int getDenominator ()
   {
      return denominator;
   }
```

listing
   4.11   continued

```java
//-----------------------------------------------------------------
//  Returns the reciprocal of this rational number.
//-----------------------------------------------------------------
public Rational reciprocal ()
{
   return new Rational (denominator, numerator);
}

//-----------------------------------------------------------------
//  Adds this rational number to the one passed as a parameter.
//  A common denominator is found by multiplying the individual
//  denominators.
//-----------------------------------------------------------------
public Rational add (Rational op2)
{
   int commonDenominator = denominator * op2.getDenominator();
   int numerator1 = numerator * op2.getDenominator();
   int numerator2 = op2.getNumerator() * denominator;
   int sum = numerator1 + numerator2;

   return new Rational (sum, commonDenominator);
}

//-----------------------------------------------------------------
//  Subtracts the rational number passed as a parameter from this
//  rational number.
//-----------------------------------------------------------------
public Rational subtract (Rational op2)
{
   int commonDenominator = denominator * op2.getDenominator();
   int numerator1 = numerator * op2.getDenominator();
   int numerator2 = op2.getNumerator() * denominator;
   int difference = numerator1 - numerator2;

   return new Rational (difference, commonDenominator);
}

//-----------------------------------------------------------------
//  Multiplies this rational number by the one passed as a
//  parameter.
//-----------------------------------------------------------------
public Rational multiply (Rational op2)
{
   int numer = numerator * op2.getNumerator();
   int denom = denominator * op2.getDenominator();
```

listing
    4.11   continued

```java
      return new Rational (numer, denom);
   }

   //-----------------------------------------------------------------
   //  Divides this rational number by the one passed as a parameter
   //  by multiplying by the reciprocal of the second rational.
   //-----------------------------------------------------------------
   public Rational divide (Rational op2)
   {
      return multiply (op2.reciprocal());
   }

   //-----------------------------------------------------------------
   //  Determines if this rational number is equal to the one passed
   //  as a parameter.  Assumes they are both reduced.
   //-----------------------------------------------------------------
   public boolean equals (Rational op2)
   {
      return ( numerator == op2.getNumerator() &&
               denominator == op2.getDenominator() );
   }

   //-----------------------------------------------------------------
   //  Returns this rational number as a string.
   //-----------------------------------------------------------------
   public String toString ()
   {
      String result;

      if (numerator == 0)
         result = "0";
      else
         if (denominator == 1)
            result = numerator + "";
         else
            result = numerator + "/" + denominator;

      return result;
   }

   //-----------------------------------------------------------------
   //  Reduces this rational number by dividing both the numerator
   //  and the denominator by their greatest common divisor.
   //-----------------------------------------------------------------
```

listing
    4.11   continued

```java
   private void reduce ()
   {
      if (numerator != 0)
      {
         int common = gcd (Math.abs(numerator), denominator);

         numerator = numerator / common;
         denominator = denominator / common;
      }
   }

   //-----------------------------------------------------------------
   //  Computes and returns the greatest common divisor of the two
   //  positive parameters. Uses Euclid's algorithm.
   //-----------------------------------------------------------------
   private int gcd (int num1, int num2)
   {
      while (num1 != num2)
         if (num1 > num2)
            num1 = num1 - num2;
         else
            num2 = num2 - num1;

      return num1;
   }
}
```

aggregation

Some objects are made up of other objects. A car, for instance, is made up of its engine, its chassis, its wheels, and lots of other parts. Each of these other parts are separate objects. Therefore we can say that a car is an *aggregation*—it is made up of other objects. Aggregation is sometimes described as a *has-a relationship*. For instance, a car *has a* chassis.

> **key concept**
>
> An aggregate object is made up, in part, of other objects, forming a has-a relationship.

In the software world, an *aggregate object* is any object that has other objects as instance data. For example, an Account object contains, among other things, a String object that is the name of the account owner. That makes each Account object an aggregate object.

Let's consider another example. The program StudentBody shown in Listing 4.12 creates two Student objects. Each Student object is made up of two Address objects, one for the student's college address and another for the student's home address. The main method just creates these objects

```
//********************************************************************
//  StudentBody.java        Author: Lewis/Loftus/Cocking
//
//  Demonstrates the use of an aggregate class.
//********************************************************************

public class StudentBody
{
    //-----------------------------------------------------------------
    //  Creates some Address and Student objects and prints them.
    //-----------------------------------------------------------------
    public static void main (String[] args)
    {
        Address school = new Address ("800 Lancaster Ave.", "Villanova",
                                      "PA", 19085);

        Address jHome = new Address ("21 Jump Street", "Lynchburg",
                                     "VA", 24551);
        Student john = new Student ("John", "Gomez", jHome, school);

        Address mHome = new Address ("123 Main Street", "Euclid", "OH",
                                     44132);
        Student marsha = new Student ("Marsha", "Jones", mHome, school);

        System.out.println (john);
        System.out.println ();
        System.out.println (marsha);
    }
}
```

output

```
John Gomez
Home Address:
21 Jump Street
Lynchburg, VA  24551
School Address:
800 Lancaster Ave.
Villanova, PA  19085

Marsha Jones
Home Address:
123 Main Street
Euclid, OH  44132
School Address:
800 Lancaster Ave.
Villanova, PA  19085
```

and prints them out. Note that we once again pass objects to the `println` method, relying on the automatic call to the `toString` method to create something suitable for printing.

The `Student` class shown in Listing 4.13 represents a single college student. This class would have to be huge if it were to represent all aspects of a student. We're keeping it simple for now so that the object aggregation is clear. The instance data of the `Student` class includes two references to

listing
4.13

```java
//********************************************************************
//  Student.java          Author: Lewis/Loftus/Cocking
//
//  Represents a college student.
//********************************************************************

public class Student
{
    private String firstName, lastName;
    private Address homeAddress, schoolAddress;

    //-----------------------------------------------------------------
    //  Sets up this Student object with the specified initial values.
    //-----------------------------------------------------------------
    public Student (String first, String last, Address home,
                    Address school)
    {
        firstName = first;
        lastName = last;
        homeAddress = home;
        schoolAddress = school;
    }

    //-----------------------------------------------------------------
    //  Returns this Student object as a string.
    //-----------------------------------------------------------------
    public String toString()
    {
        String result;

        result = firstName + " " + lastName + "\n";
        result += "Home Address:\n" + homeAddress + "\n";
        result += "School Address:\n" + schoolAddress;

        return result;
    }
}
```

Address objects: homeAddress and schoolAddress. We refer to those objects in the toString method when we create a string representation of the student. Because we are concatenating an Address object to another string, the toString method in Address is automatically called.

The Address class is shown in Listing 4.14. It contains only the parts of a street address. Note that nothing about the Address class indicates that it is part of a Student object. The Address class is general so it could be used in any situation in which a street address is needed.

listing
4.14

```java
//********************************************************************
//  Address.java        Author: Lewis/Loftus/Cocking
//
//  Represents a street address.
//********************************************************************

public class Address
{
   private String streetAddress, city, state;
   private int zipCode;

   //-----------------------------------------------------------------
   //  Sets up this Address object with the specified data.
   //-----------------------------------------------------------------
   public Address (String street, String town, String st, int zip)
   {
      streetAddress = street;
      city = town;
      state = st;
      zipCode = zip;
   }

   //-----------------------------------------------------------------
   //  Returns this Address object as a string.
   //-----------------------------------------------------------------
   public String toString()
   {
      String result;

      result = streetAddress + "\n";
      result += city + ", " + state + "  " + zipCode;

      return result;
   }
}
```

4.6 bumper cars case study: design

Using the requirements from Chapter 3, we can now design a solution to our bumper car problem. First we will identify the objects and their relationships. A good place to start is with the real-world objects: the bumper cars, the drivers, the arena, and the spectators. We could break these down into simpler objects if we need to. For example, the arena has a floor, walls, and perhaps a ceiling. A car is made up of an engine, a steering wheel, tires, a gas pedal, and so on.

In a detailed simulation, we might have the driver's foot press a gas pedal, which is part of the car, causing the car to move forward at a certain speed across the arena's floor. In this simulation, we don't have to be that detailed. We will simply have a driver tell a car to move forward.

The bumper car company wants to know how many times the cars get bumped. So the car and driver are definitely important for our simulation. The arena may be important as well, but the spectators probably are not. Looking back at the information we were given, a bump counts as bumping into another car, or into a wall, so the arena may be an important object because cars can bump into its walls.

Let's start working with the car, driver, and arena objects. We need to think about the state and behavior of each one. Take some time to think about it yourself. You might come up with a table like this:

Object	State	Behavior
Car	Year built, color, current speed, current driver, bump count	Move forward, turn, bump into another car or wall
Driver	Name, age, car being driven	Drive car
Arena	Dimensions, cars and drivers inside	??

It's not clear yet what behavior the arena might have. The real-world arena doesn't do much.

The next thing we will think about is how the objects will interact with each other. The driver controls the car by pushing the gas pedal to move forward or by turning the steering wheel to turn the car. In our program, these interactions are method calls, so an object that is a Driver might call the moveForward() method on an object that is a Car in order to make it move forward.

This leads to the question of who tells the driver to drive. Let's think about how the simulation will be run. In the real world, everything runs in real time. That is, the drivers are all driving their cars at the same time and they do so continuously, not in steps. But a computer program can only do one thing at a time and statements are executed in order. Our simulation will run in steps then. Each driver takes a turn in their car. The arena object will house the drivers and cars just like a real-world arena, so it makes sense to have the arena be the object that tells a car/driver when it is its "turn" to move. As the cars move around during the simulation, the arena will have to keep track of where each car/driver pair is located.

program flow

Now that we have decided on the main objects and their basic interactions, we need to get more detailed in our design and think about how the program will flow. During one step in the simulation we must give each car a chance to move. We will loop through all the cars in the arena and give each a chance to move. One step in the simulation looks like this:

```
Arena:          for each car in the arena
                {
Arena:              Tell car/driver it's their turn
Driver:             Determine what to do
                    Tell car to move forward or turn
Car:                Move or turn and if position changes,
                    tell arena
Arena:              Update car's position
                }
```

One object "tells" another something by using a method call. For example, the Arena might call a method go on each Car when it is that Car's turn to go.

GRAPHICS TRACK

exercises

1. Imagine a simulation of the game of tennis. List some of the real-world objects in this simulation and their state and behavior.

2. Of the "state" items listed for each object type in the bumper car table, which are most likely to be useful in the simulation and which are least likely to be useful?

3. Suppose the `Car` class has the methods `moveForward`, `turnLeft`, and `turnRight` that take no parameters. Write code showing how the driver would call these methods assuming the variable `myCar` holds a reference to the driver's car.

4.7 applet methods

In Chapter 3 we used the `paint` method to draw the contents of an applet on a screen. An applet has several other methods, too. Figure 4.8 lists several applet methods.

> **key concept**
> Several methods of the `Applet` class are designed to facilitate their execution in a Web browser.

```
public void init ()
    Initializes the applet. Called just after the applet is loaded.

public void start ()
    Starts the applet. Called just after the applet is made active.

public void stop ()
    Stops the applet. Called just after the applet is made inactive.

public void destroy ()
    Destroys the applet. Called when the browser is exited.

public URL getCodeBase ()
    Returns the URL at which this applet's bytecode is located.

public URL getDocumentBase ()
    Returns the URL at which the HTML document containing this applet is
    located.

public AudioClip getAudioClip (URL url, String name)
    Retrieves an audio clip from the specified URL.

public Image getImage (URL url, String name)
    Retrieves an image from the specified URL.
```

figure 4.8   Some methods of the `Applet` class

The init method is executed once when the applet is first loaded, such as when the browser or appletviewer first views the applet. So the init method is the place to initialize the applet's environment and permanent data.

The start and stop methods of an applet are called when the applet becomes active or inactive, respectively. For example, after we use a browser to load an applet, the applet's start method is called. When we leave that page the applet becomes inactive and the stop method is called. If we return to the page, the applet becomes active again and the start method is called again. Note that the init method is called once when the applet is loaded, but start may be called several times as the page is revisited. It is good practice to use start and stop if an applet actively uses CPU time, such as when it is showing an animation, so that CPU time is not wasted.

Reloading the Web page in the browser does not necessarily reload the applet. To force the applet to reload, most browsers need the user to press a key combination. For example, in Netscape Navigator, the user can hold down the shift key while pressing the reload button to reload the Web page and reload (and reinitialize) all applets linked to that page.

The getCodeBase and getDocumentBase methods determine where the applet's bytecode or HTML document resides. An applet could use the URL to get more resources, such as an image or audio clip, using the applet methods getImage or getAudioClip.

We use these applet methods throughout this book.

4.8   graphical objects

Often an object has a graphical representation. Consider the LineUp applet shown in Listing 4.15. It creates several StickFigure objects, of different colors and heights. The StickFigure objects are instantiated in the init method of the applet, so they are created only once, when the applet is first loaded.

The paint method asks that the stick figures redraw themselves whenever the method is called. The paint method is called whenever something happens that might change the graphic representation of the applet itself. For instance, when the window that the applet is displayed in is moved, paint redraws the applet contents.

The StickFigure class is shown in Listing 4.16. Like any other object, a StickFigure object contains data that defines its state, such as the position, color, and height of the figure. The draw method contains the individual commands that draw the figure itself.

listing
   4.15

```java
//********************************************************************
//  LineUp.java          Author: Lewis/Loftus/Cocking
//
//  Demonstrates the use of a graphical object.
//********************************************************************

import java.util.Random;
import java.applet.Applet;
import java.awt.*;

public class LineUp extends Applet
{
   private final int APPLET_WIDTH = 400;
   private final int APPLET_HEIGHT = 150;
   private final int HEIGHT_MIN = 100;
   private final int VARIANCE = 40;

   private StickFigure figure1, figure2, figure3, figure4;

   //-----------------------------------------------------------------
   //  Creates several stick figures with varying characteristics.
   //-----------------------------------------------------------------
   public void init ()
   {
      int h1, h2, h3, h4;  // heights of stick figures
      Random generator = new Random();

      h1 = HEIGHT_MIN + generator.nextInt(VARIANCE);
      h2 = HEIGHT_MIN + generator.nextInt(VARIANCE);
      h3 = HEIGHT_MIN + generator.nextInt(VARIANCE);
      h4 = HEIGHT_MIN + generator.nextInt(VARIANCE);

      figure1 = new StickFigure (100, 150, Color.red, h1);
      figure2 = new StickFigure (150, 150, Color.cyan, h2);
      figure3 = new StickFigure (200, 150, Color.green, h3);
      figure4 = new StickFigure (250, 150, Color.yellow, h4);

      setBackground (Color.black);
      setSize (APPLET_WIDTH, APPLET_HEIGHT);
   }
```

listing
    4.15   continued

```
//--------------------------------------------------------------------
//   Paints the stick figures on the applet.
//--------------------------------------------------------------------
public void paint (Graphics page)
{
    figure1.draw (page);
    figure2.draw (page);
    figure3.draw (page);
    figure4.draw (page);
}
}
```

display

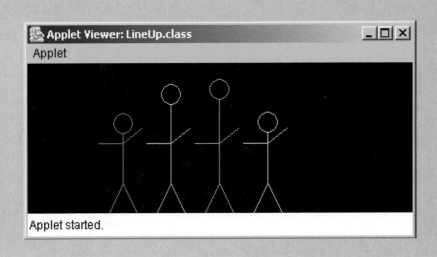

listing
   4.16

```java
//********************************************************************
//  StickFigure.java        Author: Lewis/Loftus/Cocking
//
//  Represents a graphical stick figure.
//********************************************************************

import java.awt.*;

public class StickFigure
{
   private int baseX;       // center of figure
   private int baseY;       // floor (bottom of feet)
   private Color color;     // color of stick figure
   private int height;      // height of stick figure

   //-----------------------------------------------------------------
   //  Sets up the stick figure's primary attributes.
   //-----------------------------------------------------------------
   public StickFigure (int center, int bottom, Color shade, int size)
   {
      baseX = center;
      baseY = bottom;
      color = shade;
      height = size;
   }

   //-----------------------------------------------------------------
   //  Draws this figure relative to baseX, baseY, and height.
   //-----------------------------------------------------------------
   public void draw (Graphics page)
   {
      int top = baseY - height;  // top of head

      page.setColor (color);

      page.drawOval (baseX-10, top, 20, 20);  // head

      page.drawLine (baseX, top+20, baseX, baseY-30);  // trunk

      page.drawLine (baseX, baseY-30, baseX-15, baseY);  // legs
      page.drawLine (baseX, baseY-30, baseX+15, baseY);

      page.drawLine (baseX, baseY-70, baseX-25, baseY-70);  // arms
      page.drawLine (baseX, baseY-70, baseX+20, baseY-85);
   }
}
```

summary of
key concepts

▸ Each object has a state and a set of behaviors. The values of an object's variables define its state. The methods to which an object responds define its behaviors.

▸ A class is a blueprint of an object; it saves no memory space for data. Each object has its own data space, thus its own state.

▸ The scope of a variable determines where it can be referenced and depends on where it is declared.

▸ Objects should be encapsulated. The rest of a program should interact with an object only through its public methods.

▸ Instance variables should be declared with private visibility to protect their data.

▸ A method must return a value that matches the return type in the method header.

▸ When a method is called, the actual parameters are copied into the formal parameters. The types of parameters must match.

▸ A constructor cannot have any return type, even `void`.

▸ A variable declared in a method cannot be used outside of it.

▸ The versions of an overloaded method can be told apart by their signatures. The number, type, and order of their parameters must be different.

▸ A complicated method can be broken up into simpler methods that act as private support methods.

▸ A method called through one object may take another object of the same class as a parameter.

▸ An aggregate object is made up of other objects, forming a has-a relationship.

▸ Several methods of the `Applet` class are designed to work in a Web browser.

self-review questions

4.1   What is the difference between an object and a class?

4.2   What is the scope of a variable?

4.3   Objects should be self-governing. Explain.

4.4   What is a modifier?

4.5 Describe each of the following:

a. public method

b. private method

c. public variable

d. private variable

4.6 What does the `return` statement do?

4.7 Explain the difference between an actual parameter and a formal parameter.

4.8 What are constructors used for? How are they defined?

4.9 How can you tell overloaded methods apart?

4.10 What can you do to avoid long, complex methods?

4.11 Explain how a class can have an association with itself.

4.12 What is an aggregate object?

4.13 What do the `start` and `stop` methods of an applet do?

multiple choice

4.1 Object is to class as

a. circle is to square

b. house is to blueprint

c. blueprint is to house

d. bicycle is to car

e. car is to bicycle

4.2 When a `Coin` object is passed to the `println` method,

a. a compile error occurs

b. a runtime error occurs

c. the `toString` method is called on the object to get the string to print

d. a default string that includes the class name is generated

e. the `Coin` is flipped and the result printed

4.3   Which of the following should be used for services that an object provides to client code?

a. private variables

b. public variables

c. private methods

d. public methods

e. none of the above

4.4   The values passed to a method when it is called are

a. formal parameters

b. actual parameters

c. primitive values

d. objects

e. return values

4.5   Consider the following code:

```
int cube(int x)
{
    x = 3;
    return x * x * x;
}
```

What is returned by the call cube(2)?

a. 2

b. 3

c. 8

d. 9

e. 27

4.6   Method overloading refers to

a. a method with 10 or more parameters

b. a method with a very large body

c. a method that performs too many tasks and should be divided into support methods

d. more than one method with the same name

e. more than one method with the same numbers and types of parameters

4.7   Consider the following code:

```
int sum(int n)
{
    int total = 0;
    for (int i=1; i <= n; i++)

    _____

    return total;
}
```

What statement should go in the body of the `for` loop so that the sum of the first n integers is returned?

a. `total += i;`

b. `total += 1;`

c. `total += n;`

d. `total = n + 1;`

e. `total += n - 1;`

4.8   What will be printed when the method `printStuff` is called?

```
int calc(double a, double b)
{
    int num = a * b;
    b = a;
    num = a + b;
    return num;
}
void printStuff()
{
    double x = 5.1, y = 6.2;
    System.out.println(calc(x,0) + calc(0,y));
}
```

a. `5.16.2`

b. `11.3`

c. `10.20`

d. `0`

e. There will be a compile error because a `double` cannot be assigned to an `int` without a cast.

4.9   The keyword void is placed in front of a method name when it is declared to indicate that

a. the method does not return a value

b. the method is a constructor

c. the method is overloaded

d. the method should be called only within its class

e. the method returns a value of an unknown type

4.10 Consider the following method:

```
double doIt(double x)
{
    while (x > 0)
        x -= 3;
}
```

What is it missing?

a. a declaration of the variable x

b. a return statement

c. a body

d. a name

e. a parameter

true/false

4.1   Instance variables that are declared public violate the principle of encapsulation.

4.2   Every method must have a return statement.

4.3   A constructor must have the same name as its class.

4.4   A variable declared in one method may be used in any other method in the same class.

4.5   Overloaded methods have a signature, which includes the number, type, and order of parameters.

4.6   An object may be made up of other objects.

4.7   Only one object may be created from a particular class.

4.8   Methods that provide services to clients should be made private.

4.9   Constructors should always return void.

4.10 Parameters to methods may only be primitive types.

short answer

4.1 Write a method header for a method named `translate` that takes an integer parameter and returns a `double`.

4.2 Write a method header for a method named `find` that takes a `String` and a `double` as parameters and returns an integer.

4.3 Write a method header for a method named `printAnswer` that takes three `doubles` as parameters and doesn't return anything.

4.4 Write the body of the method for the following header. The method should return a welcome message that includes the user's name and visitor number. For example, if the parameters were "Joe" and 5, the returned string would be `"Welcome Joe! You are visitor number 5."`
```
String welcomeMessage (String name, int
visitorNum)
```

4.5 Write a method called `powersOfTwo` that prints the first 10 powers of 2 (starting with 2). The method takes no parameters and doesn't return anything.

4.6 Write a method called `alarm` that prints the string `"Alarm!"` several times on separate lines. The method should accept an integer parameter that tells it how many times the string is printed. Print an error message if the parameter is less than 1.

4.7 Write a method called `sum100` that adds up all the numbers from 1 to 100, inclusive and returns the answer.

4.8 Write a method called `maxOfTwo` that accepts two integer parameters from the user and returns the larger of the two.

4.9 Write a method called `sumRange` that accepts two integer parameters that represent a range such as 50 to 75. Issue an error message and return zero if the second parameter is less than the first. Otherwise, the method should return the sum of the integers in that range (inclusive).

4.10 Write a method called `larger` that accepts two floating point parameters (of type `double`) and returns true if the first parameter is greater than the second, and false if it is less than the second.

4.11 Write a method called `countA` that accepts a `String` parameter and returns the number of times the character `'A'` is found in the string.

4.12 Write a method called `evenlyDivisible` that accepts two integer parameters and returns true if the first parameter can be evenly divided by the second, or vice versa, and false if it can't be. Return false if either parameter is zero.

4.13 Write a method called `average` that accepts two integer parameters and returns their average as a floating point value.

4.14 Overload the `average` method of Exercise 4.13 so that the method returns the average of three integers.

4.15 Overload the `average` method of Exercise 4.13 to take four integer parameters and return their average.

4.16 Write a method called `multiConcat` that takes a `String` and an integer as parameters. Return a `String` made up of the string parameter concatenated with itself `count` times, where `count` is the integer. For example, if the parameter values are `"hi"` and 4, the return value is `"hihihihi"`. Return the original string if the integer parameter is less than 2.

4.17 Overload the `multiConcat` method from Exercise 4.16 so that if the integer parameter is not provided, the method returns the string concatenated with itself. For example, if the parameter is `"test"`, the return value is `"testtest"`.

4.18 Write a method called `isAlpha` that accepts a character parameter and returns true if that character is an uppercase or lowercase alphabetic letter.

4.19 Write a method called `floatEquals` that accepts three floating point values as parameters. The method should return true if the first two parameters are no further apart from each other than the third parameter. For example, `floatEquals (2.453, 2.459, 0.01)` should return true because 2.453 and 2.459 are 0.006 apart from each other and 0.006 is less than 0.01. *Hint*: See the discussion in Chapter 3 on comparing floating point values for equality.

4.20 Write a method called `reverse` that accepts a `String` parameter and returns a string made up of the characters of the parameter in reverse order. There is a method in the `String` class that performs this operation, but for the sake of this exercise, you should write your own.

4.21 Write a method called `isIsosceles` that accepts the lengths of the sides of a triangle as its parameters. The method returns true if the triangle is isosceles but not equilateral (meaning that exactly two of the sides have an equal length), and false if all three sides are equal or if none of the sides are equal.

4.22 Write a method called `randomInRange` that accepts two integer parameters representing a range such as 30 to 50. The method should return a random integer in the specified range (inclusive). Return zero if the first parameter is greater than the second.

4.23 Write a method called `randomColor` that creates and returns a random `Color` object. Recall that a `Color` object has three values between 0 and 255, representing the contributions of red, green, and blue (its RGB value).

4.24 Write a method called `drawCircle` that draws a circle based on these parameters: a `Graphics` object through which to draw the circle, two integer values for the (x, y) coordinates of the center of the circle, another integer for the circle's radius, and a `Color` object for the circle's color. The method does not return anything.

4.25 Overload the `drawCircle` method of Exercise 4.24 so that if the `Color` parameter is not provided, the circle's color will be black.

programming projects

4.1 Change the `Account` class so that funds can be moved from one account to another. Think of this as withdrawing money from one account and depositing it into another. Change the `main` method of the `Banking` class to show this new service.

4.2 Change the `Account` class so that it also lets a user open an account with just a name and an account number, and a starting balance of zero. Change the `main` method of the `Banking` class to show this new capability.

4.3 Write an application that rolls a die and displays the result. Let the user pick the number of sides on the die. Use the `Die` class to represent the die in your program.

4.4 Design and implement a class called `PairOfDice`, with two six-sided `Die` objects. Create a driver class called `BoxCars` with a `main` method that rolls a `PairOfDice` object 1000 times, counting the number of box cars (two sixes) that occur.

4.5 Using the `PairOfDice` class from Programming Project 4.4, design and implement a class to play a game called Pig. In this game, the user competes against the computer. On each turn, the player rolls a pair of dice and adds up his or her points. Whoever reaches 100 points first, wins. If a player rolls a 1, he or she loses all points for that round and the dice go to the other player. If a player rolls two 1s in one turn, the player loses all points earned so far in the game and loses control of the dice. The player may voluntarily turn over the dice after each roll. So the player must decide to either roll again (be a pig) and risk losing points, or give up the dice, possibly letting the other player win. Set up the computer player so that it always gives up the dice after getting 20 or more points in a round.

4.6 Design and implement a class called `Card` that represents a standard playing card. Each card has a suit and a face value. Create a program that deals 20 random cards.

4.7 Write an application that lets the user add, subtract, multiply, or divide two fractions. Use the `Rational` class in your implementation.

4.8 Change the `Student` class (Listing 4.13) so that each student object also contains the scores for three tests. Provide a constructor that sets all instance values based on parameter values. Overload the constructor so that each test score starts out at zero. Provide a method called `setTestScore` that accepts two parameters: the test number (1 through 3) and the score. Also provide a method called `getTestScore` that accepts the test number and returns the score. Provide a method called `average` that computes and returns the average test score for this student. Modify the `toString` method so that the test scores and average are included in the description of the student. Modify the driver class `main` method to exercise the new `Student` methods.

4.9 Design and implement a class called `Building` that represents a drawing of a building. The parameters to the constructor should be the building's width and height. Each building should be colored black and have a few random windows colored yellow. Create an applet that draws a random skyline of buildings.

4.10 Create a class called `Crayon` that represents one crayon of a particular color and length (height). Design and implement an applet that draws a box of crayons.

answers to self-review questions

4.1   A class is the blueprint of an object. It defines the variables and methods that will be a part of every object that is instantiated from it. But a class saves no memory space for variables. Each object has its own data space and therefore its own state.

4.2   The scope of a variable is where in a program the variable can be referenced. An instance variable, declared at the class level, can be referenced in any method of the class. Local variables, including the formal parameters, declared within a particular method, can be referenced only in that method.

4.3   A self-governing object controls the values of its own data. Encapsulated objects, which don't allow an external client to reach in and change the data, are self-governing.

4.4   A modifier is a Java reserved word that can be used in the definition of a variable or method and that defines certain characteristics. For example, if a variable has private visibility, it cannot be directly accessed from outside the object.

4.5   The modifiers affect the methods and variables in the following ways:

   a. A public method is called a service method because it defines a service that the object provides.

   b. A private method is called a support method because it cannot be called from outside the object and because it supports the activities of other methods in the class.

   c. A public variable is a variable that can be directly read and changed by a client. This violates the principle of encapsulation and should be avoided.

   d. A private variable can be read and changed only from within the class. Variables almost always are declared with private visibility.

4.6   An explicit `return` statement spells out the value that is returned from a method. The type of the return value must match the return type in the method definition.

4.7   An actual parameter is a value sent to a method when the method is invoked. A formal parameter is the matching variable in the header of the method declaration; it takes on the value of the actual parameter so that it can be used inside the method.

4.8   Constructors are special methods used to initialize the object when it is instantiated. A constructor has the same name as its class, and it does not return a value.

4.9   Overloaded methods have a unique signature, which includes the number, order, and type of the parameters. The return type is not part of the signature.

4.10 Dividing a complex method into several support methods simplifies the design of the program.

4.11 A method executed through an object might take another object created from the same class as a parameter. For example, the `concat` method of the `String` class is executed through one `String` object and takes another `String` object as a parameter.

4.12 An aggregate object has other objects as instance data. That is, an aggregate object is made up of other objects.

4.13 The `Applet start` method is called automatically every time the applet becomes active, such as when a browser opens the page it is on. The `stop` method is called automatically when the applet becomes inactive.

enhancing classes

This chapter explores the design and implementation of classes. First we review object references—what they are and how they affect our processing. Then we study the `static` modifier to see how it can be applied to variables and to methods. We also discuss the interface between classes. Finally, we learn to nest one class definition in another and to use dialog boxes, then we explore the basic elements of a Java graphical user interface (GUI).

5.0   references revisited

In our examples we've declared many *object reference variables*. In this chapter we look at this in more detail. Object references play an important role in a program. We need to understand how they work so we can write sophisticated object-oriented software.

An object reference variable and an object are two different things. Remember that the declaration of the reference variable and the creation of the object that it refers to are separate steps. Although we often declare the reference variable and create an object for it to refer to on the same line, we don't have to. In fact, in many cases, we won't want to.

An object reference variable stores the address of an object even though we don't know the address ourselves. When we use the dot operator to call an object's method, we are really using the address in the reference variable to find the object, look up the method, and invoke it.

the null reference

A reference variable that does not point to an object is called a *null reference*. When a reference variable is first declared as an instance variable, it is a null reference. If we try to follow a null reference, we will get a NullPointerException, which tells us that there is no object to reference. For example, look at this code:

```
class NameIsNull
{
    String name; // not initialized, therefore null

    void printName()
    {
        System.out.println (name.length());
        // causes an exception
    }
}
```

The declaration of the instance variable name says it is a reference to a String object but doesn't create any String object for it to refer to. The variable name, therefore, contains a null reference. When the method tries to call the length method of the object, we get an error because no object exists to execute the method.

Note that this can happen only with instance variables. Suppose, for example, the following two lines of code were in a method:

```
String name;
System.out.println (name.length());
```

In this case, the variable `name` is local to whatever method we are in. The compiler would complain that we were using the `name` variable before it had been initialized. In the case of instance variables, however, the compiler can't determine whether a variable had been initialized; therefore, the danger of trying to follow a null reference is a problem.

The identifier `null` is a reserved word in Java and represents a null reference. We can set a reference to `null` on purpose, to make sure it doesn't point to any object. We can also use `null` to check whether a reference points to an object. For example, we could have used the following code in the `printName` method to keep us from following a null reference:

```
if (name == null)
    System.out.println ("Invalid Name");
else
    System.out.println (name.length());
```

> **key concept**
> The reserved word `null` represents a reference that does not point to a valid object.

the this reference

Another special reference for Java objects is called the `this` reference. The word `this` is a reserved word in Java. It lets an object refer to itself. As we have discussed, a method is always invoked through (or by) a particular object or class. Inside that method, the `this` reference can be used to refer to the currently executing object.

> **key concept**
> The `this` reference always refers to the currently executing object.

For example, in a class called `ChessPiece` there could be a method called `capture`, which could contain the following line:

```
if (piece.equals(this))
    result = false;
```

The `this` reference is being used to pass the current object to the method of another object. The `this` reference refers to the object through which the method was called. So when the next line is used to call the method, the `this` reference refers to `bishop1`:

```
bishop1.capture();
```

However, when another object is used to call the method, the `this` reference refers to the new object. So now the `this` reference in the `capture` method refers to `bishop2`:

```
bishop2.capture();
```

aliases

Because an object reference variable stores an address, you have to be careful when managing objects. In particular, you must understand the semantics of an assignment statement for objects. First, let's review assignments for primitive types. Consider the following declarations of primitive data:

```
int num1 = 5;
int num2 = 12;
```

In the following assignment statement, a copy of the value that is stored in num1 is stored in num2:

```
num2 = num1;
```

The original value of 12 in num2 is overwritten by the value 5. The variables num1 and num2 still refer to different locations in memory, and both of those locations now contain the value 5. See Figure 5.1.

Now consider the following object declarations:

```
ChessPiece bishop1 = new ChessPiece();
ChessPiece bishop2 = new ChessPiece();
```

At first, bishop1 and bishop2 refer to two different ChessPiece objects. The following assignment statement copies the value in bishop1 into bishop2.

```
bishop2 = bishop1;
```

The key issue is that when an assignment like this is made, the address stored in bishop1 is copied into bishop2. Originally, the two referred to different objects. After the assignment, both bishop1 and bishop2 contain the same address and therefore refer to the same object. See Figure 5.2.

The bishop1 and bishop2 references are now *aliases* of each other because they are two names for the same object. All references to the object

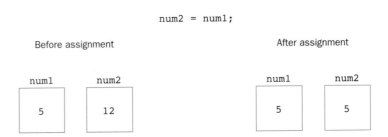

figure 5.1   Primitive data assignment

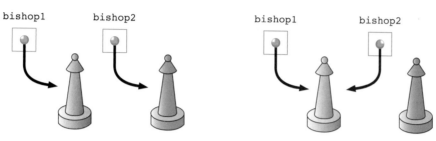

```
bishop2 = bishop1;
```

Before assignment

After assignment

bishop1   bishop2   bishop1   bishop2

figure 5.2   Reference assignment

that was originally referenced by bishop2 are now gone; that object cannot be used again in the program.

> **key concept**
>
> Several references can refer to the same object. These references are aliases of each other.

When we use one reference to change the state of the object, the state is also changed for the other object—because there is really only one object. If you change the state of bishop1, for instance, you change the state of bishop2 because they both refer to the same object. Aliases can cause problems unless you are careful.

References affect how we decide whether two objects are equal. The == operator that we use for primitive data can be used with object references, but it returns true only if the two references are aliases of each other. It does not "look inside" the objects to see whether they contain the same data. Thus the following expression is true only if bishop1 and bishop2 currently refer to the same object:

> **key concept**
>
> The == operator compares object references for equality, returning true if the references are aliases of each other.

```
bishop1 == bishop2
```

A method called equals is defined for all objects, but unless we replace it with a specific definition when we write a class, it has the same semantics as the == operator. That is, the equals method returns a boolean value that will be true if the two objects are aliases of each other. The equals method is called through one object, and takes the other one as a parameter. Therefore, the following expression returns true if both references refer to the same object:

```
bishop1.equals(bishop2)
```

> **key concept**
>
> The equals method can be defined to determine equality between objects in any way we like.

However, we could define the equals method in the ChessPiece class to mean equality for ChessPiece objects any way we would like. That is, we could define the `equals` method to return true under whatever conditions we want, to mean that one `ChessPiece` is equal to another.

As we discussed in Chapter 3, the `equals` method has been given a definition in the `String` class. When comparing two `String` objects, the `equals` method returns true only if both strings contain the same characters. A common mistake is to use the `==` operator to compare strings. The `==` operator compares the *references* for equality, when most of the time we want to compare the *characters inside the string objects* for equality. For example, consider the following:

```
String name1 = "John";
String name2 = "John";
```

The expression `name1 == name2` is false because `name1` and `name2` refer to different `String` objects. If we want to compare the characters inside the strings we should use the expression `name1.equals(name2)`, which returns true. We discuss the `equals` method in more detail in Chapter 7.

passing objects as parameters

Sometimes we want to pass an object to a method. Java passes all parameters to a method *by value*. That means the current value of the actual parameter (in the invocation) is copied into the formal parameter in the method header. Parameter passing is like an assignment statement, assigning to the formal parameter a copy of the value stored in the actual parameter.

> **key concept**
>
> When an object is passed to a method, the actual and formal parameters become aliases of each other.

We need to think about this when we make changes to a formal parameter inside a method. The formal parameter is a separate copy of the value that is passed in, so any changes made to it have no effect on the actual parameter. After control returns to the calling method, the actual parameter will have the same value as it did before the method was called.

However, when an object is passed to a method, we are actually passing a reference to that object. The value that gets copied is the address of the object. Therefore, the formal parameter and the actual parameter become aliases of each other. If we change the state of the object through the formal parameter reference inside the method, we are changing the object referenced by the actual parameter because they refer to the same object. On the other hand, if we change the formal parameter reference itself (to make it point to a new object, for instance), we have not changed the fact that the actual parameter still refers to the original object.

The program in Listing 5.1 illustrates parameter passing. Carefully trace the processing of this program and look at the values that are output. The

listing
    5.1

```
//********************************************************************
//  ParameterPassing.java        Author: Lewis/Loftus/Cocking
//
//  Demonstrates the effects of passing various types of parameters.
//********************************************************************

public class ParameterPassing
{
   //-----------------------------------------------------------------
   //  Sets up three variables (one primitive and two objects) to
   //  serve as actual parameters to the changeValues method. Prints
   //  their values before and after calling the method.
   //-----------------------------------------------------------------
   public static void main (String[] args)
   {
      ParameterTester tester = new ParameterTester();

      int a1 = 111;
      Num a2 = new Num (222);
      Num a3 = new Num (333);

      System.out.println ("Before calling changeValues:");
      System.out.println ("a1\ta2\ta3");
      System.out.println (a1 + "\t" + a2 + "\t" + a3 + "\n");

      tester.changeValues (a1, a2, a3);

      System.out.println ("After calling changeValues:");
      System.out.println ("a1\ta2\ta3");
      System.out.println (a1 + "\t" + a2 + "\t" + a3 + "\n");
   }
}
```

output

```
Before calling changeValues:
a1      a2      a3
111     222     333

Before changing the values:
f1      f2      f3
111     222     333

After changing the values:
f1      f2      f3
999     888     777

After calling changeValues:
a1      a2      a3
111     888     333
```

main method in the `ParameterPassing` class calls the `changeValues` method in a `ParameterTester` object. Two of the parameters to `changeValues` are `Num` objects, each of which simply stores an integer value. The other parameter is a primitive integer value.

Listing 5.2 shows the `ParameterTester` class, and Listing 5.3 shows the `Num` class. Inside the `changeValues` method, a change is made to each of the three formal parameters: the integer parameter is set to a different value, the value stored in the first `Num` parameter is changed using its `setValue` method, and a new `Num` object is created and assigned to the second `Num` parameter. These changes show up in the output printed at the end of the `changeValues` method.

But look at the final values that are printed after returning from the method. The primitive integer was not changed from its original value

listing
    5.2

```
//********************************************************************
//  ParameterTester.java        Author: Lewis/Loftus/Cocking
//
//  Demonstrates the effects of passing various types of parameters.
//********************************************************************

public class ParameterTester
{
    //-----------------------------------------------------------------
    //  Modifies the parameters, printing their values before and
    //  after making the changes.
    //-----------------------------------------------------------------
    public void changeValues (int f1, Num f2, Num f3)
    {
        System.out.println ("Before changing the values:");
        System.out.println ("f1\tf2\tf3");
        System.out.println (f1 + "\t" + f2 + "\t" + f3 + "\n");

        f1 = 999;
        f2.setValue (888);
        f3 = new Num (777);

        System.out.println ("After changing the values:");
        System.out.println ("f1\tf2\tf3");
        System.out.println (f1 + "\t" + f2 + "\t" + f3 + "\n");
    }
}
```

listing
   5.3

```
//*****************************************************************
//   Num.java         Author: Lewis/Loftus/Cocking
//
//   Represents a single integer as an object.
//*****************************************************************

public class Num
{
   private int value;

   //----------------------------------------------------------------
   //  Sets up the new Num object, storing an initial value.
   //----------------------------------------------------------------
   public Num (int update)
   {
      value = update;
   }

   //----------------------------------------------------------------
   //  Sets the stored value to the newly specified value.
   //----------------------------------------------------------------
   public void setValue (int update)
   {
      value = update;
   }

   //----------------------------------------------------------------
   //  Returns the stored integer value as a string.
   //----------------------------------------------------------------
   public String toString ()
   {
      return value + "";
   }
}
```

because the change was made to a copy inside the method. Likewise, the last parameter still refers to its original object with its original value. This is because the new Num object created in the method was referred to only by the formal parameter. When the method returned, that formal parameter was destroyed and the Num object it referred to could no longer be accessed. The only change that is "permanent" is the change made to the state of the second parameter. Figure 5.3 shows the step-by-step processing of this program.

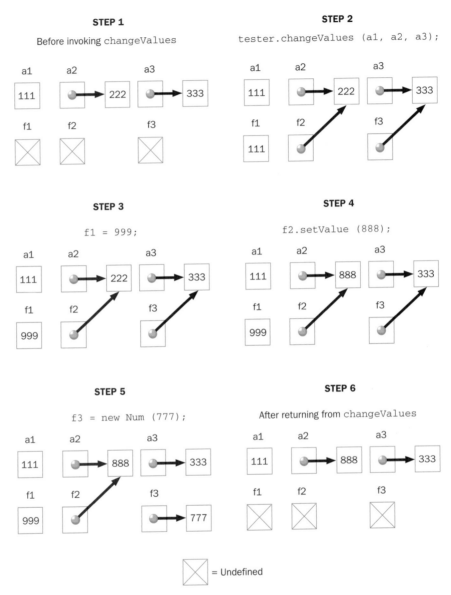

figure 5.3   Tracing the parameters in the ParameterPassing program

5.1   the static modifier

We've seen how visibility modifiers help us with encapsulation. Java has several other modifiers that determine variable and method characteristics. For example, the static modifier associates a variable or method with its class rather than with an object.

static variables

So far, we've seen two categories of variables: local variables that are declared inside a method and instance variables that are declared in a class but not inside a method. The term *instance variable* is used because an instance variable is accessed through a particular instance (an object) of a class. In general, each object has memory space for each variable so that each object can have a value for that variable.

Another kind of variable, called a *static variable* or *class variable,* is shared among all the objects in a class. Because there is only one copy of a static variable changing its value in one object changes it for all of the others. The reserved word `static` is used as a modifier to declare a static variable as follows:

> A `static` variable is shared among all instances of a class.
>
> key concept

```
private static int count = 0;
```

Memory space for a static variable is established the first time the class that contains it is referenced. A local variable declared within a method cannot be static.

Constants, which are declared using the `final` modifier, are also often declared using the `static` modifier as well. Because the value of constants cannot be changed, there might as well be only one copy of the value across all objects of the class. For example, in the `Coin` class in Listing 4.2, the `HEADS` and `TAILS` constants could have been declared static:

```
public static final int HEADS = 0;
public static final int TAILS = 1;
```

Note that static final variables (i.e., constants) are part of the AP subset, but other static variables are not.

static methods

In Chapter 2 we introduced the idea of a *static method* (also called a *class method*). We noted, for instance, that all of the methods of the `Math` class are static methods, meaning that they can be called through the class name. We don't have to instantiate an object to call a static method. For example, in the following line of code the `sqrt` method is called through the `Math` class name instead of through an object:

```
System.out.println ("Square root of 27: " + Math.sqrt(27));
```

A method is made static by using the static modifier in the method declaration. As we've seen many times, the main method of a Java program must be declared with the static modifier; this is so main can be executed by the interpreter without instantiating an object from the class that contains main. Constructors cannot be static because they are called for each instance of a class that is created.

Because static methods are not called through objects, they cannot reference instance variables, which exist only in an instance—or object—of a class. The compiler will issue an error if a static method attempts to use a nonstatic variable. A static method can, however, reference static variables because static variables are not parts of objects. This means the main method can access only static or local variables.

The methods in the Math class do basic calculations on values passed as parameters. There is no object state to maintain in these situations, so there is no good reason to create an object.

The program in Listing 5.4 instantiates several objects of the Slogan class, printing each one out in turn. At the end of the program it invokes a method called getCount through the class name. The getCount method returns the number of Slogan objects that were instantiated in the program.

Listing 5.5 shows the Slogan class. The constructor of Slogan keeps track of the number of Slogan objects that were created and printed, in a static variable called count. The variable count was initialized to zero when it was declared, and each time a Slogan object is created the constructor adds one to (increments) the count.

The getCount method of Slogan is also declared as static, so it can be called through the class name in the main method. Note that the only data the getCount method uses is the integer variable count, which is static. The getCount method could have been declared without the static modifier, but then its invocation in the main method would have to have been done through an object instead of through the Slogan class itself.

listing
5.4

```
//********************************************************************
//  CountInstances.java        Author: Lewis/Loftus/Cocking
//
//  Demonstrates the use of the static modifier.
//********************************************************************

public class CountInstances
{
   //-----------------------------------------------------------------
   //  Creates several Slogan objects and prints the number of
   //  objects that were created.
   //-----------------------------------------------------------------
   public static void main (String[] args)
   {
      Slogan obj;

      obj = new Slogan ("Remember the Alamo.");
      System.out.println (obj);

      obj = new Slogan ("Don't Worry. Be Happy.");
      System.out.println (obj);

      obj = new Slogan ("Live Free or Die.");
      System.out.println (obj);

      obj = new Slogan ("Talk is Cheap.");
      System.out.println (obj);

      obj = new Slogan ("Write Once, Run Anywhere.");
      System.out.println (obj);

      System.out.println();
      System.out.println ("Slogans created: " + Slogan.getCount());
   }
}
```

output

```
Remember the Alamo.
Don't Worry. Be Happy.
Live Free or Die.
Talk is Cheap.
Write Once, Run Anywhere.

Slogans created: 5
```

```
listing
    5.5
```

```java
//********************************************************************
//  Slogan.java         Author: Lewis/Loftus/Cocking
//
//  Represents a single slogan string.
//********************************************************************

public class Slogan
{
   private String phrase;
   private static int count = 0;

   //-----------------------------------------------------------------
   //  Sets up the slogan and counts the number of instances created.
   //-----------------------------------------------------------------
   public Slogan (String str)
   {
      phrase = str;
      count++;
   }

   //-----------------------------------------------------------------
   //  Returns this slogan as a string.
   //-----------------------------------------------------------------
   public String toString()
   {
      return phrase;
   }

   //-----------------------------------------------------------------
   //  Returns the number of instances of this class that have been
   //  created.
   //-----------------------------------------------------------------
   public static int getCount ()
   {
      return count;
   }
}
```

5.2 exceptions

Problems in a Java program may cause exceptions or errors. Recall from Chapter 2 that an *exception* is an object that defines a problem that can usually be fixed. An *error* is like an exception except that the problem usually cannot be fixed.

> **key concept**
>
> Errors and exceptions represent unusual or invalid processing.

Java has a set of exceptions and errors. Four common exceptions are explored later in this section.

We can handle an exception in one of three ways. A program can:

- not handle the exception at all,
- handle the exception where it occurs, or
- handle the exception later in the program.

Handling exceptions is not required for the AP exam and is beyond the scope of this book. In the rest of this section we discuss the exception-related topics that are required for the exam: understanding common exceptions and throwing exceptions.

exception messages

If a program does not handle the exception at all, it will crash and produce a message that describes the exception and where it happened. This information can help you track down the cause of a problem.

Let's look at an exception. The program shown in Listing 5.6 throws an `ArithmeticException` when the program tries to divide by zero.

The program crashes and prints out information about the exception. Note that the last `println` statement in the program never executes because the exception occurs first.

The first line of the output tells us which exception was thrown and gives us some information about why it was thrown. The rest of the output is the *call stack trace*. This tells us where the exception occurred. In this case, there is only one line in the call stack trace, but there could be several, depending on where the exception originated. The first trace line gives us the method, file, and line number where the exception happened. The other trace lines tell us the methods that were called just before the method that produced the exception. In this program, there is only one method, and it produced the exception, so there is only one line in the trace.

> **key concept**
>
> The messages printed by a thrown exception indicate the nature of the problem and provide a method call stack trace.

listing
  5.6

```
//********************************************************************
//  Zero.java          Author: Lewis/Loftus/Cocking
//
//  Demonstrates an uncaught exception.
//********************************************************************

public class Zero
{
   //-----------------------------------------------------------------
   //  Deliberately divides by zero to produce an exception.
   //-----------------------------------------------------------------
   public static void main (String[] args)
   {
      int numerator = 10;
      int denominator = 0;

      System.out.println (numerator / denominator);

      System.out.println ("This text will not be printed.");
   }
}
```

output

```
Exception in thread "main" java.lang.ArithmeticException: / by zero
        at Zero.main(Zero.java:17)
```

Other common exceptions include NullPointerException, ArrayIndexOutOfBoundsException, and ClassCastException. You'll get a NullPointerException if you use a null reference where you need an object reference. For example, suppose name has been declared to be a reference to a String and it has the value null, indicating that it is not referring to any String at this time. An attempt to call a method on name, such as name.length(), will cause a NullPointerException.

We will further discuss ArrayIndexOutOfBoundsException and ClassCastException in Chapter 6.

throwing exceptions

We have seen that the Java runtime environment throws exceptions in exceptional circumstances. As programmers, we too can throw exceptions. An exception is thrown with a `throw` statement: the reserved word `throw` followed by an exception object.

For example, the following statement throws a `NoSuchElementException`:

```
throw new NoSuchElementException();
```

The exception object is created with the `new` operator right in the `throw` statement. Exception classes in Java have a default constructor that takes no arguments and a constructor that takes a single `String` argument. If provided, this string appears in the exception message when the exception occurs. In later chapters we look at exceptions such as `IllegalStateException` and `NoSuchElementException` thrown in the implementation of abstract data types.

5.3 interfaces

We've used the term *interface* to mean the public methods through which the client code can interact with an object. That definition is pretty general. Now we are going to learn the formal meaning of *interface* in a particular language construct in Java. Note that students studying for the A exam are expected to have a reading knowledge of interfaces while students studying for the AB exam are expected to be able to define their own interfaces.

A Java *interface* is a collection of constants and abstract methods. An *abstract method* is a method that does not have an implementation. That is, there is no body of code defined for an abstract method. The header of the method, including its parameter list, is simply followed by a semicolon. An interface cannot be instantiated.

> **key concept**
> An interface is a collection of abstract methods. It cannot be instantiated.

Listing 5.7 shows an interface called `Complexity`. It contains two abstract methods: `setComplexity` and `getComplexity`.

An abstract method can be preceded by the reserved word `abstract`, though in interfaces it usually is not. All methods in interfaces have public visibility by default.

```
listing
   5.7
```

```
//********************************************************************
//   Complexity.java          Author: Lewis/Loftus/Cocking
//
//   Represents the interface for an object that can be assigned an
//   explicit complexity.
//********************************************************************

public interface Complexity
{
    public void setComplexity (int complexity);
    public int getComplexity();
}
```

A class *implements* an interface by providing method implementations for each of the abstract methods defined in the interface. A class
that implements an interface uses the reserved word `implements`
followed by the interface name (e.g., `Complexity`) in the class header.
When a class implements an interface, it must give a definition for all
methods in the interface. The compiler will produce errors if any of the methods in the interface are not given a definition in the class.

The `Question` class, shown in Listing 5.8, implements the `Complexity`
interface from Listing 5.7. Both the `setComplexity` and `getComplexity`
methods are implemented. They must be declared with the same signatures
as the abstract methods (`setComplexity` and `getComplexity`) in the
interface. In the `Question` class, the methods are defined simply to set or
return a numeric value representing the complexity level of the question that
the object represents.

Note that the `Question` class also implements methods that are not part
of the `Complexity` interface, methods called `getQuestion`, `getAnswer`,
`answerCorrect`, and `toString`, which have nothing to do with the interface. The interface guarantees that the class implements certain methods, but
it can also have others. In fact, a class that implements an interface usually
has other methods, too.

Listing 5.9 shows a program called `MiniQuiz`, which uses some
`Question` objects.

```
listing
   5.8
```

```java
//********************************************************************
//  Question.java        Author: Lewis/Loftus/Cocking
//
//  Represents a question (and its answer).
//********************************************************************

public class Question implements Complexity
{
   private String question, answer;
   private int complexityLevel;

   //----------------------------------------------------------------
   //  Sets up the question with a default complexity.
   //----------------------------------------------------------------
   public Question (String query, String result)
   {
      question = query;
      answer = result;
      complexityLevel = 1;
   }

   //----------------------------------------------------------------
   //  Sets the complexity level for this question.
   //----------------------------------------------------------------
   public void setComplexity (int level)
   {
      complexityLevel = level;
   }

   //----------------------------------------------------------------
   //  Returns the complexity level for this question.
   //----------------------------------------------------------------
   public int getComplexity()
   {
      return complexityLevel;
   }

   //----------------------------------------------------------------
   //  Returns the question.
   //----------------------------------------------------------------
   public String getQuestion()
   {
      return question;
   }
```

listing
  5.8   continued

```
   //---------------------------------------------------------------
   //  Returns the answer to this question.
   //---------------------------------------------------------------
   public String getAnswer()
   {
      return answer;
   }

   //---------------------------------------------------------------
   //  Returns true if the candidate answer matches the answer.
   //---------------------------------------------------------------
   public boolean answerCorrect (String candidateAnswer)
   {
      return answer.equals(candidateAnswer);
   }

   //---------------------------------------------------------------
   //  Returns this question (and its answer) as a string.
   //---------------------------------------------------------------
   public String toString()
   {
      return question + "\n" + answer;
   }
}
```

listing
  5.9

```
//********************************************************************
//  MiniQuiz.java      Author: Lewis/Loftus/Cocking
//
//  Demonstrates the use of a class that implements an interface.
//********************************************************************

import cs1.Keyboard;

public class MiniQuiz
{
   //---------------------------------------------------------------
   //  Presents a short quiz.
   //---------------------------------------------------------------
   public static void main (String[] args)
   {
```

listing
5.9   continued

```
      Question q1, q2;
      String possible;

      q1 = new Question ("What is the capital of Jamaica?",
                         "Kingston");
      q1.setComplexity (4);

      q2 = new Question ("Which is worse, ignorance or apathy?",
                         "I don't know and I don't care");
      q2.setComplexity (10);

      System.out.print (q1.getQuestion());
      System.out.println (" (Level: " + q1.getComplexity() + ")");
      possible = Keyboard.readString();
      if (q1.answerCorrect(possible))
         System.out.println ("Correct");
      else
         System.out.println ("No, the answer is " + q1.getAnswer());

      System.out.println();
      System.out.print (q2.getQuestion());
      System.out.println (" (Level: " + q2.getComplexity() + ")");
      possible = Keyboard.readString();
      if (q2.answerCorrect(possible))
         System.out.println ("Correct");
      else
         System.out.println ("No, the answer is " + q2.getAnswer());
   }
}
```

output

```
What is the capital of Jamaica? (Level: 4)
Kingston
Correct

Which is worse, ignorance or apathy? (Level: 10)
apathy
No, the answer is I don't know and I don't care
```

Several classes can implement the same interface, giving different definitions for the methods. For example, we could implement a class called `Task` that also implements the `Complexity` interface. In it we could choose to manage the complexity of a task in a different way (though it would still have to implement all the methods of the interface).

A class can implement more than one interface. In these cases, the class must implement all methods in all interfaces listed. To show that a class implements multiple interfaces, we list them in the `implements` clause, separated by commas. For example:

```
class ManyThings implements interface1, interface2, interface3
{
    // all methods of all interfaces
}
```

An interface can also contain constants, defined using the `final` modifier. When a class implements an interface, it can use all of the constants defined in it. This lets several classes share a set of constants.

The interface construct formally tells us how we can interact with a class. It is also the basis for a powerful programming technique called polymorphism, which we discuss in Chapter 7.

the Comparable interface

The Java standard class library contains a number of important interfaces. The `Comparable`, `List`, `Iterator`, and `ListIterator` interfaces are a part of the AP Java subset and are described here. The `List`, `Iterator`, and `ListIterator` interfaces are required for the AB exam only.

The `Comparable` interface is defined in the `java.lang` package. It contains only one method, `compareTo`, which takes an object as a parameter and returns an integer. This method is listed in Figure 5.4.

This interface gives us a way to compare one object to another. One object calls the method and passes another object as a parameter, like this:

```
if (obj1.compareTo(obj2) < 0)
    System.out.println ("obj1 is less than obj2");
```

AP➔

```
int compareTo (Object obj)
    Compares the executing object to the parameter to determine their relative
    ordering. Returns an integer that is less than, equal to, or greater than zero if
    the executing object is less than, equal to, or greater than the parameter,
    respectively.
```

figure 5.4   Some methods of the Comparable interface

The integer that is returned from the compareTo method should be negative if obj1 is less than obj2, 0 if they are equal, and positive if obj1 is greater than obj2. It is up to the program designer to decide what it means for one object of that class to be less than, equal to, or greater than another.

In Chapter 3, we mentioned that the String class contains a compareTo method. The String class has this method because it implements the Comparable interface. The method bases the comparison on the lexicographic ordering defined by the Unicode character set (see Appendix C).

the List interface

The List interface is implemented by classes that represent an ordered collection of elements such as numbers or strings. Four of the List interface methods—iterator, listIterator, size, and add—are shown in Figure 5.5.

The iterator and listIterator methods return an object that can be used to cycle through every element in the list. This is called *iteration*. The size method simply returns the number of elements in the list. The add method adds the element given as a parameter to the end of the list. These

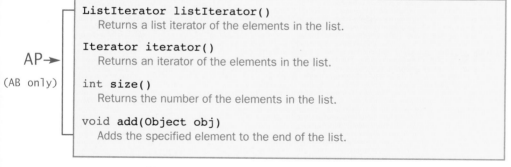

AP➔

(AB only)

```
ListIterator listIterator()
    Returns a list iterator of the elements in the list.

Iterator iterator()
    Returns an iterator of the elements in the list.

int size()
    Returns the number of the elements in the list.

void add(Object obj)
    Adds the specified element to the end of the list.
```

figure 5.5   Some methods of the List interface

methods define the interface for the list. The underlying implementation is defined by classes that implement the `List` interface. Different classes have different implementations.

the `Iterator` and `ListIterator` interfaces

The `Iterator` interface is used by classes that represent a collection of objects such as a list, giving us a way to move through the collection one object at a time. The `Iterator` interface is not used to represent the list itself, it merely represents a way to move through the elemetns of the list.

The two basic methods in the `Iterator` interface are `hasNext`, which returns a boolean result, and `next`, which returns an object. Neither of these methods takes any parameters. The `hasNext` method returns true if there are items left to process, and `next` returns the next object. It is up to the designer to decide in what order objects will be delivered by the `next` method. The methods of the `Iterator` interface are listed in Figure 5.6.

The `next` method does not remove the object from the collection; it just returns a reference to it. The `Iterator` interface also has a method called `remove`, which takes no parameters and has a `void` return type. A call to the `remove` method removes the object that was most recently returned by the `next` method from the collection.

The `ListIterator` interface contains the methods of the `Iterator` interface plus a few more, including `add` and `set`. Figure 5.7 lists some of the methods of the `ListIterator` interface. The `add` and `set` methods allow new elements to be added to the list. We will learn more about lists and iterators in Chapter 6.

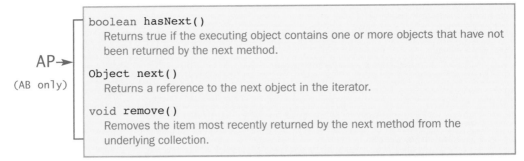

AP→
(AB only)

```
boolean hasNext()
    Returns true if the executing object contains one or more objects that have not
    been returned by the next method.

Object next()
    Returns a reference to the next object in the iterator.

void remove()
    Removes the item most recently returned by the next method from the
    underlying collection.
```

figure 5.6   Some methods of the `Iterator` interface

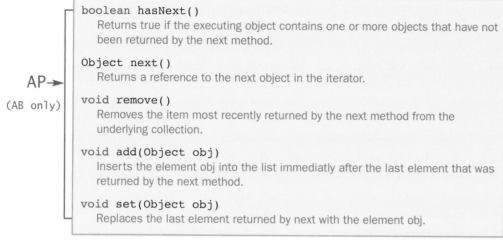

AP→

(AB only)

boolean hasNext()
    Returns true if the executing object contains one or more objects that have not been returned by the next method.

Object next()
    Returns a reference to the next object in the iterator.

void remove()
    Removes the item most recently returned by the next method from the underlying collection.

void add(Object obj)
    Inserts the element obj into the list immediatly after the last element that was returned by the next method.

void set(Object obj)
    Replaces the last element returned by next with the element obj.

figure 5.7 Some methods of the ListIterator interface

5.4 designing classes

Students planning to take the AB exam need to have experience designing classes. In this section we offer you some advice on design and go through an example.

When we design a class to represent an object, we have two pieces to think about: the state of the object (which will be the instance data) and what the object does or its behaviors (which will be the methods). When we think about the data of an object, we need to think about what is required to represent the state of the object. When we think about what an object does, we should think about how others might want to use the object. Sometimes you will know exactly how the class will be used. Other times, you won't know all the ways in which the class may be used. In any case, it is always a good idea to try to imagine what the users of the class will need, now or in the future. A class that is designed well can be reused. On the other hand, you don't want to have a class that does everything.

As an example, let's design a class that represents an alarm clock. We don't know exactly how the alarm clock will be used in a program; we must design an alarm clock that could be used in lots of programs that need to represent alarm clocks. We won't get into implementation details but we will come up with a design that includes the alarm clock's state and its public interface.

First we think about the state that is needed to represent the alarm clock. A simple alarm clock has a current time, plus a stored alarm time. A more sophisticated alarm clock could store several alarm times with a radio station setting for each alarm time. There may also be a value that indicates what type of noise to play when the alarm goes off (a beeping noise or the current radio station). Our alarm clock will have just one alarm, and the user can choose a beeping noise or a radio station. Figure 5.8 shows the data for our `AlarmClock` class. We may need to design other classes to represent some of the alarm clock data, such as a `Time` class to represent a time.

Next we need to think about what an `AlarmClock` object should do. The user can view and set the current time, view and set the alarm time, view and set the radio station, and change between waking up to a radio station and waking up to a beeping noise. So we will give our `AlarmClock` class the methods listed in Figure 5.9. These methods make up the public interface of the `AlarmClock` class. We will not worry about how the alarm clock itself works, only about what it does for the user.

`Time currentTime`
    The current time, gets updated as time passes.

`Time alarmTime`
    The time the alarm is set for.

`RadioStation radioStation`
    The radio station setting.

`boolean radioWakeUp`
    Whether to play the radio when the alarm goes off. (The default is a beeping noise.)

---

figure 5.8   Data for the `AlarmClock` class

```
void setCurrentTime(Time newTime);

Time getCurrentTime();

void setAlarmTime(Time newTime);

Time getAlarmTime();

void setRadioStation(RadioStation newStation);

RadioStation getRadioStation();

void wakeUpToRadio();

void wakeUpToBeep();
```

figure 5.9   Methods for the `AlarmClock` class

5.5 bumper cars case study: drivers

The bumper car company hasn't told us how the drivers decide where to drive their car next. So for now, we can randomly choose where each driver will go next. This is close enough to how bumper car drivers behave. However, we need to allow for different driving patterns in our design, in case the bumper car company gives us new information.

We will use an interface to provide the flexibility that we need. A `Driver` interface will contain the methods that the other classes in the simulation will need to communicate with a driver. Then we can create a driver simply by implementing the `Driver` interface. In fact, we can create as many different types of drivers as we like, as long as they use the interface. The `Driver` interface will have a single method:

```
public void drive ();
```

The `drive` method is called when it is the driver's turn to move. Each driver can implement the drive method differently, using their own algorithm to determine their next move. Listing 5.10 shows the `Driver` interface. For now, we will create only one implementation of this interface: `RandomDriver`. The random driver will randomly select his or her next move.

On each move, a driver can either drive the car forward or turn the car to face a different direction (remaining in the same spot). The random driver will choose randomly from among these options. Listing 5.11 shows our initial implementation of the `RandomDriver` class. The constructor takes a `Car` object as a parameter: A driver must know which car he or she is driving. The `drive` method uses a random number generator to decide between moving forward and turning left, right, or all the way around. The print message at the beginning of the `drive` method is for debugging purposes only.

listing
5.10

```
//********************************************************************
// Driver.java         Author: Lewis/Loftus/Cocking
//
// An interface that all drivers of bumper cars must implement.
//********************************************************************

public interface Driver
{

    //--------------------------------------------------------------
    //   Drive the car one unit. Different drivers will have different
    //   algorithms for determining where to drive the car next.
    //--------------------------------------------------------------
    public void drive();

}
```

listing
5.11

```java
//********************************************************************
// RandomDriver.java          Author: Lewis/Loftus/Cocking
//
// Represents a driver whose moves are chosen randomly.
//********************************************************************

import java.util.Random;

public class RandomDriver implements Driver
{
    // Share a random number generator among all the RandomDrivers.
    private static Random randGen = new Random();

    private Car car;

    public RandomDriver(Car aCar)
    {
        car = aCar;
    }

    //-----------------------------------------------------------------
    // Drive the car one unit. The random driver chooses a move
    // randomly.
    //-----------------------------------------------------------------
    public void drive()
    {
        System.out.println("RandomDriver:  drive");

        // Move forward 70% of the time. Turn to face another
        // direction 30% of the time. (Equal probability for
        // each of the three remaining directions.)
        final int moveForwardProb = 70;
        int probability = randGen.nextInt(100);

        if (probability < moveForwardProb)
            car.moveForward();
        else {
            int turnWhichWay = randGen.nextInt(3);
            if (turnWhichWay == 0)
                car.turnLeft();
            else if (turnWhichWay == 1)
                car.turnRight();
            else /* turnWhichWay == 2 */
                car.turnAround();
        }
    }

}
```

exercises

1. Write a class called `ForwardDriver` that implements the `Driver` interface and always moves forward.

2. What other types of drivers might the bumper car company want us to create in the future? How would we implement them?

3. The `RandomDriver` doesn't take into account its environment when selecting a move because the move is chosen randomly. What information about the environment might other types of drivers need to know in order to decide where to move?

5.6   nested classes

A class can be declared inside another class. Just as a loop written inside another loop is called a nested loop, a class written inside another class is called a *nested class*. The nested class is a member of the class it is nested in, called the *enclosing class*, just like a variable or method.

Just like any other class, a nested class produces a separate bytecode file. The name of the bytecode file is the name of the enclosing class followed by the $ character, followed by the name of the nested class. The bytecode file has an extension of `.class`. A class called `Nested` that is declared inside a class called `Enclosing` will result in a compiled bytecode file called `Enclosing$Nested.class`.

Because it is a member of the enclosing class, a nested class can use the enclosing class's instance variables and methods, even if they are private. But the enclosing class can use data in the nested class only if the data is declared public. In general, we've always said that public data is a bad idea because it violates encapsulation. However, nested classes are the exception to that rule. It is reasonable to declare the data of a private nested class with public visibility because only the enclosing class can get to that data (despite its public declaration).

A class should be nested inside another class only if it makes sense for the enclosing class. In such cases, the nesting reinforces the relationship yet simplifies the implementation by allowing direct access to the data.

The `static` modifier can be applied to a class, but only if the class is nested inside another. Like static methods, a static nested class cannot reference instance variables or methods defined in its enclosing class.

inner classes

A nonstatic nested class is called an *inner class*. Because it is not static, an inner class is associated with each instance of the enclosing class. So no member inside an inner class can be declared `static`. An instance of an inner class can exist only within an instance of the enclosing class.

The details of nested and inner classes are beyond the scope of this text, but the basic idea will be useful in certain graphics track examples.

5.7 dialog boxes

A *dialog box* is a window that pops up on top of any currently active window so that the user can interact with it. A dialog box can tell the user some information, ask the user to do something, such as click a button, or let the user to enter some information. Usually a dialog box has one purpose, and the user's interaction with it is short.

The Swing package (`javax.swing`) of the Java class library contains a class called `JOptionPane` that makes creating and using basic dialog boxes simple. Figure 5.10 lists some of the methods of `JOptionPane`.

There are three kinds of `JOptionPane` dialog boxes. A *message dialog* simply displays an output string. An *input dialog* asks the user for information and has a text field where the user can type in data. A *confirm dialog* asks the user a simple yes-or-no question.

> **key concept**
>
> `JOptionPane` is a Swing class that facilitates the creation of dialog boxes.

```
static String showInputDialog (Object msg)
   Displays a dialog box containg the specified message and an input text
field. The contents of the text field are returned.

static int showConfirmDialog (Component parent, Object msg)
   Displays a dialog box containing the specified message and Yes/No
button options. If the parent component is null, the box is centered on the screen.

static int showMessageDialog (Component parent, Object msg)
   Displays a dialog box containing the specified message. If the parent
component is null, the box is centered on the screen.
```

figure 5.10   Some methods of the `JOptionPane` class

Let's look at a program that uses each of these types of dialog boxes. Listing 5.12 shows a program that first presents an input dialog box and asks the user to enter a number. After the user presses the OK button on the input dialog, a second dialog box (this time a message dialog) appears telling the user whether the number entered was even or odd. After the user clicks the OK button, a third dialog box appears to ask if the user would like to test another number. If the user presses the Yes button, the series of dialog boxes repeats. Otherwise the program ends.

listing
   5.12

```java
//********************************************************************
//  EvenOdd.java        Author: Lewis/Loftus/Cocking
//
//  Demonstrates the use of the JOptionPane class.
//********************************************************************

import javax.swing.JOptionPane;

public class EvenOdd
{
   //-----------------------------------------------------------------
   //  Determines if the value input by the user is even or odd.
   //  Uses multiple dialog boxes for user interaction.
   //-----------------------------------------------------------------
   public static void main (String[] args)
   {
      String numStr, result;
      int num, again;

      do
      {
         numStr = JOptionPane.showInputDialog ("Enter an integer: ");

         num = Integer.parseInt(numStr);

         result = "That number is " + ((num%2 == 0) ? "even" : "odd");

         JOptionPane.showMessageDialog (null, result);
```

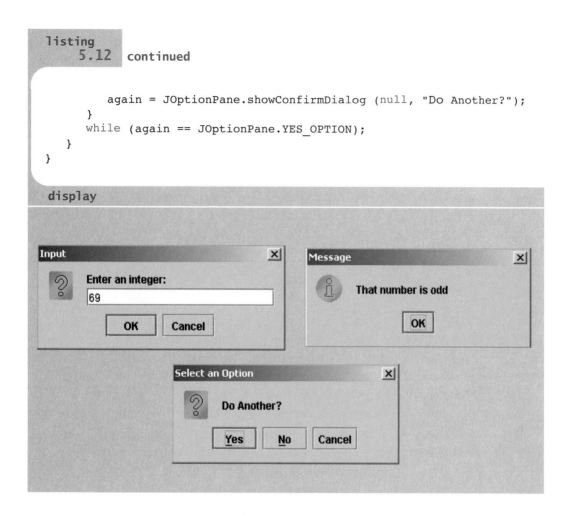

```
listing
    5.12  continued

        again = JOptionPane.showConfirmDialog (null, "Do Another?");
    }
    while (again == JOptionPane.YES_OPTION);
  }
}
```

display

The first parameter to the `showMessageDialog` and the `showConfirmDialog` methods spells out the parent window for the dialog. The dialog will appear in the center of the parent window. Using a `null` reference as this parameter makes the dialog box appear centered on the screen.

5.8   graphical user interfaces

Dialog boxes are graphical user interfaces (GUIs) that let a user interact with graphical elements such as buttons and text boxes. In general, their interaction is limited because the dialog boxes are predefined. But a GUI is far more than a series of pop-up dialog boxes. A GUI is a well-designed layout of interactive graphical components. There are a lot of ways a user can interact with a GUI.

essential GUI elements

A GUI in Java has at least three kinds of objects:

> components

> events

> listeners

A GUI *component* is an object that defines a screen element to display information or let the user interact with a program. Examples of GUI components include push buttons, text fields, labels, scroll bars, and menus. A *container* is a special type of component that holds and organizes other components. A dialog box and an applet are examples of container components.

An *event* is an object that represents an action, such as the user pressing a mouse button or typing a key on the keyboard. Most GUI components gen-

> **key concept**
>
> A GUI is made up of graphical components, events that represent user actions, and listeners that respond to those events.

erate events to indicate a user action that has to do with that component. For example, a component representing a button will generate an event to indicate that it has been pushed. A program that responds to events from the user is called *event-driven*.

A *listener* is an object that "waits" for an event and then responds in some way. The programmer must carefully establish the relationships among the listener, the event it listens for, and the component that will generate the event.

The rest of this chapter introduces these elements of a GUI. The graphics tracks in later chapters discuss additional events and components as well as additional features of components already introduced.

creating GUIs

To create a Java program that uses a GUI, we must:

▸ define and set up the necessary components

▸ create listener objects and establish the relationship between the listeners and the components that generate the events and

▸ define what happens as a result of user interactions

Let's look at an example. The PushCounter program shown in Listing 5.13 is an applet that presents the user with a single push button (labeled "Push Me!"). Each time the button is pushed, a counter is updated and displayed.

The components used in this program include a button, a label, and the applet window that contains them. These components are defined by the

listing
    5.13

```
//*********************************************************************
//  PushCounter.java        Authors: Lewis/Loftus/Cocking
//
//  Demonstrates a graphical user interface and an event listener.
//*********************************************************************

import java.awt.*;
import java.awt.event.*;
import javax.swing.*;

public class PushCounter extends JApplet
{
   private int APPLET_WIDTH = 300, APPLET_HEIGHT = 35;
   private int pushes;
   private JLabel label;
   private JButton push;

   //----------------------------------------------------------------
   //  Sets up the GUI.
   //----------------------------------------------------------------
   public void init ()
   {
      pushes = 0;

      push = new JButton ("Push Me!");
      push.addActionListener (new ButtonListener());
```

listing
   5.13   continued

```java
      label = new JLabel ("Pushes: " + Integer.toString (pushes));

      Container cp = getContentPane();
      cp.setBackground (Color.cyan);
      cp.setLayout (new FlowLayout());
      cp.add (push);
      cp.add (label);

      setSize (APPLET_WIDTH, APPLET_HEIGHT);
   }


   //*********************************************************************
   //  Represents a listener for button push (action) events.
   //*********************************************************************
   private class ButtonListener implements ActionListener
   {
      //-------------------------------------------------------------
      //  Updates the counter when the button is pushed.
      //-------------------------------------------------------------
      public void actionPerformed (ActionEvent event)
      {
         pushes++;
         label.setText("Pushes: " + Integer.toString (pushes));
         repaint ();
      }
   }
}
```

display

classes JButton, JLabel, and JApplet. These components are all part of the Swing package (javax.swing).

A *push button* is a component that lets the user start an action by clicking the button with the mouse. A *label* is a component that displays a line of text in a GUI. Labels are generally used to display information or to identify other components in the GUI. Push buttons and labels can be found in almost any GUI.

The init method of the applet sets up the GUI. The JButton constructor takes a String parameter that spells out the label on the button. The JLabel constructor also takes a String parameter, which defines the initial content of the label.

The only event of interest in this program occurs when the button is pushed. To respond to an event, we must do two things: create a listener object for the event and add that listener to the graphical component that generates the event. The listener object contains a method that is called by the component whenever that event occurs.

> A listener object contains a method that is called whenever an event occurs.
>
> key concept

A JButton generates an *action event* when it is pushed. Therefore we need an action event listener. In this program, we define the ButtonListener class as the listener for this event. In the init method, the listener object is instantiated and then added to the button using the addActionListener method.

GUI components must be added to the container in which they are displayed. In this example, the init method adds each component to the applet container. That means the button and label components are added to the *content pane* that represents the main container for the applet. The content pane is retrieved using the getContentPane method of the JApplet class. The components are then added to the content pane using the add method. The background color of the content pane is set using the setBackground method. The layout manager for the pane is set to a flow layout so that components are placed top to bottom and left to right in each row.

Now let's take a closer look at the ButtonListener class. A common way to create a listener object is to define a class that implements a *listener interface*. The Java standard class library contains a set of interfaces for event categories. For example, the interface for an action event is called ActionListener. Recall from the discussion of interfaces earlier in this chapter that an interface defines a set of methods that a class must implement. The ActionListener interface has only one method, called actionPerformed.

Inner classes are often used to define listener objects.

The ButtonListener class implements the ActionListener interface. The actionPerformed method takes one parameter of type ActionEvent. Note that ButtonListener is implemented as an inner class, nested inside the main applet class. Inner classes are often used to define listener objects.

When the button is pushed, the JButton object calls the actionPerformed method of any listener that has been added to it. The JButton object generates an ActionEvent object and passes it into the actionPerformed method. If necessary, a listener can get information about the event from this parameter. In this program, however, we just want to know that the button was pushed. The actionPerformed method responds by updating the counter used to keep track of the number of times the button has been pushed. The actionPerformed method updates the content of the label using the setText method of the JLabel class, and causing the applet to repaint itself (so that the new label is displayed).

GUI applications

Let's look at another example that uses some more components. The Fahrenheit program shown in Listing 5.14 is an application, not an applet. The main method of the program instantiates the FahrenheitGUI class and invokes its display method.

The program converts a Fahrenheit temperature into Celsius. The user types a Fahrenheit temperature into a text field. A *text field* is an area where the user can type a single line of information. Text fields are commonly used in GUI programs to accept input. In this program, when the user enters a Fahrenheit temperature and presses the enter key, the Celsius temperature is computed and displayed using a label.

In the PushCounter applet in Listing 5.13, the applet window served as the primary container of the GUI. Because the Fahrenheit program is an application, we need a different container. A *frame* is a container component that is generally used for stand-alone GUI-based applications. A frame is displayed as a separate window with its own title bar. The Fahrenheit program is executed just like any other application, but it displays its own frame containing the program's graphical interface.

A frame is a container that is often used to display the interface for a stand-alone GUI application.

Listing 5.15 shows the FahrenheitGUI class. Its constructor sets up the GUI. First it creates a frame using the JFrame class. The JFrame constructor accepts a String parameter that will be shown in the title bar of the

listing
    5.14

```
//***********************************************************************
//  Fahrenheit.java         Author: Lewis/Loftus/Cocking
//
//  Demonstrates the use of JFrame and JTextArea GUI components.
//***********************************************************************

public class Fahrenheit
{
   //-------------------------------------------------------------
   //  Creates and displays the temperature converter GUI.
   //-------------------------------------------------------------
   public static void main (String[] args)
   {
      FahrenheitGUI converter = new FahrenheitGUI();
      converter.display();
   }
}
```

display

Temperature Conversion

Enter Fahrenheit temperature: 75

Temperature in Celsius: 23

frame when it is displayed, in this case "Temperature Conversion." The `setDefaultCloseOperation` method says what will happen when the user pushes close button on the frame. In this case, the program should end when the frame is closed. This is how an event-driven application usually ends.

Another container, called a panel, is created using the `JPanel` class. A *panel* cannot be displayed on its own. A panel must be added to another container. It helps organize the components in a GUI.

The size of a panel can be set using its `setPreferredSize` method, which takes a `Dimension` object as a parameter. (A `Dimension` object encapsulates the height and width of a component into one object.) The background color of a panel can be set using the

> **key concept**
>
> A panel is a container used to organize other components. It cannot be displayed on its own.

listing
    5.15

```java
//********************************************************************
//   FahrenheitGUI.java        Author: Lewis/Loftus/Cocking
//
//   Demonstrates the use of JFrame and JTextArea GUI components.
//********************************************************************

import java.awt.*;
import java.awt.event.*;
import javax.swing.*;

public class FahrenheitGUI
{
   private int WIDTH = 300;
   private int HEIGHT = 75;

   private JFrame frame;
   private JPanel panel;
   private JLabel inputLabel, outputLabel, resultLabel;
   private JTextField fahrenheit;

   //-----------------------------------------------------------------
   //  Sets up the GUI.
   //-----------------------------------------------------------------
   public FahrenheitGUI()
   {
      frame = new JFrame ("Temperature Conversion");
      frame.setDefaultCloseOperation (JFrame.EXIT_ON_CLOSE);

      inputLabel = new JLabel ("Enter Fahrenheit temperature:");
      outputLabel = new JLabel ("Temperature in Celsius: ");
      resultLabel = new JLabel ("---");

      fahrenheit = new JTextField (5);
      fahrenheit.addActionListener (new TempListener());

      panel = new JPanel();
      panel.setPreferredSize (new Dimension(WIDTH, HEIGHT));
      panel.setBackground (Color.yellow);
      panel.add (inputLabel);
      panel.add (fahrenheit);
      panel.add (outputLabel);
      panel.add (resultLabel);

      frame.getContentPane().add (panel);
   }
```

listing
5.15 continued

```java
//---------------------------------------------------------------
//   Displays the primary application frame.
//---------------------------------------------------------------
public void display()
{
   frame.pack();
   frame.show();
}

//***************************************************************
//   Represents an action listener for the temperature input field.
//***************************************************************
private class TempListener implements ActionListener
{
   //------------------------------------------------------------
   //   Performs the conversion when the enter key is pressed in
   //   the text field.
   //------------------------------------------------------------
   public void actionPerformed (ActionEvent event)
   {
      int fahrenheitTemp, celsiusTemp;

      String text = fahrenheit.getText();

      fahrenheitTemp = Integer.parseInt (text);
      celsiusTemp = (fahrenheitTemp-32) * 5/9;

      resultLabel.setText (Integer.toString (celsiusTemp));
   }
}
}
```

setBackground method. Components are added to the panel using the add method. In the Fahrenheit example, once the entire panel is set up, it is added to the content pane of the frame.

The components added to the panel in this program are three labels and a text field. A text field is defined by the JTextField class. The constructor of the JTextField class accepts an integer that indicates how many characters the text field should be able to display.

Note that the order in which the labels and text field are added to the panel is the order in which they appear. The size of the panel determines how the components line up. This is actually a function of the layout manager. Panels have a flow layout, which puts as many components on a row as possible, moving to the next row when one row fills up.

The `display` method of the `FahrenheitGUI` class calls the `pack` and `show` methods of the frame. The `pack` method changes the size of the frame to fit the components that have been added to it, which in this case is the panel. The `show` method displays the frame on the monitor screen.

Note that the program responds only when the user presses the enter key inside the text field. A `JTextField` object generates an action event when the user presses the enter key. This is the same event that occurs when a button is pressed, as we saw in the `PushCounter` example. The `TempListener` class is set up as the action listener for this program. Note that it is implemented as an inner class, which gives it easy access to the components stored in the enclosing class.

In the `actionPerformed` method, the `getText` method of the `JTextField` class gets the input string—the temperature that the user typed in. Then the temperature is converted to a numeric value, the Celsius temperature is computed, and the text of the output label is set.

summary of key concepts

▸ An object reference variable stores the address of an object.

▸ The reserved word `null` represents a reference that does not point to a valid object.

▸ The `this` reference always refers to the currently executing object.

▸ Several references can refer to the same object. These references are aliases of each other.

▸ The `==` operator compares object references, returning true if the references are aliases of each other.

▸ The `equals` method can be defined so it compares objects in any way we want.

▸ When an object is passed to a method, the actual and formal parameters become aliases of each other.

▸ A static variable is shared among all instances of a class.

▸ A method is made static by using the `static` modifier in the method declaration.

▸ An interface is a collection of abstract methods. It cannot be instantiated.

▸ A class implements an interface, which formally defines a set of methods used to interact with objects of that class.

▸ If designed well, inner classes preserve encapsulation and simplify the implementation of related classes.

▸ `JOptionPane` is a Swing class that makes creating dialog boxes easier.

▸ A GUI is made up of graphical components, events that represent user actions, and listeners that respond to those events.

▸ A listener object contains a method that is called whenever an event occurs.

▸ Inner classes are often used to define listener objects.

▸ A frame is often used to display the interface for a stand-alone GUI application.

▸ A panel is used to organize other components. It cannot be displayed on its own.

self-review questions

5.1   What is a null reference?

5.2   What does the `this` reference refer to?

5.3   What is an alias?

5.4   How are objects passed as parameters?

5.5   What is the difference between a static variable and an instance variable?

5.6   What is the difference between a class and an interface?

5.7   Why might you declare an inner class?

5.8   What is a dialog box?

5.9   What is an event? What is a listener?

5.10 Can a GUI-based program be a stand-alone application? Explain.

multiple choice

5.1   The `this` reference refers to

a. the currently executing object

b. the first parameter in a method

c. the current class

d. a reference that doesn't point to any object

e. the object that called the current method

5.2   Which of the following should be used for an object reference variable that does not refer to any object?

a. `this`

b. `static`

c. `null`

d. `0`

e. `−1`

5.3   Which of the following expressions can be used to test whether two objects, o1 and o2, are aliases of each other?

   a. `o1 == o2`

   b. `o1.equals(o2)`

   c. `o2.equals(o1)`

   d. `o1.compareTo(o2) == 0`

   e. `o1.compareTo(o2) != 0`

5.4   Which of the following reserved words is used in the class header of a class that implements an interface?

   a. `interface`

   b. `implements`

   c. `abstract`

   d. `void`

   e. `final`

5.5   Which of the following is often static?

   a. local variables

   b. all instance variables

   c. parameters to methods

   d. object reference variables

   e. constants

5.6   Suppose s1 comes before s2 in the Unicode character set. What will be returned by this `compareTo` method?

`s2.compareTo(s1)`

   a. a number less than 0

   b. 0

   c. a number greater than 0

   d. `null`

   e. the `String` object s1

5.7 A class that implements an interface must implement which methods of the interface?

   a. only those that return a value

   b. only those that are not abstract

   c. only those that are marked with the word "required"

   d. the class is not required to implement any methods

   e. all methods must be implemented

5.8 Given the declarations

```
String s1 = "James Gosling";
String s2 = "James Gosling";
```

which of the following statements is true?

   a. s1 and s2 are aliases of each other

   b. s1 == s2 is true

   c. s1 < s2 because capital letters come before lowercase in the Unicode character set

   d. s1.equals(s2) is true

   e. s1 and s2 are the same because they have the same number of characters

5.9 A method that does not have an implementation

   a. is not allowed by the Java compiler

   b. takes no parameters and returns the integer 0

   c. is a static method

   d. is a null method

   e. is an abstract method

5.10 What is output by the following code?

```
String word1 = "blue";
String word2 = "red";
String word3 = "green";
word2 = word3;
word1 = word3;
word3 = word1;
System.out.println(word1 + " " + word2 + " " + word3);
```

a. blue red green

b. green green blue

c. blue blue blue

d. green green green

e. red red blue

true/false

5.1   A reference variable that does not currently point to an object is called a `null` reference.

5.2   The `this` reference lets an object refer to iself.

5.3   Two objects are aliases of each other if they are equal using the `equals` method.

5.4   The `==` operator and the `equals` method do the same thing for all objects.

5.5   When an object is passed to a method, what is actually passed is a reference to that object.

5.6   Static variables and methods are accessed through a class rather than through an instance of a class.

5.7   A static method may use instance variables in the same class.

5.8   Constructors may not be static.

5.9   Constants may be declared in interfaces.

5.10 A class may implement more than one interface.

short answer

5.1 Discuss how Java passes parameters to a method. Is this technique the same for primitive types and objects? Explain.

5.2 Explain why a static method cannot refer to an instance variable.

5.3 Can a class implement two interfaces that each contain the same method signature? Explain.

5.4 Create an interface called `Visible` that includes two methods: `makeVisible` and `makeInvisible`. Both methods should take no parameters and should return a `boolean` result. Describe how a class might implement this interface.

5.5 Create an interface called `VCR` with methods that represent what a video cassette recorder does (play, stop, etc.). Define the method signatures any way you want. Describe how a class might implement this interface.

5.6 Given the `Num` and `ParameterTester` classes listed earlier in the chapter, what is the result of executing the following lines of code?

```
ParameterTester myTester = new ParameterTester();
int an Integer = 27;
Num aNum = new Num(38);
Num anotherNum = new Num(49);
myTester.changeValues(anInteger, aNum, anotherNum);
System.out.println("anInteger: " + anInteger);
System.out.println("aNum: " + aNum);
System.out.println("anotherNum: " + anotherNum);
```

programming projects

5.1 Change the `PigLatinTranslator` class from Chapter 4 so that its `translate` method is static. Change the `PigLatin` class so it invokes the method correctly.

5.2 Change the `Rational` class from Chapter 4 so it implements the `Comparable` interface. To do the comparison, compute a floating point value from the numerator and denominator for both `Rational` objects, then compare them using a tolerance value of 0.0001. Write a main driver to test your changes.

5.3 Design a Java interface called `Priority` that has two methods: `setPriority` and `getPriority`. The interface should let us number a set of objects in the order of their importance. Design and implement a class called `Task` that implements the `Priority` interface. Create a driver class to use some `Task` objects.

5.4 Change the `Task` class from Programming Project 5.3 so that it also implements the `Complexity` interface defined in this chapter. Change the driver class to show these new features of `Task` objects.

5.5 Change the `Task` class from Programming Projects 5.3 and 5.4 so that it also implements the `Comparable` interface from the Java standard class library. Implement the interface so that the tasks are listed in the order of their importance. Create a driver class whose `main` method shows these new features of `Task` objects.

5.6 Design a Java interface called `Lockable` that includes the following methods: `setKey`, `lock`, `unlock`, and `locked`. The `setKey`, `lock`, and `unlock` methods take an integer parameter that represents the key. The `setKey` method establishes the key. The `lock` and `unlock` methods lock and unlock the object, but only if the key used is correct. The `locked` method returns a boolean of true for locked and false for unlocked. A `Lockable` object is an object whose regular methods are protected: if the object is locked, the methods cannot be invoked; if it is unlocked, they can be invoked. Redesign and implement a version of the `Coin` class from Chapter 4 so that it is `Lockable`.

5.7 Redesign and implement a version of the `Account` class from Chapter 4 so that it is `Lockable`, as described in Programming Project 5.6.

5.8 Design and implement an application that uses dialog boxes to get two integer values (one dialog box for each value) and display the sum and product of the values. Use another dialog box to ask whether the user wants to process another pair of values.

5.9 Redesign and implement a version of the `PalindromeTester` program from Chapter 3 so that it uses dialog boxes to get the input string, display the results, and ask whether the user wants to test another palindrome.

5.10 Design and implement an application that shows the user two buttons and a label. Name the buttons `Add` and `Subtract`, respectively. Display a number (initially 50) using the label. Each time the `Add` button is pushed, increase the value by one. Likewise, each time the `Subtract` button is pressed, decrease the value by one.

answers to self-review questions

5.1   A null reference does not refer to any object. The reserved word `null` can be used to check for null references before following them.

5.2   The `this` reference always refers to the currently executing object. A nonstatic method of a class is written for all objects of the class, but it is invoked through a particular object. The `this` reference refers to the object through which that method is currently being executed.

5.3   Two references are aliases of each other if they refer to the same object. Changing the state of the object through one reference changes it for the other because there is actually only one object.

5.4   Objects are passed to methods by copying the reference to the object (its address). Therefore the actual and formal parameters of a method become aliases of each other.

5.5   Memory space for an instance variable is created for each object that is instantiated from a class. A static variable is shared among all objects of a class.

5.6   A class can be instantiated; an interface cannot. An interface contains a set of abstract methods which a class implements.

5.7   An inner class is useful when one class regularly changes the state of another. If designed well, an inner class can preserve encapsulation and simplify the implementations of both classes.

5.8   A dialog box is a small window that gives the user information, confirms an action, or accepts input. Generally, dialog boxes are used for brief user interactions.

5.9   Events usually represent user actions. A listener object "listens" for a certain event to be generated from a particular component.

5.10 A GUI-based program can be implemented as a stand-alone application. The application needs a window, such as a frame, for the GUI elements of the program.

We often want to organize objects or primitive data in a way that makes them easy to access and change. This chapter introduces arrays, which are a way of grouping data into lists. Arrays are basic to most high-level languages. We also explore the `ArrayList` class in the Java standard class library.

chapter objectives

- ▶ Define and use arrays.

- ▶ Describe how arrays and array elements are passed as parameters.

- ▶ Explore how arrays and other objects can be combined to manage complex information.

- ▶ Explore searching and sorting with arrays.

- ▶ Learn to use multidimensional arrays.

- ▶ Examine the `ArrayList` class.

6.0 arrays

An *array* is a simple but powerful way to group and organize data. When we have a large amount of information, such as a list of 100 names, it is not practical to declare separate variables for each piece of data. Arrays solve this problem by letting us declare one variable that can hold many values.

array indexing

An array is a list of values. Each value is stored at a numbered position in the array. The number for each position is called an *index* or a *subscript*. Figure 6.1 shows an array of integers and the indexes for each position. The array is called `height` and the integers are several peoples' heights in inches.

In Java, array indexes always begin at zero just as the section numbers in each chapter of this book begin with zero (instead of one). So the value stored at index 5 is actually the sixth value in the array. The array shown in Figure 6.1 has 11 values, indexed from 0 to 10.

To get a value in an array, we use the name of the array followed by the index in square brackets. For example, the following expression refers to the ninth value in the array `height`:

`height[8]`

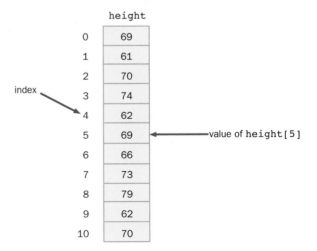

figure 6.1   An array called `height` containing integer values

According to Figure 6.1, `height[8]` (pronounced "height-sub-eight") contains the value 79. Don't confuse the value of the index, in this case 8, with the value stored in the array at that index, in this case 79.

The expression `height[8]` refers to a single integer stored at a particular memory location. It can be used wherever an integer variable can be used. This means you can assign a value to it, use it in calculations, print its value, and so on. Furthermore, because array indexes are integers, you can use integer expressions to specify the index used to access an array. For example, in the following lines of code we see the index in the `height` array given by a number (2), a variable (`count`), and an expression (`MAX/2` and `rand.nextInt(11)`).

```
height[2] = 72;
height[count] = feet * 12;
average = (height[0] + height[1] + height[2]) / 3;
System.out.println ("The middle value is " + height[MAX/2]);
pick = height[rand.nextInt(11)];
```

declaring and using arrays

In Java, arrays are objects. To create an array, we must declare the reference to the array. The array can then be instantiated using the `new` operator, which reserves memory space to store values. The following code is the declaration for the array shown in Figure 6.1:

> In Java, an array is an object. Memory space for the array elements is reserved by instantiating the array using the `new` operator.
>
> **key concept**

```
int[] height = new int[11];
```

In this declaration the variable `height` is declared to be an array of integers whose type is written as `int[]`. All values stored in an array have the same type (or are at least compatible). For example, we can create an array that can hold integers or an array that can hold strings, but not an array that can hold *both* integers and strings. An array can hold any primitive type or any object (class) type. A value stored in an array is sometimes called an *array element*, and the type of values that an array holds is called the *element type* of the array.

Note that the type of the array variable (`int[]`) does not include the size of the array. The instantiation of `height`, using the `new` operator, reserves the memory space to store 11 integers indexed from 0 to 10. Once an array is declared to be a certain size, the number of values it can hold cannot be changed.

The example shown in Listing 6.1 creates an array called `list` that can hold 15 integers. It then changes the value of the sixth element in the array (at index 5). Finally, it prints all values stored in the array.

```
//********************************************************************
//  BasicArray.java       Author: Lewis/Loftus/Cocking
//
//  Demonstrates basic array declaration and use.
//********************************************************************

public class BasicArray
{
   final static int LIMIT = 15;
   final static int MULTIPLE = 10;

   //-----------------------------------------------------------------
   //  Creates an array, fills it with various integer values,
   //  modifies one value, then prints them out.
   //-----------------------------------------------------------------
   public static void main (String[] args)
   {
      int[] list = new int[LIMIT];

      //  Initialize the array values
      for (int index = 0; index < LIMIT; index++)
         list[index] = index * MULTIPLE;

      list[5] = 999;   // change one array value

      for (int index = 0; index < LIMIT; index++)
         System.out.print (list[index] + "   ");

      System.out.println ();
   }
}
```

output

```
0   10   20   30   40   999   60   70   80   90   100   110   120   130   140
```

Figure 6.2 shows the array as it changes during the execution of the BasicArray program. It is often a good idea to use for loops when handling arrays because the number of positions in the array is constant. Note that a constant called LIMIT is used in several places in the BasicArray program. This constant is used to declare the size of the array, to control the for loop that initializes the array values, and to control the for loop that prints the values. Using constants in this way is a good practice. It makes a program more readable and easier to change. For instance, if you needed to change the size of the array, you would only have to change one line of code

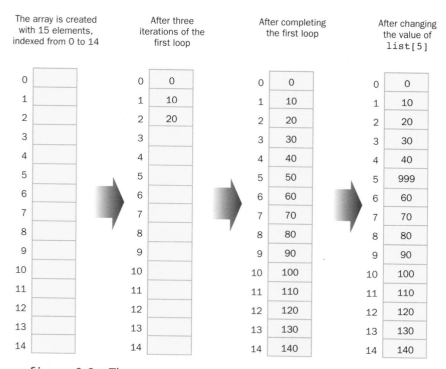

The array is created with 15 elements, indexed from 0 to 14

After three iterations of the first loop

After completing the first loop

After changing the value of list[5]

figure 6.2   The array `list` as it changes in the `BasicArray` program

(the constant declaration). We'll see another way to handle this situation later in this chapter.

The square brackets used to indicate the index of an array are treated as an operator in Java. Therefore, just like the + operator or the <= operator, the index operator ([ ]) has a precedence. In fact, it has the highest precedence of all Java operators.

The index operator performs *automatic bounds checking*. Bounds checking makes sure that the index is within the range for the array being referenced. Whenever a reference to an array element is made, the index must be greater than or equal to zero and less than the size of the array. For example, suppose an array called `prices` is created with 25 elements. The valid indexes for the array are from 0 to 24. Whenever a reference is made to a particular element in the array (such as `prices[count]`), the value of the index is checked. If it is between zero and 24 inclusive, the reference is carried out. If the index is not valid, if for example it is 25, the exception `ArrayIndexOutOfBoundsException` is thrown.

> **key concept**
>
> Bounds checking ensures that an index used to refer to an array element is in range. The Java index operator performs automatic bounds checking.

Because array indexes begin at zero and go up to one less than the size of the array, it is easy to create *off-by-one errors* in a program. When referencing array elements, be careful to make sure that the index stays within the array bounds.

Another important characteristic of Java arrays is that their size is held in a constant called `length` in the array object. It is a public constant and therefore can be referenced directly. For example, after the array `prices` is created with 25 elements, the constant `prices.length` contains the value 25. Its value is set once when the array is first created and cannot be changed. The `length` constant, which is an integral part of each array, can be used when the array size is needed without having to create a separate constant.

Let's look at another example. The program shown in Listing 6.2 reads 10 integers into an array called `numbers` and then prints them in reverse order.

Note that in the `ReverseOrder` program, the array `numbers` is declared to have 10 elements and therefore is indexed from 0 to 9. The index range is controlled in the `for` loops by using the `length` field of the array object. You should carefully set the initial value of loop control variables and the

listing
   6.2

```
//********************************************************************
//   ReverseOrder.java        Author: Lewis/Loftus/Cocking
//
//   Demonstrates array index processing.
//********************************************************************

import cs1.Keyboard;

public class ReverseOrder
{
    //-----------------------------------------------------------------
    //   Reads a list of numbers from the user, storing them in an
    //   array, then prints them in the opposite order.
    //-----------------------------------------------------------------
    public static void main (String[] args)
    {
        double[] numbers = new double[10];

        System.out.println ("The size of the array: " + numbers.length);
```

listing
6.2   continued

```java
        for (int index = 0; index < numbers.length; index++)
        {
            System.out.print ("Enter number " + (index+1) + ": ");
            numbers[index] = Keyboard.readDouble();
        }

        System.out.println ("The numbers in reverse order:");

        for (int index = numbers.length-1; index >= 0; index--)
            System.out.print (numbers[index] + "   ");

        System.out.println ();
    }
}
```

output

```
The size of the array: 10
Enter number 1: 18.36
Enter number 2: 48.9
Enter number 3: 53.5
Enter number 4: 29.06
Enter number 5: 72.404
Enter number 6: 34.8
Enter number 7: 63.41
Enter number 8: 45.55
Enter number 9: 69.0
Enter number 10: 99.18
The numbers in reverse order:
99.18   69.0   45.55   63.41   34.8   72.404   29.06   53.5   48.9   18.36
```

conditions that terminate loops to guarantee that all elements are processed and only valid indexes are used to reference an array element.

The LetterCount example, shown in Listing 6.3, uses two arrays and a String object. The array called upper is used to store the number of times each uppercase alphabetic letter is found in the string. The array called lower stores the number of times each lowercase letter is found.

Because there are 26 letters in the English alphabet, both the upper and lower arrays are declared with 26 elements. Each element contains an integer that is initially zero by default. The for loop scans through the string one character at a time. The counter in the array increases once for each character found in the string.

listing
6.3

```
//*********************************************************************
//  LetterCount.java         Author: Lewis/Loftus/Cocking
//
//  Demonstrates the relationship between arrays and strings.
//*********************************************************************

import cs1.Keyboard;

public class LetterCount
{
   //-------------------------------------------------------------------
   //  Reads a sentence from the user and counts the number of
   //  uppercase and lowercase letters contained in it.
   //-------------------------------------------------------------------
   public static void main (String[] args)
   {
      final int NUMCHARS = 26;

      int[] upper = new int[NUMCHARS];
      int[] lower = new int[NUMCHARS];

      char current;   // the current character being processed
      int other = 0;  // counter for non-alphabetics

      System.out.println ("Enter a sentence:");
      String line = Keyboard.readString();

      // Count the number of each letter occurence
      for (int ch = 0; ch < line.length(); ch++)
      {
         current = line.charAt(ch);
         if (current >= 'A' && current <= 'Z')
            upper[current-'A']++;
         else
            if (current >= 'a' && current <= 'z')
               lower[current-'a']++;
            else
               other++;
      }

      // Print the results
      System.out.println ();
      for (int letter=0; letter < upper.length; letter++)
```

listing
   6.3   continued

```
    {
        System.out.print ( (char) (letter + 'A') );
        System.out.print (": " + upper[letter]);
        System.out.print ("\t\t" + (char) (letter + 'a') );
        System.out.println (": " + lower[letter]);
    }

    System.out.println ();
    System.out.println ("Non-alphabetic characters: " + other);
  }
}
```

output

```
Enter a sentence:
In Casablanca, Humphrey Bogart never says "Play it again, Sam."
A: 0          a: 10
B: 1          b: 1
C: 1          c: 1
D: 0          d: 0
E: 0          e: 3
F: 0          f: 0
G: 0          g: 2
H: 1          h: 1
I: 1          i: 2
J: 0          j: 0
K: 0          k: 0
L: 0          l: 2
M: 0          m: 2
N: 0          n: 4
O: 0          o: 1
P: 1          p: 1
Q: 0          q: 0
R: 0          r: 3
S: 1          s: 3
T: 0          t: 2
U: 0          u: 1
V: 0          v: 1
W: 0          w: 0
X: 0          x: 0
Y: 0          y: 3
Z: 0          z: 0

Non-alphabetic characters: 14
```

Both of the counter arrays are indexed from 0 to 25. We have to match each character to a counter. A logical way to do this is to use upper[0] to count the number of 'A' characters found, upper[1] to count the number of 'B' characters found, and so on. Likewise, lower[0] is used to count 'a' characters, lower[1] is used to count 'b' characters, and so on. A separate variable called other is used to count any nonalphabetic characters that are encountered.

We use the current character to calculate which index in the array to reference. Remember that each character has a numeric value based on the Unicode character set, and that the uppercase and lowercase letters are continuous and in order (see Appendix B). Therefore, taking the numeric value of an uppercase letter such as 'E' (which is 69) and subtracting the numeric value of the character 'A' (which is 65) yields 4, which is the correct index for the counter of the character 'E' as shown in Figure 6.3. Note that nowhere in the program do we actually need to know the specific numeric values for each letter.

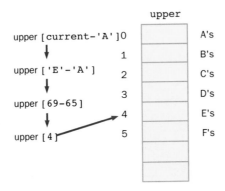

figure 6.3   When current is 'E' , upper[current-'A'] is the array cell that the number of Es is stored in

initializer lists

Another way to instantiate arrays is to use an *initializer list*. An initializer list provides the initial values for the elements of the array. It is basically the same idea as initializing a variable of a primitive data type in its declaration except that an array requires several values.

The items in an initializer list are separated by commas and enclosed in braces (`{}`). When an initializer list is used, the `new` operator is not used. The size of the array is the same as the number of items in the initializer list. For example, the following declaration instantiates the array `scores` as an array of eight integers, indexed from 0 to 7 with these initial values:

```
int[] scores = {87, 98, 69, 54, 65, 76, 87, 99};
```

An initializer list can be used only when an array is first declared.

> **key concept**
>
> An initializer list can be used to instantiate an array object instead of using the `new` operator. The size of the array is the same as the number of items in the initializer list.

The type of each value in an initializer list must match the type of the array elements. Let's look at another example:

```
char[] letterGrades = {'A', 'B', 'C', 'D', 'F'};
```

In this case, the variable `letterGrades` is declared to be an array of five characters, and the initializer list contains character literals: the letters A, B, C, D, and F. The program shown in Listing 6.4 shows an initializer list used to instantiate an array.

arrays as parameters

An entire array can be passed as a parameter to a method. Because an array is an object, when an entire array is passed as a parameter, a copy of the reference to the original array is passed. We discussed objects passed as parameters in Chapter 5.

A method that gets an array as a parameter can permanently change an element of the array because it is referring to the original element value. The method cannot permanently change the reference to the array itself because only a copy of the original reference is sent to the method. These are the same as the rules for any object type.

> **key concept**
>
> An entire array can be passed as a parameter, making the formal parameter an alias of the original.

An element of an array can be passed to a method as well. If the element type is a primitive type, a copy of the value is passed. If that element is a reference to an object, a copy of the object reference is passed. As always, the impact of changes made to a parameter inside the method depends on the type of the parameter. We discuss arrays of objects further in the next section.

listing
   6.4

```
//***************************************************************
//   Primes.java        Author: Lewis/Loftus/Cocking
//
//   Demonstrates the use of an initializer list for an array.
//***************************************************************

public class Primes
{
   //---------------------------------------------------------------
   //  Stores some prime numbers in an array and prints them.
   //---------------------------------------------------------------
   public static void main (String[] args)
   {
      int[] primeNums = {2, 3, 5, 7, 11, 13, 17, 19};

      System.out.println ("Array length: " + primeNums.length);

      System.out.println ("The first few prime numbers are:");

      for (int scan = 0; scan < primeNums.length; scan++)
         System.out.print (primeNums[scan] + "  ");

      System.out.println ();
   }
}
```

output

```
Array length: 8
The first few prime numbers are:
2  3  5  7  11  13  17  19
```

6.1   arrays of objects

In our examples so far, the arrays stored primitive types, such as integers and characters. Arrays can also store references to objects. Fairly complicated information management structures can be created using only arrays and other objects. For example, an array could contain objects, and each of those objects could have several variables and the methods that use them. Those variables could themselves be arrays, and so on. When you design a program you can use this to create the best representation for the information.

arrays of string objects

Consider the following declaration:

```
String[] words = new String[25];
```

The variable words is an array of references to String objects. The new operator in the declaration instantiates the array and reserves space for 25 String references. Note that this declaration does not create any String objects; it merely creates an array that holds references to String objects.

The program called GradeRange shown in Listing 6.5 creates an array of String objects called grades, which stores letter grades for a course. The String objects are created using string literals in the initializer list. Note that this array could not have been declared as an array of characters because the plus and minus grades create two-character strings. The output for the GradeRange program shown in Listing 6.5 lists letter grades and their lower numeric cutoff values (the lowest score you can have to get an A is 95, for example), which have been stored in an array of integers.

Sometimes two arrays with corresponding elements like this are called *parallel arrays*. Parallel arrays can be tricky because they can get out of synch with each other. You are usually better off creating one array that holds a single object containing all necessary information. For example, the GradeRange program could be changed to use a single array of objects that contain both the grade string and the numeric cutoff value. This change is left as a programming project.

command-line arguments

The formal parameter to the main method of a Java application is always an array of String objects. We've ignored that parameter in previous examples, but now we can discuss how it might be useful. (Note that this topic is not part of the AP subset.)

In Java the main method is invoked when an application is submitted to the interpreter. The String[] parameter, which we typically call args (for "arguments"), represents *command-line arguments* that are provided when the interpreter is invoked. Any extra information on the command line when the interpreter is invoked is stored in the args array for use by the program. This is another way to provide input to a program.

> **key concept**
>
> Command-line arguments are stored in an array of String objects and are passed to the main method.

The program shown in Listing 6.6 uses command-line arguments to print a name tag. It assumes the first argument represents some type of greeting and the second argument represents a person's name.

listing
6.5

```java
//********************************************************************
//  GradeRange.java        Author: Lewis/Loftus/Cocking
//
//  Demonstrates the use of an array of String objects.
//********************************************************************

public class GradeRange
{
    //-----------------------------------------------------------------
    //  Stores the possible grades and their numeric lowest value,
    //  then prints them out.
    //-----------------------------------------------------------------
    public static void main (String[] args)
    {
        String[] grades = {"A", "A-", "B+", "B", "B-", "C+", "C", "C-",
                           "D+", "D", "D-", "F"};

        int[] cutoff = {95, 90, 87, 83, 80, 77, 73, 70, 67, 63, 60, 0};

        for (int level = 0; level < cutoff.length; level++)
            System.out.println (grades[level] + "\t" + cutoff[level]);
    }
}
```

output

```
A       95
A-      90
B+      87
B       83
B-      80
C+      77
C       73
C-      70
D+      67
D       63
D-      60
F       0
```

If two strings are not provided on the command line for the NameTag program, the args array will not contain enough (if any) elements, and the references in the program will cause an ArrayIndexOutOfBoundsException to be thrown. If extra information is included on the command line, it would be stored in the args array but ignored by the program.

listing
6.6

```java
//************************************************************************
//  NameTag.java         Author: Lewis/Loftus/Cocking
//
//  Demonstrates the use of command line arguments.
//************************************************************************

public class NameTag
{
   //----------------------------------------------------------------
   //  Prints a simple name tag using a greeting and a name that is
   //  specified by the user.
   //----------------------------------------------------------------
   public static void main (String[] args)
   {
      System.out.println ();
      System.out.println ("     " + args[0]);
      System.out.println ("My name is " + args[1]);
      System.out.println ();
   }
}
```

output

```
>java NameTag Howdy John

     Howdy
My name is John

>java NameTag Hello William

     Hello
My name is William
```

Remember that the parameter to the `main` method is always an array of `String` objects. If you want numeric information to be input as a command-line argument, the program has to convert it from its string representation.

Sometimes a command line is not used to submit a program to the interpreter. When that happens the command-line information can be specified in some other way. Consult the manual for your particular software for these specifics.

filling arrays of objects

There is something else you need to know about object arrays: Creating the array and creating the objects that we store in the array are two separate steps. When we declare an array of `String` objects, for example, we create an array that holds `String` references. We have to create the `String` objects separately. In previous examples, we created the `String` objects using string literals in an initializer list or, in the case of command-line arguments, they were created by the Java runtime environment.

> **key concept**
>
> Instantiating an array of objects reserves room to store references only. The objects that are stored in each element must be instantiated separately.

This is demonstrated in the `Tunes` program in Listing 6.7. Listing 6.7 shows the `Tunes` class, which contains a `main` method that creates, changes, and looks at a compact disc (CD) collection. Each CD added to the collection has a title, artist, purchase price, and number of tracks.

listing 6.7

```
//********************************************************************
//  Tunes.java        Author: Lewis/Loftus/Cocking
//
//  Driver for demonstrating the use of an array of objects.
//********************************************************************

public class Tunes
{
   //-----------------------------------------------------------------
   //  Creates a CDCollection object and adds some CDs to it. Prints
   //  reports on the status of the collection.
   //-----------------------------------------------------------------
   public static void main (String[] args)
   {
      CDCollection music = new CDCollection ();

      music.addCD ("By the Way", "Red Hot Chili Peppers", 14.95, 10);
      music.addCD ("Come On Over", "Shania Twain", 14.95, 16);
      music.addCD ("Soundtrack", "The Producers", 17.95, 33);
      music.addCD ("Play", "Jennifer Lopez", 13.90, 11);

      System.out.println (music);

      music.addCD ("Double Live", "Garth Brooks", 19.99, 26);
      music.addCD ("Greatest Hits", "Stone Temple Pilots", 15.95, 13);

      System.out.println (music);
   }
}
```

listing 6.7 continued

output

```
*******************************************
My CD Collection

Number of CDs: 4
Total value: $61.75
Average cost: $15.44

CD List:

$14.95   10      By the Way      Red Hot Chili Peppers
$14.95   16      Come On Over    Shania Twain
$17.95   33      Soundtrack      The Producers
$13.90   11      Play            Jennifer Lopez

*******************************************
My CD Collection

Number of CDs: 6
Total value: $97.69
Average cost: $16.28

CD List:

$14.95   10      By the Way      Red Hot Chili Peppers
$14.95   16      Come On Over    Shania Twain
$17.95   33      Soundtrack      The Producers
$13.90   11      Play            Jennifer Lopez
$19.99   26      Double Live     Garth Brooks
$15.95   13      Greatest Hits   Stone Temple Pilots
```

Listing 6.8 shows the CDCollection class. It contains an array of CD objects representing the collection. It counts the CDs in the collection and their combined value. It also keeps track of the size of the collection array so that a larger array can be created if too many CDs are added to the collection.

The collection array is instantiated in the CDCollection constructor. Every time a CD is added to the collection (using the addCD method), a new CD object is created and a reference to it is stored in the collection array.

listing
  6.8

```java
//********************************************************************
//  CDCollection.java       Author: Lewis/Loftus/Cocking
//
//  Represents a collection of compact discs.
//********************************************************************

import java.text.NumberFormat;

public class CDCollection
{
   private CD[] collection;
   private int count;
   private double totalCost;

   //-----------------------------------------------------------------
   //  Creates an initially empty collection.
   //-----------------------------------------------------------------
   public CDCollection ()
   {
      collection = new CD[100];
      count = 0;
      totalCost = 0.0;
   }

   //-----------------------------------------------------------------
   //  Adds a CD to the collection, increasing the size of the
   //  collection if necessary.
   //-----------------------------------------------------------------
   public void addCD (String title, String artist, double cost,
                      int tracks)
   {
      if (count == collection.length)
         increaseSize();

      collection[count] = new CD (title, artist, cost, tracks);
      totalCost += cost;
      count++;
   }

   //-----------------------------------------------------------------
   //  Returns a report describing the CD collection.
   //-----------------------------------------------------------------
   public String toString()
   {
      NumberFormat fmt = NumberFormat.getCurrencyInstance();
```

```
listing
  6.8      continued

    String report = "*****************************************\n";
    report += "My CD Collection\n\n";

    report += "Number of CDs: " + count + "\n";
    report += "Total cost: " + fmt.format(totalCost) + "\n";
    report += "Average cost: " + fmt.format(totalCost/count);

    report += "\n\nCD List:\n\n";


    for (int cd = 0; cd < count; cd++)
       report += collection[cd].toString() + "\n";

    return report;
  }


  //-----------------------------------------------------------------
  //  Doubles the size of the collection by creating a larger array
  //  and copying the existing collection into it.
  //-----------------------------------------------------------------
  private void increaseSize ()
  {
     CD[] temp = new CD[collection.length * 2];

     for (int cd = 0; cd < collection.length; cd++)
        temp[cd] = collection[cd];

     collection = temp;
  }
}
```

Each time a CD is added to the collection, we check to see whether we
have filled up the collection array. If we didn't check this, we would get
an exception when we tried to store a new CD object at an invalid index. If
the array is full, the private increaseSize method is invoked, which first
creates an array that is twice as big as the current collection array. Each
CD in the collection is then copied into the new array. Finally, the collection reference is set to the larger array. This means we never run out of
room in our CD collection. The user of the CDCollection object (the main
method) never has to worry about running out of space because it's all handled internally.

The toString method of the CDCollection class returns a report summarizing the collection. The report is created, in part, using calls to the toString method of each CD object stored in the collection. Listing 6.9 shows the CD class.

listing
    6.9

```java
//************************************************************
//  CD.java          Author: Lewis/Loftus/Cocking
//
//  Represents a compact disc.
//************************************************************

import java.text.NumberFormat;

public class CD
{
   private String title, artist;
   private double cost;
   private int tracks;

   //-----------------------------------------------------------
   //  Creates a new CD with the specified information.
   //-----------------------------------------------------------
   public CD (String name, String singer, double price, int numTracks)
   {
      title = name;
      artist = singer;
      cost = price;
      tracks = numTracks;
   }

   //-----------------------------------------------------------
   //  Returns a description of this CD.
   //-----------------------------------------------------------
   public String toString()
   {
      NumberFormat fmt = NumberFormat.getCurrencyInstance();

      String description;

      description = fmt.format(cost) + "\t" + tracks + "\t";
      description += title + "\t" + artist;

      return description;
   }
}
```

6.2   searching

A common problem with arrays is searching for a particular element in the array. For example, in the CDCollection class, we may want to be able to search for a particular CD in the collection. The most basic search is called a *linear* or *sequential search*. In a sequential search, we look at each element of the array in turn, starting with the first, until we find the element we're looking for or we reach the end of the array.

The program shown in Listing 6.10 searches an array for a particular name. The boolean variable found is used to record whether the name was found or not. It starts out false. If the name is found in the array, found is set to true. The for loop in the program goes through the elements of the array, testing whether each element is the one we are looking for. Note the use of the equals method to compare the strings.

You may need to search an array in more than one place in a program, so you will need to implement a search in a separate method. Listing 6.11 shows the Searches class, which contains methods that implement searches. The linearSearch method returns the index in the array at which the element was found, or –1 if the element was not found. Notice that the if statement inside the for loop returns the index right away if it is found. Once the element is found, there is no need to keep searching the array. If the array does not contain the element we're looking for, then the for loop will end after the last element has been examined and –1 will be returned. We use –1 to indicate that the element was not found because –1 is not a valid index into an array.

> **key concept**
> A sequential search starts with the first element of an array and looks at elements one at a time, in order.

The main problem with a linear search is that it can be slow when working on large amounts of data. For example, in an array with 10,000 elements, if the element we're looking for is at position 9,999, we have to look at every element in the array before we find it. Sometimes, a linear search is our only option. However, if we know something about the way the data in the array are arranged, we can use a *binary search* instead. For example, consider an array of numbers in which the numbers are arranged from smallest to largest. If we are looking for a particular number, we could start with the middle element of the array. If the number we're looking for is less than the middle element, then we only have to look in the first half of the array. In fact, we can now examine the element that is in the middle of the first half and decide which quarter of the array the element we're looking for is in. We keep going until we find the element we're looking for or decide it is not in the array. Each time we look at an element in the array, we eliminate half the remaining elements from consideration. In this way, we look at far fewer elements than we do in a linear

> **key concept**
> A binary search is more efficient than a linear search but it only works if the data is stored in order in the array.

listing
    6.10

```java
//************************************************************
//  Guests.java        Author: Lewis/Loftus/Cocking
//
//  Demonstrates a linear search.
//************************************************************

import cs1.Keyboard;

public class Guests
{
    //-----------------------------------------------------------
    //  Creates an array of guests' names and allows the user to
    //  search the array for a particular name.
    //-----------------------------------------------------------
    public static void main (String[] args)
    {
        String[] guests = {"Paul", "Wendy", "Jared", "Eric", "Ayame",
                           "Ian", "Isobel", "Hakem"};
        String name;
        boolean found = false;
        System.out.print ("Enter a name: ");
        name = Keyboard.readString();

        // Perform a linear search
        for (int index = 0; index < guests.length; index++)
            if (name.equals(guests[index]))
                found = true;

        if (found)
            System.out.println (name + " is on the guest list.");
        else
            System.out.println (name + " is not on the guest list.");
    }
}
```

output

```
Enter a name: Wendy
Wendy is on the guest list.
```

listing
6.11

```java
//********************************************************************
//  Searches.java          Author: Lewis/Loftus/Cocking
//
//  Demonstrates the linear and binary search algorithms.
//********************************************************************

public class Searches
{
   //-----------------------------------------------------------------
   //  Searches the array of integers for the specified element using
   //  a linear search. The index where the element was found is
   //  returned, or -1 if the element is not found.
   //-----------------------------------------------------------------
   public static int linearSearch (int[] numbers, int key)
   {
      for (int index = 0; index < numbers.length; index++)
         if (key == numbers[index])
            return index;
      return -1;
   }

   //-----------------------------------------------------------------
   //  Searches the array of integers for the specified element using
   //  a binary search. The index where the element was found is
   //  returned, or -1 if the element is not found.
   //  NOTE: The array must be sorted!
   //-----------------------------------------------------------------
   public static int binarySearch (int[] numbers, int key)
   {
      int low = 0, high = numbers.length-1, middle = (low + high) / 2;

      while (numbers[middle] != key && low <= high)
      {
         if (key < numbers[middle])
            high = middle - 1;
         else
            low = middle + 1;
         middle = (low + high) / 2;
      }

      if (numbers[middle] == key)
         return middle;
      else
         return -1;
   }

}
```

search. This is the idea behind the binary search. Figure 6.4 demonstrates the binary search algorithm on a list of integers where 7 is the number being searched for.

In a binary search the data must be arranged in order, or *sorted* for it to work. In the next section we discuss how to sort an array. For now, we assume that when a binary search is being used, the data are already sorted.

The `Searches` class in Listing 6.11 shows a binary search used by the `FindGrade` program shown in Listing 6.12. In the binary search, the integer variables `low` and `high` keep track of the part of the array to be searched. At first they are set to the first and last index in the array. The element at index `middle` is compared to `key`, the element being searched for. If `key` is less than the element at `middle`, then `high` is set to `middle-1`, eliminating those elements in the upper half of the array. Likewise, if `key` is greater than the element at `middle`, then we know it must be in the upper half of the array (if it is in the array at all), and we change `low` to `middle+1`. The loop continues until either the element is found (`numbers[middle] == key`) or `low` becomes greater than `high`. If `low` is greater than `high`, then the element is not in the array.

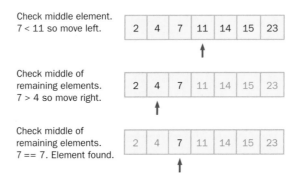

figure 6.4   Searching for the element 7 using a binary search

listing
6.12

```java
//**********************************************************************
//  FindGrade.java        Author: Lewis/Loftus/Cocking
//
//  Driver for testing a numeric binary search.
//**********************************************************************

public class FindGrade
{
   //---------------------------------------------------------------
   //  Creates an array of grades, sorts them, then prints them.
   //---------------------------------------------------------------
   public static void main (String[] args)
   {
      int[] grades = {60, 68, 70, 72, 73, 77, 85, 86, 89, 93, 95, 98};

      // Search for the grade 77
      int lookFor = 77;
      int pos = Searches.binarySearch (grades, lookFor);

      if (pos != -1)
         System.out.println ("The grade " + lookFor + " was found at "
            + "position " + pos);
      else
         System.out.println ("The grade " + lookFor + " was not found");

      // Search for the grade 94
      lookFor = 94;
      pos = Searches.binarySearch (grades, lookFor);

      if (pos != -1)
         System.out.println ("The grade " + lookFor + " was found at "
            + "position " + pos);
      else
         System.out.println ("The grade " + lookFor + " was not found");
   }
}
```

output

```
The grade 77 was found at position 5
The grade 94 was not found
```

6.3   sorting

Sorting is the process of arranging a list of items in order. For example, you may want to alphabetize a list of names. Many sorting algorithms have been developed over the years. In fact, sorting is considered to be a classic area of study in computer science.

> **key concept**
>
> Selection sort and insertion sort are two sorting algorithms for putting a list of values in order.

This section examines two sorting algorithms: selection sort and insertion sort. Other sorting algorithms are explored in later chapters.

selection sort

> **key concept**
>
> Selection sort works by putting each value in its final position, one at a time.

The *selection sort* algorithm sorts a list of values by successively putting particular values in their final, sorted positions. In other words, for each position in the list, the algorithm selects the value that should go in that position and puts it there. Let's look at the problem of putting a list of numeric values into ascending order.

1. First we scan the list to find the smallest value.

2. Then we swap that value with the value in the first position of the list.

3. Next we scan the rest of the list (all but the first value) to find the smallest value and swap it with the value in the second position of the list.

4. Then we scan the rest of the list (all but the first two values) to find the smallest value and exchange it with the value in the third position of the list.

5. We keep doing this until we get to the last position in the list (which will end up containing the largest value). When we are done, the list is sorted.

Figure 6.5 demonstrates the selection sort algorithm.

The program shown in Listing 6.13 uses a selection sort to arrange a list of values into ascending order. The SortGrades class has a main method that creates an array of integers. It calls the static method selectionSort in the Sorts class to put them in ascending order.

> **key concept**
>
> Swapping requires three assignment statements.

Listing 6.14 shows the Sorts class. It contains three sorting algorithms. The SortGrades program uses only the selectionSort method. The other methods are discussed later in this section.

The selectionSort method uses two for loops. The outer loop controls where the next smallest value will be stored. The inner loop finds the

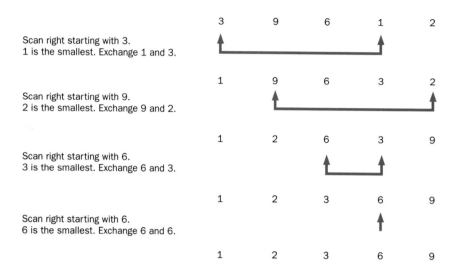

figure 6.5   Selection sort processing

listing
6.13

```java
//********************************************************************
//   SortGrades.java        Author: Lewis/Loftus/Cocking
//
//   Driver for testing a numeric selection sort.
//********************************************************************

public class SortGrades
{
   //-----------------------------------------------------------------
   //  Creates an array of grades, sorts them, then prints them.
   //-----------------------------------------------------------------
   public static void main (String[] args)
   {
      int[] grades = {89, 94, 69, 80, 97, 85, 73, 91, 77, 85, 93};

      Sorts.selectionSort (grades);

      for (int index = 0; index < grades.length; index++)
         System.out.print (grades[index] + "   ");
   }
}
```

output

```
69   73   77   80   85   85   89   91   93   94   97
```

listing
    6.14

```java
//********************************************************************
//  Sorts.java          Author: Lewis/Loftus/Cocking
//
//  Demonstrates the selection sort and insertion sort algorithms,
//  as well as a generic object sort.
//********************************************************************

public class Sorts
{
   //-----------------------------------------------------------------
   //  Sorts the specified array of integers using the selection
   //  sort algorithm.
   //-----------------------------------------------------------------
   public static void selectionSort (int[] numbers)
   {
      int min, temp;

      for (int index = 0; index < numbers.length-1; index++)
      {
         min = index;
         for (int scan = index+1; scan < numbers.length; scan++)
            if (numbers[scan] < numbers[min])
               min = scan;

         // Swap the values
         temp = numbers[min];
         numbers[min] = numbers[index];
         numbers[index] = temp;
      }
   }

   //-----------------------------------------------------------------
   //  Sorts the specified array of integers using the insertion
   //  sort algorithm.
   //-----------------------------------------------------------------
   public static void insertionSort (int[] numbers)
   {
      for (int index = 1; index < numbers.length; index++)
      {
         int key = numbers[index];
         int position = index;

         // shift larger values to the right
         while (position > 0 && numbers[position-1] > key)
         {
            numbers[position] = numbers[position-1];
            position--;
```

```
listing
   6.14  continued

        }

        numbers[position] = key;
      }
   }

   //--------------------------------------------------------------------
   //  Sorts the specified array of objects using the insertion
   //  sort algorithm.
   //--------------------------------------------------------------------
   public static void insertionSort (Comparable[] objects)
   {
      for (int index = 1; index < objects.length; index++)
      {
         Comparable key = objects[index];
         int position = index;

         // shift larger values to the right
         while (position > 0 && objects[position-1].compareTo(key) > 0)
         {
            objects[position] = objects[position-1];
            position--;
         }

         objects[position] = key;
      }
   }
}
```

smallest value in the rest of the list by scanning all positions greater than or
equal to the index specified by the outer loop. When the smallest value is
found, it swaps that with the value stored at the index. This is done in three
assignment statements by using an extra variable called temp. This is often
called *swapping*.

Note that because this algorithm finds the smallest value each time, the
result is an array sorted from smallest to largest. The algorithm can easily be
changed to put values in order from largest to smallest by finding the largest
value each time.

insertion sort

The `Sorts` class also has a method that does an insertion sort on an array of integers. If used to sort the array of grades in the `SortGrades` program, it would produce the same results as the selection sort did. However, the way the numbers are put in order is different.

The *insertion sort* algorithm sorts a list of values by repeatedly inserting a particular value into a subset of the list that has already been sorted. One at a time, each unsorted element is inserted into its proper position in the sorted subset until the entire list is in order. You can use this strategy to sort a hand of cards as it is being dealt. Each time a new card is dealt you pick it up and insert it into its proper position in your hand. Here are the steps:

1. We begin with a "sorted" list containing only one value.

2. We "pick up" a new value and sort the first two values, swapping them if necessary.

3. Then we insert the list's third value in the proper place, and so on.

4. We continue until all values are inserted in their proper places, at which point the list is completely sorted.

In the insertion process the other values in the array shift to make room for the inserted element. Figure 6.6 demonstrates the insertion sort algorithm.

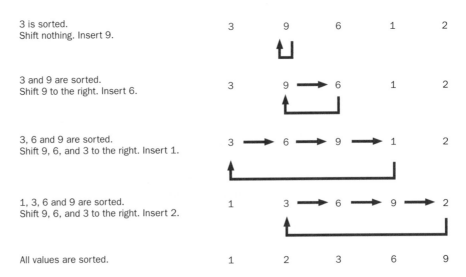

figure 6.6   Insertion sort processing

Like a selection sort, the insertionSort method uses two for loops. In the insertion sort, however, the outer loop controls the index in the array of the next value to be inserted. The inner loop compares the current insert value with values stored at lower indexes (which make up a sorted subset of the entire list). If the current insert value is less than the value at position, that value is shifted to the right. Shifting continues until the proper position is opened to accept the insert value. Each iteration of the outer loop adds one more value to the sorted subset of the list, until the entire list is sorted.

sorting an array of objects

The Sorts class in Listing 6.14 has an overloaded insertionSort method. This version of the method accepts an array of Comparable objects and uses the insertion sort algorithm to put the objects in sorted order.

The main difference between the two versions of the insertionSort method is that one sorts an array of integers and the other sorts an array of objects. We know what it means for one integer to be less than another integer, but what does it mean for one object to be less than another object? Basically, that depends on the objects being sorted and what kind of order we want them in. If you think of sorting a hand of cards, for example, you might sort them by suit, or by value, depending on whether you are playing bridge or "war."

The key is that the parameter to the method is an array of Comparable objects. That is, the array is filled with objects that have implemented the Comparable interface, which we discussed in Chapter 5. Recall that the Comparable interface contains one method, compareTo, which is designed to return an integer that is less than zero, equal to zero, or greater than zero if the object is less than, equal to, or greater than the object to which it is being compared.

Let's look at an example. The SortPhoneList program shown in Listing 6.15 creates an array of Contact objects, sorts these objects using a call to the insertionSort method, and prints the sorted list.

Each Contact object represents a person with a last name, a first name, and a phone number. Listing 6.16 shows the Contact class.

The Contact class implements the Comparable interface and provides a definition of the compareTo method. In this case, the contacts are sorted by last name; if two contacts have the same last name, their first names are used.

When the insertionSort method executes, it uses the compareTo method of each object to determine the order. We know that the objects in the array have implemented the compareTo method because they are all

listing
    6.15

```
//********************************************************************
//  SortPhoneList.java        Author: Lewis/Loftus/Cocking
//
//  Driver for testing an object sort.
//********************************************************************

public class SortPhoneList
{
    //-----------------------------------------------------------------
    //  Creates an array of Contact objects, sorts them, then prints
    //  them.
    //-----------------------------------------------------------------
    public static void main (String[] args)
    {
        Contact[] friends = new Contact[7];

        friends[0] = new Contact ("Barika", "Favaken", "610-555-7384");
        friends[1] = new Contact ("Lorenz", "Lowski", "215-555-3827");
        friends[2] = new Contact ("Ely", "Kassakian", "733-555-2969");
        friends[3] = new Contact ("Galen", "Powers", "663-555-3984");
        friends[4] = new Contact ("Laura", "Getz", "464-555-3489");
        friends[5] = new Contact ("Ching", "Lee", "322-555-2284");
        friends[6] = new Contact ("Susan", "Getz", "243-555-2837");

        Sorts.insertionSort(friends);

        for (int index = 0; index < friends.length; index++)
            System.out.println (friends[index]);
    }
}
```

output

```
Favaken, Barika   610-555-7384
Getz, Laura       464-555-3489
Getz, Susan       243-555-2837
Kassakian, Ely    733-555-2969
Lee, Ching        322-555-2284
Lowski, Lorenz    215-555-3827
Powers, Galen     663-555-3984
```

```
listing
   6.16
```

```java
//********************************************************************
//   Contact.java        Author: Lewis/Loftus/Cocking
//
//   Represents a phone contact.
//********************************************************************

public class Contact implements Comparable
{
   private String firstName, lastName, phone;

   //-----------------------------------------------------------------
   //   Sets up this contact with the specified information.
   //-----------------------------------------------------------------
   public Contact (String first, String last, String telephone)
   {
      firstName = first;
      lastName = last;
      phone = telephone;
   }

   //-----------------------------------------------------------------
   //   Returns a description of this contact as a string.
   //-----------------------------------------------------------------
   public String toString ()
   {
      return lastName + ", " + firstName + "\t" + phone;
   }

   //-----------------------------------------------------------------
   //   Uses both last and first names to determine lexical ordering.
   //-----------------------------------------------------------------
   public int compareTo (Object other)
   {
      int result;

      if (lastName.equals(((Contact)other).lastName))
         result = firstName.compareTo(((Contact)other).firstName);
      else
         result = lastName.compareTo(((Contact)other).lastName);

      return result;
   }
}
```

Comparable objects (according to the parameter type). We will get an error message if we try to pass an array to this method that does not contain Comparable objects. This version of the insertionSort method can be used to sort any array of objects as long as the objects have implemented the Comparable interface. This example shows a classic and powerful way interfaces can be used to create generic algorithms that work on a variety of data.

6.4   comparing sorts

There are lots of reasons for choosing one sorting algorithm over another. We might choose an algorithm because it is simple, fast, uses less memory, or works well on the kind of data we have. An algorithm that is easier to understand is also easier to write and debug. However, often the simplest sorts are not efficient. Efficiency is usually the first thing we look for. There are several algorithms that are more efficient than the two we examined, but they are also more complicated. We discuss some of these algorithms in later chapters.

In this section we explore how to compare algorithms in terms of time and space efficiency. We introduce big-oh notation (which is required for the AB exam) to help us.

Time efficiency refers to how long it takes an algorithm to run. *Space efficiency* refers to the amount of space that an algorithm uses. An algorithm that uses less space and runs faster is more efficient.

> **key concept**
>
> Sorting algorithms are ranked according to their time efficiency, which is denoted with big-oh notation.

We measure efficiency by the size of the input. For a sorting algorithm the input is the array of elements to be sorted, so the size of the input is the number of elements. We will use n for the number of elements being sorted.

We can measure the time efficiency of an algorithm by counting how many statements get executed when the algorithm runs. We are most interested in how the running time grows as the size of the input grows, so we can ignore statements that get executed the same number of times each time the algorithm is run. Instead we look at those statements that get executed a different number of times depending on the size of the input. In sorting algorithms the common operation is a comparison, so we usually count comparisons when we consider sorting algorithms. As the number of elements to be sorted grows, the number of comparisons required grows as well. We want to find the relationship between the two growth rates.

> **key concept**
>
> Both selection sort and insertion sort algorithms have time efficiency $O(n^2)$.

The selection sort in Listing 6.14 has an outer loop that runs $n-1$ times, where n is the size of the input array. The inner loop runs a variable number of times, ranging from 1 to $n-1$, depending on the index of the outer loop. So we can say that the time efficiency of the selection sort algorithm is on the *order* of n^2. We use big-oh notation saying that selection sort is $O(n^2)$. This means that the running time of the selection sort algorithm will be no worse than on the order of n^2 units of time, where n is the size of the input. We are not interested in how long a unit of time is because we use big-oh notation only to compare algorithms to each other; we are not trying to find out how long the algorithm takes to run.

Note that because $O(n^2)$ is an efficiency no worse than n^2, we could also say that selection sort is $O(n^3)$ or $O(n^4)$ or $O(2^n)$. However, we want to get as close as possible to an algorithm's real time efficiency.

We can analyze insertion sort in almost the same way. Its two nested loops run n times each, so the statements (comparisons) inside get executed approximately n^2 times. The insertion sort algorithm is therefore also $O(n^2)$.

An algorithm that was $O(n)$ would be more efficient than one that is $O(n^2)$. Likewise, $O(n^3)$ and $O(2^n)$ algorithms are less efficient than $O(n^2)$. Figure 6.7 shows various efficiency values for algorithms ranked from most efficient to least efficient. Note that for small values of n there is not much difference, but when n gets large, the efficiency of an algorithm makes a big difference.

Next let's consider space efficiency. In most sorting algorithms the sort occurs *in place*, meaning that the elements are moved around and sorted in the array they were originally stored in. So the amount of space being used is

Order	n=1	n=2	n=10	n=100	n=1000
$\log_2 n$	0	1	3.32	6.64	9.97
n	1	2	10	100	1000
$n\log_2 n$	0	2	33.22	664.4	9965.8
n^2	1	4	100	10,000	1,000,000
n^3	1	8	1000	1,000,000	1,000,000,000
2^n	2	4	1024	1.27E+30	1.07E+301

figure 6.7   A few efficiencies ranked from most efficient to least

approximately *n* memory locations, or the size of the array. (We don't consider the space needed for loop indices and temporary variables because it remains constant and does not increase as the size of the input increases.) Therefore, in terms of space efficiency, both the selection and insertion sort algorithms are O(*n*).

Because both selection sort and insertion sort have the same general efficiency, the choice between them is up to the programmer. Selection sort is usually easy to understand and each value moves exactly once to its final place in the list. That is, although the selection and insertion sorts have the same general efficiency, selection sort makes fewer swaps. Some people find insertion sort to be a good choice when they are continually adding values to a list while keeping the list in sorted order, because that is the strategy that the insertion sort technique uses anyway.

6.5   hashing

Hashing is a technique that is used to efficiently store and retrieve data in an array. An array used for hashing is often called a *hash table*. Each item in the data set has a *hash code* that tells where in the array the data item should be stored. The hash code is calculated from properties of the data item itself using a *hash function*. When storing an item, we simply calculate its hash code to determine which cell of the array to store it in. When we want to look up an item in the array, we calculate the item's hash code to find the cell where it should be stored. If the item is not there, it is not in the array at all. This makes searching for an item very fast (assuming the hash function is fast). Neither a linear search nor a binary search is required; instead we can jump straight to the appropriate cell.

The hash function can be any function that maps a data element to an index in the array. When defining a hash function, you need to know how many cells there are in the array. A good hash function will spread the data elements out evenly in the array. Suppose we are storing important dates in an array of size 10 using hashing. We could define the hash function to be (year + month + day)%10. The remainder of any number divided by 10 will be in the range 0 to 9, so the hash function will map every date to a valid cell in the array. We use the remainder operator (%) to produce a number in the correct range.

Figure 6.8 shows some dates and cells in an array, stored by the hash function. The date July 4, 1776 has hash code 7 because July is the seventh month and (7 + 4 + 1776) % 10 = 1787 % 10 = 7. Another way we can state this is that July 4, 1776 *hashes* to 7.

Date	Hash Code
July 4, 1776	$(7 + 4 + 1776)\% \, 10 = 7$
January 1, 2000	$(1 + 1 + 2000)\% \, 10 = 2$
February 12, 1809	$(2 + 12 + 1809)\% \, 10 = 3$
December 7, 1941	$(12 + 7 + 1941)\% \, 10 = 0$

December 7, 1941		January 1, 2000	February 12, 1809				July 4, 1776		
0	1	2	3	4	5	6	7	8	9

figure 6.8   Dates stored in an array via hashing

Suppose we want to find out if the date January 1, 2000 is in the array. First we calculate its hash code: $(1 + 1 + 2000) \% \, 10 = 2$. Since the hash code is 2, the date will be at index 2 if it is in the array at all. Looking at the cell at index 2 shows us that the date is indeed in the array. If we are looking for the date October 31, 1515, we calculate a hash code of 6 $((10 + 31 + 1515) \% \, 10 = 6)$. Since the cell at index 6 is empty, that date is not in the array. There is no need to look at the other cells because the date could only be at index 6.

Now suppose we want to add the date May 1, 1981. Its hash code is $(5 + 1 + 1981) \% \, 10 = 7$. Now we have two data values that hash to the same array cell; this is called a *collision*. The more data values we need to store, the more likely we are to get a collision. We would like to avoid collisions as much as possible. A rule of thumb is to use an array twice the size of the number of elements that will be stored in it. However, there is always the possibility that a collision will occur, so we must be able to deal with it. In later chapters we explore methods for handling collisions in hash tables.

6.6   two-dimensional arrays

The arrays we've looked at so far have all been *one-dimensional arrays* because they store a simple list of values. A *two-dimensional array* has values in two "dimensions," which are like the rows and columns of a table. Figure 6.9 compares a one-dimensional array with a two-dimensional array. We must use two indexes to refer to a value in a two-dimensional array, one for the row and another for the column. Note that two-dimensional arrays are an AB topic and will not be on the A exam.

Each dimension ("row" and "column") is enclosed in square brackets. So a two-dimensional array that stores integers is `int[][]`.

The `TwoDArray` program shown in Listing 6.17 instantiates a two-dimensional array of integers. The size of the dimensions is specified when the array is created. The size of the dimensions can be different.

Nested `for` loops are used in the `TwoDArray` program to load the array with values and to print them in a table. Carefully trace the processing to see how the nested loops visit each element in the two-dimensional array. Note that the outer loops are governed by `table.length`, which is the number of rows, and the inner loops are governed by `table[row].length`, which is the number of columns in that row.

As with one-dimensional arrays, an initializer list can be used to instantiate a two-dimensional array, where each element is itself an array initializer list. This technique is used in the `SodaSurvey` program, shown in Listing 6.18.

Suppose a soda company held a taste test for four new flavors to see how teens liked them. The company got 10 students to try each new flavor and give it a score from 1 to 5, where 1 means "gross" and 5 means "awesome." The two-dimensional array called `scores` in the `SodaSurvey` program stores the results of that survey. Each row is a soda and each column in that row is the student who tasted it. More generally, each row holds the responses that all students gave for one particular soda flavor, and each column holds the responses of one student for all sodas.

The `SodaSurvey` program computes and prints the average responses for each soda and for each student. The sums of each soda and student are first stored in one-dimensional arrays of integers. Then the averages are computed and printed.

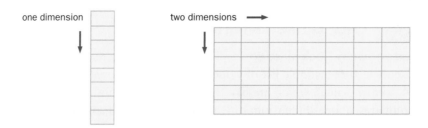

figure 6.9   A one-dimensional array and a two-dimensional array

```
listing
    6.17

//************************************************************************
//  TwoDArray.java              Author: Lewis/Loftus/Cocking
//
//  Demonstrates the use of a two-dimensional array.
//************************************************************************

public class TwoDArray
{
   //-----------------------------------------------------------------
   //  Creates a 2D array of integers, fills it with increasing
   //  integer values, then prints them out.
   //-----------------------------------------------------------------
   public static void main (String[] args)
   {
      int[][] table = new int[5][10];

      // Load the table with values
      for (int row=0; row < table.length; row++)
         for (int col=0; col < table[row].length; col++)
            table[row][col] = row * 10 + col;

      // Print the table
      for (int row=0; row < table.length; row++)
      {
         for (int col=0; col < table[row].length; col++)
            System.out.print (table[row][col] + "\t");
         System.out.println();
      }
   }
}
```

```
output

0       1       2       3       4       5       6       7       8       9
10      11      12      13      14      15      16      17      18      19
20      21      22      23      24      25      26      27      28      29
30      31      32      33      34      35      36      37      38      39
40      41      42      43      44      45      46      47      48      49
```

Arrays can have one, two, three, or even more dimensions, though arrays with more than two dimensions are rare and are not included in the AP Java subset.

```
//************************************************************************
//  SodaSurvey.java        Author: Lewis/Loftus/Cocking
//
//  Demonstrates the use of a two-dimensional array.
//************************************************************************

import java.text.DecimalFormat;

public class SodaSurvey
{
   //-------------------------------------------------------------------
   //  Determines and prints the average of each row (soda) and each
   //  column (respondent) of the survey scores.
   //-------------------------------------------------------------------
   public static void main (String[] args)
   {
      int[][] scores = { {3, 4, 5, 2, 1, 4, 3, 2, 4, 4},
                         {2, 4, 3, 4, 3, 3, 2, 1, 2, 2},
                         {3, 5, 4, 5, 5, 3, 2, 5, 5, 5},
                         {1, 1, 1, 3, 1, 2, 1, 3, 2, 4} };

      final int SODAS = scores.length;
      final int PEOPLE = scores[0].length;

      int[] sodaSum = new int[SODAS];
      int[] personSum = new int[PEOPLE];

      for (int soda=0; soda < SODAS; soda++)
         for (int person=0; person < PEOPLE; person++)
         {
            sodaSum[soda] += scores[soda][person];
            personSum[person] += scores[soda][person];
         }

      DecimalFormat fmt = new DecimalFormat ("0.#");
      System.out.println ("Averages:\n");

      for (int soda=0; soda < SODAS; soda++)
         System.out.println ("Soda #" + (soda+1) + ": " +
                   fmt.format ((double)sodaSum[soda]/PEOPLE));

      System.out.println ();
      for (int person =0; person < PEOPLE; person++)
         System.out.println ("Person #" + (person+1) + ": " +
                   fmt.format ((double)personSum[person]/SODAS));
   }
}
```

listing
6.18   continued

output

```
Averages:

Soda #1: 3.2
Soda #2: 2.6
Soda #3: 4.2
Soda #4: 1.9

Person #1: 2.2
Person #2: 3.5
Person #3: 3.2
Person #4: 3.5
Person #5: 2.5
Person #6: 3
Person #7: 2
Person #8: 2.8
Person #9: 3.2
Person #10: 3.8
```

6.7   the ArrayList class

The ArrayList class is part of the java.util package of the Java standard class library. It works like an array in that it can store a list of values and reference them by an index. But an array remains a fixed size throughout its existence, and an ArrayList object grows and shrinks as needed. You can insert or remove a data element from any location (index) of an ArrayList object by invoking a single method.

> **key concept**
>
> An ArrayList object is like an array, but it changes size as needed, and elements can be inserted and removed.

The ArrayList class is part of the Collections API, a group of classes that serve to organize and manage other objects. We discuss collection classes in Chapter 9.

Unlike an array, an ArrayList is not declared to store a particular type. An ArrayList object stores a list of references to the Object class. A reference to any type of object can be added to an ArrayList object. Because an ArrayList stores references, a primitive value must be stored in a wrapper class in order to be stored in an ArrayList. Figure 6.10 lists several methods of the ArrayList class. Students studying for the AB exam should note that ArrayList implements the List interface.

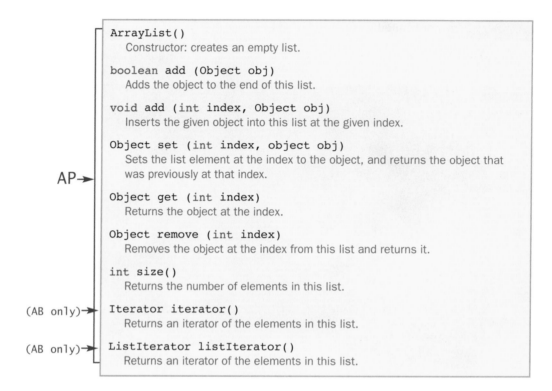

AP→

(AB only)→

(AB only)→

```
ArrayList()
    Constructor: creates an empty list.

boolean add (Object obj)
    Adds the object to the end of this list.

void add (int index, Object obj)
    Inserts the given object into this list at the given index.

Object set (int index, object obj)
    Sets the list element at the index to the object, and returns the object that
    was previously at that index.

Object get (int index)
    Returns the object at the index.

Object remove (int index)
    Removes the object at the index from this list and returns it.

int size()
    Returns the number of elements in this list.

Iterator iterator()
    Returns an iterator of the elements in this list.

ListIterator listIterator()
    Returns an iterator of the elements in this list.
```

figure 6.10   Some methods of the `ArrayList` class

The program shown in Listing 6.19 instantiates an `ArrayList` called band. The method `add` is used to add several `String` objects to the `ArrayList` in a particular order. Then one string is deleted and another is inserted at a particular index. As with any other object, the `toString` method of the `ArrayList` class is automatically called whenever it is sent to the `println` method.

Note that when an element from an `ArrayList` is deleted, the list of elements "collapses" so that there are no "holes" in the list. Likewise, when an element is inserted the list "expands."

The objects stored in an `ArrayList` object can be of different reference types. The methods of the `ArrayList` class accept references to the `Object` class as parameters, which means a reference to any kind of object can be passed to it. Because of this, the `get` method's return type is an `Object` reference. In order to retrieve a specific object from the `ArrayList`, the

listing
6.19

```
//***************************************************************
//  DestinysChild.java        Author: Lewis/Loftus/Cocking
//
//  Demonstrates the use of a ArrayList object.
//***************************************************************

import java.util.ArrayList;

public class DestinysChild
{
   //------------------------------------------------------------
   //  Stores and modifies a list of band members.
   //------------------------------------------------------------
   public static void main (String[] args)
   {
      ArrayList band = new ArrayList();

      band.add ("Michelle");
      band.add ("Kelly");
      band.add ("Beyonce");
      band.add ("Farrah");

      System.out.println (band);

      int location = band.indexOf ("Farrah");
      band.remove (location);

      System.out.println (band);
      System.out.println ("At index 1: " + band.get(1));

      System.out.println (band);
      System.out.println ("Size of the band: " + band.size());
   }
}
```

output

```
[Michelle, Kelly, Beyonce, Farrah]
[Michelle, Kelly, Beyonce]
At index 1: Kelly
Size of the band: 3
```

returned object must be cast to its original class. If you use a cast to convert an object to an incompatible type you will get a `ClassCastException`. You have to watch out for this in an `ArrayList`. If a is an `ArrayList` storing a `String` at position 0 then the statement

```
r = (Double)a.get(0);
```

will cause a `ClassCastException`.

using a ListIterator

The `listIterator` method on `ArrayList` returns a `ListIterator` object that can be used to iterate through the items in the list. Listing 6.20 shows a `ListIterator` being used. Once the iterator is obtained from the `ArrayList`, the `hasNext` and `next` methods are used to loop through each of the elements in the list.

ArrayList efficiency

The `ArrayList` class is implemented, as you might imagine, using an array. That is, the `ArrayList` class stores an array of `Object` references as instance data. The methods provided by the class move things around that array so that the indexes are always continuous as elements are added and removed.

When an `ArrayList` object is instantiated, the number of references the internal array can handle is set. Elements can be added to the list until it reaches this limit. At that point more memory is added. We did something like this in the `Tunes` program earlier in this chapter.

When an element is inserted into an `ArrayList`, all of the elements at higher indexes are copied into their new locations to make room for the new element. Figure 6.11 illustrates this. The same sort of thing happens when an element is removed from an `ArrayList`, except that the items are shifted in the other direction, closing the gap. As elements are inserted or deleted, this copying is repeated.

> **key concept**
>
> `ArrayList` processing can be inefficient depending on how it is used.

If, in general, elements are added to or removed from the end of an `ArrayList`, its efficiency is not affected. But if elements are added to or removed from the front part of a long `ArrayList`, a huge amount of element copying will occur. An `ArrayList` is a useful abstraction of an array, but the abstraction hides some activity that can be fairly inefficient depending on how it is used.

listing
   6.20

```java
//********************************************************************
//  Recipe.java        Author: Lewis/Loftus/Cocking
//
//  Demonstrates the use of a ListIterator to iterate through the
//  elements of an ArrayList.
//********************************************************************

import java.util.ArrayList;
import java.util.ListIterator;

public class Recipe
{
   //-----------------------------------------------------------------
   //  Stores and then prints a list of ingredients for a recipe.
   //-----------------------------------------------------------------
   public static void main (String[] args)
   {
      ArrayList ingredients = new ArrayList();

      ingredients.add ("flour");
      ingredients.add ("sugar");
      ingredients.add ("cocoa");
      ingredients.add ("oil");
      ingredients.add ("butter");
      ingredients.add ("eggs");
      ingredients.add ("baking soda");

      System.out.println ("To make a chocolate cake, use the following " +
         ingredients.size() + " ingredients:");

      ListIterator iterator = ingredients.listIterator();
      while (iterator.hasNext())
         System.out.println(iterator.next());
   }
}
```

output

```
To make a chocolate cake, use the following 7 ingredients:
flour
sugar
cocoa
oil
butter
eggs
baking soda
```

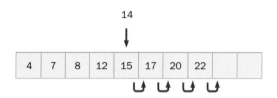

figure 6.11   Inserting an element into an `ArrayList` object

6.8 bumper cars case study: the arena

Before implementing our bumper cars program we need to look at the `Arena` class and add some detail to our design. In our simulation, cars move around the arena, controlled by drivers, sometimes bumping into each other. We need to answer some questions about the arena:

1. What kind of data structure will we use to store the cars?

2. How will we represent the arena?

3. How will we know each car's position in the arena?

The arena is a rectangle, so a good representation for the arena would be a two-dimensional array, also known as a matrix. Each space in the array would be a space that could be occupied by a single car. The array could be declared like this:

```
Car[][] arena = new Car[length][width];
```

Because one of the requirements is that the arena can change size from one run of the simulation to the next, the user should input the size of the arena. The length and width variables in the array declaration have values that come from the user's input.

Using this data structure answers all three of our questions about the arena and the cars. We will represent the arena with a two-dimensional array, where we will store the cars. Each cell in the array can hold a car or it can be empty. A car's position in the arena is given by its position in the array. Figure 6.12 shows an arena with six cars in it.

We know the relationship between the `Arena` and `Car` objects (an `Arena` *has-a* `Car`, or many `Car`s), but where do the drivers fit in? There are many ways we can handle the relationship between the `Driver` and the `Arena` and `Car` classes. Let's look at the solution used in this case study, then look at other solutions.

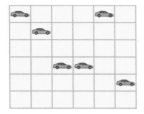

figure 6.12   A 6x6 arena with 6 cars in it

The cars have a close relationship with the drivers. One car and one driver form an inseparable pair throughout the simulation. We can only store one object in each spot in an array though, so we cannot store both a car and its driver in the array. We could give each `Car` a reference to the `Driver` that is driving it. Then a car "knows" which driver is driving it. Therefore, even though drivers are not stored in the arena array, each car that is stored knows which driver is driving it.

Now if the `Arena` object needs to communicate with a driver, it will have to communicate through the car. Is that okay? At this point, we don't see any problems with that design. We will stick with this design decision, but keep in mind that if it causes problems later in the design process, it could be changed. Figure 6.13 shows the interactions between the `Arena`, `Car`, and `Driver` objects.

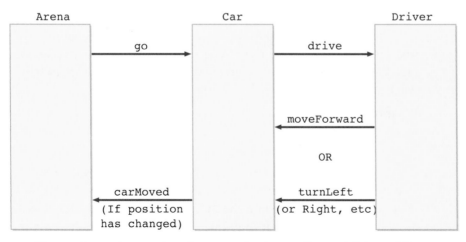

figure 6.13   Interactions between the Arena, Car, and Driver objects

an alternate arena

A different data structure we could have used for the `Arena` is simply an array of `Cars`, such as

```
Car[] arena = new Car[numCars];
```

In this case, information about the position of each car would have to be stored somewhere else because it is not part of each `Car`'s location in the array. Position information could be stored inside each `Car` object, or it could be stored in a parallel array. We could write a simple class, called `Position`, that represents a position. Then a position array, parallel to the `Car` array, could be declared like this:

```
Position[] positions = new Position[numCars];
```

In this situation, the car at `arena[0]` would have a position indicated by `positions[0]`. In a very big arena with a small number of cars, this design would need less memory space than the previous design, which is an advantage. But there is no quick way to test whether a particular cell in the arena is occupied. The entire `positions` array would have to be searched. Finding out whether a cell is occupied is something we will do often. Whenever a car moves, we need to know if it bumps into another car. Also, the drivers need to know whether the cells around them are empty so they can decide where to drive next.

exercises

1. In our program, the length and width of the arena are measured in units of space, about equal to the space a car takes up. Suppose this space is equal to 8 square feet. Write a segment of code that asks the user for the dimensions of the arena in feet and converts that to the size needed for the array that represents the arena.

2. What operations will we have to do on the `arena` array when a car moves? What would we have to do if we were using the parallel `arena` and `positions` arrays?

3. In our code, the arena stores `Cars` in its matrix and calls the `go()` method on each car when it is that car's turn to go. The car then calls the `drive()` method on the `Driver` to tell the driver to drive. But maybe we should do it this way: The arena stores `Drivers` in its matrix and calls the `drive()` method on the `Driver` directly when it is that driver's turn to drive. Discuss the advantages and disadvantages of this solution.

first-stage implementation

We can't write the whole program just yet, but we have enough to get
started. You should write large programs in stages rather than all at once.
That way you can test each stage and make sure it works before moving on
to the next. Once you have one piece of the program working, you can move
on to the next piece. Each time you do this, you are refining your design.
After the last refinement, the program will be complete.

Implementing our design so far, we come up with the classes Arena, Car,
Driver, and RandomDriver, shown in Listings 6.21, 6.22, 6.23, and 6.24.
Notice that the Arena class has a main program. When we're done, we'll
have a separate class (a driver program) that contains the main program and
gets the simulation started. At this point though, we put a main program in
Arena for testing purposes. Note also that not all methods are implemented
yet. In the Car class, the moveForward method and the turn methods print
a message so we know that they were called, but they do not do anything
"real" yet. A printArena method was added to the Arena class so that we
can see what the arena looks like. This method can help you during debugging. It will also show you a snapshot of the arena during the simulation.

listing 6.21

```
//********************************************************************
// Arena.java          Author: Lewis/Loftus/Cocking
//
// Represents a bumper car arena with cars in it.
//********************************************************************

import java.util.ArrayList;

public class Arena
{
    // The size of the arena
    private int length;
    private int width;

    // A 2-d array representing the arena. The upper-left corner is
    // position 0,0. A null entry indicates that that position in the
    // arena is unoccupied.
    private Car[][] arena;

    //-------------------------------------------------------------
    // Create an Arena of the given dimensions.
    //-------------------------------------------------------------
```

listing
6.21 continued

```java
public Arena(int length_, int width_)
{
    length = length_;
    width = width_;
    arena = new Car[length][width];
}

//-----------------------------------------------------------------
// Returns the length of this arena.
//-----------------------------------------------------------------
public int getLength()
{
    return length;
}

//-----------------------------------------------------------------
// Returns the width of this arena.
//-----------------------------------------------------------------
public int getWidth()
{
    return width;
}

//-----------------------------------------------------------------
// Add a car to the arena at the position given.
//-----------------------------------------------------------------
public void addCar(Car car, int len, int wid)
{
    // If the positions given are out of bounds, an
    // exception will automatically be thrown.
    arena[len][wid] = car;
}

//-----------------------------------------------------------------
// Let all cars take a turn to move.
//-----------------------------------------------------------------
public void step()
{
    // Use an ArrayList to keep track of which cars have gone
    // already, so that no car will go more than once.
    ArrayList movedAlready = new ArrayList();

    for (int len=0; len < length; len++)
    {
        for (int wid=0; wid < width; wid++)
        {
            if ((arena[len][wid] != null) &&
```

listing
6.21   continued

```java
                    (!movedAlready.contains(arena[len][wid])))
            {
                System.out.println("Arena:  car at " + len + ","
                                    + wid + " is going.");
                movedAlready.add(arena[len][wid]);
                arena[len][wid].go();
            }
        }
    }

    System.out.println("Arena:  1 step taken.");
}

//------------------------------------------------------------
// Display the arena in a textual format.
//------------------------------------------------------------
public void printArena()
{
    // Print a top line
    for (int wid=0; wid < width; wid++)
        System.out.print("-");
    System.out.println();

    // Print the cars in the arena
    for (int len=0; len < length; len++)
    {
        for (int wid=0; wid < width; wid++)
        {
            if (arena[len][wid] == null)
                System.out.print(" ");
            else
                System.out.print(arena[len][wid].carAsChar());
        }
        System.out.println();
    }

    // Print a bottom line
    for (int wid=0; wid < width; wid++)
        System.out.print("-");
    System.out.println();
}

//------------------------------------------------------------
// A main so that this class can be tested and debugged alone.
//------------------------------------------------------------
public static void main(String[] args)
{
```

listing
    6.21   continued

```
        Arena arena = new Arena(10, 10);
        Car car = new Car(arena);
        Driver driver = new RandomDriver(car);
        car.setDriver(driver);
        car.turnLeft();
        arena.addCar(car, 0, 0);

        car = new Car(arena);
        driver = new RandomDriver(car);
        car.setDriver(driver);
        car.turnAround();
        arena.addCar(car, 9, 9);

        car = new Car(arena);
        driver = new RandomDriver(car);
        car.setDriver(driver);
        arena.addCar(car, 0, 9);

        car = new Car(arena);
        driver = new RandomDriver(car);
        car.setDriver(driver);
        arena.addCar(car, 9, 0);

        car = new Car(arena);
        car.turnRight();
        driver = new RandomDriver(car);
        car.setDriver(driver);
        arena.addCar(car, 7, 4);

        // Do some steps
        arena.printArena();
        arena.step();

        arena.printArena();
        arena.step();

        arena.printArena();
    }
}
```

listing
  6.22

```java
//********************************************************************
//  Car.java           Author: Lewis/Loftus/Cocking
//
//  Represents a car in a bumper car arena.
//********************************************************************

public class Car
{
    private Arena arena; // the arena this car is in
    private Driver driver = null; // the driver controlling this car
    private int bumpCount;

    //-----------------------------------------------------------------
    //  Create a Car.
    //-----------------------------------------------------------------
    public Car(Arena theArena)
    {
        bumpCount = 0;
        arena = theArena;
    }

    //-----------------------------------------------------------------
    //  Sets the driver of this car.
    //-----------------------------------------------------------------
    public void setDriver(Driver theDriver)
    {
        driver = theDriver;
    }

    //-----------------------------------------------------------------
    //  Returns the number of times that this car has bumped into
    //  other cars or a wall.
    //-----------------------------------------------------------------
    public int getBumpCount()
    {
        return bumpCount;
    }

    //-----------------------------------------------------------------
    //  Tell the driver to drive. This function is called by the
    //  Arena when it is this car's turn to go.
    //-----------------------------------------------------------------
    public void go()
    {
        if (driver != null)
            driver.drive();
    }
```

listing
6.22   **continued**

```java
//--------------------------------------------------------------------
// Move forward one unit. This function is used by the driver.
//--------------------------------------------------------------------
public void moveForward()
{
    System.out.println("Car:  moved forward");
}


//--------------------------------------------------------------------
// Turn to the left. The turn left, right, and around functions
// are used by the driver to control the car.
//--------------------------------------------------------------------
public void turnLeft()
{
    System.out.println("Car:  turned left");
}


//--------------------------------------------------------------------
// Turn to the right.
//--------------------------------------------------------------------
public void turnRight()
{
    System.out.println("Car:  turned right");
}


//--------------------------------------------------------------------
// Turn around.
//--------------------------------------------------------------------
public void turnAround()
{
    System.out.println("Car:  turned around");
}


//--------------------------------------------------------------------
// Returns a one-character string representing this car.
//--------------------------------------------------------------------
public String carAsChar()
{
    return "C";
}

}
```

listing
     6.23

```java
//********************************************************************
//  Driver.java          Author: Lewis/Loftus/Cocking
//
//  An interface that all drivers of bumper cars must implement.
//********************************************************************

public interface Driver
{

    //---------------------------------------------------------------
    //  Drive the car one unit. Different drivers will have different
    //  algorithms for determining where to drive the car next.
    //---------------------------------------------------------------
    public void drive();

}
```

managing the simulation

We will now design and implement more pieces until we have a program that satisfies all the bumper car company's requirements.

In addition to the classes representing real-world objects, we need to write a class that manages the simulation. Code in this class will break the simulation into steps. In addition, the simulation object will set up the simulation—create the arena, create all the cars and drivers, and put them in the arena. It will also handle printing out the summary of bump counts after the simulation is over. We will name this class Simulation.

In order to run the simulation and print the summary, Simulation will need to keep references to the arena and the cars inside it. The setup tasks can be done in the constructor of Simulation. One step of the simulation can be run by calling the step method on Simulation. The step method will call a method on the Arena, telling it to give each car a chance to move.

Finally, Simulation will have a method that displays the bump count summary. Our program is text-based, but we want to keep the design flexible so it could be changed to a graphical interface in the future. So we will keep the code that prints to the screen in one method. The printBumpCounts method will display the bump counts by printing text to the screen.

listing
    6.24

```java
//********************************************************************
//  RandomDriver.java         Author: Lewis/Loftus/Cocking
//
//  Represents a driver whose moves are chosen randomly.
//********************************************************************

import java.util.Random;

public class RandomDriver implements Driver
{
    // Share a random number generator among all the RandomDrivers.
    private static Random randGen = new Random();

    private Car car;

    public RandomDriver(Car aCar)
    {
        car = aCar;
    }

    //----------------------------------------------------------------
    //  Drive the car one unit. The random driver chooses a move
    //  randomly.
    //----------------------------------------------------------------
    public void drive()
    {
        System.out.println("RandomDriver:  drive");

        // Move forward 70% of the time. Turn to face another direction
        // 30% of the time. (Equal probability for each of the three
        // remaining directions.)
        final int moveForwardProb = 70;
        int probability = randGen.nextInt(100);

        if (probability < moveForwardProb)
            car.moveForward();
        else {
            int turnWhichWay = randGen.nextInt(3);
            if (turnWhichWay == 0)
                car.turnLeft();
            else if (turnWhichWay == 1)
                car.turnRight();
            else /* turnWhichWay == 2 */
                car.turnAround();
        }
    }
}
```

The outline of our `Simulation` class looks like this:

```
public class Simulation
{
    public Simulation()
    {
        set up the simulation
    }

    public void step()
    {
        perform one step in the simulation
    }

    public void printBumpCounts()
    {
        print summary information to the screen
    }
}
```

The setup tasks for the simulation will be done in the `Simulation` constructor. Part of this setup is to create the arena, cars, and drivers, so the constructor should take parameters for the size of the arena and the number of car-driver pairs. Then the objects can be created.

The next part of the setup is to place the cars in the arena. The bumper car company told us the bumper cars are randomly placed in the arena. We will use a random number generator to determine where each car will be placed. We need to make sure that two cars do not occupy the same spot.

We can use the size of the arena to pick a random position in the arena. Let's lay out the arena with a North-South dimension and an East-West dimension. Then we need to generate a car's North-South coordinate and its East-West coordinate. This also gives us a convenient way to say which direction a car is facing—North, South, East, or West. The `Simulation` constructor will have two local variables called `arenaNSsize` and `arenaEWsize`, for the size of the arena. To get a random set of coordinates, (ns, ew), for each car, we can use the following code, assuming `randomGen` is a reference to a `Random` object:

```
ns = randomGen.nextInt(arenaNSsize);
ew = randomGen.nextInt(arenaEWsize);
```

We still need to make sure that two cars don't get assigned the same coordinates. An algorithm for doing that is as follows:

```
for each car
{
    generate random coordinates
    while (a car already occupies those coordinates)
        generate new random coordinates
    assign the car the generated coordinates
}
```

We need a way to find whether there's already a car in a given position. When we assign a car its coordinates we will be telling the arena where the car is. The arena will then have a record of where the cars are. So all we have to do is create a method on the `Arena` class that will tell us whether or not a particular spot is occupied. This method will also be useful for drivers when they are deciding where to move next. Drivers may want to know whether the space in front of them (or beside them) is empty, is occupied by a car, or is a wall. (Our `RandomDriver` doesn't take that into account, but other types of drivers may want to.) We will design a method with the following signature:

```
int occupiedBy(int ns, int ew)
```

The `occupiedBy` method will return a constant indicating what's in the space. The constants `EMPTY`, `CAR`, and `WALL` will be defined publicly in the `Arena` class to be used as return values. We can use this method as we are placing cars to make sure we don't put two cars in the same spot. Listing 6.25 shows the `occupiedBy` method in the `Arena` class.

listing
6.25

```
//********************************************************************
// Arena.java          Author: Lewis/Loftus/Cocking
//
// Represents a bumper car arena with cars in it.
//********************************************************************

import java.util.ArrayList;

public class Arena
{
    // Constants returned by the occupiedBy() method
    public static final int EMPTY = 0;
    public static final int CAR = 1;
    public static final int WALL = 2;
```

listing
6.25 **continued**

```java
    // The size of the arena
    private int nsSize;
    private int ewSize;

    // A 2-d array representing the arena. The upper left corner is
    // position 0,0. A null entry indicates that that position in the
    // arena is unoccupied.
    private Car[][] arena;

    //----------------------------------------------------------------
    // Create an Arena of the given dimensions.
    //----------------------------------------------------------------
    public Arena(int nsSize_, int ewSize_)
    {
        nsSize = nsSize_;
        ewSize = ewSize_;
        arena = new Car[nsSize][ewSize];
    }


    // other methods as previously shown, with length and width
    // changed to nsSize and ewSize ...


    //----------------------------------------------------------------
    // Returns a constant indicating what the given position in the
    // arena is occupied by - either EMPTY, CAR, or WALL.
    //----------------------------------------------------------------
    public int occupiedBy(int ns, int ew)
    {
        if (ns < 0 || ns >= nsSize || ew < 0 || ew >= ewSize)
            return WALL;
        else if (arena[ns][ew] != null)
            return CAR;
        else
            return EMPTY;
    }
}
```

This brings up another issue: We can only have as many cars as there are positions in the arena. For example, in an arena that is 5 by 5, the maximum number of cars is 25. If the number of cars is 26 or more, the while loop in our pseudocode will be an infinite loop! The size of the arena and the number of cars in the simulation is entered by the user, so when we collect the user's input, we must remember to validate it. Listing 6.26 shows the Simulation class as it now stands.

**listing
6.26**

```
//****************************************************************
// Simulation.java          Author: Lewis/Loftus/Cocking
//
// The class used to control the simulation of the bumper car arena.
//****************************************************************

import java.util.Random;
import java.util.ListIterator;
import java.util.ArrayList;

public class Simulation
{
    private Arena arena;

    public Simulation(int numCars, int arenaNSsize, int arenaEWsize)
    {
        arena = new Arena(arenaNSsize, arenaEWsize);

        Random randomGen = new Random();
        Car car;
        Driver driver;
        int ns, ew;

        // Create the given number of cars and place them in the arena.
        for (int k=0; k < numCars; k++)
        {
            // Create a car-driver pair with a randomly-generated
            // position in the arena.
            ns = randomGen.nextInt(arenaNSsize);
            ew = randomGen.nextInt(arenaEWsize);
            // Assume that numCars < arenaNSsize * arenaEWsize
            // If not, the loop below would go on forever once the
            // arena is filled!
            while (arena.occupiedBy(ns, ew) != Arena.EMPTY)
            {
                ns = randomGen.nextInt(arenaNSsize);
                ew = randomGen.nextInt(arenaEWsize);
            }
```

```
listing
    6.26  continued

            car = new Car(arena);
            // Turn the car to face a random direction
            car.turn(Direction.randomDirection());
            driver = new RandomDriver(car);
            car.setDriver(driver);
            arena.addCar(car, ns, ew);
        }
    }

    //-----------------------------------------------------------
    // Perform one step in the simulation.
    //-----------------------------------------------------------
    public void step()
    {
        arena.step();
    }

    //-----------------------------------------------------------
    // Prints the bump count totals for all the drivers in a
    // textual format.
    //-----------------------------------------------------------
    public void printBumpCounts()
    {
        // not implemented yet
    }
}
```

exercises

1. Suppose the number of cars in the simulation was going to be randomly generated. Given `arenaNSsize` and `arenaEWsize`, write code that will generate this random number. There should be at least one car and no more than can fit in the arena.

2. Instead of placing the cars randomly we could have asked the user where to place each car. Discuss the advantages and disadvantages of these two approaches.

3. Suppose we were using parallel `arena` and `position` arrays. Write pseudocode that checks to see if a particular position is occupied or not.

6.9   polygons and polylines

Arrays can help you draw complex shapes. A polygon, for example, is a multisided shape that is defined in Java using a series of (*x, y*) coordinates. Arrays are often used to store the list of coordinates.

Polygons are drawn using methods of the `Graphics` class, something like the way we draw rectangles and ovals. Like other shapes, a polygon can be drawn filled or unfilled. The methods used to draw a polygon are called `drawPolygon` and `fillPolygon`. Both of these methods are overloaded. One version uses arrays of integers to define the polygon, and the other uses an object of the `Polygon` class to define the polygon. We discuss the `Polygon` class later in this section.

In the version that uses arrays, the `drawPolygon` and `fillPolygon` methods take three parameters. The first is an array of integers representing the *x* coordinates of the points in the polygon. The second is an array of integers representing the *y* coordinates of those points. The third is an integer that indicates how many points are used from each of the two arrays. The first two parameters represent the (*x, y*) coordinates of the corners of the polygon.

> **key concept**
> A polygon is always a closed shape. The last point is automatically connected back to the first one.

A polygon is always closed. A line is always drawn from the last point in the list to the first point in the list.

> **key concept**
> A polyline is similar to a polygon except that a polyline is not a closed shape.

Like a polygon, a *polyline* contains a series of points connected by line segments. But in polylines the first and last coordinates are not automatically connected. Since a polyline is not closed, it cannot be filled. Therefore there is only one method, called `drawPolyline`, used to draw a polyline.

The first two parameters of the `drawPolyline` method are both arrays of integers. Taken together, the first two parameters represent the (*x, y*) coordinates of the end points of the line segments. The third parameter is the number of points in the coordinate list.

The program shown in Listing 6.27 uses polygons to draw a rocket. The arrays called `xRocket` and `yRocket` define the points of the polygon that make up the main body of the rocket. The first point in the arrays is the upper tip of the rocket, and they go clockwise from there. The `xWindow` and `yWindow` arrays hold the points for the window in the rocket. Both the rocket and the window are filled polygons.

listing
    6.27

```java
//********************************************************************
//  Rocket.java        Author: Lewis/Loftus/Cocking
//
//  Demonstrates the use of polygons and polylines.
//********************************************************************

import javax.swing.JApplet;
import java.awt.*;

public class Rocket extends JApplet
{
   private final int APPLET_WIDTH = 200;
   private final int APPLET_HEIGHT = 200;

   private int[] xRocket = {100, 120, 120, 130, 130, 70, 70, 80, 80};
   private int[] yRocket = {15, 40, 115, 125, 150, 150, 125, 115, 40};

   private int[] xWindow = {95, 105, 110, 90};
   private int[] yWindow = {45, 45, 70, 70};

   private int[] xFlame = {70, 70, 75, 80, 90, 100, 110, 115, 120,
                           130, 130};
   private int[] yFlame = {155, 170, 165, 190, 170, 175, 160, 185,
                           160, 175, 155};

   //--------------------------------------------------------------
   //  Sets up the basic applet environment.
   //--------------------------------------------------------------
   public void init()
   {
      setBackground (Color.black);
      setSize (APPLET_WIDTH, APPLET_HEIGHT);
   }

   //--------------------------------------------------------------
   //  Draws a rocket using polygons and polylines.
   //--------------------------------------------------------------
   public void paint (Graphics page)
   {
      page.setColor (Color.cyan);
      page.fillPolygon (xRocket, yRocket, xRocket.length);

      page.setColor (Color.gray);
      page.fillPolygon (xWindow, yWindow, xWindow.length);
```

listing
    6.27   continued

```
      page.setColor (Color.red);
      page.drawPolyline (xFlame, yFlame, xFlame.length);
   }
}
```

display

Applet started.

The `xFlame` and `yFlame` arrays define the points of a polyline that look like flames shooting out of the tail of the rocket. Because it is a polyline, and not a polygon, the flame is not closed or filled.

the Polygon class

A polygon can also be defined using an object of the `Polygon` class, which is defined in the `java.awt` package of the Java standard class library. Two versions of the overloaded `drawPolygon` and `fillPolygon` methods take a single `Polygon` object as a parameter.

A `Polygon` object encapsulates the coordinates of the polygon sides. The constructors of the `Polygon` class allow the creation of an empty polygon, or one defined by arrays of integers representing the point coordinates. The

`Polygon` class contains methods to add points to the polygon and to determine whether a given point is inside the polygon shape. It also has methods that create a bounding rectangle for the polygon, as well as a method to translate all of the points in the polygon to another position. Figure 6.14 lists these methods.

6.10 other button components

In the graphics track of Chapter 5, we introduced the basics of graphical user interface (GUI) construction: components, events, and listeners. Recall that the `JButton` class represents a push button. When the button is pushed, an action event is generated and a listener responds. Now let's look at buttons of a different kind.

```
Polygon ()
    Constructor: Creates an empty polygon.

Polygon (int[] xpoints, int[] ypoints, int npoints)
    Constructor: Creates a polygon using the (x, y) coordinate pairs
    in corresponding entries of xpoints and ypoints    .

void addPoint (int x, int y)
    Appends the specified point to this polygon.

boolean contains (int x, int y)
    Returns true if the specified point is contained in this polygon.

boolean contains (Point p)
    Returns true if the specified point is contained in this polygon.

Rectangle getBounds ()
    Gets the bounding rectangle for this polygon.

void translate (int deltaX, int deltaY)
    Translates the vertices of this polygon by deltaX along the x axis
    and deltaY along the y axis.
```

figure 6.14   Some methods of the `Polygon` class

check boxes

A check box allows the user to set the status of a boolean condition.

A *check box* is a button that can be on or off, checked or unchecked, indicating that a boolean condition is set or unset. For example, a check box labeled `Collate` might indicate whether a print job should be collated. When check boxes appear together, each check box operates independently. That is, each can be set to on or off and the status of one does not influence the others.

The program in Listing 6.28 displays two check boxes and a label. The check boxes determine whether the text of the label is displayed in bold, italic, both, or neither. Any combination of bold and italic is valid. For example, both check boxes could be checked (on), in which case the text is both bold and italic. If neither is checked, the text of the label is displayed in a plain style.

The GUI for the `StyleOptions` program is in the `StyleGUI` class shown in Listing 6.29. This organization is different than what we used in the `Fahrenheit` program in Chapter 5. In this example, the frame is created in the `main` method. The `StyleGUI` object creates a panel for the label and check boxes. The panel is returned to the `main` method using a call to `getPanel` and is added to the application frame.

A check box is represented by the `JCheckBox` class. When a check box changes from on (checked) to off (unchecked), or vice versa, it generates an *item event*. The `ItemListener` interface has one method, called `itemStateChanged`. In this example, we use the same listener object to handle both check boxes.

Listing 6.29 also uses the `Font` class, which represents a particular *character font*. A `Font` object has a font name, font style, and font size. We are using the Helvetica font in this program. The style of a Java font can be plain, bold, italic, or bold and italic combined. The check boxes in our GUI are set up to change the characteristics of our font style.

The style of a font is represented as an integer, and integer constants defined in the `Font` class are used to represent the various possibilities for the style. The constant `PLAIN` is used to represent a plain style. The constants `BOLD` and `ITALIC` are used to represent bold and italic, respectively. The sum of the `BOLD` and `ITALIC` constants indicates a style that is both bold and italic.

The `itemStateChanged` method of the listener determines what the revised style should be when one of the check boxes changes the style to plain. Then each check box is consulted in turn using the `isSelected` method, which returns a boolean value. First, if the bold check box is

```
listing
   6.28
```

```
//*****************************************************************
//   StyleOptions.java        Author: Lewis/Loftus/Cocking
//
//   Demonstrates the use of check boxes.
//*****************************************************************

import javax.swing.*;

public class StyleOptions
{
    //--------------------------------------------------------------
    //   Creates and presents the program frame.
    //--------------------------------------------------------------
    public static void main (String[] args)
    {
        JFrame styleFrame = new JFrame ("Style Options");
        styleFrame.setDefaultCloseOperation (JFrame.EXIT_ON_CLOSE);

        StyleGUI gui = new StyleGUI();
        styleFrame.getContentPane().add (gui.getPanel());

        styleFrame.pack();
        styleFrame.show();
    }
}
```

display

selected (checked), then the style is set to bold. Then, if the italic check box is selected, the ITALIC constant is added to the style variable. Finally, the font of the label is set to a new font with its revised style.

Note that it doesn't matter which check box was clicked first. Both check boxes are processed by the same listener. It also doesn't matter whether the check box was changed from on to off or vice versa. The listener looks at both check boxes if either is changed.

listing
    6.29

```java
//********************************************************************
//  StyleGUI.java        Author: Lewis/Loftus/Cocking
//
//  Represents the user interface for the StyleOptions program.
//********************************************************************

import javax.swing.*;
import java.awt.*;
import java.awt.event.*;

public class StyleGUI
{
   private final int WIDTH = 300, HEIGHT = 100, FONT_SIZE = 36;
   private JLabel saying;
   private JCheckBox bold, italic;
   private JPanel primary;

   //-----------------------------------------------------------------
   //  Sets up a panel with a label and some check boxes that
   //  control the style of the label's font.
   //-----------------------------------------------------------------
   public StyleGUI()
   {
      saying = new JLabel ("Say it with style!");
      saying.setFont (new Font ("Helvetica", Font.PLAIN, FONT_SIZE));

      bold = new JCheckBox ("Bold");
      bold.setBackground (Color.cyan);
      italic = new JCheckBox ("Italic");
      italic.setBackground (Color.cyan);

      StyleListener listener = new StyleListener();
      bold.addItemListener (listener);
      italic.addItemListener (listener);

      primary = new JPanel();
      primary.add (saying);
      primary.add (bold);
      primary.add (italic);
      primary.setBackground (Color.cyan);
      primary.setPreferredSize (new Dimension(WIDTH, HEIGHT));
   }
```

listing
6.29 continued

```
//------------------------------------------------------------
//   Returns the primary panel containing the GUI.
//------------------------------------------------------------
public JPanel getPanel()
{
    return primary;
}


//*************************************************************
//   Represents the listener for both check boxes.
//*************************************************************
private class StyleListener implements ItemListener
{
    //------------------------------------------------------------
    //   Updates the style of the label font style.
    //------------------------------------------------------------
    public void itemStateChanged (ItemEvent event)
    {
        int style = Font.PLAIN;

        if (bold.isSelected())
            style = Font.BOLD;

        if (italic.isSelected())
            style += Font.ITALIC;

        saying.setFont (new Font ("Helvetica", style, FONT_SIZE));
    }
}
}
```

radio buttons

A *radio button* is used with other radio buttons to provide a set of mutually exclusive options. That means you can only pick one of the buttons. Unlike a check box, a radio button is not useful by itself. It has meaning only when it is used with one or more other radio buttons. Only one option out of the group is valid. One and only one button of the group of radio buttons can be selected (on) at a time. When a radio button from the group is pushed, the other button in the group that is currently on is automatically off.

> **key concept**
>
> Radio buttons work together as a group, giving the user mutually exclusive options. When one button is selected, the currently selected button turns off.

The term "radio buttons" comes from the way the buttons worked on an old-fashioned car radio. At any point, one button was pushed to pick a station; when another button was pushed, the current one automatically popped out. This makes sense if you think about it: You can't listen to two stations at the same time.

The QuoteOptions program, shown in Listing 6.30, displays a label and a group of radio buttons. The radio buttons determine which quote is dis-

listing
    6.30

```
//********************************************************************
//   QuoteOptions.java        Author: Lewis/Loftus/Cocking
//
//   Demonstrates the use of radio buttons.
//********************************************************************

import javax.swing.*;

public class QuoteOptions
{
   //-----------------------------------------------------------------
   //  Creates and presents the program frame.
   //-----------------------------------------------------------------
   public static void main (String[] args)
   {
      JFrame quoteFrame = new JFrame ("Quote Options");
      quoteFrame.setDefaultCloseOperation (JFrame.EXIT_ON_CLOSE);

      QuoteGUI gui = new QuoteGUI();
      quoteFrame.getContentPane().add (gui.getPanel());

      quoteFrame.pack();
      quoteFrame.show();
   }
}
```

display

played in the label. Because only one of the quotes can be displayed at a time, using radio buttons makes sense. For example, if the Comedy radio button is selected, the comedy quote is displayed in the label. If the Philosophy button is then pressed, the Comedy radio button is automatically turned off and the comedy quote is replaced by a philosophical one.

This program is something like the StyleOptions program from the previous section. The label and radio buttons are displayed on a panel defined in the QuoteGUI class, shown in Listing 6.31. A radio button is represented by the JRadioButton class. Because the radio buttons in a set work together, the ButtonGroup class is used to define a set of related radio buttons.

Note that each button is added to the button group, and also that each button is added individually to the panel. A ButtonGroup object is not a container to organize and display components like a panel or a frame; it is simply a way to define the group of radio buttons that work together. The ButtonGroup object makes sure that the currently selected radio button is turned off when another button in the group is selected.

A radio button produces an action event when it is selected. The actionPerformed method of the listener first determines the source of the event using the getSource method, and then compares it to each of the three radio buttons in turn. The text of the label is set to the quote that matches the button.

Unlike push buttons, both check boxes and radio buttons are *toggle buttons*, meaning that at any time they are either on or off. The difference is in how they are used. Independent options (choose any combination) are controlled with check boxes. Dependent options (choose one of a set) are controlled with radio buttons. If there is only one option, a check box can be used by itself. As we mentioned earlier, a radio button makes sense only in a group with other radio buttons.

Also note that check boxes and radio buttons produce different types of events. A check box produces an *item event* and a radio button produces an *action event*. This is because the buttons work differently. A check box produces an event when it is selected or deselected. A radio button, on the other hand, only produces an event when it is selected.

listing
6.31

```java
//********************************************************************
//  QuoteGUI.java        Author: Lewis/Loftus/Cocking
//
//  Represents the user interface for the QuoteOptions program.
//********************************************************************

import javax.swing.*;
import java.awt.*;
import java.awt.event.*;

public class QuoteGUI
{
   private final int WIDTH = 300, HEIGHT = 100;
   private JPanel primary;
   private JLabel quote;
   private JRadioButton comedy, philosophy, carpentry;
   private String comedyQuote = "Take my wife, please.";
   private String philosophyQuote = "I think, therefore I am.";
   private String carpentryQuote = "Measure twice. Cut once.";

   //-----------------------------------------------------------------
   //  Sets up a panel with a label and a set of radio buttons
   //  that control its text.
   //-----------------------------------------------------------------
   public QuoteGUI()
   {
      quote = new JLabel (comedyQuote);
      quote.setFont (new Font ("Helvetica", Font.BOLD, 24));

      comedy = new JRadioButton ("Comedy", true);
      comedy.setBackground (Color.green);
      philosophy = new JRadioButton ("Philosophy");
      philosophy.setBackground (Color.green);
      carpentry = new JRadioButton ("Carpentry");
      carpentry.setBackground (Color.green);

      ButtonGroup group = new ButtonGroup();
      group.add (comedy);
      group.add (philosophy);
      group.add (carpentry);

      QuoteListener listener = new QuoteListener();
      comedy.addActionListener (listener);
      philosophy.addActionListener (listener);
      carpentry.addActionListener (listener);
```

listing
6.31 continued

```
    primary = new JPanel();
    primary.add (quote);
    primary.add (comedy);
    primary.add (philosophy);
    primary.add (carpentry);
    primary.setBackground (Color.green);
    primary.setPreferredSize (new Dimension(WIDTH, HEIGHT));
  }

  //-----------------------------------------------------------------
  //  Returns the primary panel containing the GUI.
  //-----------------------------------------------------------------
  public JPanel getPanel()
  {
    return primary;
  }

  //*****************************************************************
  //  Represents the listener for all radio buttons
  //*****************************************************************
  private class QuoteListener implements ActionListener
  {
    //-----------------------------------------------------------
    //  Sets the text of the label depending on which radio
    //  button was pressed.
    //-----------------------------------------------------------
    public void actionPerformed (ActionEvent event)
    {
      Object source = event.getSource();

      if (source == comedy)
        quote.setText (comedyQuote);
      else
        if (source == philosophy)
          quote.setText (philosophyQuote);
        else
          quote.setText (carpentryQuote);
    }
  }
}
```

summary of
key concepts

▸ An array of size N is indexed from 0 to $N - 1$.

▸ In Java, an array is an object. Memory space for the array elements is reserved by instantiating the array using the new operator.

▸ Bounds checking makes sure that an index used to refer to an array element is in range. The Java index operator does automatic bounds checking.

▸ An initializer list can be used instead of using the new operator to instantiate an array object. The size of the array and its initial values are determined by the initializer list.

▸ An entire array can be passed as a parameter, making the formal parameter an alias of the original array.

▸ Command-line arguments are stored in an array of String objects and are passed to the main method.

▸ Instantiating an array of objects only reserves room to store references to the objects. The objects must be instantiated separately.

▸ Selection sort and insertion sort define the steps for putting a list of values in order.

▸ Selection sort works by putting each value in its final position, one at a time.

▸ Swapping means exchanging two values. Swapping requires three assignment statements.

▸ Insertion sort works by inserting each value into an already sorted list.

▸ The efficiency of sorting algorithms is measured by the number of comparisons they have to do to perform the sort.

▸ Both selection sort and insertion sort algorithms are of order n^2. Other sorts are more efficient.

▸ An ArrayList object is like an array, but it changes size as needed, and elements can be inserted and removed.

▸ ArrayList processing can be inefficient depending on how it is used.

▸ A polygon is always a closed shape. The last point is automatically connected back to the first one.

▸ A polyline is like a polygon except that a polyline is not a closed shape.

▸ A check box lets the user pick between two or more choices.

▸ Radio buttons work as a group, and ask the user to pick one and only one of a set of choices. When the user picks one button, the currently selected button is toggled off.

self-review questions

6.1   Explain array bounds checking. What happens when a Java array is indexed with an invalid value?

6.2   Describe how an array is created. When is memory reserved for the array?

6.3   What is an off-by-one error? How does it relate to arrays?

6.4   What does an array initializer list do?

6.5   Can an entire array be passed as a parameter? How is this done?

6.6   How is an array of objects created?

6.7   What is a command-line argument?

6.8   What are parallel arrays?

6.9   Compare and contrast a sequential search and a binary search.

6.10 Which is better: selection sort or insertion sort? Explain.

6.11 What is hashing?

6.12 What are the advantages of using an `ArrayList` object instead of an array? What are the disadvantages?

6.13 What is a polyline? How do we create one?

6.14 Compare and contrast check boxes and radio buttons.

multiple choice

6.1. Given the declarations

```
int[] a = new int[10];
int[] b;
```

which of the following will cause an
`ArrayIndexOutOfBoundsException`?

a. `a[0] = 10;`

b. `a[6] = 10;`

c. `b[0] = 10;`

d. `b = a;`

e. none of the above

6.2 Which of the following code segments correctly creates a four-element array and initializes it so that each element stores its index? For example, the element stored at index 2 is 2.

I

```
int[] a = {0, 1, 2, 3};
```

II

```
int[] a = {1, 2, 3, 4};
```

III

```
int[] a = new int[4];
    for (int i=0; i < 4; i++)
        a[i] = i;
```

a. I only

b. I and II

c. II and III

d. I and III

e. I, II, and III

6.3 Which of the following loops will reach every element in the array a?

a. `for (int j=0; j < a.length+1; j++)`

b. `for (int j=0; j < a.length; j++)`

c. `for (int j=1; j < a.length; j++)`

d. `for (int j=1; j <= a.length; j++)`

e. `for (int j=0; j <= a.length; j++)`

6.4 Assuming all variables are declared correctly, which of the following swaps the values of x and y?

I

```
x = y;
y = x;
```

II

```
tmp = x;
y = x;
x = tmp;
```

III

```
tmp = x;
x = y;
y = tmp;
```

a. I only

b. II only

c. III only

d. II and III

e. I, II, and III

6.5 When looking for an element in a sorted array, which algorithm is most efficient?

a. sequential search

b. binary search

c. selection sort

d. insertion sort

e. They are all equally efficient.

6.6 Which of the following complexities is the *least* efficient for large values of n?

a. $\log n$

b. $n \log n$

c. n

d. n^2

e. 2^n

6.7   In which of the following situations must we use an `ArrayList` instead of an array?

a. We will be storing primitive data.

b. We will be storing objects.

c. Our array must be able to change size.

d. We need to be able to sort the data.

e. We need to be able to perform calculations on the data.

6.8   Suppose we are adding up all the values in an array called a, using a `for` loop with loop index k. Which statement, if placed in the body of the loop, will correctly add the current element to the sum?

a. `sum += a[k];`

b. `sum = a[k];`

c. `sum += k;`

d. `sum = k;`

e. `sum += k[a];`

6.9   Suppose an `ArrayList`, `list`, stores `String` objects. Which expression gives the length of the string at index 0?

a. `list[0].length()`

b. `list.get(0).length()`

c. `((String)list).get(0).length()`

d. `((String)list.get(0)).length()`

e. `(String)(list.get(0).length())`

6.10 Suppose a hash table is implemented with an array of size 13. Which of the following would be the best hash function for storing the integer num in the hash table?

a. `num`

b. `num + 13`

c. `num % 13`

d. `num + 3`

e. `num % 3`

true/false

6.1   An array in Java is an object.

6.2   When an array is passed as a parameter and changed inside the method, the changes will be gone when the method returns.

6.3   An array in Java can change size as needed.

6.4   The index of the last element in the array a is `a.length` − 1.

6.5   An initializer list can be used only when an array is first declared.

6.6   When an array of objects is declared, the objects themselves are also created.

6.7   Since a binary search is more efficient, there is never any reason to use a linear search.

6.8. Selection sort and insertion sort both have time complexity $O(n^2)$.

6.9   A hash function matches a data element to a hash code that can be used as an index in an array.

6.10 An algorithm that is $O(n \log n)$ is probably more efficient than one that is $O(n^2)$.

short answer

6.1   Which of the following are valid declarations? Which instantiate an array object? Explain your answers.

```
int primes = {2, 3, 4, 5, 7, 11};
double[] elapsedTimes = {11.47, 12.04, 11.72, 13.88};
int[] scores = int[30];
int[] primes = new {2,3,5,7,11};
int[] scores = new int[30];
char[] grades = {'a', 'b', 'c', 'd', 'f'};
char[] grades = new char[];
```

6.2   Describe two programs that would be difficult to implement without using arrays.

6.3 Describe the problem in the following code. What changes would fix the problem?

```
int[] numbers = {3, 2, 3, 6, 9, 10, 12, 32, 3, 12, 6};
for (int count = 1; count <= numbers.length; count++)
    System.out.println (numbers[count]);
```

6.4 Write an array declaration and any necessary supporting classes to represent the following statements:

a. students' names for a class of 25 students

b. students' test grades for a class of 40 students

c. credit-card transactions that contain a transaction number, a store name, and a charge

d. students' names for a class and homework grades for each student

e. for each employee of the L&L International Corporation: the employee number, hire date, and the amount of the last five raises

6.5 Write a method called `sumArray` that accepts an array of floating point values and returns the sum of the values stored in the array.

6.6 Write a method called `switchThem` that accepts two integer arrays as parameters and switches the contents of the arrays. Take into account that the arrays may be different sizes.

6.7 Describe a program that would use the `ArrayList` class instead of arrays. Describe a program that would use arrays instead of the `ArrayList` class. Explain your choices.

6.8 Explain what would happen if the radio buttons used in the `QuoteOptions` program were not organized into a `ButtonGroup` object. Change the program to test your answer.

programming projects

6.1 Design and implement an application that reads a number of integers that are in the range 0 to 50 inclusive and counts how many times each one is entered. After all input has been processed, print all of the values, with the number of times each one was entered.

6.2   Change the program from Programming Project 6.1 so that it works for numbers in the range between –25 and 25.

6.3   Rewrite the `Sorts` class so that both sorting algorithms put the values in descending order. Create a driver class with a `main` method that calls the new versions of the methods.

6.4   Design and implement an application that reads a set of values in the range 1 to 100 from the user and then creates a chart showing how often the values appeared. The chart should look like the one shown here. It shows how many values fell in the range 1 to 10, 11 to 20, and so on. Print one asterisk for each value entered.

```
1   -  10  | * * * * *
11  -  20  | * *
21  -  30  | * * * * * * * * * * * * * * * * * *
31  -  40  |
41  -  50  | * * *
51  -  60  | * * * * * * * *
61  -  70  | * *
71  -  80  | * * * * *
81  -  90  | * * * * * * *
91  - 100  | * * * * * * * *
```

6.5   The lines of asterisks in Programming Project 6.4 will be too long if a lot of values are entered. Change the program so that it prints an asterisk for every five values in each category. Ignore leftovers. For example, if a category had 17 values, print three asterisks in that row. If a category had 4 values, do not print any asterisks in that row.

6.6   The L&L Bank can handle up to 30 customers who have savings accounts. Design and implement a program that manages the accounts. Keep track of key information and let each customer make deposits and withdrawals. Produce error messages for invalid transactions. *Hint*: You may want to base your accounts on the `Account` class from Chapter 4. Also provide a method to add 3 percent interest to all accounts whenever the method is invoked.

6.7   Modify the `GradeRange` program (Listing 6.5) from this chapter so that it doesn't use parallel arrays. Instead, design a new class called `Grade` that stores both the grade string and its cutoff value (the lowest score for that grade). Set both values using the

Grade constructor and provide methods that return the values. In the main method of the new GradeRange program, fill a single array with Grade objects, and then produce the same output as the original GradeRange program did.

6.8   The programming projects of Chapter 4 discussed a Card class that represents a standard playing card. Create a class called DeckOfCards that stores 52 objects of the Card class. Include methods to shuffle the deck, deal a card, and report the number of cards left in the deck. The shuffle method should assume you have a full deck. Create a driver class with a main method that deals each card from a shuffled deck, printing each card as it is dealt.

6.9   Use the Question class from Chapter 5 to define a Quiz class. A quiz can be composed of up to 25 questions. Define the add method of the Quiz class to add a question to a quiz. Define the giveQuiz method of the Quiz class to present each question in turn to the user, accept an answer for each one, and keep track of the results. Define a class called QuizTime with a main method that chooses questions for a quiz, presents the quiz to the user, collects and checks the answers, and prints the final results.

6.10 Change your answer to Programming Project 6.10 so that the quiz questions are ordered by how hard they are. Overload the giveQuiz method so that it accepts two integer parameters that specify the minimum and maximum difficulty levels for the quiz questions and only shows the user questions in that range. Change the main method to match this feature.

6.11 Change the Tunes program (Listing 6.7) so that it keeps the CDs sorted by title. Use the general object sort defined in the Sorts class from this chapter.

6.12 Change the Sorts class to include an overloaded version of the SelectionSort method that performs a general object sort. Change the SortPhoneList program to test the new sort.

6.13 Design and implement an applet that displays a graph of the processing of a selection sort. Use bars to represent the values being sorted. Display the set of bars after each swap. Put a delay in the processing of the sort to give the user a chance to see how the order of the values changes.

6.14 Repeat Programming Project 6.13 using an insertion sort.

6.15 Design a class that represents a star. Use a filled polygon to draw the star. Design and implement an applet that draws 10 stars of random sizes in random locations.

6.16 Design and implement an applet that draws a checkerboard with five red and eight black checkers on it. Store the checkerboard as a two-dimensional array.

answers to self-review questions

6.1 The index operator makes sure that the value of an index is greater than or equal to zero and less than the size of the array. If it is not, an `ArrayIndexOutOfBoundsException` is thrown.

6.2 An array is created like any other object. First we name the array. We then instantiate the array itself, which reserves memory space to store the array elements. The only difference between a regular object instantiation and an array instantiation is the bracket syntax.

6.3 An off-by-one error happens when a reference to an index is off by one. These errors often happen because we go past the boundary of the array. Off-by-one errors come up in array processing because indexes begin at zero and run to one less than the size of the array.

6.4 An array initializer list is used when an array is created, to set up the initial values of its elements. An initializer list instantiates the array object, so the `new` operator is needed.

6.5 An entire array can be passed as a parameter. Because an array is an object, a reference to the array is passed to the method. Any changes made to the array elements will be seen outside the method.

6.6 An array of objects is really an array of object references. The array itself must be instantiated, and the objects that are stored in the array must be created separately.

6.7 A command-line argument is data that is included on the command line when the interpreter is invoked to execute the program. Command-line arguments are another way to provide input. They are accessed using the array of strings that is passed into the `main` method as a parameter.

6.8 Parallel arrays are two or more arrays whose elements are related in some way. Because parallel arrays can easily get out of synch, it is often better to create a single array of objects that encapsulate the related elements.

6.9   Sequential and binary searches look for an element in an array. A sequential search starts with the first element and looks at each element in turn. A binary search is more efficient than a sequential search but it only works on sorted data.

6.10 Selection sort and insertion sort are generally equally efficient, because they both take about n^2 number of comparisons to sort a list of n numbers, giving them $O(n^2)$ time efficiency. Selection sort, though, generally makes fewer swaps. Several sorting algorithms are more efficient than either of these.

6.11 Hashing is a technique for efficiently storing and retrieving data in an array. A hash function matches each data value to a hash code that tells us where the value is stored in the array.

6.12 An `ArrayList` keeps the indexes of its objects continuous as they are added and removed, and an `ArrayList` expands as needed. In addition, an `ArrayList` is implemented so that it stores references to the `Object` class, so any object can be stored in it. A disadvantage of the `ArrayList` class is that it copies a lot of data as it inserts and deletes elements, which is inefficient.

6.13 A polyline is a series of points connected by lines that do not make a closed figure. The `drawPolyline` method takes three parameters. The first is an array of integers that represent the x coordinates of the points. The second is an array of integers that represent the y coordinates of the points. The third parameter is a single integer that indicates the number of points to be used from the arrays.

6.14 Both check boxes and radio buttons are either on or off. However, radio buttons work as a group in which only one button can be "on" at a time. Check boxes can be used alone or in a set in which any combination of off and on is valid.

This chapter explains inheritance, a basic technique for organizing and creating classes. It is a simple but powerful idea that influences the way we design object-oriented software. Inheritance helps us to reuse classes in other situations and programs. We explore how we can use classes to form inheritance hierarchies and create polymorphic references. We review Java interfaces and discuss how inheritance affects graphical user interfaces (GUIs) in Java.

chapter
objectives

- Derive new classes from existing ones.

- Explain how inheritance supports software reuse.

- Add and modify methods in child classes.

- Discuss how to design class hierarchies.

- Define polymorphism and how it can be done.

- Discuss the use of inheritance in Java GUI frameworks.

- Examine and use the GUI component class hierarchy.

7.0 creating subclasses

In Chapter 4 we learned that a class is like a blueprint for an object. A class lays out the characteristics and behaviors of an object but it does not reserve memory space for variables (unless those variables are `static`). Classes are the floor plan, and objects are the finished house.

Many houses can be created from the same blueprint. They are basically the same house in different locations with different people living in them. But suppose you want a house that has some different or additional features. You start with the same basic blueprint but make a few changes to suit your needs. Many housing developments are created this way. The houses in the development have the same layout, but they have unique features. For instance, some might have a fireplace or full basement while others do not, or an attached garage instead of a carport.

It's likely that the housing developer hired an architect to create a single blueprint for the basic design, then a series of new blueprints that include variations designed to appeal to different buyers. The act of creating the new blueprints was simple because they all begin with the same structure.

This is the basic idea of inheritance, a powerful software development technique in object-oriented programming.

derived classes

> **key concept**
> Inheritance is how a new class is created from an existing one.

Inheritance is how a new class is created from an existing class. The new class automatically contains some or all of the variables and methods in the original class. Then, the programmer can add new variables and methods to the derived class or change the inherited ones.

Inheritance lets us create new classes faster, easier, and cheaper than by writing them from scratch. At the heart of inheritance is the idea of *software reuse*. By using existing software we are reusing the design, implementation, and testing done on the existing software.

> **key concept**
> One purpose of inheritance is to reuse existing software.

Keep in mind that the word *class* comes from the idea of classifying groups of objects with similar characteristics. Classification often uses levels of classes that relate to each other. For example, all mammals share certain characteristics: They are warmblooded, have hair, and bear live offspring. Horses are a subset of mammals. All horses are mammals and have all of the characteristics of mammals, but they also have unique features that make them different from other mammals.

In software terms, a class called `Mammal` would have certain variables and methods that describe the state and behavior of mammals. A `Horse` class created from the `Mammal` class would automatically inherit the variables and methods contained in `Mammal`. The `Horse` class can refer to the inherited variables and methods as if they had been declared locally in that class. New variables and methods can then be added to the `Horse` class to make a horse different from other mammals. Inheritance is like many situations found in the natural world.

> **key concept**
>
> Inherited variables and methods can be used in the derived class as if they had been declared locally.

The original class that is used to create, or *derive*, a new one is called the *parent class, superclass,* or *base class.* The new class is called a *child class,* or *subclass.* Java uses the reserved word `extends` to indicate that a new class is being created from the original class.

When we create a child class from a parent class, we say they have an *is-a relationship.* This means that the new class should be a more specific version of the original. For example, a horse *is a* mammal. Not all mammals are horses, but all horses are mammals.

> **key concept**
>
> Inheritance creates an is-a relationship between all parent and child classes.

Let's look at an example. The program shown in Listing 7.1 instantiates an object of class `Dictionary`, which we created from a class called `Book`. In the `main` method, two methods are invoked through the `Dictionary`

listing 7.1

```
//********************************************************************
//  Words.java        Author: Lewis/Loftus/Cocking
//
//  Demonstrates the use of an inherited method.
//********************************************************************

public class Words
{
   //-----------------------------------------------------------------
   //  Instantiates a derived class and invokes its inherited and
   //  local methods.
   //-----------------------------------------------------------------
   public static void main (String[] args)
   {
      Dictionary webster = new Dictionary ();

      webster.pageMessage();
      webster.definitionMessage();
   }
}
```

output

```
Number of pages: 1500
Number of definitions: 52500
Definitions per page: 35
```

object: one that was declared locally in the `Dictionary` class and one that was inherited from the `Book` class.

The `Book` class (see Listing 7.2) is used to create the `Dictionary` class (see Listing 7.3) using the reserved word `extends` in the header of `Dictionary`. The `Dictionary` class automatically inherits the definition of the `pageMessage` method and the `pages` variable. It is as if the `pageMessage` method and the `pages` variable were declared inside the `Dictionary` class. Note that the `definitionMessage` method refers to the `pages` variable.

Also, note that although the `Book` class is needed to create the definition of `Dictionary`, no `Book` object is ever instantiated in the program. An instance of a child class does not rely on an instance of the parent class.

Inheritance is a one-way street. The `Book` class cannot use variables or methods that are declared explicitly in the `Dictionary` class. For instance, if we created an object from the `Book` class, it could not be used to invoke the `definitionMessage` method. This makes sense because a child class is a more specific version of the parent class. A dictionary has pages because all books have pages; but not all books have definitions like a dictionary does.

listing
   7.2

```
//********************************************************************
//  Book.java        Author: Lewis/Loftus/Cocking
//
//  Represents a book. Used as the parent of a derived class to
//  demonstrate inheritance.
//********************************************************************

public class Book
{
    public int pages = 1500;

    //-----------------------------------------------------------
    //  Prints a message about the pages of this book.
    //-----------------------------------------------------------
    public void pageMessage ()
    {
        System.out.println ("Number of pages: " + pages);
    }
}
```

```
                                listing
                                   7.3

//************************************************************************
//   Dictionary.java         Author: Lewis/Loftus/Cocking
//
//   Represents a dictionary, which is a book. Used to demonstrate
//   inheritance.
//************************************************************************

public class Dictionary extends Book
{
   private int definitions = 52500;

   //----------------------------------------------------------------
   //  Prints a message using both local and inherited values.
   //----------------------------------------------------------------
   public void definitionMessage ()
   {
      System.out.println ("Number of definitions: " + definitions);

      System.out.println ("Definitions per page: " + definitions/pages);
   }
}
```

Inheritance relationships are often shown graphically. Figure 7.1 shows the inheritance relationship between the `Book` and `Dictionary` classes. An arrow points from the child class to the parent class.

Not all variables and methods are inherited in a derivation. The visibility modifiers used to declare the members of a class determine which ones are inherited and which ones are not. So the child class inherits variables and methods that are declared public and does not inherit those that are declared private. The `pageMessage` method and the `pages` variable are inherited by `Dictionary` because they are declared with public visibility. However, when we declare a variable with public visibility so that the new class can use it, we violate the principle of encapsulation. Instead, we should create methods that can use the variable.

> **key concept**
>
> Visibility modifiers determine which variables and methods are inherited. The child class inherits public, but not private, variables and methods.

Each inherited variable or method keeps the effect of its original visibility modifier. For example, the `pageMessage` method is public in the `Books` class, so it is public in the `Dictionary` class too.

Constructors are not inherited in a child class, even though they have public visibility. This is an exception to the rule about public members being inherited. Constructors are special methods that are used to set up a partic-

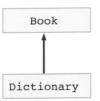

figure 7.1   A class diagram showing an inheritance relationship

ular type of object, so it wouldn't make sense for a class called `Dictionary` to have a constructor called `Book`.

the super reference

The reserved word `super` can be used in a class to refer to its parent class. Using the `super` reference, we can use a parent's members, even if they aren't inherited. Like the `this` reference, what the word `super` refers to depends on the class in which it is used. However, unlike the `this` reference, which refers to a particular instance of a class, `super` is a general reference to the members of the parent class.

One use of the `super` reference is to invoke a parent's constructor. Let's look at an example. Listing 7.4 shows a modification of the original `Words` program shown in Listing 7.1. Like the original version, we use a class called `Book2` (see Listing 7.5) as the parent of the class `Dictionary2` (see Listing 7.6). However, unlike earlier versions of these classes, `Book2` and `Dictionary2` have explicit constructors used to initialize their instance variables. The output of the `Words2` program is the same as it is for the original `Words` program.

The `Dictionary2` constructor takes two integer values as parameters, for the number of pages and definitions in the book. The `Book2` class already has a constructor that sets up the parts of the dictionary that were inherited. But because the constructor is not inherited, we cannot invoke it directly, so we use the `super` reference to get to it in the parent class. The `Dictionary2` constructor then initializes its `definitions` variable.

```
listing
   7.4
```

```
//************************************************************************
//  Words2.java        Author: Lewis/Loftus/Cocking
//
//  Demonstrates the use of the super reference.
//************************************************************************

public class Words2
{
    //-----------------------------------------------------------------
    //  Instantiates a derived class and invokes its inherited and
    //  local methods.
    //-----------------------------------------------------------------
    public static void main (String[] args)
    {
        Dictionary2 webster = new Dictionary2 (1500, 52500);

        webster.pageMessage();
        webster.definitionMessage();
    }
}
```

output

```
Number of pages: 1500
Number of definitions: 52500
Definitions per page: 35
```

A child's constructor calls its parent's constructor. Generally, the first line of a constructor uses the super reference call to a constructor of the parent class. Otherwise Java will automatically make a call to super() at the beginning of the constructor. This way a parent class always initializes its variables before the child class constructor begins to execute. We can only use the super reference to invoke a parent's constructor in the child's constructor. If we do this, the super reference must be the first line of the constructor.

The super reference can also be used to reference other variables and methods defined in the parent's class. We discuss this later in this chapter.

listing
   7.5

```
//************************************************************************
//  Book2.java        Author: Lewis/Loftus/Cocking
//
//  Represents a book. Used as the parent of a dervied class to
//  demonstrate inheritance and the use of the super reference.
//************************************************************************

public class Book2
{
   public int pages;

   //-----------------------------------------------------------------
   //  Sets up the book with the specified number of pages.
   //-----------------------------------------------------------------
   public Book2 (int numPages)
   {
      pages = numPages;
   }

   //-----------------------------------------------------------------
   //  Prints a message about the pages of this book.
   //-----------------------------------------------------------------
   public void pageMessage ()
   {
      System.out.println ("Number of pages: " + pages);
   }
}
```

multiple inheritance

Java's approach to inheritance is called *single inheritance*. This term means that a child class can have only one parent. Some object-oriented languages let a child class have two or more parents. This is called *multiple inheritance*. Multiple inheritance is useful for describing objects that are in between two categories or classes. For example, suppose we had a class Car and a class Truck and we wanted to create a new class called PickupTruck. A pickup truck is somewhat like a car and somewhat like a truck. With single inheritance, we must decide whether it is better to create the new class from Car or Truck. With multiple inheritance, we can create it from both, as shown in Figure 7.2.

Multiple inheritance works well in some situations, but it comes with a price. What if both Truck and Car have methods with the same name?

```
listing
   7.6
```

```
//***********************************************************************
//  Dictionary2.java        Author: Lewis/Loftus/Cocking
//
//  Represents a dictionary, which is a book. Used to demonstrate
//  the use of the super reference.
//***********************************************************************

public class Dictionary2 extends Book2
{
   private int definitions;

   //-------------------------------------------------------------------
   //  Sets up the dictionary with the specified number of pages
   //  (maintained by the Book parent class) and defintions.
   //-------------------------------------------------------------------
   public Dictionary2 (int numPages, int numDefinitions)
   {
      super (numPages);

      definitions = numDefinitions;
   }

   //-------------------------------------------------------------------
   //  Prints a message using both local and inherited values.
   //-------------------------------------------------------------------
   public void definitionMessage ()
   {
      System.out.println ("Number of definitions: " + definitions);

      System.out.println ("Definitions per page: " + definitions/pages);
   }
}
```

Which method would `PickupTruck` inherit? The answer to this question is complicated, and it depends on the rules of the language.

We can't use multiple inheritance in Java, but interfaces can do some of the same things. A Java class can be derived from only one parent class, but it can have many different interfaces. So we can interact with a particular class in particular ways while inheriting the basic information from one parent.

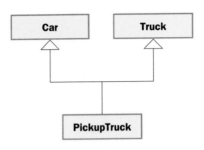

figure 7.2   A class diagram showing multiple inheritance

7.1 overriding methods

When a child class defines a method with the same name and signature as a method in the parent class, we say that the child's version *overrides* the parent's version in favor of its own. Overriding happens often in inheritance.

The program in Listing 7.7 demonstrates method overriding in Java. The `Messages` class contains a `main` method that instantiates two objects: one from class `Thought` and one from class `Advice`. The `Thought` class is the parent of the `Advice` class.

Both the `Thought` class (see Listing 7.8) and the `Advice` class (see Listing 7.9) have a method called `message`. The version of `message` in the `Thought` class is inherited by `Advice`, but `Advice` overrides it with its own version. The new version of the method prints out an entirely different message and then invokes the parent's version of the `message` method using the `super` reference.

Which object invokes a method decides which version of the method is executed. When `message` is invoked using the `parked` object in the `main` method, the `Thought` version of `message` is executed. When `message` is invoked using the `dates` object, the `Advice` version of `message` is executed. This means two objects related by inheritance can use the same names for methods that do the same task in different ways.

```
listing
  7.7
```

```
//**************************************************************
//   Messages.java          Author: Lewis/Loftus/Cocking
//
//   Demonstrates the use of an overridden method.
//**************************************************************

public class Messages
{
   //-----------------------------------------------------------
   //   Instantiates two objects and invokes the message method in each.
   //-----------------------------------------------------------
   public static void main (String[] args)
   {
      Thought parked = new Thought();
      Advice dates = new Advice();

      parked.message();

      dates.message();   // overridden
   }
}
```

output

```
I feel like I'm diagonally parked in a parallel universe.

Warning: Dates in calendar are closer than they appear.

I feel like I'm diagonally parked in a parallel universe.
```

7.2 class hierarchies

A child class can be the parent of its own child class. What's more, many classes can be created from a single parent. We call the "family tree" of classes a *class hierarchy*. Figure 7.3 shows a class hierarchy for the `Mammal` and `Horse` classes.

> **key concept**
> The child of one class can be the parent of one or more other classes, creating a class hierarchy.

There is no limit to the number of children a class can have or to the number of levels a class hierarchy can have. Two children of the same parent are called *siblings*. Although siblings share the characteristics of their common parent, they are not related by inheritance because one is not used to create the other.

```
listing
  7.8

//****************************************************************
//  Thought.java        Author: Lewis/Loftus/Cocking
//
//  Represents a stray thought. Used as the parent of a derived
//  class to demonstrate the use of an overridden method.
//****************************************************************

public class Thought
{
   //-----------------------------------------------------------
   //  Prints a message.
   //-----------------------------------------------------------
   public void message()
   {
      System.out.println ("I feel like I'm diagonally parked in a " +
                          "parallel universe.");

      System.out.println();
   }
}
```

In class hierarchies, common features should be kept as high in the hierarchy as possible. That way, the only characteristics established in a child class will be those that make the class different from its parent and from its siblings. This lets us get the most out of our classes. It also makes changes easier, because when changes are made to the parent, the child classes are affected automatically. Always remember to keep the is-a relationship when building class hierarchies.

The inheritance goes all the way down a heirarchy. That is, a parent passes along a trait to a child class, and that child class passes it along to its children, and so on. An inherited feature might have started in the immediate parent or several levels higher.

There is no single best hierarchy organization for all situations. The decisions you make when you are designing a class hierarchy affect other design decisions, so you must make them carefully.

listing
  7.9

```java
//************************************************************************
//  Advice.java        Author: Lewis/Loftus/Cocking
//
//  Represents a piece of advice. Used to demonstrate the use of an
//  overridden method.
//************************************************************************

public class Advice extends Thought
{
   //-----------------------------------------------------------------
   //  Prints a message. This method overrides the parent's version.
   //  It also invokes the parent's version explicitly using super.
   //-----------------------------------------------------------------
   public void message()
   {
      System.out.println ("Warning: Dates in calendar are closer " +
                          "than they appear.");

      System.out.println();

      super.message();
   }
}
```

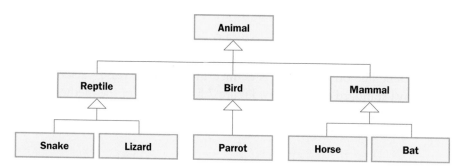

figure 7.3   A class diagram showing a class hierarchy

Figure 7.3 shows animals organized by their major biological classifications, such as `Mammal`, `Bird`, and `Reptile`. In a different situation, the same animals might logically be organized in a different way. For example, as shown in Figure 7.4, the class hierarchy might be organized around a function of the animals, such as their ability to fly. In this case, a `Parrot` class and a `Bat` class would be siblings created from a `FlyingAnimal` class. This class hierarchy is as reasonable as the original one. The needs of the programs that use the classes will determine which is best for the particular situation.

the `Object` class

In Java, all classes are created from the `Object` class. If a class definition doesn't use the `extends` clause to create itself from another class, then that class is automatically created from the `Object` class. This means the following two class definitions are equivalent:

```
class Thing
{
    // whatever
}
```

and

```
class Thing extends Object
{
    // whatever
}
```

Because all classes are created from `Object`, any public method of `Object` can be invoked through any object created in any Java program. The `Object` class is defined in the `java.lang` package of the Java standard class library. Figure 7.5 lists some of the methods of the `Object` class.

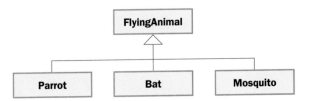

figure 7.4   Another hierarchy for organizing animals

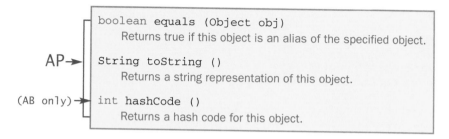

AP→

(AB only)→

```
boolean equals (Object obj)
     Returns true if this object is an alias of the specified object.
String toString ()
     Returns a string representation of this object.
int hashCode ()
     Returns a hash code for this object.
```

figure 7.5   Some methods of the Object class

As it turns out, we've been using Object methods quite often in our examples. The toString method, for instance, is defined in the Object class, so the toString method can be called on any object. As we've seen several times, when a println method is called with an object parameter, toString is called to determine what to print.

The definition for toString provided by the Object class returns a string containing the object's class name followed by a number that is unique for that object. Usually, we override the Object version of toString to fit our own needs. The String class has overridden the toString method so that it returns its stored string value.

The equals method of the Object class is also useful. It decides whether two objects are equal. The definition of the equals method provided by the Object class behaves the same as the == operator: it returns true if the two object references actually refer to the same object (that is, if they are aliases). Classes often override the inherited definition of the equals method in favor of a better definition. For instance, the String class overrides equals so that it returns true only if both strings contain the same characters in the same order.

> **key concept**
>
> The toString and equals methods are defined in the Object class and therefore are inherited by every class in every Java program.

The hashCode method returns a hash code for an object so that any object can be stored in a hash table (see Chapter 6). A class may override the hashCode method to provide a good hash function for the given object type. If two objects are equal according to the equals method, then calling the hashCode method on each should produce the same result.

Listing 7.10 shows the program called Academia with a Student object and a StudentAthlete object. The Student class (see Listing 7.11) is the parent of StudentAthlete (see Listing 7.12). A student athlete is a student who also plays on a sports team for the school.

listing
    7.10

```
//***************************************************************
//  Academia.java        Author: Lewis/Loftus/Cocking
//
//  Demonstrates the use of methods inherited from the Object class.
//***************************************************************

public class Academia
{
    //---------------------------------------------------------------
    //  Creates objects of two student types, prints some information
    //  about them, then checks them for equality.
    //---------------------------------------------------------------
    public static void main (String[] args)
    {
        Student Frank = new Student ("Frank", 5);
        StudentAthlete Suki = new StudentAthlete ("Suki", 4, "Soccer");

        System.out.println (Frank);
        System.out.println ();

        System.out.println (Suki);
        System.out.println ();

        if (! Frank.equals(Suki))
            System.out.println ("These are two different students.");
    }
}
```

output

```
Student name: Frank
Number of courses: 5

Student name: Suki
Number of courses: 4
Sport: Soccer

These are two different students.
```

The StudentAthlete class inherits the method toString that was defined in Student (overriding the version from Object). The StudentAthlete constructor uses the super reference to invoke the constructor of Student, then initializes its own variables.

> **listing**
> **7.11**

```java
//********************************************************************
//  Student.java       Author: Lewis/Loftus/Cocking
//
//  Represents a student. Used to demonstrate inheritance.
//********************************************************************

public class Student
{
   private String name;
   private int numCourses;

   //-----------------------------------------------------------------
   //  Sets up a student with the specified name and number of
   //  courses.
   //-----------------------------------------------------------------
   public Student (String studentName, int courses)
   {
      name = studentName;
      numCourses = courses;
   }

   //-----------------------------------------------------------------
   //  Returns information about this student as a string.
   //-----------------------------------------------------------------
   public String toString()
   {
      String result = "Student name: " + name + "\n";

      result += "Number of courses: " + numCourses;

      return result;
   }
}
```

The StudentAthlete class adds to its inherited definition with a variable representing the student's sport, and it overrides toString (yet again) to print more information. Note that the StudentAthlete version of toString invokes the Student version of toString using the super reference.

listing
      7.12

```java
//********************************************************************
//  StudentAthlete.java        Author: Lewis/Loftus/Cocking
//
//  Represents a student athlete who plays a sports team for the school.
//  Used to demonstrate inheritance.
//********************************************************************

public class StudentAthlete extends Student
{
   private String sport;

   //-----------------------------------------------------------------
   //  Sets up the student athlete using the specified information.
   //-----------------------------------------------------------------
   public StudentAthlete (String studentName, int courses,
                     String sportName)
   {
      super (studentName, courses);

      sport = sportName;
   }

   //-----------------------------------------------------------------
   //  Returns a description of this graduate student as a string.
   //-----------------------------------------------------------------
   public String toString()
   {
      String result = super.toString();

      result += "\nSport: " + sport;

      return result;
   }
}
```

abstract classes

An *abstract class* is a kind of ghost class. It can pass along methods and variables but it can't ever be instantiated itself. That is, we can never create an object of an abstract class. In this sense, an abstract class is like an interface. Unlike interfaces, however, an abstract class can contain methods that are not abstract. It can also contain data declarations other than constants.

A class is declared as abstract by including the `abstract` modifier in the class header. Any class that contains one or more abstract methods must be declared as abstract. In abstract classes (unlike interfaces) the `abstract` modifier must be applied to each abstract method. A class declared as abstract does not have to contain abstract methods.

Abstract classes act as placeholders in a class hierarchy. For example, an abstract class may contain a partial description that is inherited by all of its descendants in the class hierarchy. Its children, which are more specific, fill in the gaps.

> **key concept**
> An abstract class cannot be instantiated. It represents a concept on which other classes can build their definitions.

Consider the class hierarchy shown in Figure 7.6. The `Vehicle` class at the top of the hierarchy may be too general to be used by the application, so we implement it as an abstract class. Still, general ideas that apply to all vehicles can be represented in the `Vehicle` class and are inherited by its child classes. That way, each of its child classes doesn't have to define the same idea. For example, we may say that all vehicles have a particular speed. Therefore we declare a `speed` variable in the `Vehicle` class, and all the cars and boats and planes automatically have that variable because of inheritance. Any change we make to the speed in the abstract class `Vehicle` automatically shows up in all the child classes. Or we may declare an abstract method called `fuelConsumption`, which we're going to use to calculate mileage. The details of the `fuelConsumption` method will be different for each type of vehicle, but the `Vehicle` class establishes that all vehicles consume fuel and it gives us a consistent way to calculate mileage.

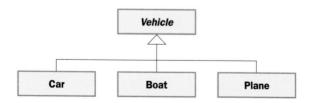

figure 7.6   A `vehicle` class hierarchy

Some things don't apply to all vehicles, so we wouldn't represent them at the `Vehicle` level. For instance, we wouldn't include a variable called `numberOfWheels` in the `Vehicle` class, because boats don't have wheels. The child classes that have wheels can add that at the appropriate level in the hierarchy.

An abstract class can be defined anywhere in a class hierarchy. Usually they're in the upper levels, but we could create an abstract class from a non-abstract parent.

Usually, a child of an abstract class will have a specific definition for an abstract method inherited from its parent. Note that this is just a case of overriding a method, giving a different definition than the one the parent provides. If a child of an abstract class does not give a definition for every abstract method that it inherits from its parent, the child class is also considered abstract.

An abstract method cannot be made `static`. A `static` method can be invoked using the class name without declaring an object of the class. Because abstract methods are never implemented, an abstract `static` method would make no sense.

Choosing which classes and methods to make abstract is an important part of the design process, so you should give them a lot of thought. By using abstract classes wisely, you can create flexible software designs that can be used over and over.

A program called `Pets` is shown in Listing 7.13. In this program, a `Dog` object and a `Snake` object are created and then information about each one is printed out. Both `Dog` and `Snake` inherit from the abstract class `Pet` (Listing 7.14) as shown in Figure 7.7. `Pet` contains a variable `name` and a constructor that initializes the name. It provides the methods `getName` and `toString` along with their implementations. It also declares the abstract methods `speak` and `move`. All pets can speak and move, but in different ways. The `Dog` and `Snake` classes, shown in Listings 7.15 and 7.16 provide implementations of `speak` and `move` for dogs and snakes.

listing
7.13

```java
//********************************************************************
//  Pets.java          Author: Lewis/Loftus/Cocking
//
//  Demonstrates the use of abstract classes.
//********************************************************************

public class Pets
{
   //-----------------------------------------------------------------
   //  Instantiates a dog and a snake object and prints information
   //  about them.
   //-----------------------------------------------------------------
   public static void main (String[] args)
   {
      Dog fido = new Dog("Fido", 45);
      Snake sam = new Snake("Sam", 30);

      System.out.println(fido);
      System.out.println(fido.getName() + " says " + fido.speak());
      System.out.println(fido.move() + " " + fido.getName() + " "
                         + fido.move());

      System.out.println();
      System.out.println(sam);
      System.out.println(sam.getName() + " says " + sam.speak());
      System.out.println(sam.move() + " " + sam.getName() + " "
                         + sam.move());
   }
}
```

output

```
pet Fido is a dog, weighing 45 pounds
Fido says woof
run Fido run

pet Sam is a snake, 30 inches long
Sam says hiss
slither Sam slither
```

listing
     7.14

```
//*****************************************************************
//   Pet.java          Author: Lewis/Loftus/Cocking
//
//   Represents a pet.
//*****************************************************************

public abstract class Pet
{
   private String name;

   //---------------------------------------------------------------
   //   Creates a pet with the given name.
   //---------------------------------------------------------------
   public Pet(String petName)
   {
      name = petName;
   }

   //---------------------------------------------------------------
   //   Returns this pet's name.
   //---------------------------------------------------------------
   public String getName()
   {
      return name;
   }

   //---------------------------------------------------------------
   // Returns a string representation of this pet.
   //---------------------------------------------------------------
   public String toString()
   {
      return "pet " + name;
   }

   //---------------------------------------------------------------
   // This method should return a string indicating what this pet says.
   //---------------------------------------------------------------
   abstract public String speak();

   //---------------------------------------------------------------
   // This method should return a string indicating how this pet moves.
   //---------------------------------------------------------------
   abstract public String move();
}
```

listing
    7.15

```java
//********************************************************************
//  Dog.java         Author: Lewis/Loftus/Cocking
//
//  Represents a dog, which is a pet.
//********************************************************************

public class Dog extends Pet
{
   private int weight;

   //-----------------------------------------------------------------
   // Creates a dog with the given name and weight.
   //-----------------------------------------------------------------
   public Dog(String dogName, int dogWeight)
   {
      super(dogName);
      weight = dogWeight;
   }

   //-----------------------------------------------------------------
   // Returns this dog's weight.
   //-----------------------------------------------------------------
   public int getWeight()
   {
      return weight;
   }

   //-----------------------------------------------------------------
   // Returns a string representation of this dog.
   //-----------------------------------------------------------------
   public String toString()
   {
      return super.toString() + " is a dog, weighing " + weight + " pounds";
   }

   //-----------------------------------------------------------------
   // Returns a string indicating what this dog says.
   //-----------------------------------------------------------------
   public String speak()
   {
      return "woof";
   }

   //-----------------------------------------------------------------
   // Returns a string indicating how this dog moves.
   //-----------------------------------------------------------------
   public String move()
   {
      return "run";
   }
}
```

```
listing
    7.16
```

```java
//********************************************************************
//   Snake.java          Author: Lewis/Loftus/Cocking
//
//   Represents a snake, which is a pet.
//********************************************************************

public class Snake extends Pet
{
   private int length;

   //---------------------------------------------------------------
   // Creates a snake with the given name and length.
   //---------------------------------------------------------------
   public Snake(String snakeName, int snakeLength)
   {
      super(snakeName);
      length = snakeLength;
   }

   //---------------------------------------------------------------
   // Returns this snake's length.
   //---------------------------------------------------------------
   public int getLength()
   {
      return length;
   }

   //---------------------------------------------------------------
   // Returns a string representation of this snake.
   //---------------------------------------------------------------
   public String toString()
   {
      return super.toString() + " is a snake, " + length + " inches long";
   }

   //---------------------------------------------------------------
   // Returns a string indicating what this snake says.
   //---------------------------------------------------------------
   public String speak()
   {
      return "hiss";
   }
   //---------------------------------------------------------------
   // Returns a string indicating how this snake moves.
   //---------------------------------------------------------------
   public String move()
   {
      return "slither";
   }
```

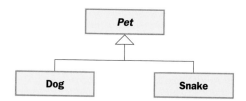

figure 7.7   A class hierarchy of pets

7.3   indirect use of class members

There is another feature of inheritance that we should look at. The visibility modifiers determine whether a variable or method is inherited into a subclass. If a variable or method is inherited, it can be referenced directly in the child class by name, as if it were declared locally in the child class. However, all variables and methods in a parent class exist for an object of a child class, even though they can't be referenced directly. They can, however, be referenced indirectly.

Let's look at an example. The program shown in Listing 7.17 has a `main` method that instantiates a `Pizza` object and invokes a method to figure out how many calories the pizza has per serving.

The `FoodItem` class shown in Listing 7.18 represents a general type of food. The constructor of `FoodItem` accepts the number of grams of fat and the number of servings of that food. The `calories` method returns the number of calories due to fat, which the `caloriesPerServing` method invokes to get the number of fat calories per serving.

The `Pizza` class, shown in Listing 7.19, is created from the `FoodItem` class, but it adds no special function or information. Its constructor calls the constructor of `FoodItem`, using the `super` reference, assuming that there are eight servings per pizza.

Note that the `Pizza` object called `special` in the `main` method is used to invoke the method `caloriesPerServing`, which is a public method of `FoodItem` and is therefore inherited by `Pizza`. Then `caloriesPerServing` calls `calories`, which is `private` and is not inherited by `Pizza`. Next `calories` references the variable `fatGrams` and the constant `CALORIES_PER_GRAM`, which are also `private`.

> **key concept**
>
> All members of a superclass exist for a subclass, but they are not necessarily inherited. Only inherited members can be referenced by name in the subclass.

```
listing
     7.17

//**************************************************************
//  FoodAnalysis.java        Author: Lewis/Loftus/Cocking
//
//  Demonstrates indirect referencing through inheritance.
//**************************************************************

public class FoodAnalysis
{
   //------------------------------------------------------------
   //  Instantiates a Pizza object and prints its calories per
   //  serving.
   //------------------------------------------------------------
   public static void main (String[] args)
   {
      Pizza special = new Pizza (275);

      System.out.println ("Calories per serving: " +
                          special.caloriesPerServing());
   }
}
```

output

```
Calories per serving: 309
```

Even though `Pizza` did not inherit `calories`, `fatGrams`, or `CALORIES_PER_GRAM` it can use them indirectly like this. The `Pizza` class cannot refer to them directly by name because they are not inherited, but they do exist. Note that a `FoodItem` object was never created or needed.

Figure 7.8 lists each variable and method declared in the `FoodItem` class and whether it exists in or is inherited by the `Pizza` class. Note that every `FoodItem` member exists in the `Pizza` class, no matter how it is declared. The items that are not inherited can be referenced only indirectly.

```
listing
   7.18
```

```
//********************************************************************
//  FoodItem.java        Author: Lewis/Loftus/Cocking
//
//  Represents an item of food. Used as the parent of a derived class
//  to demonstrate indirect referencing through inheritance.
//********************************************************************

public class FoodItem
{
   final private int CALORIES_PER_GRAM = 9;
   private int fatGrams;
   private int servings;

   //-----------------------------------------------------------------
   //  Sets up this food item with the specified number of fat grams
   //  and number of servings.
   //-----------------------------------------------------------------
   public FoodItem (int numFatGrams, int numServings)
   {
      fatGrams = numFatGrams;
      servings = numServings;
   }

   //-----------------------------------------------------------------
   //  Computes and returns the number of calories in this food item
   //  due to fat.
   //-----------------------------------------------------------------
   private int calories()
   {
      return fatGrams * CALORIES_PER_GRAM;
   }

   //-----------------------------------------------------------------
   //  Computes and returns the number of fat calories per serving.
   //-----------------------------------------------------------------
   public int caloriesPerServing()
   {
      return (calories() / servings);
   }
}
```

```
listing
   7.19

//****************************************************************
//  Pizza.java         Author: Lewis/Loftus/Cocking
//
//  Represents a pizza, which is a food item. Used to demonstrate
//  indirect referencing through inheritance.
//****************************************************************

public class Pizza extends FoodItem
{
   //----------------------------------------------------------------
   //  Sets up a pizza with the specified amount of fat (assumes
   //  eight servings).
   //----------------------------------------------------------------
   public Pizza (int fatGrams)
   {
      super (fatGrams, 8);
   }
}
```

Declared in FoodItem **class**	Defined in Pizza **class**	Inherited in Pizza **class**
CALORIES_PER_GRAM	yes	no, because the constant is private
fatGrams	yes	no, because the variable is private
servings	yes	no, because the variable is private
FoodItem	yes	no, because the constructors are not inherited
calories	yes	no, because the method is private
caloriesPerServing	yes	yes, because the method is public

figure 7.8   The relationship between FoodItem members and the Pizza class

7.4 polymorphism

Usually, the type of a reference variable matches exactly the class of the object to which it refers. That is, if we declare a reference as follows, `bishop` refers to an object created from the `ChessPiece` class.

```
ChessPiece bishop;
```

But it doesn't always have to work like that.

The term *polymorphism* means "having many forms." A *polymorphic reference* is a reference variable that can refer to different types of objects at different times. The method invoked through a polymorphic reference can change from one time to the next.

> **key concept**
> A polymorphic reference can refer to different types of objects at different times.

Look at the following line of code:

```
obj.doIt();
```

If the reference `obj` is polymorphic, it can refer to different types of objects at different times. If that line of code is in a loop or in a method that is called more than once, that line of code might call a different version of the `doIt` method each time it is invoked.

At some point, the computer has to execute the code to carry out a method invocation. This is called *binding* a method invocation to a method definition. Most of the time binding happens at compile time. For polymorphic references, however, binding can't be done until runtime. This is because which object is being referenced can change. This is called *late binding* or *dynamic binding*. It is less efficient than binding at compile time because the decision must be made during the execution of the program. But the flexibility that a polymorphic reference gives us makes up for that.

We can create a polymorphic reference in Java in two ways: using inheritance and using interfaces. This section describes how we can create a polymorphic reference using inheritance. In Section 7.5 we describe how we can create a polymorphic reference using interfaces.

references and class hierarchies

In Java, a reference can refer to an object of any class related to it by inheritance. For example, if the class `Mammal` is used to derive the class `Horse`, then a `Mammal` reference can refer to an object of class `Horse`:

> **key concept**
> A reference variable can refer to any object created from any class related to it by inheritance.

```
Mammal pet;
Horse secretariat = new Horse();
pet = secretariat;  // a valid assignment
```

The reverse operation, assigning the `Mammal` object to a `Horse` reference, is possible, but requires an explicit cast, as shown:

```
secretariat = (Horse)pet;
```

This type of assignment is only valid if the `Mammal` object that is being cast to a `Horse` is actually a `Horse` object. (Otherwise, you'll get a `ClassCastException`.) Although a horse *is-a* mammal, the reverse is not necessarily true.

This relationship works throughout a class hierarchy. If the `Mammal` class were derived from a class called `Animal`, the following assignment would also be valid:

```
Animal creature = new Horse();
```

Carrying this to the limit, an `Object` reference can be used to refer to any object because all classes are descendants of the `Object` class. An `ArrayList`, for example, uses polymorphism because it has `Object` references. That's why an `ArrayList` can be used to store any kind of object. In fact, a particular `ArrayList` can be used to hold several different types of objects at one time because they are all `Object` objects.

Because an `ArrayList` stores `Object` references, when we get elements from an `ArrayList`, we must cast them back to the type of object they really are if we want to be able to use them as anything other than a general `Object`. Suppose `words` is an `ArrayList` containing `String` objects and we want to get the first two letters of the first word in the list. We can use the `substring` method to get the first two letters, but it is a method defined in the `String` class and won't work if we use it through a variable that is a reference to an `Object` object. The following code segment illustrates how we can use a cast on an object retrieved from the list `words`, then perform the desired action.

```
String firstWord = (String)words.get(0);
String twoLetters = firstWord.substring(0,2);
```

polymorphism and inheritance

The reference variable `creature`, as defined in the previous section, can be polymorphic because at any point in time it can refer to an `Animal` object, a `Mammal` object, or a `Horse` object. Suppose that all three of these classes have a method called `move` that is implemented in different ways (because the child class overrode the definition it inherited). The following invocation calls the move method, but the particular version of the method it calls is determined at runtime:

```
creature.move();
```

If `creature` currently refers to an `Animal` object when this line is executed, the move method of the `Animal` class is invoked. Likewise, if `creature` currently refers to a `Mammal` or `Horse` object when this line is executed, the `Mammal` or `Horse` version of move is invoked.

A polymorphic reference uses the type of the object, not the type of the reference, to determine which version of a method to invoke.

key concept

If `Animal` and `Mammal` are defined as abstract classes, we can still have polymorphic references. Suppose the move method in the `Mammal` class is abstract, and is given unique definitions in the `Horse`, `Dog`, and `Whale` classes (all derived from `Mammal`). A `Mammal` reference variable can be used to refer to any objects created from any of the `Horse`, `Dog`, and `Whale` classes, and can be used to execute the move method on any of them.

Let's look at Figure 7.9. The classes in it represent kinds of employees at a company. Let's use this hierarchy to demonstrate several inheritance issues, including polymorphism.

The `Firm` class shown in Listing 7.20 contains a `main` driver that creates a `Staff` of employees and invokes the `payday` method to pay them all. The program output includes information about each employee and how much each is paid (if anything).

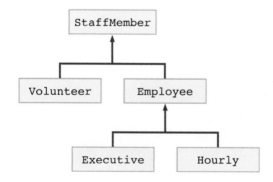

figure 7.9   A class hierarchy of employees

```
listing
  7.20
```

```java
//***********************************************************************
//  Firm.java        Author: Lewis/Loftus/Cocking
//
//  Demonstrates polymorphism via inheritance.
//***********************************************************************

public class Firm
{
    //--------------------------------------------------------------
    //  Creates a staff of employees for a firm and pays them.
    //--------------------------------------------------------------
    public static void main (String[] args)
    {
        Staff personnel = new Staff();

        personnel.payday();
    }
}
```

output

```
Name: Elliot
Address: 123 Main Line
Phone: 555-0469
Social Security Number: 123-45-6789
Paid: 2923.07
-----------------------------------
Name: Dr. Kelso
Address: 456 Off Line
Phone: 555-0101
Social Security Number: 987-65-4321
Paid: 1246.15
-----------------------------------
Name: Turk
Address: 789 Off Rocker
Phone: 555-0000
Social Security Number: 010-20-3040
Paid: 1169.23
-----------------------------------
Name: Dr. Cox
Address: 678 Fifth Ave.
Phone: 555-0690
Social Security Number: 958-47-3625
Current hours: 40
Paid: 422.0
```

listing
   7.20   continued

```
------------------------------------
Name: J.D.
Address: 987 Suds Blvd.
Phone: 555-8374
Thanks!
------------------------------------
Name: Carla
Address: 321 Duds Lane
Phone: 555-7282
Thanks!
------------------------------------
```

The Staff class shown in Listing 7.21 is an array of objects that represent individual employees. Note that the array is declared to hold StaffMember references, but it is actually filled with objects created from several other classes, such as Executive and Employee. These classes are all descendants of the StaffMember class, so the assignments are valid.

The payday method of the Staff class scans through the list of employees, printing their information and invoking their pay methods to determine how much each employee should be paid. The invocation of the pay method is polymorphic because each class has its own version of the pay method.

The StaffMember class shown in Listing 7.22 is abstract. It does not represent a particular type of employee and is not meant to be instantiated. Rather, it serves as the parent of all employee classes and contains information that applies to all employees. Each employee has a name, address, and phone number, so variables to store these values are declared in the StaffMember class.

The StaffMember class contains a toString method to return the information managed by the StaffMember class. It also contains an abstract method called pay, which takes no parameters and returns a value of type double. We can't define this method at the StaffMember level because each type of employee gets paid in a different way. The descendants of StaffMember each provide their own definition for pay. Because pay is abstract in StaffMember, the payday method of Staff can polymorphically pay each employee.

listing
    7.21

```java
//********************************************************************
//  Staff.java        Author: Lewis/Loftus/Cocking
//
//  Represents the personnel staff of a particular business.
//********************************************************************

public class Staff
{
   private StaffMember[] staffList;

   //-----------------------------------------------------------------
   //  Sets up the list of staff members.
   //-----------------------------------------------------------------
   public Staff ()
   {
      staffList = new StaffMember[6];

      staffList[0] = new Executive ("Elliot", "123 Main Line",
         "555-0469", "123-45-6789", 2423.07);

      staffList[1] = new Employee ("Dr. Kelso", "456 Off Line",
         "555-0101", "987-65-4321", 1246.15);
      staffList[2] = new Employee ("Turk", "789 Off Rocker",
         "555-0000", "010-20-3040", 1169.23);

      staffList[3] = new Hourly ("Dr. Cox", "678 Fifth Ave.",
         "555-0690", "958-47-3625", 10.55);

      staffList[4] = new Volunteer ("J.D.", "987 Suds Blvd.",
         "555-8374");
      staffList[5] = new Volunteer ("Carla", "321 Duds Lane",
         "555-7282");

      ((Executive)staffList[0]).awardBonus (500.00);

      ((Hourly)staffList[3]).addHours (40);
   }

   //-----------------------------------------------------------------
   //  Pays all staff members.
   //-----------------------------------------------------------------
   public void payday ()
   {
      double amount;

      for (int count=0; count < staffList.length; count++)
      {
```

```
listing
   7.21   continued

        System.out.println (staffList[count]);

        amount = staffList[count].pay();   // polymorphic

        if (amount == 0.0)
            System.out.println ("Thanks!");
        else
            System.out.println ("Paid: " + amount);

        System.out.println ("----------------------------------");
      }
   }
}
```

The Volunteer class shown in Listing 7.23 represents a person who does not get paid. We keep track only of a volunteer's basic information, which is passed into the constructor of Volunteer, which in turn passes it to the StaffMember constructor using the super reference. The pay method of Volunteer simply returns a zero pay value. If pay had not been overridden, the Volunteer class would have been considered abstract and could not have been instantiated.

Note that when a volunteer gets "paid" in the payday method of Staff, a simple expression of thanks is printed. In all other situations, where the pay value is greater than zero, the payment itself is printed.

The Employee class shown in Listing 7.24 represents an employee who gets paid at a particular rate each pay period. The pay rate, as well as the employee's Social Security number, is passed to the Employee constructor. The basic information is passed to the constructor of StaffMember using the super reference.

The toString method of Employee is overridden to match the additional information that Employee manages to the information returned by the parent's version of toString, which is called using the super reference. The pay method of an Employee simply returns the pay rate for that employee.

The Executive class shown in Listing 7.25 represents an employee that may earn a bonus in addition to his or her normal pay rate. The Executive class is derived from Employee and therefore inherits from both StaffMember and Employee. The constructor of Executive passes along

listing
     7.22

```java
//********************************************************************
//  StaffMember.java        Author: Lewis/Loftus/Cocking
//
//  Represents a generic staff member.
//********************************************************************

abstract public class StaffMember
{
   private String name;
   private String address;
   private String phone;

   //-----------------------------------------------------------------
   //  Sets up a staff member using the specified information.
   //-----------------------------------------------------------------
   public StaffMember (String eName, String eAddress, String ePhone)
   {
      name = eName;
      address = eAddress;
      phone = ePhone;
   }

   //-----------------------------------------------------------------
   //  Returns a string including the basic employee information.
   //-----------------------------------------------------------------
   public String toString()
   {
      String result = "Name: " + name + "\n";

      result += "Address: " + address + "\n";
      result += "Phone: " + phone;

      return result;
   }

   //-----------------------------------------------------------------
   //  Derived classes must define the pay method for each type of
   //  employee.
   //-----------------------------------------------------------------
   public abstract double pay();
}
```

```
listing
    7.23

//*********************************************************************
//   Volunteer.java        Author: Lewis/Loftus/Cocking
//
//   Represents a staff member that works as a volunteer.
//*********************************************************************

public class Volunteer extends StaffMember
{
    //-----------------------------------------------------------------
    //   Sets up a volunteer using the specified information.
    //-----------------------------------------------------------------
    public Volunteer (String eName, String eAddress, String ePhone)
    {
        super (eName, eAddress, ePhone);
    }

    //-----------------------------------------------------------------
    //   Returns a zero pay value for this volunteer.
    //-----------------------------------------------------------------
    public double pay()
    {
        return 0.0;
    }
}
```

its information to the Employee constructor and sets the executive bonus to zero.

A bonus is awarded to an executive using the awardBonus method. This method is called in the payday method in Staff for the only executive who is part of the personnel array. Note that the general StaffMember reference must be cast into an Executive reference to invoke the awardBonus method (which doesn't exist for a StaffMember).

The Executive class overrides the pay method so that it first determines the payment as it would for any employee, then adds the bonus. The pay method of the Employee class is invoked using super to obtain the normal payment amount. After the bonus is awarded, it is reset to zero.

listing
      7.24

```
//********************************************************************
//   Employee.java         Author: Lewis/Loftus/Cocking
//
//   Represents a general paid employee.
//********************************************************************

public class Employee extends StaffMember
{
   private String socialSecurityNumber;
   private double payRate;

   //------------------------------------------------------------------
   //   Sets up an employee with the specified information.
   //------------------------------------------------------------------
   public Employee (String eName, String eAddress, String ePhone,
                    String socSecNumber, double rate)
   {
      super (eName, eAddress, ePhone);

      socialSecurityNumber = socSecNumber;
      payRate = rate;
   }

   //------------------------------------------------------------------
   //   Returns the pay rate for this employee.
   //------------------------------------------------------------------
   public double getPayRate()
   {
      return payRate;
   }

   //------------------------------------------------------------------
   //   Returns information about an employee as a string.
   //------------------------------------------------------------------
   public String toString()
   {
      String result = super.toString();

      result += "\nSocial Security Number: " + socialSecurityNumber;

      return result;
   }
```

```
listing
    7.24  continued

   //----------------------------------------------------------------
   //  Returns the amount this employee should be paid.
   //----------------------------------------------------------------
   public double pay()
   {
      return payRate;
   }
}
```

The `Hourly` class shown in Listing 7.26 represents an employee whose pay rate is applied on an hourly basis. It keeps track of the number of hours worked in the current pay period, which can be modified by calls to the `addHours` method. This method is called from the `payday` method of `Staff`. The `pay` method of `Hourly` determines the payment based on the number of hours worked, and then resets the hours to zero.

7.5 interfaces

We introduced interfaces in Chapter 5. We review them here because they have a lot in common with inheritance. Just as we can use polymorphism in inheritance, we can also use it with interfaces.

polymorphism with interfaces

As we've seen many times, a class name is used to declare the type of an object reference variable. In the same way, an interface name can be used as the type of a reference variable as well. An interface reference variable can be used to refer to any object of any class that implements that interface.

> **key concept**
> An interface name can be used to declare an object reference variable. An interface reference can refer to any object of any class that implements that interface.

Suppose we declare an interface called `Speaker` as follows:

```
public interface Speaker
{
   public void speak();
   public void announce (String str);
}
```

listing
     7.25

```java
//***********************************************************************
//   Executive.java          Author: Lewis/Loftus/Cocking
//
//   Represents an executive staff member, who can earn a bonus.
//***********************************************************************

public class Executive extends Employee
{
   private double bonus;

   //------------------------------------------------------------------
   //   Sets up an executive with the specified information.
   //------------------------------------------------------------------
   public Executive (String eName, String eAddress, String ePhone,
                     String socSecNumber, double rate)
   {
      super (eName, eAddress, ePhone, socSecNumber, rate);

      bonus = 0;   // bonus has yet to be awarded
   }

   //------------------------------------------------------------------
   //   Awards the specified bonus to this executive.
   //------------------------------------------------------------------
   public void awardBonus (double execBonus)
   {
      bonus = execBonus;
   }

   //------------------------------------------------------------------
   //   Computes and returns the pay for an executive, which is the
   //   regular employee payment plus a one-time bonus.
   //------------------------------------------------------------------
   public double pay()
   {
      double payment = super.pay() + bonus;

      bonus = 0;

      return payment;
   }
}
```

listing
    7.26

```
//********************************************************************
//  Hourly.java        Author: Lewis/Loftus/Cocking
//
//  Represents an employee that gets paid by the hour.
//********************************************************************

public class Hourly extends Employee
{
    private int hoursWorked;

    //----------------------------------------------------------------
    //  Sets up this hourly employee using the specified information.
    //----------------------------------------------------------------
    public Hourly (String eName, String eAddress, String ePhone,
                   String socSecNumber, double rate)
    {
        super (eName, eAddress, ePhone, socSecNumber, rate);

        hoursWorked = 0;
    }

    //----------------------------------------------------------------
    //  Adds the specified number of hours to this employee's
    //  accumulated hours.
    //----------------------------------------------------------------
    public void addHours (int moreHours)
    {
        hoursWorked += moreHours;
    }

    //----------------------------------------------------------------
    //  Computes and returns the pay for this hourly employee.
    //----------------------------------------------------------------
    public double pay()
    {
        double payment = getPayRate() * hoursWorked;

        hoursWorked = 0;

        return payment;
    }

    //----------------------------------------------------------------
    //  Returns information about this hourly employee as a string.
    //----------------------------------------------------------------
```

listing
7.26 continued

```
public String toString()
{
    String result = super.toString();

    result += "\nCurrent hours: " + hoursWorked;

    return result;
}
}
```

The interface name, Speaker, can now be used to declare an object reference variable:

```
Speaker current;
```

The reference variable current can be used to refer to any object of any class that implements the Speaker interface. For example, if we define a class called Philosopher such that it implements the Speaker interface, we can then assign a Philosopher object to a Speaker reference as follows:

```
current = new Philosopher();
```

This assignment is valid because a Philosopher is, in fact, a Speaker.

The flexibility of an interface reference lets us create polymorphic references. As we saw earlier in this chapter, we can create a polymorphic reference for objects related by inheritance. We can create polymorphic references using interfaces except that the objects being referenced all implement the same interface.

> **key concept**
> Interfaces let us make polymorphic references with methods that are based on the object being referenced at the time.

For example, if we create a class called Dog that also implements the Speaker interface, it can be assigned to a Speaker reference variable. The same reference, in fact, can at one point refer to a Philosopher object and then later refer to a Dog object. The following lines of code illustrate this:

```
Speaker guest;
guest = new Philosopher();
guest.speak();
guest = new Dog();
guest.speak();
```

In this code, the first time the `speak` method is called, it invokes the `speak` method defined in the `Philosopher` class. The second time it is called, it invokes the `speak` method of the `Dog` class. It is not the type of the reference that determines which method gets invoked, it's the type of the object that the reference points to when it is invoked.

Note that when we are using an interface reference variable, we can invoke only the methods defined in the interface, even if the object it refers to has other methods. For example, suppose the `Philosopher` class also defined a public method called `lecture`. The second line of the following code would give us a compiler error, even though the object can in fact respond to the `lecture` method:

```
Speaker special = new Philosopher();
special.lecture();   // generates a compiler error
```

The problem is that the compiler knows only that the object is a `Speaker`, and therefore can guarantee only that the object can respond to the `speak` and `announce` methods. Because the reference variable `special` could refer to a `Dog` object (which cannot lecture), it does not allow the reference. If we know that such an invocation is valid, we can cast the object into the appropriate reference so that the compiler will accept it, as follows:

```
((Philosopher)special).lecture();
```

Like polymorphic references based in inheritance, an interface name can be used as the type of a method parameter. Then any object of any class that implements the interface can be passed into the method. For example, the following method takes a `Speaker` object as a parameter. Now both a `Dog` object and a `Philosopher` object can be passed into it separately:

```
public void sayIt (Speaker current)
{
   current.speak();
}
```

7.6 bumper cars case study: the driver program

One thing we haven't talked about yet is how we will get input from the user about the size of the arena and the number of cars in the simulation. We could write a `main` method in the `Simulation` class to do that, but instead we will create a separate class that will be the driver for the simulation. (Our driver program should not be confused with the drivers of cars in the bumper

AP CASE STUDY

car simulation!) A driver program drives the use of other, more interesting, parts of the program. The other parts do most or all of the work in the application: The driver is just used to get them started.

We will call our driver `BumperCarSimulation` since it drives the whole bumper car simulation. This class will only have one method: `main`. In this method we must collect the necessary input from the user (making sure the input is valid), create objects to set up the simulation, run the simulation, and then display the final summary information (by calling `printBumpCounts` on the `Simulation` object).

The input we need includes the number of cars and the size of the arena. Once that information is entered, we need to make sure that the arena is big enough to hold the number of cars. If not, we should ask the user to re-enter the data. We can use a boolean variable called `badInput` to control a `while` loop that keeps executing until the input is valid. This is what our code looks like:

```java
int ew = 0;
int ns = 0;
int numCars = 0;
boolean badInput = true;

// Get the number of cars and size of the arena from the user.
while (badInput) {
    System.out.println("How many cars?");
    numCars = Keyboard.readInt();
    System.out.println("Size of the arena's north-south dimension?");
    ns = Keyboard.readInt();
    System.out.println("Size of the arena's east-west dimension?");
    ew = Keyboard.readInt();
    if (numCars > ew*ns)
    {
        System.out.println("Too many cars to fit in that size arena!");
        System.out.println("Please enter the information again:");
    }
    else
        badInput = false;
}
```

When this code finishes, we have a valid set of input data. Next we create a `Simulation` object, passing it the size of the arena and the number of cars. The simulation should run as many times as the user wants it to. We have two possibilities:

1. Ask the user how many steps he or she would like in the simulation, then run that many steps.

2. Run the simulation one step at a time and ask the user after each step whether to continue.

The second option is more flexible, but requires more input from the user. With the first option, we don't need much user input but after seeing how the simulation is going, the user can't add more steps. We will go with option two since it is more flexible and we can always change it later if the bumper car company prefers option one.

We'll call our `Simulation` object `sim` and make initializations before the loop, so our code will look like this:

```
while (keepGoing.equalsIgnoreCase("y"))
  {
    sim.step();
    System.out.println("Keep going? Type 'y' for yes or 'n' for no.");
    keepGoing = Keyboard.readString();
  }
```

At this point we notice that there is no output between steps in the simulation. In order for the user to see what is going on we need output between steps. We can use the `printArena` method, which prints a grid representing the arena, including where the cars are in the arena. After each step in the simulation, we will call that method on the `Arena` object. This means that the main program will have to create the `Arena` object so that it can call `printArena` on it between steps. We can change the `Simulation` constructor to take an already-created `Arena` object rather than arena dimensions. Now the second half of our `main` function will look like this:

```
Arena arena = new Arena(ns, ew);
Simulation sim = new Simulation(numCars, arena);

String keepGoing;
arena.printArena();
System.out.println("Keep going? Type 'y' for yes or 'n' for no.");
keepGoing = Keyboard.readString();
while (keepGoing.equalsIgnoreCase("y"))
  {
```

```
        sim.step();
        arena.printArena();
        System.out.println("Keep going? Type 'y' for yes or 'n' for no.");
        keepGoing = Keyboard.readString();
    }

    sim.printBumpCounts();
```

Listing 7.27 shows the BumperCarSimulation class.

listing
   7.27

```
//********************************************************************
// BumperCarSimulation.java       Author: Lewis/Loftus/Cocking
//
// This program runs a bumper car simulation.
//********************************************************************

import cs1.Keyboard;

public class BumperCarSimulation
{

    //---------------------------------------------------------------
    // Creates a Simulation object to control the bumper car
    // simulation. The user specifies the size of the arena and
    // how many bumper cars are in the arena. The simulation
    // continues until the user decides to stop it.
    //---------------------------------------------------------------
    public static void main(String[] args)
    {
        System.out.println("Bumper Cars Simulation");
        int ew = 0;
        int ns = 0;
        int numCars = 0;
        boolean badInput = true;

        // Get the number of cars and size of the arena from the user.
        while (badInput) {
            System.out.println("How many cars?");
            numCars = Keyboard.readInt();
            System.out.println("Size of the arena's north-south"
                                + " dimension?");
            ns = Keyboard.readInt();
            System.out.println("Size of the arena's east-west "
                                + "dimension?");
            ew = Keyboard.readInt();
            if (numCars > ew*ns)
```

listing
    7.27   continued

```java
        {
            System.out.println("Too many cars to fit in that "
                                + "size arena!");
            System.out.println("Please enter the information "
                                + "again:");
        }
        else if (numCars <= 0)
        {
            System.out.println("The number of cars must be greater"
                                + " than 0!");
            System.out.println("Please enter the information "
                                + "again:");
        }
        else
            badInput = false;
    }

    Arena arena = new Arena(ns, ew);
    Simulation sim = new Simulation(numCars, arena);

    int iterations = 0;
    String keepGoing;
    arena.printArena();
    System.out.println("Keep going? Type 'y' for yes or 'n' for"
                        + " no.");
    keepGoing = Keyboard.readString();
    while (keepGoing.equalsIgnoreCase("y"))
    {
        sim.step();
        iterations++;
        arena.printArena();
        System.out.println("Keep going? Type 'y' for yes or 'n'"
                            + " for no.");
        keepGoing = Keyboard.readString();
    }

    System.out.println("Number of iterations: " + iterations);
    sim.printBumpCounts();
    }
}
```

exercises

1. Why are driver programs useful?

2. Our input validation code doesn't check for a negative number of cars. Change it so that it makes sure the user enters a number of cars that is greater than 0.

3. Look at the code in the `BumperCarSimulation` class. What will happen if the user enters negative numbers for the dimensions of the arena?

7.7   inheritance and GUIs

We can use inheritance when we create graphics and GUIs. This section explores some of these issues.

It's important to note that there are two primary GUI APIs used in Java: the Abstract Windowing Toolkit (AWT) and the Swing classes. The AWT is the original set of graphics classes in Java. Swing classes were introduced later and have more functionality than AWT. In general, we use Swing components in our examples in this book.

applets

In previous chapters, we've created applets using inheritance. At first, we extended the `Applet` class, which is an original AWT component that is part of the `java.applet` package. In Chapter 5 and beyond, we've created our applets from the `JApplet` class, which is the Swing version. The main difference between these two classes is that a `JApplet` has a content pane to which GUI components are added. Also, in general, a `JApplet` component should not be drawn on directly. It's better to draw on a panel and add that panel to the applet, especially if there is going to be user interaction.

> **key concept**
>
> An applet is a good example of inheritance. The `JApplet` parent class handles characteristics common to all applets.

An applet is a good example of inheritance. It lets the parent class shoulder the responsibilities that apply to all of its descendants. The `JApplet` class is already designed to handle all of the details of applet creation and execution. For example, an applet program interacts with a browser, can accept parameters through HTML code, and has security limitations. The `JApplet` class already takes care of these details in a way that applies to all applets.

Because of inheritance, the applet class that we write (the one created from `JApplet`) is ready to focus on the purpose of that particular program.

In other words, the only thing we have to think about in our applet is what makes it different from other applets.

Note that we've been using applets even before we knew what inheritance does and what the parent applet class does in particular. We used the parent applet classes simply for the services they provide. Therefore applets are another wonderful example of abstraction in which certain details can be ignored.

the component class hierarchy

All of the Java classes that define GUI components are part of a class hierarchy, shown in part in Figure 7.10. Almost all Swing GUI components are derived from the JComponent class, which defines how all components

> **key concept**
> The classes that represent Java GUI components are organized into a class hierarchy.

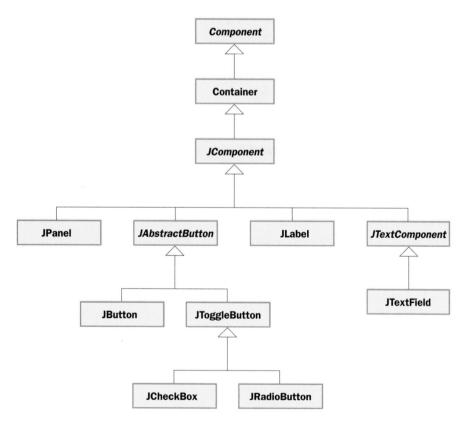

figure 7.10 Part of the GUI component class hierarchy

work in general. `JComponent` is derived from the `Container` class, which in turn is derived from the `Component` class.

Both `Container` and `Component` are original AWT classes. The `Component` class contains functions that apply to all GUI components, such as basic painting and event handling. So although we may like to use some of the Swing components, they are based on AWT concepts and respond to the same events as AWT components. Because they are derived from `Container`, many Swing components can serve as containers, with some limits. For example, a `JLabel` object can contain an image but it cannot be used as a general container for any component.

Many features that apply to all Swing components are defined in the `JComponent` class and are inherited by its descendants. For example, we can put a border on any Swing component. This ability is defined, only once, in the `JComponent` class and is inherited by any class that is derived from it.

Some component classes, such as `JPanel` and `JLabel`, are derived directly from `JComponent`. Other component classes are nested further down in the inheritance hierarchy. For example, the `JAbstractButton` class is an abstract class that defines all types of GUI buttons. `JButton` is derived directly from it. However, note that `JCheckBox` and `JRadioButton` are both derived from a class called `JToggleButton`, which has the characteristics for all buttons that can be in one of two states. The set of classes that define GUI buttons shows once again how common characteristics are put at high levels of the class hierarchy rather than duplicated in multiple classes.

Text components demonstrate this too. The `JTextField` class is one of many Java GUI components that help us manage text data. They are organized under a class called `JTextComponent`. Keep in mind that there are many GUI component classes that are not shown in the diagram in Figure 7.10.

Painting is another GUI feature affected by inheritance. The `paint` method we've used in applets is defined in the `Component` class. The `Applet` class inherits the default version of this method, which we have regularly overridden in our applet programs. Most Swing classes, however, use a method called `paintComponent` to do custom painting. Usually, we draw on a `JPanel` using its `paintComponent` method and use the `super` reference to invoke the version of the `paintComponent` method defined in `JComponent`, which draws the background and outline of the component. This technique is demonstrated in the next section.

7.8 mouse events

Let's look at what happens when we use a mouse. Java divides this into two categories: *mouse events* and *mouse motion events*. The table in Figure 7.11 defines these events.

When you click the mouse button over a Java GUI component, three events are generated: one when you push the mouse button down (*mouse pressed*) and two when you let it up (*mouse released* and *mouse clicked*). A mouse click is defined as pressing and releasing the mouse button in the same location. If you press the mouse button down, move the mouse, and then release the mouse button, a mouse clicked event is not generated.

A component will generate a *mouse entered* event when the mouse pointer passes into its graphical space. Likewise, it generates a *mouse exited* event when the mouse pointer leaves.

Mouse motion events occur while the mouse is moving. The *mouse moved* event indicates simply that the mouse is moving. The *mouse dragged* event is generated when you press the mouse button down and move the mouse without releasing the button. Mouse motion events are generated many times, very quickly, while the mouse is in motion.

> **key concept**
> Moving the mouse and clicking the mouse button generate mouse events to which a program can respond.

Sometimes, we care about only one or two mouse events. What we listen for depends on what we are trying to do.

Mouse Event	Description
mouse pressed	The mouse button is pressed down.
mouse released	The mouse button is released.
mouse clicked	The mouse button is pressed down and released without moving the mouse in between.
mouse entered	The mouse pointer is moved onto (over) a component.
mouse exited	The mouse pointer is moved off of a component.

Mouse Motion Event	Description
mouse moved	The mouse is moved.
mouse dragged	The mouse is moved while the mouse button is pressed down.

figure 7.11   Mouse events and mouse motion events

The Dots program shown in Listing 7.28 responds to one mouse event. It draws a green dot where the mouse pointer is, whenever the mouse button is pressed.

listing
7.28

```
//********************************************************************
//  Dots.java        Author: Lewis/Loftus/Cocking
//
//  Demonstrates mouse events and drawing on a panel.
//********************************************************************

import javax.swing.*;

public class Dots
{
   //-----------------------------------------------------------------
   //  Creates and displays the application frame.
   //-----------------------------------------------------------------
   public static void main (String[] args)
   {
      JFrame dotsFrame = new JFrame ("Dots");
      dotsFrame.setDefaultCloseOperation (JFrame.EXIT_ON_CLOSE);

      dotsFrame.getContentPane().add (new DotsPanel());

      dotsFrame.pack();
      dotsFrame.show();
   }
}
```

display

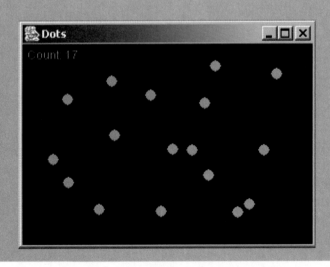

The `main` method of the `Dots` class creates a frame and adds one panel to it. That panel is defined by the `DotsPanel` class shown in Listing 7.29. The `DotsPanel` class is derived from `JPanel`. This panel is the surface on which the dots are drawn.

listing
   7.29

```java
//********************************************************************
//  DotsPanel.java        Author: Lewis/Loftus/Cocking
//
//  Represents the primary panel for the Dots program on which the
//  dots are drawn.
//********************************************************************

import javax.swing.*;
import java.awt.*;
import java.awt.event.*;
import java.util.*;

public class DotsPanel extends JPanel
{
   private final int WIDTH = 300, HEIGHT = 200;
   private final int RADIUS = 6;

   private ArrayList pointList;
   private int count;

   //-----------------------------------------------------------------
   //  Sets up this panel to listen for mouse events.
   //-----------------------------------------------------------------
   public DotsPanel()
   {
      pointList = new ArrayList();
      count = 0;

      addMouseListener (new DotsListener());

      setBackground (Color.black);
      setPreferredSize (new Dimension(WIDTH, HEIGHT));
   }

   //-----------------------------------------------------------------
   //  Draws all of the dots stored in the list.
   //-----------------------------------------------------------------
   public void paintComponent (Graphics page)
   {
      super.paintComponent(page);
```

listing
    7.29 continued

```java
      page.setColor (Color.green);

      // Retrieve an iterator for the ArrayList of points
      Iterator pointIterator = pointList.iterator();

      while (pointIterator.hasNext())
      {
         Point drawPoint = (Point) pointIterator.next();
         page.fillOval (drawPoint.x - RADIUS, drawPoint.y - RADIUS,
                        RADIUS * 2, RADIUS * 2);
      }

      page.drawString ("Count: " + count, 5, 15);
   }

   //*****************************************************************
   //  Represents the listener for mouse events.
   //*****************************************************************
   private class DotsListener implements MouseListener
   {
      //--------------------------------------------------------------
      //  Adds the current point to the list of points and redraws
      //  whenever the mouse button is pressed.
      //--------------------------------------------------------------
      public void mousePressed (MouseEvent event)
      {
         pointList.add (event.getPoint());
         count++;
         repaint();
      }

      //--------------------------------------------------------------
      //  Provide empty definitions for unused event methods.
      //--------------------------------------------------------------
      public void mouseClicked (MouseEvent event) {}
      public void mouseReleased (MouseEvent event) {}
      public void mouseEntered (MouseEvent event) {}
      public void mouseExited (MouseEvent event) {}
   }
}
```

The `DotsPanel` class keeps track of a list of `Point` objects that represent all of the places where the user clicked the mouse. A `Point` class represents the (x, y) coordinates of a given point. It provides public access to the instance variables `x` and `y` for the point. Each time the panel is painted, all of the points stored in the list are drawn. The list is an `ArrayList` object. To draw the points, an `Iterator` object is obtained from the `ArrayList` so that each point can be processed in turn. We discussed the `ArrayList` class in Chapter 6 and the `Iterator` interface in Chapter 5.

The listener for the mouse pressed event is a private inner class that implements the `MouseListener` interface. The `mousePressed` method is invoked by the panel each time the user presses down on the mouse button while it is over the panel.

A mouse event always happens at some point in space, and the object that represents that event keeps track of that location. In a mouse listener, we can get and use that point whenever we need it. In the `Dots` program, each time the `mousePressed` method is called, the location of the event is obtained using the `getPoint` method of the `MouseEvent` object. That point is stored in the `ArrayList`, and the panel is then repainted.

Note that, unlike the `ActionListener` and `ItemListener` interfaces that we've used in previous examples, which contain one method each, the `MouseListener` interface contains five methods. For this program, the only event we are interested in is the mouse pressed event. So, the only method we are interested in is the `mousePressed` method. However, implementing an interface means we must provide definitions for all methods in the interface. Therefore we provide empty methods for the other events. When those events are generated, the empty methods are called, but no code is executed.

Let's look at an example that responds to two mouse-oriented events. The `RubberLines` program shown in Listing 7.30 draws a line between two points. The first point is where the mouse is first pressed down. The second point changes as the mouse is dragged while the mouse button is held down. When the button is released, a line appears between the first and second points. When the mouse button is pressed again, a new line is started. This program is an applet.

The panel on which the lines are drawn is represented by the `RubberLinesPanel` class shown in Listing 7.31. Because we need to listen for both a mouse pressed event and a mouse dragged event, we need a listener that responds to both mouse events and mouse motion events. Note that the listener class implements both the `MouseListener` and `MouseMotionListener` interfaces. So it must implement all methods of both classes. The two methods, `mousePressed` and `mouseDragged`, are implemented, and the rest are given empty definitions.

listing
    7.30

```
//**********************************************************************
//   RubberLines.java        Author: Lewis/Loftus/Cocking
//
//   Demonstrates mouse events and rubberbanding.
//**********************************************************************

import javax.swing.*;

public class RubberLines extends JApplet
{
   private final int WIDTH = 300, HEIGHT = 200;

   //--------------------------------------------------------------------
   //   Sets up the applet to contain the drawing panel.
   //--------------------------------------------------------------------
   public void init()
   {
      getContentPane().add (new RubberLinesPanel());

      setSize (WIDTH, HEIGHT);
   }
}
```

display

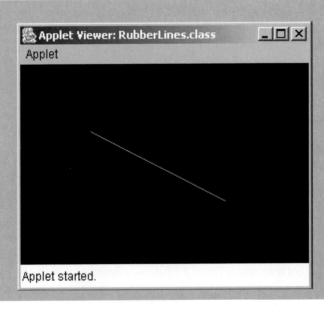

listing
    7.31

```java
//********************************************************************
//  RubberLinesPanel.java       Author: Lewis/Loftus/Cocking
//
//  Represents the primary drawing panel for the RubberLines applet.
//********************************************************************

import java.awt.*;
import java.awt.event.*;
import javax.swing.*;

public class RubberLinesPanel extends JPanel
{
   private Point point1 = null, point2 = null;

   //-----------------------------------------------------------------
   //  Sets up the applet to listen for mouse events.
   //-----------------------------------------------------------------
   public RubberLinesPanel()
   {
      LineListener listener = new LineListener();
      addMouseListener (listener);
      addMouseMotionListener (listener);

      setBackground (Color.black);
   }

   //-----------------------------------------------------------------
   //  Draws the current line from the intial mouse down point to
   //  the current position of the mouse.
   //-----------------------------------------------------------------
   public void paintComponent (Graphics page)
   {
      super.paintComponent (page);

      page.setColor (Color.green);
      if (point1 != null && point2 != null)
         page.drawLine (point1.x, point1.y, point2.x, point2.y);
   }

   //********************************************************************
   //  Represents the listener for all mouse events.
   //********************************************************************
   private class LineListener implements MouseListener,
                                         MouseMotionListener
   {
```

listing
7.31   continued

```java
        //----------------------------------------------------------------
        //  Captures the initial position at which the mouse button is
        //  pressed.
        //----------------------------------------------------------------
        public void mousePressed (MouseEvent event)
        {
            point1 = event.getPoint();
        }

        //----------------------------------------------------------------
        //  Gets the current position of the mouse as it is dragged and
        //  draws the line to create the rubberband effect.
        //----------------------------------------------------------------
        public void mouseDragged (MouseEvent event)
        {
            point2 = event.getPoint();
            repaint();
        }

        //----------------------------------------------------------------
        //  Provide empty definitions for unused event methods.
        //----------------------------------------------------------------
        public void mouseClicked (MouseEvent event) {}
        public void mouseReleased (MouseEvent event) {}
        public void mouseEntered (MouseEvent event) {}
        public void mouseExited (MouseEvent event) {}
        public void mouseMoved (MouseEvent event) {}
    }
}
```

> **key concept**
>
> Rubberbanding is when a graphical shape seems to stretch and contract as the mouse is dragged.

When the `mousePressed` method is called, the variable `point1` is set. Then, as the mouse is dragged, the variable `point2` is reset again and again, and the panel repainted. That is, the line is constantly being redrawn as the mouse is dragged, so that it looks like one line is being stretched. This is called *rubberbanding* and is common in graphical programs.

Note that, in the `RubberLinesPanel` constructor, the listener object is added to the panel twice: once as a mouse listener and once as a mouse motion listener. The method called to add the listener must match the object passed as the parameter. In this case, we had one object for both events. We could have had two listener classes if we wanted: one listening for mouse events and one listening for mouse motion events. A component can have a listener for each event category.

Also note that this program draws one line at a time. That is, when the user begins to draw another line with a new mouse click, the old line disappears. This is because the paintComponent method redraws its background, erasing the line every time. To see the old lines, we'd have to keep track of them, perhaps using an ArrayList as we did in the Dots program.

extending event adapter classes

In previous event-based examples, we created the listener classes by implementing a particular listener interface. For instance, to create a class that listens for mouse events, we created a listener class that implements the MouseListener interface. As we saw in the Dots and RubberLines programs, a listener interface often has event methods that are not important to a particular program, which we give empty definitions.

Another way to create a listener class is to use an *event adapter class*. Each listener interface that contains more than one method has a matching adapter class that already contains empty definitions. We can derive a new listener class from the adapter class and override any event methods in which we are interested. This means we don't have to provide empty definitions for unused methods.

> **key concept**
>
> A listener class can be created by deriving it from an event adapter class.

The applet in Listing 7.32 responds to mouse click events. Whenever the mouse button is clicked over the applet, a line is drawn from the mouse pointer to the center of the applet. The distance that line represents in pixels is displayed.

The OffCenter program is like the RubberLines program. It loads a display panel, represented by the OffCenterPanel class shown in Listing 7.33, into the applet window.

The listener class, instead of implementing the MouseListener interface directly as we have done in previous examples, extends the MouseAdapter class, which is defined in the java.awt.event package of the Java standard class library. The MouseAdapter class implements the MouseListener interface and contains empty definitions for all of the mouse event methods. In our listener class, we override the definition of the mouseClicked method to suit our needs. Because we inherit the other empty methods that go with the rest of the mouse events, we don't have to provide our own empty definitions.

listing
    7.32

```
//********************************************************************
//  OffCenter.java        Author: Lewis/Loftus/Cocking
//
//  Demonstrates the use of an event adapter class.
//********************************************************************

import javax.swing.*;

public class OffCenter extends JApplet
{
   private final int WIDTH = 300, HEIGHT = 300;

   //-----------------------------------------------------------------
   //  Sets up the applet.
   //-----------------------------------------------------------------
   public void init()
   {
      getContentPane().add(new OffCenterPanel (WIDTH, HEIGHT));

      setSize (WIDTH, HEIGHT);
   }
}
```

display

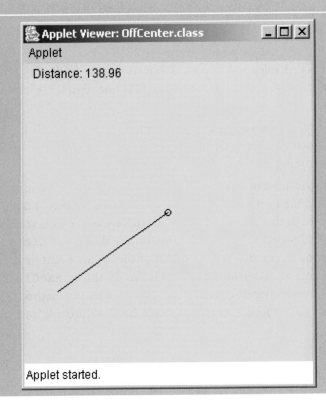

listing
    7.33

```java
//********************************************************************
//  OffCenterPanel.java       Author: Lewis/Loftus/Cocking
//
//  Represents the primary drawing panel for the OffCenter applet.
//********************************************************************

import java.awt.*;
import java.awt.event.*;
import java.text.DecimalFormat;
import javax.swing.*;

public class OffCenterPanel extends JPanel
{
    private DecimalFormat fmt;
    private Point current;
    private int centerX, centerY;
    private double length;

    //----------------------------------------------------------------
    //  Sets up the panel and necessary data.
    //----------------------------------------------------------------
    public OffCenterPanel (int width, int height)
    {
        addMouseListener (new OffCenterListener());

        centerX = width / 2;
        centerY = height / 2;

        fmt = new DecimalFormat ("0.##");

        setBackground (Color.yellow);
    }

    //----------------------------------------------------------------
    //  Draws a line from the mouse pointer to the center point of
    //  the applet and displays the distance.
    //----------------------------------------------------------------
    public void paintComponent (Graphics page)
    {
        super.paintComponent (page);

        page.setColor (Color.black);
        page.drawOval (centerX-3, centerY-3, 6, 6);
```

listing
7.33   **continued**

```
    if (current != null)
    {
       page.drawLine (current.x, current.y, centerX, centerY);
       page.drawString ("Distance: " + fmt.format(length), 10, 15);
    }
}


//****************************************************************
//   Represents the listener for mouse events.
//****************************************************************
private class OffCenterListener extends MouseAdapter
{
   //-----------------------------------------------------------
   //   Computes the distance from the mouse pointer to the center
   //   point of the applet.
   //-----------------------------------------------------------
   public void mouseClicked (MouseEvent event)
   {
      current = event.getPoint();
      length = Math.sqrt(Math.pow((current.x-centerX), 2) +
                            Math.pow((current.y-centerY), 2));
      repaint();
   }
}
}
```

Because of inheritance, we can now choose how we create event listeners. We can implement an event listener interface, or we can extend an event adapter class. This is a design decision that should be considered carefully. The best technique depends on the situation.

- Inheritance is the process of creating a new class from an old one.
- Inheritance lets us reuse existing software.
- Inherited variables and methods can be used in the child class as if they had been declared locally.
- Inheritance creates an is-a relationship between all parent and child classes.
- Visibility modifiers determine which variables and methods are inherited.
- A parent's constructor can be invoked using the `super` reference.
- A child class can override the parent's definition of an inherited method.
- The child of one class can be the parent of one or more other classes, creating a class hierarchy.
- Common features should be located as high in a class hierarchy as possible.
- All Java classes are derived, directly or indirectly, from the `Object` class.
- The `toString` and `equals` methods are defined in the `Object` class, so they are inherited by every class in every Java program.
- An abstract class cannot be instantiated.
- A class derived from an abstract parent must override all of its parent's abstract methods, or the child class will also be considered abstract.
- All members of a superclass exist for a subclass, but they are not necessarily inherited. Only inherited members can be referenced by name in the subclass.
- A polymorphic reference can refer to different types of objects at different times.
- A reference variable can refer to any object created from any class related to it by inheritance.
- A polymorphic reference uses the type of the object, not the type of the reference, to determine which version of a method to invoke.

▸ An interface name can be used to declare an object reference variable. An interface reference can refer to any object of any class that implements that interface.

▸ Interfaces let us make polymorphic references in which the method that is invoked is based on the object being referenced at the time.

▸ An applet is a good example of inheritance. The `JApplet` parent class handles characteristics that all applets have.

▸ The classes for Java GUI components are organized into a class hierarchy.

▸ Moving the mouse and clicking the mouse button generate mouse events that a program can respond to.

▸ Rubberbanding is when a graphical shape seems to expand and contract as the mouse is dragged.

▸ A listener class can be created from an event adapter class.

self-review questions

7.1 Describe the relationship between a parent class and a child class.

7.2 How does inheritance support software reuse?

7.3 What relationship should every pair of parent-child classes represent?

7.4 Why would a child class override the methods of its parent class?

7.5 Why is the `super` reference important to a child class?

7.6 What is the relationship of the `Object` class to all other classes?

7.7 What is an abstract class?

7.8 Are all members of a parent class inherited by the child? Explain.

7.9 What is polymorphism?

7.10 How does inheritance support polymorphism?

7.11 How is overriding related to polymorphism?

7.12 How can polymorphism be done using interfaces?

7.13 What is an adapter class?

multiple choice

7.1 Superclass is to subclass as

a. child is to parent

b. this is to super

c. object is to primitive data

d. base class is to derived class

e. instance variable is to local variable

7.2 Look back at Figure 7.3 in the chapter. Which class in the diagram is both a subclass and a superclass?

a. Animal

b. Bird

c. Parrot

d. Lizard

e. Horse

7.3 Suppose a class M inherits from a class P. In the constructor of M, how would you call the default (no arguments) constructor of P?

a. P()

b. this()

c. super()

d. parent()

e. sub()

7.4 Which of the following does a child class inherit from its parent?

a. public constants

b. private variables

c. local variables

d. private methods

e. static methods

7.5   Look at Figure 7.3. Suppose animal is declared to be a reference to an Animal. Which of the following is a valid assignment?

a. animal = new Reptile();

b. animal = new Parrot();

c. animal = new Horse();

d. animal = new Bat();

e. all of the above

7.6   Given the classes A and B,

```
class A {
  void foo() {
     System.out.println("A's foo");
  }
}
class B extends A {
  void foo() {
     System.out.println("B's foo");
  }
}
```

what will be output by the following code?

```
A aRef = new B();
aRef.foo();
```

a. A's foo

b. B's foo

c. There will be a compile error because aRef may only refer to A objects.

d. There will be a compile error because the compiler can't tell which foo method is being called.

e. There will be a runtime error because the call to foo is ambiguous.

7.7 Given the following variable declaration

```
Object obj = new String("hello");
```

which of the following expressions will *not* cause a compile error?

a. `obj.toUpperCase()`

b. `obj.substring(0, 5)`

c. `obj.equals("hi")`

d. `obj.compareTo("hi")`

e. All of them will cause compile errors.

7.8 Given the method header

```
void doSomething(Object param)
```

which of the following is *not* a valid call to the method?

a. `doSomething("Java")`

b. `doSomething(new String("Java"))`

c. `doSomething(14)`

d. `doSomething(new Integer(14))`

e. All are valid calls

7.9 In this class header, which keyword should go in the blank to create an inheritance relationship?

```
public class Child _____ Parent
```

a. `super`

b. `extends`

c. `implements`

d. `inherits`

e. `interface`

7.10 If A inherits from B, B inherits from C, and C inherits from D, which of the following is true?

a. A is the grandparent of B, C, and D.

b. D is derived from B.

c. C may use public variables that are declared in A.

d. B may use public variables that are declared in A.

e. A may use public variables that are declared in D.

true/false

7.1   In an inheritance relationship, the parent class should be a more specific version of the child class.

7.2   A child class inherits all public data and methods from its parent class.

7.3   The super reference means the same thing as the this reference, but it is only used in subclasses.

7.4   In Java, a subclass may inherit from many superclasses.

7.5   If a child class defines a method with the same signature as a method in its parent class, an error will occur.

7.6   A class in Java can be both a superclass and a subclass.

7.7   All classes are derived from the Object class.

7.8   An abstract class cannot be instantiated.

7.9   A polymorphic reference variable can refer to different types of objects at different times.

7.10 Polymorphism may occur with inheritance but not with interfaces.

short answer

7.1   Draw an inheritance hierarchy containing classes that represent different types of clocks. Show the variables and method names for two of these classes.

7.2   Show another diagram for the hierarchy in Exercise 7.1. Explain why it may be better or worse than the original.

7.3   Draw a class hierarchy for types of teachers at a high school. Show what characteristics would be represented in the various classes of the hierarchy. Explain how polymorphism could play a role in assigning courses to each teacher.

7.4   Experiment with a simple is-a relationship between two classes. Put println statements in constructors of both the parent and child classes. Do not call the constructor of the parent in the child. What happens? Why? Change the child's constructor to call the constructor of the parent. Now what happens?

7.5   What would happen if the pay method were not defined as an abstract method in the StaffMember class of the program in Listing 7.20?

7.6 What would happen if, in the Dots program (Listing 7.28), we did not provide empty definitions for one or more of the unused mouse events?

7.7 What would happen if the call to super.paintComponent were removed from the paintComponent method of the DotsPanel class? Remove it and run the program to test your answer.

programming projects

7.1 Design and implement a class called MonetaryCoin that is derived from the Coin class presented in Chapter 4. Store a value in the monetary coin that represents its value and add a method that returns its value. Create a main driver class to instantiate and compute the sum of several MonetaryCoin objects. Show that a monetary coin inherits its parent's ability to be flipped.

7.2 Design and implement a set of classes that define the employees of a hospital: doctor, nurse, administrator, surgeon, receptionist, janitor, and so on. Include methods in each class that are named according to the services provided by that person and that print an appropriate message. Create a main driver class to instantiate several of the classes.

7.3 Design and implement a set of classes that define types of reading material: books, novels, magazines, technical journals, textbooks, and so on. Include data values that describe the material, such as the number of pages and the names of the authors. Include methods that are named for each class and that print an appropriate message. Create a main driver class to instantiate several of the classes.

7.4 Design and implement a set of classes that keeps track of sports statistics. Have each low-level class represent a specific sport. Tailor the services of the classes to the sport in question, and move common attributes to the higher-level classes. Create a main driver class to instantiate several of the classes.

7.5 Design and implement a set of classes that keeps track of information about a set of people, such as age, nationality, occupation, income, and so on. Design each class to focus on a particular aspect of data collection. Create a main driver class to instantiate several of the classes.

7.6   Design and implement an application that draws a traffic light and uses a push button to change the light. Derive the drawing surface from the `JPanel` class and use another panel to organize the drawing surface and the button.

7.7   Design and implement an application that draws a circle using rubberbanding. The circle size is determined by a mouse drag. Use the first mouse click location as a fixed center point. Compute the distance between the location of the mouse pointer and the center point to determine the radius of the circle.

7.8   Design and implement an application that acts like a mouse odometer, displaying how far, in pixels, the mouse has moved (while it is over the program window). Display the current odometer value using a label. *Hint*: Use the mouse movement event to determine the current position, and compare it to the last position of the mouse. Use the distance formula to see how far the mouse has traveled, and add that to a running total distance.

answers to self-review questions

7.1   A child class is derived from a parent class using inheritance. The methods and variables of the parent class automatically become a part of the child class, according to the rules of the visibility modifiers used to declare them.

7.2   Because a new class can be derived from an existing class, the characteristics of the parent class can be reused without the error-prone process of copying and modifying code.

7.3   Each inheritance should represent an is-a relationship: the child *is-a* version of the parent.

7.4   A child class may use its own definition of a method instead of the definition provided by its parent. In this case, the child overrides the parent's definition with its own.

7.5   The super reference can be used to call the parent's constructor, which cannot be invoked directly by name. It can also be used to invoke the parent's version of an overridden method.

7.6   All classes in Java are derived, directly or indirectly, from the `Object` class. Therefore all public methods of the `Object` class, such as `equals` and `toString`, are available to every object.

7.7 An abstract class is a representation of a general idea. Common characteristics and method signatures can be defined in an abstract class so that they are inherited by its child classes.

7.8 A class member is not inherited if it is private, meaning that it cannot be referenced by name in the child class. However, such members can be referenced indirectly.

7.9 Polymorphism is the ability of a reference variable to refer to different types of objects at different times. A method invoked through such a reference is bound to different method definitions at different times, depending on the type of the object referenced.

7.10 In Java, a reference variable declared using a parent class can be used to refer to an object of the child class. If both classes contain a method with the same signature, the parent reference can be polymorphic.

7.11 When a child class overrides the definition of a parent's method, two versions of that method exist. If a polymorphic reference is used to invoke the method, the version of the method that is invoked is determined by the type of the object being referred to, not by the type of the reference variable.

7.12 An interface name can be used as the type of a reference. This reference variable can refer to any object of any class that uses that interface. Because all classes use the same interface, they have methods with common signatures, which can be dynamically bound.

7.13 An adapter class implements a listener interface, providing empty definitions for all of its methods. A listener class can be created by extending the adapter class and overriding the methods of interest.

Recursion is a powerful programming
technique. This chapter introduces
recursive processing. It explains the basic
ideas of recursion and then
explores the use of recursion
in programming. Several
problems are solved using
recursion, demonstrating its
versatility, simplicity, and
elegance.

chapter objectives

▶ Explain the underlying ideas of recursion.

▶ Examine recursive methods and processing steps.

▶ Define infinite recursion and discuss ways to avoid it.

▶ Explain when recursion should and should not be used.

▶ Demonstrate the use of recursion to solve problems.

▶ Examine the use of recursion in sorting.

8.0 recursive thinking

We've seen many times how one method can call another method. What we haven't seen is a method calling itself. *Recursion* is a programming technique in which a method calls itself. But before we get into the details of how we use recursion in a program, we need to explore the general idea of recursion. We have to be able to *think* recursively before we can use recursion as a programming technique.

In general, recursion means defining something in terms of itself. For example, consider the following definition of the word *decoration*:

decoration: n. any ornament or adornment used to decorate something

The word *decorate* is used to define the word *decoration*. Your English teacher may tell you not to use recursion when explaining the meaning of a word. However, in many situations, recursion is a good way to express an idea or definition. For example, suppose we wanted to formally define a list of one or more numbers, separated by commas. We could define the list recursively as being made up of either a number or a number followed by a comma followed by a list. This definition can be expressed as follows:

A *List* is a: `number`
      or a: `number   comma   List`

This recursive definition of *List* works for all of the following lists of numbers:

```
24, 88, 40, 37
96, 43
14, 64, 21, 69, 32, 93, 47, 81, 28, 45, 81, 52, 69
70
```

No matter how long a list is, the recursive definition describes it. A list with only one element, such as in the last example, 70, is defined completely by the first (nonrecursive) part of the definition. For any list longer than one element, the recursive part of the definition (the part that refers to itself) is used over and over until the last element is reached. The last element in the list is always defined by the nonrecursive part of the definition, in this case "number" instead of "number comma *List*." Figure 8.1 shows how one list of numbers matches to the recursive definition of *List*.

```
LIST: number    comma    LIST
      24           ,       88,  40,  37
                          number   comma   LIST
                            88       ,      40,  37
                                          number   comma   LIST
                                            40        ,       37
                                                            number
                                                              37
```

figure 8.1   Tracing the recursive definition of *List*

infinite recursion

Note that the definition of *List* contains one part that is recursive and one part that is not. The part of the definition that is not recursive is called the *base case*. If all the parts were recursive, the recursion would never end. For example, if the definition of *List* was simply "a number followed by a comma followed by a *List*," no list could ever end. This problem is called *infinite recursion*. It is like an infinite loop except that the "loop" occurs in the definition itself.

You should be careful to avoid infinite recursion. Any recursive definition must have a base case that does not result in recursion. The base case of the *List* definition is a single number that is not followed by anything. In other words, when the last number in the list is reached, the base case option ends the recursion.

recursion in math

Let's look at an example of recursion in math. The value referred to as *N*! (pronounced *N factorial*) is defined for any positive integer *N* as the product of all integers between 1 and *N* inclusive. Therefore, 3! is defined as:

```
3!  =  3*2*1  =  6
```

and 5! is defined as:

```
5!  =  5*4*3*2*1  =  120.
```

Mathematical formulas are often expressed recursively. The definition of N! can be expressed recursively as:

```
1! = 1
N! = N * (N-1)! for N > 1
```

The base case of this definition is 1!, which is defined as 1. All other values of N! (for N > 1) are defined recursively as N times the value (N–1)!. In other words, the factorial function is defined in terms of the factorial function: which is recursion!

By this definition, 50! is equal to 50 * 49!. And 49! is equal to 49 * 48!. And 48! is equal to 48 * 47!. This continues until we get to the base case of 1. Because N! is defined only for positive integers, this definition is complete and will always conclude with the base case.

The next section describes how recursion is used in programs.

8.1 recursive programming

Let's use some simple math to demonstrate the concept of recursive programming. Consider adding up the values between 1 and N inclusive, where N is any positive number. We can express this as N plus the sum of the values from 1 to N–1, as shown in Figure 8.2.

For example, the sum of the values between 1 and 20 is equal to 20 plus the sum of the values between 1 and 19. Continuing this approach, the sum of the values between 1 and 19 is equal to 19 plus the sum of the values between 1 and 18. This may sound like a strange way to think about this problem, but it is a straightforward example that can be used to demonstrate how recursion is programmed.

As we mentioned earlier, in Java, as in many other programming languages, a method can call itself. Each call to the method creates a new environment in which to work. That is, all local variables and parameters are newly defined with their own unique data space every time the method is called. Each parameter is given an initial value based on the new call. Each time a method ends, processing returns to the method that called it (which may be an earlier invocation of the same method). These rules are no different from those for "regular" method invocation.

$$\sum_{i=1}^{N} i \;=\; N + \sum_{i=1}^{N-1} i \;=\; N + N-1 + \sum_{i=1}^{N-2} i$$

$$=\; N + N-1 + N-2 + \sum_{i=1}^{N-3} i$$

$$\vdots$$

$$=\; N + N-1 + N-2 + \cdots + 2 + 1$$

figure 8.2   The sum of the numbers 1 through N, defined recursively

A recursive solution to the summation problem is defined by the following recursive method called sum:

```java
// This method returns the sum of 1 to num
public int sum (int num)
{
   int result;
   if (num == 1)
      result = 1;
   else
      result = num + sum (num-1);
   return result;
}
```

Note that this method is basically our recursive definition that the sum of the numbers between 1 and N is equal to N plus the sum of the numbers between 1 and $N-1$. The sum method is recursive because sum calls itself. The parameter passed to sum is reduced by one each time sum is called until it reaches the base case of 1. Recursive methods always have an if-else statement, with one of the branches, usually the first one, representing the base case, as in this example.

Suppose the main method calls sum, passing it an initial value of 1, which is stored in the parameter num. Since num is equal to 1, the result of 1 is returned to main and no recursion occurs.

Now let's trace the execution of the sum method when it is passed an initial value of 2. Since num does not equal 1, sum is called again with an argument of num-1, or 1. This is a new call to the method sum, with a new parameter num and a new local variable result. Since this num is equal to 1 in this invocation, the result of 1 is returned without any more recursive calls. Control returns to the first version of sum that was invoked. The return value of 1 is added to the initial value of num in that call to sum, which is 2. Therefore, result is assigned the value

> Carefully tracing recursive processing shows us how it solves a problem.
>
> **key concept**

3, which is returned to the main method. The method called from main correctly calculates the sum of the integers from 1 to 2 and returns the result of 3.

The base case in the summation example is when N equals 1, at which point no more recursive calls are made. The recursion begins to fold back into the earlier versions of the sum method, returning the appropriate value each time. Each return value contributes to the computation of the sum at the next higher level. Without the base case, infinite recursion would result. Each call to a method requires additional memory space; therefore infinite recursion often results in a runtime error indicating that memory has been used up.

Trace the sum function with different beginning values of num until this processing becomes familiar. Figure 8.3 illustrates the recursive calls when main invokes sum to determine the sum of the integers from 1 to 4. Each box represents a copy of the method as it is invoked, allocating space to store the formal parameters and any local variables. Invocations are shown as solid lines, and returns as dotted lines. The return value result is shown at each step. The recursive path is followed completely until the base case is reached; the calls then begin to return their result up through the chain.

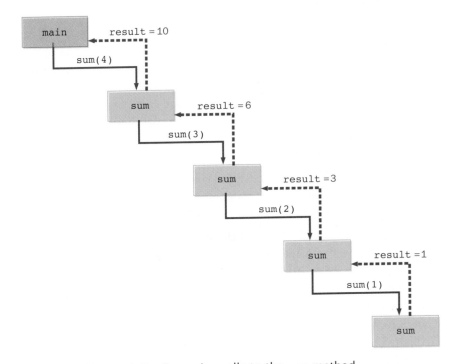

figure 8.3   Recursive calls to the sum method

recursion vs. iteration

Of course, there is a nonrecursive solution to the summation problem we just explored. One way to add up the numbers between 1 and num inclusive in an iterative manner is as follows:

```
sum = 0;
for (int number = 1; number <= num; number++)
    sum += number;
```

This solution is certainly more straightforward than the recursive version. We used the summation problem to demonstrate recursion because it is simple, not because you would normally use recursion to solve it. Recursion requires many method invocations so, in this case, it is a more complicated solution than doing with iteration.

A programmer must learn when to use recursion and when not to use it. Which approach is best depends on the problem being solved. All problems can be solved in an iterative manner, but in some cases the iterative version is much more complicated. Recursion, for some problems, lets us create relatively short, elegant programs.

> **key concept**
>
> Recursion is the most elegant and appropriate way to solve some problems, but for others it is less intuitive than an iterative solution.

direct vs. indirect recursion

Direct recursion is when a method invokes itself, such as when sum calls sum. *Indirect recursion* is when a method invokes another method, eventually resulting in the original method being invoked again. For example, if method m1 invokes method m2, and m2 invokes method m1, we can say that m1 is indirectly recursive. The amount of indirection could be several levels deep, as when m1 invokes m2, which invokes m3, which invokes m4, which invokes m1. Figure 8.4 shows indirect recursion. The method invocations are the solid lines, and returns are the dotted lines. The entire invocation path is followed, and then the recursion unravels following the return path.

Indirect recursion requires all of the same attention to base cases that direct recursion requires. Indirect recursion can be harder to trace because of the method calls in between. So we need to be extra careful when designing or evaluating indirectly recursive methods. Make sure that the indirection is truly necessary and clearly explained in documentation.

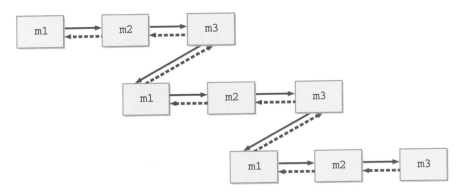

figure 8.4   Indirect recursion

8.2 using recursion

Each of the following sections describes a particular recursive problem. For each one, we look at exactly how recursion works and how a base case ends the recursion. As you examine these examples, think about how complicated a nonrecursive solution for each problem would be.

solving a maze

Solving a maze involves a great deal of trial and error: you follow a path, backtrack when you cannot go farther, and try other routes. Recursion can handle this nicely. The program shown in Listing 8.1 creates a Maze object and attempts to solve it.

The Maze class shown in Listing 8.2 uses a two-dimensional array of integers to represent the maze. The goal is to move from the top-left corner (the entry point) to the bottom-right corner (the exit point). At first, a 1 indicates a clear path and a 0 indicates a blocked path. As the maze is solved, these array elements are changed to other values to indicate attempted paths and finally a successful path through the maze, if there is one.

The only valid moves through the maze are in the four directions down, right, up, and left. No diagonal moves are allowed. In this example, the maze is 8 rows by 13 columns, although the code is designed to handle a maze of any size.

Let's think this through recursively. We start at position (0, 0). We must now move to position (1, 0), position (0, 1), position (-1, 0), or position (0, -1). Picking one, say (1, 0), we find ourselves with similar choices. At any

listing
  8.1

```
//************************************************************************
//  MazeSearch.java          Author: Lewis/Loftus/Cocking
//
//  Demonstrates recursion.
//************************************************************************

public class MazeSearch
{
   //--------------------------------------------------------------
   //  Creates a new maze, prints its original form, tries to
   //  solve it, and prints out its final form.
   //--------------------------------------------------------------
   public static void main (String[] args)
   {
      Maze labyrinth = new Maze();

      System.out.println (labyrinth);

      if (labyrinth.traverse (0, 0))
         System.out.println ("The maze was successfully solved!");
      else
         System.out.println ("There is no possible path.");

      System.out.println (labyrinth);
   }
}
```

output

```
1110110001111
1011101111001
0000101010100
1110111010111
1010000111001
1011111101111
1000000000000
111111111111

The maze was successfully solved!

7770110001111
3077707771001
0000707070300
7770777070333
7070000773003
7077777703333
7000000000000
7777777777777
```

```
//*****************************************************************
//   Maze.java          Author: Lewis/Loftus/Cocking
//
//   Represents a maze of characters. The goal is to get from the
//   top left corner to the bottom right, following a path of 1s.
//*****************************************************************

public class Maze
{
   private final int TRIED = 3;
   private final int PATH = 7;

   private int[][] grid = { {1,1,1,0,1,1,0,0,0,1,1,1,1},
                            {1,0,1,1,1,0,1,1,1,1,0,0,1},
                            {0,0,0,0,1,0,1,0,1,0,1,0,0},
                            {1,1,1,0,1,1,1,0,1,0,1,1,1},
                            {1,0,1,0,0,0,0,1,1,1,0,0,1},
                            {1,0,1,1,1,1,1,1,0,1,1,1,1},
                            {1,0,0,0,0,0,0,0,0,0,0,0,0},
                            {1,1,1,1,1,1,1,1,1,1,1,1,1} };

   //----------------------------------------------------------------
   //   Tries to recursively follow the maze. Inserts special
   //   characters for locations that have been tried and that
   //   eventually become part of the solution.
   //----------------------------------------------------------------
   public boolean traverse (int row, int column)
   {
      boolean done = false;

      if (valid (row, column))
      {
         grid[row][column] = TRIED;  // this cell has been tried

         if (row == grid.length-1 && column == grid[0].length-1)
            done = true;  // the maze is solved
         else
         {
            done = traverse (row+1, column);    // down
            if (!done)
               done = traverse (row, column+1);  // right
            if (!done)
               done = traverse (row-1, column);  // up
            if (!done)
               done = traverse (row, column-1);  // left
         }
```

listing
8.2   continued

```
        if (done)  // this location is part of the final path
            grid[row][column] = PATH;
    }

    return done;
}

//------------------------------------------------------------------
//  Determines if a specific location is valid.
//------------------------------------------------------------------
private boolean valid (int row, int column)
{
    boolean result = false;

    // check if cell is in the bounds of the matrix
    if (row >= 0 && row < grid.length &&
        column >= 0 && column < grid[row].length)

        //  check if cell is not blocked and not previously tried
        if (grid[row][column] == 1)
            result = true;

    return result;
}

//------------------------------------------------------------------
//  Returns the maze as a string.
//------------------------------------------------------------------
public String toString ()
{
    String result = "\n";

    for (int row=0; row < grid.length; row++)
    {
        for (int column=0; column < grid[row].length; column++)
            result += grid[row][column] + "";
        result += "\n";
    }

    return result;
}
}
```

point, some of choices of where to move may be invalid, may be blocked, or may be a possible successful path. We continue this process recursively. When the base case, position (7, 12) is reached, we have solved the maze.

The recursive method in the `Maze` class is called `traverse`. It returns a boolean value that tells us whether a solution was found. First the method decides whether a move is valid. A move is valid if it stays within the grid and if the grid contains a 1 in that location, meaning that a move in that direction is not blocked. The first call to `traverse` passes in the upper-left location (0, 0).

If the move is valid, the grid entry is changed from a 1 to a 3, marking this location as visited so that later we don't retrace our steps. The `traverse` method then decides whether the maze has been solved by having reached the bottom-right location. There are three possibilities of the base case for this problem that will end any particular recursive path:

▸ an invalid move because the move is out of bounds

▸ an invalid move because the move has been tried before

▸ a move that arrives at the final location

If the current location is not the bottom-right corner, we search for a solution in each of the primary directions. First, we look down by recursively calling the `traverse` method and passing in the new location. The `traverse` method starts all over again using this new position. A solution is either found by first trying to move down from the current location, or it's not found. If it's not found, we try moving right. If that fails, we try up. Finally, if no other direction works, we try left. If no direction from the current location works, then there is no path from this location, and `traverse` returns false.

If a solution is found from the current location, the grid entry is changed to a 7. The first 7 is placed in the bottom-right corner. The next 7 is placed in the location that led to the bottom-right corner, and so on until the final 7 is placed in the upper-left corner. Therefore, when the final maze is printed, the zeros still indicate a blocked path, a 1 indicates an open path that was never tried, a 3 indicates a path that was tried but failed to yield a correct solution, and a 7 indicates a part of the final solution of the maze.

Note that there are several opportunities for recursion in each call to the `traverse` method. Any or all of them might be followed, depending on how the maze is set up. Although there may be many paths through the maze, the recursion ends when a path is found. Carefully trace the execution of this code while following the maze array to see how the recursion solves the problem. Then think about how hard it would be to get a nonrecursive solution.

the Towers of Hanoi

The *Towers of Hanoi* puzzle was invented in the 1880s by Edouard Lucas, a French mathematician. It is a favorite of computer scientists because its solution is an excellent demonstration of recursion.

The puzzle consists of three pegs and a set of disks with holes in the middle so that they slide onto the pegs. Each disk is a different size. At first, all of the disks are stacked on one peg in order of size, with the largest disk on the bottom, as shown in Figure 8.5.

The goal is to move all of the disks from the first peg to the third peg so that they are in the same order, from largest on the bottom to smallest on the top. We can use the middle peg as a temporary place to put disks, but we must obey the following three rules:

 ▸ We can move only one disk at a time.

 ▸ We cannot place a larger disk on top of a smaller disk.

 ▸ All disks must be on some peg except for the disk being moved between pegs.

These rules mean that we must move smaller disks "out of the way" in order to move a larger disk from one peg to another. Figure 8.6 shows the step-by-step solution for the Towers of Hanoi puzzle using three disks. In order to move all three disks from the first peg to the third peg, we first have to get to the point where the smaller two disks are out of the way on the second peg so that the largest disk can be moved from the first peg to the third peg.

The first three moves shown in Figure 8.6 move the smaller disks out of the way. The fourth move puts the largest disk in its final place. The last three moves then put the smaller disks in their final places on top of the largest one.

Let's use this idea to form a general strategy. To move a stack of N disks from the first peg to the third peg:

 ▸ Move the topmost $N-1$ disks from the first peg to the middle peg.

 ▸ Move the largest disk from the first peg to the third peg.

 ▸ Move the $N-1$ disks from the middle peg to the third peg.

figure 8.5   The Towers of Hanoi puzzle

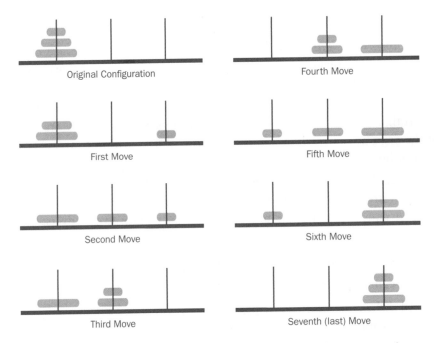

figure 8.6   A solution to the three-disk Towers of Hanoi puzzle

This strategy lends itself nicely to a recursive solution. The step to move the *N*–1 disks out of the way is the same problem all over again: moving a stack of disks. For this subtask, though, there is one less disk, and our destination is the middle peg. A similar thing happens after we've moved the largest disk, and we have to move the original *N*–1 disks again.

The base case for this problem happens when we want to move a "stack" that consists of only one disk. That step doesn't need recursion.

The program in Listing 8.3 creates a `TowersOfHanoi` object and invokes its `solve` method. The output is a step-by-step list of how the disks should be moved to solve the puzzle. This example uses four disks, which is specified by a parameter to the `TowersOfHanoi` constructor.

The `TowersOfHanoi` class shown in Listing 8.4 uses the `solve` method to make the first call to `moveTower`, the recursive method. The first call indicates that all of the disks should be moved from peg 1 to peg 3, using peg 2 as the extra position.

The `moveTower` method first considers the base case (a "stack" of one disk). When that happens, it calls the `moveOneDisk` method, which prints a single line describing that move. If the stack contains more than one disk, we call `moveTower` again to get the *N*–1 disks out of the way, then move the

listing
8.3

```
//********************************************************************
//  SolveTowers.java          Author: Lewis/Loftus/Cocking
//
//  Demonstrates recursion.
//********************************************************************

public class SolveTowers
{
   //-----------------------------------------------------------------
   //  Creates a TowersOfHanoi puzzle and solves it.
   //-----------------------------------------------------------------
   public static void main (String[] args)
   {
      TowersOfHanoi towers = new TowersOfHanoi (4);

      towers.solve();
   }
}
```

output

```
Move one disk from 1 to 2
Move one disk from 1 to 3
Move one disk from 2 to 3
Move one disk from 1 to 2
Move one disk from 3 to 1
Move one disk from 3 to 2
Move one disk from 1 to 2
Move one disk from 1 to 3
Move one disk from 2 to 3
Move one disk from 2 to 1
Move one disk from 3 to 1
Move one disk from 2 to 3
Move one disk from 1 to 2
Move one disk from 1 to 3
Move one disk from 2 to 3
```

largest disk, then move the N–1 disks to their final destination with yet another call to moveTower.

Note that the parameters to moveTower describing the pegs are switched around as needed to move the partial stacks. This code follows our general strategy and uses the moveTower method to move all partial stacks. Trace the code carefully for a stack of three disks to understand the processing. Compare the processing steps to Figure 8.6.

listing
   8.4

```
//********************************************************************
//   TowersOfHanoi.java          Author: Lewis/Loftus/Cocking
//
//   Represents the classic Towers of Hanoi puzzle.
//********************************************************************

public class TowersOfHanoi
{
   private int totalDisks;

   //-----------------------------------------------------------------
   //  Sets up the puzzle with the specified number of disks.
   //-----------------------------------------------------------------
   public TowersOfHanoi (int disks)
   {
      totalDisks = disks;
   }

   //-----------------------------------------------------------------
   //  Performs the initial call to moveTower to solve the puzzle.
   //  Moves the disks from tower 1 to tower 3 using tower 2.
   //-----------------------------------------------------------------
   public void solve ()
   {
      moveTower (totalDisks, 1, 3, 2);
   }

   //-----------------------------------------------------------------
   //  Moves the specified number of disks from one tower to another
   //  by moving a subtower of n-1 disks out of the way, moving one
   //  disk, then moving the subtower back. Base case of 1 disk.
   //-----------------------------------------------------------------
   private void moveTower (int numDisks, int start, int end, int temp)
   {
      if (numDisks == 1)
         moveOneDisk (start, end);
      else
      {
         moveTower (numDisks-1, start, temp, end);
         moveOneDisk (start, end);
         moveTower (numDisks-1, temp, end, start);
      }
   }

   //-----------------------------------------------------------------
   //  Prints instructions to move one disk from the specified start
   //  tower to the specified end tower.
   //-----------------------------------------------------------------
```

> **listing**
> **8.4** continued

```
    private void moveOneDisk (int start, int end)
    {
        System.out.println ("Move one disk from " + start + " to " +
                            end);
    }
}
```

Solving the Towers of Hanoi puzzle using recursion is pretty simple, but the solution is actually terribly inefficient. To solve the puzzle with a stack of N disks, we have to make 2^N-1 moves, thus the algorithm is $O(2^N)$. This is an example of *exponential complexity*. As the number of disks increases, the number of required moves increases exponentially.

> **key concept**
>
> The Towers of Hanoi solution has exponential complexity, which is very inefficient. Yet the implementation of the solution is incredibly short and elegant.

Legend has it that priests of Brahma are working on this puzzle in a temple at the center of the world. They are using 64 gold disks, moving them between pegs of pure diamond. The downside is that when the priests finish the puzzle, the world will end. The upside is that even if they move one disk every second of every day, it will take them over 584 billion years to complete it. That's with a puzzle of only 64 disks! So you can see just how inefficient exponential algorithms are.

8.3 recursion in sorting

We will now look at sorting algorithms (see Chapter 6) that use recursion. In particular, we will look at *merge sort* and *quick sort*. Both of these algorithms divide the list to be sorted into smaller sublists, recursively sort each sublist, and then combine the sublists into the final sorted list. In each algorithm the base case of the recursion is a list of one item.

merge sort

The merge sort algorithm sorts a list by dividing the list in half, recursively sorting the two half lists, and then *merging* the two sorted half lists together. At the deepest level of the recursion, we have lists of length one. The work of the sorting is in merging the pairs of half lists together, maintaining sorted order.

Consider the list of eight numbers shown in Figure 8.7. Merge sort divides the list in half, then into quarters, then into eighths. We end up with eight sublists of one element each, as shown at the top of the figure. As the recursion unravels, these lists are merged into lists of two elements, which are then merged into lists of four elements. Finally, the two lists of four elements are merged to form the final sorted list, as shown.

Listing 8.5 shows the `RecursiveSorts` class with methods for the merge sort and quick sort algorithms. The `mergeSort` method simply calls a helper method, `doMergeSort`, with some extra parameters telling it that the entire array should be sorted. The `doMergeSort` method does the recursion. It calculates the middle index of the portion of the array that should be sorted, then calls itself twice to sort the first half of the list and then the second half of the list. Once both halves are sorted, the `merge` method merges them together. Note that the recursion only happens when `start` is less than `end`. In a one-element sublist, `start` is equal to `end`, and, since nothing needs to be done to sort a one-element list, no recursion takes place.

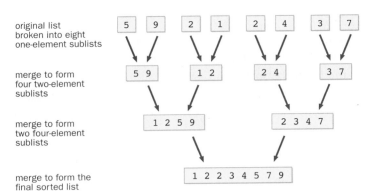

figure 8.7   Merge sort processing

listing
   8.5

```java
//********************************************************************
//  RecursiveSorts.java       Author: Lewis/Loftus/Cocking
//
//  Demonstrates the merge sort and quick sort algorithms.
//********************************************************************

public class RecursiveSorts
{
   //-----------------------------------------------------------------
   //  Sorts the specified array of integers using merge sort.
   //-----------------------------------------------------------------
   public static void mergeSort (int[] numbers)
   {
      doMergeSort(numbers, 0, numbers.length - 1);
   }

   //-----------------------------------------------------------------
   //  Recursively sorts the the portion of the given array beginning
   //  at start and ending at end.
   //-----------------------------------------------------------------
   private static void doMergeSort (int[] numbers, int start, int end)
   {
      if (start < end)
      {
         int middle = (start + end) / 2;
         doMergeSort (numbers, start, middle);
         doMergeSort (numbers, middle + 1, end);
         merge (numbers, start, middle, end);
      }
   }

   //-----------------------------------------------------------------
   //  Merges in sorted order the two sorted subarrays
   //  [start, middle] and [middle + 1, end].
   //-----------------------------------------------------------------
   private static void merge (int[] numbers, int start, int middle,
                    int end)
   {
      // This temporary array will be used to build the merged list.
      int[] tmp = new int[end - start + 1];

      int index1 = start;
      int index2 = middle + 1;
      int indexTmp = 0;

      // Loop until one of the sublists is exhausted, adding the smaller
      // of the first elements of each sublist to the merged list.
```

listing
8.5   continued

```java
      while (index1 <= middle && index2 <= end)
      {
         if (numbers[index1] < numbers[index2])
         {
            tmp[indexTmp] = numbers[index1];
            index1++;
         }
         else
         {
            tmp[indexTmp] = numbers[index2];
            index2++;
         }
          indexTmp++;
      }

      // Add to the merged list the remaining elements of whichever sublist
      // is not yet exhausted.
      while (index1 <= middle)
      {
         tmp[indexTmp] = numbers[index1];
         index1++;
         indexTmp++;
      }
      while (index2 <= end)
      {
         tmp[indexTmp] = numbers[index2];
         index2++;
         indexTmp++;
      }

      // Copy the merged list from tmp into numbers.
      for (indexTmp = 0; indexTmp < tmp.length; indexTmp++)
      {
         numbers[start + indexTmp] = tmp[indexTmp];
      }
   }

   //------------------------------------------------------------------
   //  Sorts the specified array of integers using quick sort.
   //------------------------------------------------------------------
   public static void quickSort (int[] numbers)
   {
      doQuickSort(numbers, 0, numbers.length - 1);
   }
```

listing
   8.5   continued

```java
//------------------------------------------------------------------
//  Recursively sorts the portion of the given array beginning
//  at start and ending at end.
//------------------------------------------------------------------
private static void doQuickSort (int[] numbers, int start, int end)
{
   if (start < end)
   {
      int middle = partition(numbers, start, end);
      doQuickSort(numbers, start, middle);
      doQuickSort(numbers, middle + 1, end);
   }
}


//------------------------------------------------------------------
//  Partitions the array such that each value in [start, middle]
//  is less than or equal to each value in [middle + 1, end].
//  The index middle is determined in the procedure and returned.
//------------------------------------------------------------------
private static int partition (int[] numbers, int start, int end)
{
   int pivot = numbers[start];
   int i = start - 1;
   int j = end + 1;

   // As the loop progresses, the indices i and j move towards each other.
   // Elements at i and j that are on the wrong side of the partition are
   // exchanged. When i and j pass each other, the loop ends and j is
   // returned as the index at which the elements are partitioned around.
   while (true)
   {
      i = i + 1;
      while (numbers[i] < pivot)
         i = i + 1;

      j = j - 1;
      while (numbers[j] > pivot)
         j = j - 1;

      if (i < j)
      {
         int tmp = numbers[i];
         numbers[i] = numbers[j];
         numbers[j] = tmp;
      }
      else return j;
   }
}
}
```

The merge method in Listing 8.5 merges the start to middle sublist with the middle + 1 to end sublist. A temporary array, tmp, is used to build up the final sorted list. Once the merge is done, the elements of tmp are copied back into the original array.

Since the two sublists are sorted, we need only look at the first element of each list to decide which is the first element of the merged list. We can keep adding elements to the merged list this way, comparing the first elements of the remaining portions of each sublist and adding the smaller as the next element in the merged list. When one of the sublists runs out of elements, we take the remaining elements from the other sublist to complete the merged list. Study the code for the merge method carefully to make sure you understand it. Listing 8.6 shows a program that sorts a list of grades using merge sort, something like the SortGrades class in Chapter 6.

listing
   8.6

```java
//********************************************************************
//   SortGrades.java        Author: Lewis/Loftus/Cocking
//
//   Driver for testing a numeric merge sort.
//********************************************************************

public class SortGrades
{
   //-----------------------------------------------------------------
   //   Creates an array of grades, sorts them, then prints them.
   //-----------------------------------------------------------------
   public static void main (String[] args)
   {
      int[] grades = {89, 94, 69, 80, 97, 85, 73, 91, 77, 85, 93};

      RecursiveSorts.mergeSort (grades);

      for (int index = 0; index < grades.length; index++)
         System.out.print (grades[index] + "   ");
   }
}
```

output

```
69   73   77   80   85   85   89   91   93   94   97
```

Now let's look at the efficiency of merge sort. We will let n be the number of elements in the list. The merge algorithm makes no more than one comparison for each element it places in the merged list, so it has a time complexity of $O(n)$. At each level of recursion a total of n elements are merged together by the merge method. For example, the final merge merges two halves of the list into the final sorted list, merging a total of n elements. Before that, merge was called twice to merge the first two and the second two quarters of the list, each call merging $n/2$ elements for a total of n elements merged at that level of recursion. We can keep working back like this until we get to one-element lists at the deepest level of recursion. At each level we merge a total of n elements. Now we need only know how many levels of recursion there are. Since we cut the list in half each time, there are $\log_2 n$ levels of recursion. Thus, the time complexity of the merge sort algorithm is $O(n\log n)$.

quick sort

The quick sort algorithm sorts a list of values by dividing the list into two sublists so that every value in the first sublist is less than or equal to every value in the second sublist. The two sublists are then sorted recursively. Unlike a merge sort, a quick sort does most of its work when it divides the list. It doesn't need to combine sublists after the recursive steps; the list is already sorted at that point. Also, unlike a merge sort, the two sublists need not be the same size.

> **key concept**
> Quick sort works by partitioning a list into two sublists and recursively sorting each sublist.

The partitioning works by selecting a *pivot* value. Every element less than or equal to the pivot is moved to the front of the array, while every element greater than or equal to the pivot is moved to the back of the array. There are several ways to pick the pivot element; we will use the first element in the list as the pivot. The two parts of the partitioned array will vary in size depending on the value of the pivot. The partition procedure returns the index that separates the two partitions. The quick sort algorithm uses the index returned by the partitioning to decide which sublists to recurse on.

> **key concept**
> Quick sort partitioning works by selecting a pivot value and moving every element less than or equal to the pivot to the front and every element greater than or equal to the pivot to the back of the array.

The code for quick sort is in the doQuickSort and partition methods in Listing 8.5. The partition method sets a variable, pivot, equal to the value of the first element in the part of the list to be partitioned. The variables i and j are used as indices into the list: i first points to the beginning and j points to the end, as shown at the top of Figure 8.8. The index i is increased by one as long as it points to a value less than the pivot; these elements are already on the proper side of the list. Likewise, j is decreased by one as long as it points to a value greater than the pivot. When i and j stop moving, they each point to an element that is on the wrong side of the list, as seen in the second and third steps in Figure 8.8. The two elements at indices i and j are swapped. If i and j pass each other (as shown in the fourth step in Figure 8.8), then the list has been partitioned and j is returned as the index that divides the two sublists. Study the code for the partition method carefully to make sure you understand it.

To determine the time efficiency of quick sort, we can use an analysis like the one we used for merge sort. The partition method, like the merge method, runs in O(n) time. If the partitioning divides the list into halves each time, then quick sort is also O(*nlogn*). This is what happens in the best case. If we have an uneven partitioning, we could end up with more than log$n$ levels of recursion. In the worst case each partitioning will divide the list into a sublist containing one element and a sublist containing the remaining elements. In this case there will be $n–1$ levels of recursion. So, in the worst case, quick sort has complexity O(n^2). The average time efficiency of quick sort is much closer to the best case than the worst case. The details are beyond the scope of this book, but quick sort's time efficiency for the average case is O($nlogn$).

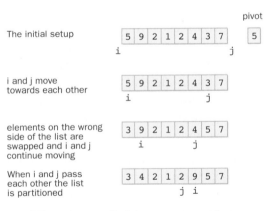

figure 8.8   Quick sort processing

AP CASE STUDY

8.4 bumper cars case study: putting it all together

We have worked out enough design details now to finish implementing our bumper cars program. The code is shown in Listings 8.7 through 8.13. Note the use of a boolean constant, DEBUG, defined in the Simulation class to control whether or not informational messages are printed while the simulation is running. While we debug our program these messages will be helpful. Once the program is complete, we can turn off the messages, so that they don't clutter the output, simply by changing the value of the constant.

listing
8.7

```java
//************************************************************************
// BumperCarSimulation.java        Author: Lewis/Loftus/Cocking
//
// This program runs a bumper car simulation.
//************************************************************************

import cs1.Keyboard;

public class BumperCarSimulation
{

    //-------------------------------------------------------------------
    // Creates a Simulation object to control the bumper car
    // simulation. The user types in the size of the arena and
    // how many bumper cars are in the arena. The simulation
    // continues until the user decides to stop it.
    //-------------------------------------------------------------------
    public static void main(String[] args)
    {
        System.out.println("Bumper Cars Simulation");
        int ew = 0;
        int ns = 0;
        int numCars = 0;
        boolean badInput = true;

        // Get the number of cars and size of the arena from the user.
        while (badInput) {
            System.out.println("How many cars?");
            numCars = Keyboard.readInt();
            System.out.println("Size of the arena's north-south"
                              + " dimension?");
            ns = Keyboard.readInt();
```

listing
    8.7   continued

```
            System.out.println("Size of the arena's east-west "
                                + "dimension?");
            ew = Keyboard.readInt();
            if (numCars > ew*ns)
            {
                System.out.println("Too many cars to fit in that "
                                    + "size arena!");
                System.out.println("Please enter the information "
                                    + "again:");
            }
            else if (numCars <= 0)
            {
                System.out.println("The number of cars must be greater"
                                    + " than 0!");
                System.out.println("Please enter the information "
                                    + "again:");
            }
            else
                badInput = false;
        }

        Arena arena = new Arena(ns, ew);
        Simulation sim = new Simulation(numCars, arena);

        int iterations = 0;
        String keepGoing;
        arena.printArena();
        System.out.println("Keep going? Type 'y' for yes or 'n' for"
                            + " no.");
        keepGoing = Keyboard.readString();
        while (keepGoing.equalsIgnoreCase("y"))
        {
            sim.step();
            iterations++;
            arena.printArena();
            System.out.println("Keep going? Type 'y' for yes or 'n'"
                                + " for no.");
            keepGoing = Keyboard.readString();
        }

        System.out.println("Number of iterations: " + iterations);
        sim.printBumpCounts();
    }

}
```

listing
    8.8

```java
//***********************************************************************
// Simulation.java          Author: Lewis/Loftus/Cocking
//
// The class used to control the simulation of the bumper car arena.
//***********************************************************************

import java.util.Random;
import java.util.ListIterator;
import java.util.ArrayList;

public class Simulation
{
    public static final boolean DEBUG = false;

    private Arena arena;
    private ArrayList allCars;

    public Simulation(int numCars, Arena theArena)
    {
        allCars = new ArrayList();
        arena = theArena;
        int arenaNSsize = arena.getNSsize();
        int arenaEWsize = arena.getEWsize();

        Random randomGen = new Random();
        Car car;
        Driver driver;
        int ns, ew;

        // Create the given number of cars and place them in the arena.
        for (int k=0; k < numCars; k++)
        {
            // Create a car-driver pair with a randomly-generated
            // position in the arena.
            ns = randomGen.nextInt(arenaNSsize);
            ew = randomGen.nextInt(arenaEWsize);
            // Assume that numCars < arenaNSsize * arenaEWsize
            // If not, the loop below would go on forever once the
            // arena is filled!
            while (arena.occupiedBy(ns, ew) != Arena.EMPTY)
            {
                ns = randomGen.nextInt(arenaNSsize);
                ew = randomGen.nextInt(arenaEWsize);
            }

            car = new Car(arena);
```

listing
  8.8   continued

```java
        // Turn the car to face a random direction
        car.turn(Direction.randomDirection());
        driver = new RandomDriver(car);
        car.setDriver(driver);
        arena.addCar(car, ns, ew);
        allCars.add(car);
    }
}

//-------------------------------------------------------------
// Perform one step in the simulation.
//-------------------------------------------------------------
public void step()
{
    arena.step();
}

//-------------------------------------------------------------
// Prints the bump count totals for all the drivers as text.
//-------------------------------------------------------------
public void printBumpCounts()
{
    System.out.println("Bump Counts:");
    int total = 0;

    // 'AB' way using ListIterator
    /*
    ListIterator listIterator = allCars.listIterator();
    while (listIterator.hasNext())
    {
        Car car = (Car)(listIterator.next());
        System.out.println(car.getBumpCount());
        total += car.getBumpCount();
    }
    */

    // 'A' way not using ListIterator
    for (int c=0; c < allCars.size(); c++)
    {
        Car car = (Car)(allCars.get(c));
        System.out.println(car.getBumpCount());
        total += car.getBumpCount();
    }

    System.out.println("Average bump count: " +
                    total / allCars.size());
}
}
```

listing
   8.9

```java
//********************************************************************
// Arena.java          Author: Lewis/Loftus/Cocking
//
// Represents a bumper car arena with cars in it.
//********************************************************************

import java.util.ArrayList;

public class Arena
{
    // Constants returned by the occupiedBy() method
    public static final int EMPTY = 0;
    public static final int CAR = 1;
    public static final int WALL = 2;

    // The size of the arena
    private int nsSize;
    private int ewSize;

    // A 2-d array representing the arena. The NW corner is position
    // 0,0. A null entry indicates that that position in the arena
    // is unoccupied.
    private Car[][] arena;

    //------------------------------------------------------------
    // Create an Arena of the given dimensions.
    //------------------------------------------------------------
    public Arena(int nsSize_, int ewSize_)
    {
        nsSize = nsSize_;
        ewSize = ewSize_;
        arena = new Car[nsSize][ewSize];
    }

    //------------------------------------------------------------
    // Returns the north-south size of this arena.
    //------------------------------------------------------------
    public int getNSsize()
    {
        return nsSize;
    }

    //------------------------------------------------------------
    // Returns the east-west size of this arena.
    //------------------------------------------------------------
    public int getEWsize()
    {
```

listing
    8.9   continued

```
        return ewSize;
    }

    //---------------------------------------------------------------
    // Add a car to the arena at the position given.
    //---------------------------------------------------------------
    public void addCar(Car car, int ns, int ew)
    {
        // If the positions given are out of bounds, an
        // exception will automatically be thrown.
        arena[ns][ew] = car;
    }

    //---------------------------------------------------------------
    // Let all cars take a turn to move. The order in which they
    // get to move is determined by scanning from west to east,
    // starting with the north-most row and continuing south after
    // each west-east scan.
    //---------------------------------------------------------------
    public void step()
    {
        // Use an ArrayList to keep track of which cars have gone
        // already. If a car moves east or south, it will come up again
        // in our search, but we don't want to move it again.
        ArrayList movedAlready = new ArrayList();

        for (int ns=0; ns < nsSize; ns++)
        {
            for (int ew=0; ew < ewSize; ew++)
            {
                if ((arena[ns][ew] != null) &&
                    (!movedAlready.contains(arena[ns][ew])))
                {
                    if (Simulation.DEBUG)
                        System.out.println("Arena: car at " + ns + ","
                                            + ew + " is going.");
                    movedAlready.add(arena[ns][ew]);
                    arena[ns][ew].go();
                }
            }
        }

        if (Simulation.DEBUG)
            System.out.println("Arena: 1 step taken.");
    }
```

listing
    8.9   continued

```java
//----------------------------------------------------------------
// Called by a car when it wants to move forward. If there is no
// obstacle in front of the car, it moves forward. Otherwise,
// it bumps into something and stays where it is.
//----------------------------------------------------------------
public void carMove(Car car, Direction dir)
{
    int[] posTo = null;
    int nsFrom = 0;
    int ewFrom = 0;
    // First find where the car is to begin with
    for (int ns=0; ns < nsSize; ns++)
    {
        for (int ew=0; ew < ewSize; ew++)
        {
            if ((arena[ns][ew] != null) &&
                (arena[ns][ew].equals(car)))
            {
                // Found the car
                nsFrom = ns;
                ewFrom = ew;
                posTo = newPos(ns, ew, dir);
            }
        }
    }

    // Try to move the car
    if (posTo != null)
    {
        int nsTo = posTo[0];
        int ewTo = posTo[1];
        // See if the car runs into a wall
        if (occupiedBy(nsTo, ewTo) == WALL)
            arena[nsFrom][ewFrom].gotBumped();
        // See if the car bumps another car
        else if (occupiedBy(nsTo, ewTo) == CAR)
        {
            arena[nsTo][ewTo].gotBumped();
            arena[nsFrom][ewFrom].gotBumped();
        }
        // Move the car
        else
        {
            arena[nsTo][ewTo] = arena[nsFrom][ewFrom];
            arena[nsFrom][ewFrom] = null;
        }
    }
}
```

listing
8.9   continued

```java
//------------------------------------------------------------
// Returns a constant indicating what the given position in the
// arena is occupied by - either EMPTY, CAR, or WALL.
//------------------------------------------------------------
public int occupiedBy(int ns, int ew)
{
    if (ns < 0 || ns >= nsSize || ew < 0 || ew >= ewSize)
        return WALL;
    else if (arena[ns][ew] != null)
        return CAR;
    else
        return EMPTY;
}


//------------------------------------------------------------
// Display the arena in a textual format.
//------------------------------------------------------------
public void printArena()
{
    // Print a top line
    for (int ew=0; ew < ewSize; ew++)
        System.out.print("-");
    System.out.println();

    // Print the cars in the arena
    for (int ns=0; ns < nsSize; ns++)
    {
        for (int ew=0; ew < ewSize; ew++)
        {
            if (arena[ns][ew] == null)
                System.out.print(" ");
            else
                System.out.print(arena[ns][ew].carAsChar());
        }
        System.out.println();
    }

    // Print a bottom line
    for (int ew=0; ew < ewSize; ew++)
        System.out.print("-");
    System.out.println();
}


//------------------------------------------------------------
// Returns the position that is in the direction indicated from
// the given position.
//------------------------------------------------------------
```

listing
    8.9   **continued**

```java
    private int[] newPos(int ns, int ew, Direction dir)
    {
        int[] pos = new int[2];
        pos[0] = ns;
        pos[1] = ew;
        if (dir.equals(Direction.NORTH)) pos[0] = ns - 1;
        else if (dir.equals(Direction.EAST)) pos[1] = ew + 1;
        else if (dir.equals(Direction.SOUTH)) pos[0] = ns + 1;
        else /* WEST */ pos[1] = ew - 1;

        return pos;
    }
}
```

listing
    8.10

```java
//************************************************************************
// Car.java            Author: Lewis/Loftus/Cocking
//
// Represents a car in a bumper car arena.
//************************************************************************

public class Car
{
    private Arena arena; // the arena this car is in
    private Driver driver = null; // the driver controlling this car
    private Direction direction = Direction.NORTH;
    private int bumpCount;

    //----------------------------------------------------------------
    // Create a Car.
    //----------------------------------------------------------------
    public Car(Arena theArena)
    {
        bumpCount = 0;
        arena = theArena;
    }

    //----------------------------------------------------------------
    // Sets the driver of this car.
    //----------------------------------------------------------------
    public void setDriver(Driver theDriver)
    {
        driver = theDriver;
    }
```

listing
8.10 continued

```
//----------------------------------------------------------------
// Returns the direction this car is facing. This function,
// though not used currently, could be useful to drivers as they
// decide what to do next.
//----------------------------------------------------------------
public Direction getDirection()
{
    return direction;
}

//----------------------------------------------------------------
// Returns the number of times that this car has bumped into
// obstacles (either other cars or a wall).
//----------------------------------------------------------------
public int getBumpCount()
{
    return bumpCount;
}

//----------------------------------------------------------------
// Tell the driver to drive. This function is called by the
// Arena when it is this car's turn to go.
//----------------------------------------------------------------
public void go()
{
    if (driver != null)
        driver.drive();
}

//----------------------------------------------------------------
// Move forward one unit. This function is used by the driver.
//----------------------------------------------------------------
public void moveForward()
{
    arena.carMove(this, direction);
}

//----------------------------------------------------------------
// Called when another car bumps into this car.
//----------------------------------------------------------------
public void gotBumped()
{
    bumpCount++;
}

//----------------------------------------------------------------
// Turn to face the given direction.
//----------------------------------------------------------------
```

listing
  8.10   continued

```java
public void turn(Direction newDirection)
{
    direction = newDirection;
}

//-----------------------------------------------------------------
// Turn to the left. The turn left, right, and around functions
// are used by the driver to control the car.
//-----------------------------------------------------------------
public void turnLeft()
{
    if (Simulation.DEBUG)
        System.out.println("Car:  turned left");

    turn(direction.toLeft());
}

//-----------------------------------------------------------------
// Turn to the right.
//-----------------------------------------------------------------
public void turnRight()
{
    if (Simulation.DEBUG)
        System.out.println("Car:  turned right");

    turn(direction.toRight());
}

//-----------------------------------------------------------------
// Turn around.
//-----------------------------------------------------------------
public void turnAround()
{
    if (Simulation.DEBUG)
        System.out.println("Car:  turned around");

    turn(direction.toOpposite());
}

//-----------------------------------------------------------------
// Returns a one-character string representing this car. The
// character returned indicates which direction the car is facing.
//-----------------------------------------------------------------
public String carAsChar()
{
    if (direction.equals(Direction.NORTH)) return "^";
    else if (direction.equals(Direction.EAST)) return ">";
```

listing
    8.10   continued

```
        else if (direction.equals(Direction.SOUTH)) return "v";
        else /* WEST */ return "<";
    }

}
```

listing
    8.11

```
//***********************************************************************
// Direction.java          Author: Lewis/Loftus/Cocking
//
// Represents a compass direction.
//***********************************************************************

import java.util.Random;

public class Direction
{

    public static final Direction NORTH = new Direction();
    public static final Direction EAST =  new Direction();
    public static final Direction SOUTH = new Direction();
    public static final Direction WEST =  new Direction();

    // For generating random numbers
    private static Random randGen = new Random();

    //----------------------------------------------------------------
    // The constructor is private so that Directions cannot be
    // created. The public Direction constants NORTH, EAST, SOUTH
    // and WEST should be used.
    //----------------------------------------------------------------
    private Direction()
    {
    }

    //----------------------------------------------------------------
    // Returns the direction to the right of this direction.
    //----------------------------------------------------------------
```

listing
   8.11   continued

```java
    public Direction toRight()
    {
        if (NORTH.equals(this)) return EAST;
        else if (EAST.equals(this)) return SOUTH;
        else if (SOUTH.equals(this)) return WEST;
        else /* WEST */ return NORTH;
    }

    //----------------------------------------------------------------
    // Returns the direction to the left of this direction.
    //----------------------------------------------------------------
    public Direction toLeft()
    {
        if (NORTH.equals(this)) return WEST;
        else if (EAST.equals(this)) return NORTH;
        else if (SOUTH.equals(this)) return EAST;
        else /* WEST */ return SOUTH;
    }

    //----------------------------------------------------------------
    // Returns the direction that is opposite this direction.
    //----------------------------------------------------------------
    public Direction toOpposite()
    {
        if (NORTH.equals(this)) return SOUTH;
        else if (EAST.equals(this)) return WEST;
        else if (SOUTH.equals(this)) return NORTH;
        else /* WEST */ return EAST;
    }

    //----------------------------------------------------------------
    // Returns a randomly-generated direction.
    //----------------------------------------------------------------
    public static Direction randomDirection()
    {
        int rand = randGen.nextInt(4);
        if (rand == 0) return NORTH;
        else if (rand == 1) return EAST;
        else if (rand == 2) return SOUTH;
        else /* rand == 3 */ return WEST;
    }

}
```

```
listing
   8.12
```

```
//***********************************************************************
// Driver.java          Author: Lewis/Loftus/Cocking
//
// An interface that all drivers of bumper cars must implement.
//***********************************************************************

public interface Driver
{

    //-------------------------------------------------------------
    // Drive the car one unit. Different drivers will have different
    // algorithms for determining where to drive the car next.
    //-------------------------------------------------------------
    public void drive();

}
```

Besides the classes we have already discussed, we created a `Direction` class to represent a direction (either North, South, East, or West) in the arena. This was necessary for each car to keep track of which way it is facing.

To represent the four possible directions, the `Direction` class contains constants `NORTH`, `SOUTH`, `EAST`, and `WEST`. Note that these constants are `Direction` objects themselves and are public. Users of the `Direction` class can access these constants to represent the desired direction. The constructor of `Direction` is private because only the public constants should be used. This is a common design pattern. This pattern means there can be only one `Direction` object representing each of the four directions. Thus comparisons can be done with `==` or `equals` and we don't need to override the `equals` method.

The `Direction` class also contains useful methods that operate on `Direction` objects. The methods `toRight`, `toLeft`, and `toOpposite` return the direction that is to the right, left, or opposite of the current direction. The method `randomDirection` randomly selects a direction and returns it.

listing
    8.13

```java
//********************************************************************
// RandomDriver.java          Author: Lewis/Loftus/Cocking
//
// Represents a driver whose moves are chosen randomly.
//********************************************************************

import java.util.Random;

public class RandomDriver implements Driver
{
    // Share a random number generator among all the RandomDrivers.
    private static Random randGen = new Random();

    private Car car;

    public RandomDriver(Car aCar)
    {
        car = aCar;
    }

    //-----------------------------------------------------------------
    // Drive the car one unit. The random driver chooses a move
    // randomly.
    //-----------------------------------------------------------------
    public void drive()
    {
        if (Simulation.DEBUG)
            System.out.println("RandomDriver: drive");

        // Move forward 70% of the time. Turn to face another direction
        // 30% of the time. (Equal probability for each of the three
        // remaining directions.)
        final int moveForwardProb = 70;
        int probability = randGen.nextInt(100);

        if (probability < moveForwardProb)
            car.moveForward();
        else {
            int turnWhichWay = randGen.nextInt(3);
            if (turnWhichWay == 0)
                car.turnLeft();
            else if (turnWhichWay == 1)
                car.turnRight();
            else /* turnWhichWay == 2 */
                car.turnAround();
        }
    }

}
```

testing

We tested our first stage implementation by putting a `main` method in the `Arena` class. Now we can run the program as it will be run by users. We should create a complete set of test cases for our program so we know it works.

When we think about testing any program, we should create test cases that cause errors and that test unusual or boundary inputs. By boundaries we mean the edges of the input—for example, testing a simulation with zero cars or only one car.

For our bumper cars simulation, the only user inputs are the number of cars, the size of the arena, and then a yes or no after each step to tell us whether the user wants to continue the simulation. We should test several arena sizes and numbers of cars, including invalid configurations, such as too many cars to fit in the arena. We should test an arena that is very full and one that is nearly empty as well as a very small arena and a large arena. As to the number of steps in the simulation, we should test not running any steps (that is, answering "no" the first time we are asked if we want to continue), as well as running more than one step. The table below summarizes the test cases we will run our program through.

Type of Test Case	Example Input for Test Case
Error: too many cars to fit in arena	5 × 5 arena, 28 cars
Full arena: cars won't be able to move	4 × 4 arena, 16 cars, run for 2 steps
Large, nearly empty arena, few cars	20 × 40 arena, 2 cars, run for 3 steps
Very small arena, one car	1 × 2 arena, 1 car, run for 3 steps
No steps in simulation	7 × 3 arena, 5 cars, run 0 steps
Average case: medium-size arena	8 × 10 arena, 10 cars, run 10 steps

extensions

The program we have written satisfies the basic needs of the bumper car company. We also tried to write the code so that the program could be extended in the future with only a few changes to the code. One obvious extension is to have different kinds of drivers. The bumper car company could do some research and discover that most bumper car drivers fall into categories. Perhaps one type of driver is an aggressive one who always tries to bump into the nearest car. With the `Driver` interface, it is easy to add new kinds of drivers to the simulation. We only need to write a class that implements the `Driver` interface.

If there are different kinds of drivers, there must be some way of choosing how many of each type will be in the simulation. This could be decided automatically by the program using statistics collected by the bumper car company. For example, perhaps 25 percent of drivers drive aggressively. Or the program might be modified to let the user pick the types of drivers.

Another extension might be to add a mode where the simulation runs in real time, not pausing between steps. The user could stop the simulation at any point. This would be useful with a graphical display showing the cars moving around the arena, instead of a scrolling text display.

exercises

1. Add a `toString` method to the `Direction` class that prints a string version of the direction. Write a driver program that tests your new method.

2. List more sample inputs for each of the types of test cases given.

3. What other extensions could we add to the simulation in the future?

8.5 recursion in graphics

Recursion has several uses in images and graphics. The following section explores some image and graphics-based recursion examples.

tiled pictures

Carefully look at the display for the `TiledPictures` applet shown in Listing 8.14. There are actually three images. The entire area is divided into four equal sections. A picture of the world (with a circle indicating the Himalayan mountain region) is shown in the bottom-right section. The bottom-left section has a picture of Mt. Everest. In the top-right section is a picture of a mountain goat.

The interesting part of the picture is the top-left section. It contains a copy of the entire collage, including itself. In this smaller version you can see the three simple pictures in their three sections. And again, in the top-left corner, the picture is repeated (including itself). This repetition continues for several

listing
   8.14

```
//***********************************************************************
//  TiledPictures.java         Author: Lewis/Loftus/Cocking
//
//  Demonstrates the use of recursion.
//***********************************************************************

import java.awt.*;
import javax.swing.JApplet;

public class TiledPictures extends JApplet
{
   private final int APPLET_WIDTH = 320;
   private final int APPLET_HEIGHT = 320;
   private final int MIN = 20;   // smallest picture size

   private Image world, everest, goat;

   //----------------------------------------------------------------
   //  Loads the images.
   //----------------------------------------------------------------
   public void init()
   {
      world = getImage (getDocumentBase(), "world.gif");
      everest = getImage (getDocumentBase(), "everest.gif");
      goat = getImage (getDocumentBase(), "goat.gif");

      setSize (APPLET_WIDTH, APPLET_HEIGHT);
   }

   //----------------------------------------------------------------
   //  Draws the three images, then calls itself recursively.
   //----------------------------------------------------------------
   public void drawPictures (int size, Graphics page)
   {
      page.drawImage (everest, 0, size/2, size/2, size/2, this);
      page.drawImage (goat, size/2, 0, size/2, size/2, this);
      page.drawImage (world, size/2, size/2, size/2, size/2, this);

      if (size > MIN)
         drawPictures (size/2, page);
   }
```

listing
    8.14   continued

```
    //----------------------------------------------------------------
    //  Performs the initial call to the drawPictures method.
    //----------------------------------------------------------------
    public void paint (Graphics page)
    {
        drawPictures (APPLET_WIDTH, page);
    }
}
```

display

levels. It is like what you see when you look in a mirror in the reflection of another mirror.

This effect is created quite easily using recursion. The applet's `init` method first loads the three images. The `paint` method then invokes the `drawPictures` method, which accepts a parameter that defines the size of the picture area. It draws the three images using the `drawImage` method, making the picture the correct size. The `drawPictures` method is then called recursively to draw the upper-left quadrant.

Each time, if the drawing area is large enough, the `drawPictures` method is invoked again, using a smaller drawing area. Eventually, the drawing area becomes so small that the recursive call is not performed. Note that `drawPictures` assumes the beginning (0, 0) coordinate as the relative location of the new images, no matter what their size is.

The base case of the recursion in this problem is a minimum size for the drawing area. Because the size is decreased each time, the base case eventually is reached and the recursion stops. This is why the upper-left corner is empty in the smallest version of the collage.

fractals

A *fractal* is a geometric shape made up of the same pattern repeated at different sizes and positions. Recursion is good at creating fractals. Interest in fractals has grown immensely in recent years, largely due to Benoit Mandelbrot, a Polish mathematician born in 1924. He demonstrated that

> **key concept**
>
> A fractal is a geometric shape made up of repeated patterns.

there are fractals in many places in mathematics and nature. Computers have made fractals much easier to create and study. Over the past quarter century, the bright, interesting images that can be created with fractals have become as much an art form as a mathematical interest.

One example of a fractal is called the *Koch snowflake*, named after Helge von Koch, a Swedish mathematician. It begins with an equilateral triangle, which we call the Koch fractal of order 1. Koch fractals of higher orders are made by repeatedly changing all of the line segments in the shape.

To create the next higher order Koch fractal, the middle third of each line segment is replaced by two line segments, each having the same length as the replaced part. The line segments always come to an outward point. Figure 8.9 shows several orders of Koch fractals. As the order increases, the shape begins to look like a snowflake.

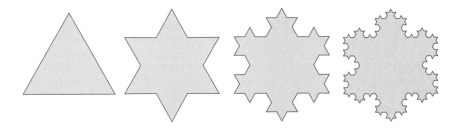

figure 8.9   Several orders of the Koch snowflake

The applet shown in Listing 8.15 draws a Koch snowflake. The buttons at the top of the applet let the user increase and decrease the order of the fractal. Each time a button is pressed, the fractal image is redrawn. The applet serves as the listener for the buttons.

The fractal image is drawn on a canvas defined by the KochPanel class shown in Listing 8.16. The paint method makes the first calls to the recursive method drawFractal. The three calls to drawFractal in the paint method draw the original three sides of the equilateral triangle that make up a Koch fractal of order 1.

The variable current is the order of the fractal to be drawn. Each recursive call to drawFractal decreases the order by 1. The base case is the fractal with the order 1, which is a simple line.

If the order of the fractal is more than 1, three additional points are computed. Together with the parameters, these points form the four line segments of the new fractal. Figure 8.10 shows the transformation.

Based on the position of the two end points of the original line, a point one-third of the way and a point two-thirds of the way between them are computed. The calculations to determine the three new points actually have nothing to do with the recursive technique used to draw the fractal, so we won't discuss the details of these computations here.

An interesting mathematical feature of a Koch snowflake is that it has an infinite perimeter but a finite area. That is, the outline of the snowflake gets longer and longer because it jogs in and out, but the snowflake stays the same size. The outline can be an infinite length, but a rectangle drawn around the snowflake will never get bigger.

listing
   8.15

```
//********************************************************************
//  KochSnowflake.java       Author: Lewis/Loftus/Cocking
//
//  Demonstrates the use of recursion.
//********************************************************************

import java.awt.*;
import java.awt.event.*;
import javax.swing.*;

public class KochSnowflake extends JApplet implements ActionListener
{
    private final int APPLET_WIDTH = 400;
    private final int APPLET_HEIGHT = 440;

    private final int MIN = 1, MAX = 9;

    private JButton increase, decrease;
    private JLabel titleLabel, orderLabel;
    private KochPanel drawing;
    private JPanel appletPanel, tools;

    //-----------------------------------------------------------------
    //  Sets up the components for the applet.
    //-----------------------------------------------------------------
    public void init()
    {
        tools = new JPanel ();
        tools.setLayout (new BoxLayout(tools, BoxLayout.X_AXIS));
        tools.setBackground (Color.yellow);
        tools.setOpaque (true);

        titleLabel = new JLabel ("The Koch Snowflake");
        titleLabel.setForeground (Color.black);

        increase = new JButton (new ImageIcon ("increase.gif"));
        increase.setPressedIcon (new ImageIcon ("increasePressed.gif"));
        increase.setMargin (new Insets (0, 0, 0, 0));
        increase.addActionListener (this);
```

listing
     8.15   continued

```
      decrease = new JButton (new ImageIcon ("decrease.gif"));
      decrease.setPressedIcon (new ImageIcon ("decreasePressed.gif"));
      decrease.setMargin (new Insets (0, 0, 0, 0));
      decrease.addActionListener (this);

      orderLabel = new JLabel ("Order: 1");
      orderLabel.setForeground (Color.black);

      tools.add (titleLabel);
      tools.add (Box.createHorizontalStrut (20));
      tools.add (decrease);
      tools.add (increase);
      tools.add (Box.createHorizontalStrut (20));
      tools.add (orderLabel);

      drawing = new KochPanel (1);

      appletPanel = new JPanel();
      appletPanel.add (tools);
      appletPanel.add (drawing);

      getContentPane().add (appletPanel);

      setSize (APPLET_WIDTH, APPLET_HEIGHT);
   }

   //-----------------------------------------------------------------
   //  Determines which button was pushed, and sets the new order
   //  if it is in range.
   //-----------------------------------------------------------------
   public void actionPerformed (ActionEvent event)
   {
      int order = drawing.getOrder();

      if (event.getSource() == increase)
         order++;
      else
         order--;

      if (order >= MIN && order <= MAX)
      {
         orderLabel.setText ("Order: " + order);
         drawing.setOrder (order);
```

listing
8.15   continued

```
        repaint();
    }
  }
}
```

display

listing
   8.16

```
//****************************************************************
//   KochPanel.java       Author: Lewis/Loftus/Cocking
//
//   Represents a drawing surface on which to paint a Koch Snowflake.
//****************************************************************

import java.awt.*;
import javax.swing.JPanel;

public class KochPanel extends JPanel
{
   private final int PANEL_WIDTH = 400;
   private final int PANEL_HEIGHT = 400;

   private final double SQ = Math.sqrt(3.0) / 6;

   private final int TOPX = 200, TOPY = 20;
   private final int LEFTX = 60, LEFTY = 300;
   private final int RIGHTX = 340, RIGHTY = 300;

   private int current; //current order

   //----------------------------------------------------------------
   //   Sets the initial fractal order to the value specified.
   //----------------------------------------------------------------
   public KochPanel (int currentOrder)
   {
      current = currentOrder;
      setBackground (Color.black);
      setPreferredSize (new Dimension(PANEL_WIDTH, PANEL_HEIGHT));
   }

   //----------------------------------------------------------------
   //   Draws the fractal recursively. Base case is an order of 1 for
   //   which a simple straight line is drawn. Otherwise three
   //   intermediate points are computed, and each line segment is
   //   drawn as a fractal.
   //----------------------------------------------------------------
   public void drawFractal (int order, int x1, int y1, int x5, int y5,
                       Graphics page)
   {
      int deltaX, deltaY, x2, y2, x3, y3, x4, y4;
```

listing
    8.16   continued

```java
    if (order == 1)
        page.drawLine (x1, y1, x5, y5);
    else
    {
        deltaX = x5 - x1;   // distance between end points
        deltaY = y5 - y1;

        x2 = x1 + deltaX / 3;   // one third
        y2 = y1 + deltaY / 3;

        x3 = (int) ((x1+x5)/2 + SQ * (y1-y5));   // tip of projection
        y3 = (int) ((y1+y5)/2 + SQ * (x5-x1));

        x4 = x1 + deltaX * 2/3;   // two thirds
        y4 = y1 + deltaY * 2/3;

        drawFractal (order-1, x1, y1, x2, y2, page);
        drawFractal (order-1, x2, y2, x3, y3, page);
        drawFractal (order-1, x3, y3, x4, y4, page);
        drawFractal (order-1, x4, y4, x5, y5, page);
    }
}

//-----------------------------------------------------------------
//  Performs the initial calls to the drawFractal method.
//-----------------------------------------------------------------
public void paintComponent (Graphics page)
{
    super.paintComponent (page);

    page.setColor (Color.green);

    drawFractal (current, TOPX, TOPY, LEFTX, LEFTY, page);
    drawFractal (current, LEFTX, LEFTY, RIGHTX, RIGHTY, page);
    drawFractal (current, RIGHTX, RIGHTY, TOPX, TOPY, page);
}
```

listing
8.16   **continued**

```java
//---------------------------------------------------------------
//  Sets the fractal order to the value specified.
//---------------------------------------------------------------
public void setOrder (int order)
{
    current = order;
}


//---------------------------------------------------------------
//  Returns the current order.
//---------------------------------------------------------------
public int getOrder ()
{
    return current;
}
}
```

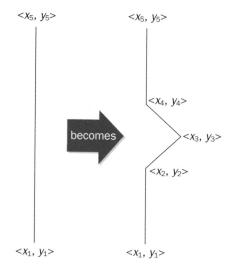

figure 8.10   The transformation of each line segment of a Koch snowflake

summary of
key concepts

▶ Recursion is a programming technique in which a method calls itself. To program recursively we need to think recursively.

▶ Any recursive definition must have a nonrecursive part, called the base case, so that the recursion will eventually end.

▶ Math problems are often expressed recursively.

▶ Each recursive call to a method creates new local variables and parameters.

▶ Recursion is the best way to solve some problems, but for others it does not work as efficiently as an iterative solution.

▶ The Towers of Hanoi solution is very inefficient. Yet the implementation of the solution is incredibly short and elegant.

▶ Merge sort works by dividing a list in half, recursively sorting the two sublists, an then merging them together.

▶ Quick sort works by partitioning a list into two sublists and recursively sorting each sublist.

▶ Quick sort partitioning works by selecting a pivot value and moving every element less than or equal to the pivot to the front and every element greater than or equal to the pivot to the back of the array.

▶ Quick sort runs in time $O(n\log n)$ on the average but has time complexity $O(n^2)$ in the worst case.

▶ A fractal is a geometric shape that can be defined naturally in a recursive manner.

self-review questions

8.1 What is recursion?

8.2 What is infinite recursion?

8.3 When is a base case needed for recursive processing?

8.4 Is recursion necessary?

8.5 When should recursion be avoided?

8.6 What is indirect recursion?

8.7 Explain the general approach to solving the Towers of Hanoi puzzle. How does it relate to recursion?

8.8   How does merge sort work?

8.9   How does quick sort partition an array?

8.10 What is a fractal? What does it have to do with recursion?

multiple choice

Questions 8.1 through 8.6 refer to the following method:

```
int mystery (int w)
{
   if (w < 0)  return 0;
   int x = mystery (w - 2);
   return w - x;
}
```

8.1   Which line of code is the base case in the recursion?

   a. int mystery (int w)

   b. if (w < 0) return 0;

   c. int x = mystery (w - 2);

   d. return w - x;

   e. There is no base case.

8.2   Which line of code is the recursive case?

   a. int mystery (int w)

   b. if (w < 0) return 0;

   c. int x = mystery (w - 2);

   d. return w - x;

   e. There is no recursive case.

8.3   What is returned by the call mystery(2)?

   a. 0

   b. 1

   c. 2

   d. 3

   e. 4

8.4   What is returned by the call `mystery(5)`?

   a. 0

   b. 2

   c. 3

   d. 4

   e. 5

8.5. Which line's removal would cause infinite recursion?

   a. `int mystery (int w)`

   b. `if (w < 0)   return 0;`

   c. `int x = mystery (w — 2);`

   d. `return w — x;`

   e. The recursion is already infinite.

8.6. The `mystery` method is an example of

   a. direct recursion

   b. indirect recursion

   c. iteration

   d. inheritance

   e. interpretation

Questions 8.7 and 8.8 refer to the following method:

```
void arrayTraverse (int curIndex, int[] array)
{
    if (curIndex == array.length)
       return;

    // process array[curIndex]

    arrayTraverse (_____ , array);
}
```

8.7   The method `arrayTraverse` recursively visits each element in an array, processing each in some way. Which expression should go in the blank?

   a. 0

   b. `array.length — 1`

   c. `curIndex`

   d. `curIndex — 1`

   e. `curIndex + 1`

8.8   How should `arrayTraverse` be called to process every element in the array nums?

a. `arrayTraverse (nums.length, nums)`

b. `arrayTraverse (nums.length - 1, nums)`

c. `arrayTraverse (1, nums)`

d. `arrayTraverse (0, nums)`

e. `arrayTraverse (nums.length + 1, nums)`

8.9   Which definitions recursively define an exercise set to be made up of one or more problems?

I
```
ExSet: problem
    or problem problem
```

II
```
ExSet: problem
    or ExSet problem
```

III
```
ExSet: problem
    or problem ExSet
```

a. I only

b. II only

c. III only

d. I and III

e. II and III

8.10 Consider different types of solutions to the same problem. Which type of solution involves the fewest number of method calls?

a. iterative solution

b. direct recursive solution

c. indirect recursive solution

d. infinite recursive solution

e. recursive solution with no base case

true/false

8.1 Recursion is a technique in which a method calls itself.

8.2 Each recursive call to a method creates new local variables and parameters.

8.3 Method `f1` calling method `f2` and `f2` calling `f1` is an example of direct recursion.

8.4 Any problem that can be solved recursively can be solved iteratively.

8.5 A recursive method must have a return value.

8.6 Indirect recursion is the same thing as iteration.

8.7 Any recursive definition must have a base case that causes the recursion to end.

8.8 A good use of recursion would be to calculate how much an employee should be paid given their pay rate and hours worked.

8.9 Merge sort is a recursive sort with time complexity $O(n\log n)$.

8.10 When indirect recursion is used, a base case is unnecessary.

short answer

8.1 Write a recursive definition of a valid Java identifier (see Chapter 1).

8.2 Write a recursive definition of x^y (x raised to the power y), where x and y are integers and $y > 0$.

8.3 Write a recursive definition of $i * j$ (integer multiplication), where $i > 0$. Define the multiplication process in terms of integer addition. For example, 4×7 is equal to 7 added to itself 4 times.

8.4 Write a recursive definition of the Fibonacci numbers. The Fibonacci numbers are a sequence of integers, each of which is the sum of the previous two numbers. The first two numbers in the sequence are 0 and 1. Explain why you would not normally use recursion to solve this problem.

8.5 Modify the method that calculates the sum of the integers between 1 and N shown in this chapter. Have the new version match the following recursive definition: The sum of 1 to N is the sum of 1 to $(N/2)$ plus the sum of $(N/2 + 1)$ to N. Trace your solution using an N of 7.

8.6 Write a recursive method that returns the value of N! (N factorial) using the definition given in this chapter. Explain why you would not normally use recursion to solve this problem.

8.7 Write a recursive method to reverse a string. Explain why you would not normally use recursion to solve this problem.

8.8 Design a new maze for the MazeSearch program in this chapter and rerun the program. Explain how the program works, giving examples of a path that was tried but failed, a path that was never tried, and the final solution.

8.9 Make notes next to the lines of output of the SolveTowers program in this chapter to show the recursive steps.

8.10 Produce a chart showing the number of moves needed to solve the Towers of Hanoi puzzle using the following number of disks: 2, 3, 4, 5, 6, 7, 8, 9, 10, 15, 20, and 25.

8.11 Describe a strategy for choosing a pivot value in quick sort so that the list will always be partitioned into two equal halves. Does your strategy change the time efficiency of quick sort?

8.12 How many line segments are used to make a Koch snowflake of order N? Make a chart showing the number of line segments that make up a Koch snowflake for orders 1 through 9.

programming projects

8.1 Design and implement a recursive version of the PalindromeTester program from (Listing 3.9) Chapter 3.

8.2 Design and implement a program for finding the greatest common divisor of two positive numbers using Euclid's algorithm. The greatest common divisor is the largest number that divides both numbers without producing a remainder. An iterative version of this method was part of the Rational class presented in Chapter 4. In a class called DivisorCalc, define a static method called gcd that accepts two integers, num1 and num2. Create a driver to test your implementation. The recursive algorithm is defined as follows:

a. gcd (num1, num2) is num2 if num2 <= num1 and num2 divides num1

b. gcd (num1, num2) is gcd (num2, num1) if num1 < num2

c. gcd (num1, num2) is gcd (num2, num1%num2) otherwise

8.3   Modify the `Maze` class (Listing 8.2) so that it prints out the path of the final solution as it is discovered, without storing it.

8.4   Design and implement a program that solves a 3D maze.

8.5   Change the `TiledPictures` program (Listing 8.14) so that the repeated images appear in the lower-right quadrant.

8.6   Design and implement a recursive program that solves the Nonattacking Queens problem. The Nonattacking Queens problem is how eight queens can be positioned on an eight-by-eight chessboard so that none of them are in the same row, column, or diagonal as any other queen. There are no other chess pieces on the board.

8.7   In the language of an alien race, all words take the form of Blurbs. A Blurb is a Whoozit followed by one or more Whatzits. A Whoozit is the character x followed by zero or more ys. A Whatzit is a q followed by either a z or a d, followed by a Whoozit. Design and implement a recursive program that generates random Blurbs in this alien language.

8.8   Design and implement a recursive program to decide whether a string is a valid Blurb as defined in Programming Project 8.7.

8.9   Design and implement a recursive program to print the Nth line of Pascal's Triangle, as shown here. Each inside value is the sum of the two values above it. *Hint*: Use an array to store the values on each line.

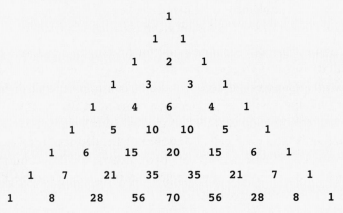

8.10   Change the quick sort code in Listing 8.5 to use the middle element as the pivot, rather than the first. Write a program that sorts prices (doubles) to test your quick sort.

8.11 Design and implement a graphic version of the Towers of Hanoi puzzle. Let the user set the number of disks used in the puzzle. The user should be able to interact with the puzzle in two ways. The user can move the disks from one peg to another using the mouse, in which case the program should make sure that each move is legal. The user can also watch a solution take place as an animation, with pause/resume buttons. Let the user control the speed of the animation.

answers to self-review questions

8.1 Recursion is a programming technique in which a method calls itself, solving a smaller version of the problem each time, until the base case is reached.

8.2 Infinite recursion is when there is no base case to end the recursion or when the base case doesn't work. The recursive path is followed forever. In a recursive program, infinite recursion will often result in an error that tells us available memory has been used up.

8.3 A base case is always needed to end recursion. Without the base case, infinite recursion results.

8.4 Recursion is not necessary. Every recursive algorithm can be written in an iterative manner. However, some problem solutions are much more elegant and straightforward when written recursively.

8.5 Avoid recursion when the iterative solution is simpler and more easily understood and programmed. Recursion has many method calls and is not always easy to follow.

8.6 Indirect recursion occurs when a method calls another method, which calls another method, and so on until one of the called methods invokes the original. Indirect recursion is usually more difficult to trace than direct recursion, in which a method calls itself.

8.7 The Towers of Hanoi puzzle of N disks is solved by moving $N-1$ disks out of the way onto an extra peg, moving the largest disk to the last peg, then moving the $N-1$ disks from the extra peg to the last peg. This solution is recursive because, to move the sub-stack of $N-1$ disks, we can use the same process.

8.8   Merge sort works by dividing a list in half, recursively sorting the two sublists, and then merging them together.

8.9   Quick sort partitioning works by selecting a pivot value and moving every element less than or equal to the pivot to the front and every element greater than or equal to the pivot to the back of the array.

8.10 A fractal is a geometric shape made of many versions of the same shape of different sizes, in different positions. Recursion can be used to draw the shapes over and over again.

To solve problems we need ways to organize and manage information. The term *data structures* refers to the ways information can be organized and used. Many data structures have been developed over the years, and some of them have become classics. Often, a data structure can be used in many ways. This chapter explains how data structures can be used with references to link one object to another. This chapter also introduces queues and stacks.

chapter
objectives

- Explore the idea of a collection.

- Introduce the predefined collection classes in the Java standard class library.

- Examine the difference between fixed and dynamic implementations.

- Define and use dynamically linked lists.

- Define queue and stack data structures.

9.0 collections

A *collection* is an object that holds other objects. It can be used in many situations, but we usually use a collection to add, remove, and otherwise manage the elements in it. For example, the `ArrayList` class (discussed in Chapter 6) is a collection. It gives us ways to add or remove elements of a list.

Some collections keep their elements in a specific order, while others do not. Some collections are *homogeneous,* meaning that they can hold all of the same type of object; other collections are *heterogeneous,* which means they can have objects of different types. An `ArrayList` is heterogeneous because it can hold an object of any type. An `ArrayList` stores `Object` references, which means it can store any object because of inheritance and polymorphism (as discussed in Chapter 7).

separating interface from implementation

Collections can be implemented in several ways. That is, the data structure that stores the objects can be implemented using different techniques. The `ArrayList` class from the Java standard library, for instance, is implemented using an array. All operations on an `ArrayList` are done by invoking methods that work with the array.

An *abstract data type* (ADT) is a collection of data and the operations that are allowed on that data. An ADT has a name, a domain of values, and a set of operations that can be performed. An ADT is abstract because the details of its data and methods are "hidden" behind an interface.

Objects are perfect for defining ADTs. An object has a well-defined interface that is "hidden" in the class. The data and the operations that manage the data are encapsulated together inside the object. This type of encapsulated ADT is reusable and reliable, because its interaction with the rest of the system is controlled.

Java API collection classes

The Java standard class library has several classes that represent collections. These are called the *Java Collections API* (Application Programmer Interface).

The names of the classes in this set generally include both the collection type and the implementation. One example is the `ArrayList` class, which represents a *list* collection with an *array* implementation. In addition, a `LinkedList` class represents a *list* collection with a *linked* implementation.

Several interfaces are used to define the collection operations themselves. These interfaces include `List`, `Set`, and `Map`. A `Set` is a collection of elements without duplicates. A `Map` is a group of elements that can be referenced by a key value. The `Set` and `Map` interfaces are explored in the next chapter.

9.1 representing data structures

An array is only one way to organize a list. Arrays are limited because they have a fixed size. Sometimes we don't know how big to make an array because we don't know how much information we will store. The `ArrayList` class handles this by creating a larger array and copying everything over into it. This is not very efficient. Fortunately, there's another way to do this.

A *dynamic data structure* is implemented using links. Using references as links between objects, we can create whatever type of structure we need. If we are careful, the structure can be easy to search and modify. Structures created this way are called dynamic because their size changes dynamically, as they are used.

> **key concept**
> A fixed data structure has a specific size for the duration of its existence, whereas a dynamic data structure grows and shrinks as needed.

dynamic structures

Remember from Chapter 4 that all objects are created dynamically using the `new` operator. A variable used to keep track of an object is actually a reference to the object, meaning that it stores the address of the object. So a declaration such as:

```
House home = new House ("602 Greenbriar Court");
```

does two things: it declares `home` to be a reference to a `House` object, and it instantiates an object of class `House`. Now consider an object that has a reference to another object of the same type. For example:

```
class ListNode
{
    Object value;
    ListNode next;
}
```

Two objects of this class can be instantiated and chained together by having the `next` reference of one `ListNode` object refer to the other

> **key concept**
> A dynamically linked list is managed by storing and updating references to objects.

ListNode object. The second object's `next` reference can refer to a third object, and so on, creating a *linked list*. Each `ListNode` object in the list is called a node. The first node in the list could be referenced using a separate variable. The last node in the list would have a `next` reference that is `null`, which means this is the end of the list. Figure 9.1 shows how this works. In this example, the information stored in each `ListNode` class is an `Object` so it can contain any type of information.

Listing 9.1 shows the class `ListNode`, which is an implementation of a node in a linked list. This class was written by the AP committee and will be provided on the AP exam.

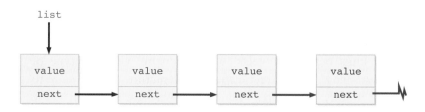

figure 9.1   A linked list

---

listing
9.1

```
//********************************************************************
//   ListNode.java          Author: AP Committee, comments added by
//                                  Lewis/Loftus/Cocking
//
//   A node in a linked list.
//********************************************************************


public class ListNode
{
    private Object value;
    private ListNode next;
```

listing
   9.1   continued

```
//-------------------------------------------------------------
//  Initializes this node.
//-------------------------------------------------------------
public ListNode (Object initValue, ListNode initNext)
{
   value = initValue;
   next = initNext;
}


//-------------------------------------------------------------
//  Returns the value of this node.
//-------------------------------------------------------------
public Object getValue ()
{
   return value;
}


//-------------------------------------------------------------
//  Returns the next reference in this node.
//-------------------------------------------------------------
public ListNode getNext ()
{
   return next;
}


//-------------------------------------------------------------
//  Sets the value of this node.
//-------------------------------------------------------------
public void setValue (Object theNewValue)
{
   value = theNewValue;
}


//-------------------------------------------------------------
//  Sets the next reference in this node.
//-------------------------------------------------------------
public void setNext (ListNode theNewNext)
{
   next = theNewNext;
}
}
```

managing linked lists

No matter what is stored in a linked list, there are a few basic ways to manage the nodes on the list: nodes are added to a list and they are removed from the list. We have to be careful when we're dealing with the first node because that affects the reference to the whole list.

inserting nodes

A node may be inserted anywhere: at the front of the list, in the middle of the list, or at the end of the list. When we add a node to the front of the list we have to reset the reference to the whole list, as shown in Figure 9.2. First, the next reference of the added node is set to point to the current first node in the list. Second, the reference to the front of the list is reset to point to the added node.

> **key concept**
>
> When adding a node to the beginning of a linked list, the next reference of the added node must be set before the reference to the old first node is changed.

You would have problems if you did this the other way around—if you set the reference to the added node list first—because you would lose the only reference to the existing list and wouldn't be able to get any of the nodes in the list.

Inserting a node into the middle of a list is a little more complicated. First we have to find the node in the list that will come before the new node. Unlike an array, in a linked list we use a separate reference to move through the nodes of the list until we find the one we want. This is often called a `current` reference, because it indicates the current node in the list.

At first, `current` is set to point to the first node in the list. Then a loop is used to move the current reference along the list nodes until the node before the inserted node is found. Then the new node can be inserted, as shown in Figure 9.3.

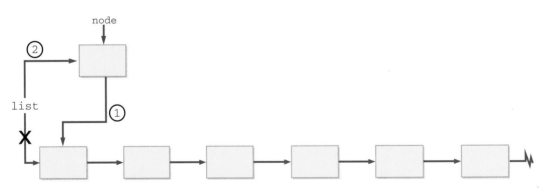

figure 9.2   Inserting a node at the front of a linked list

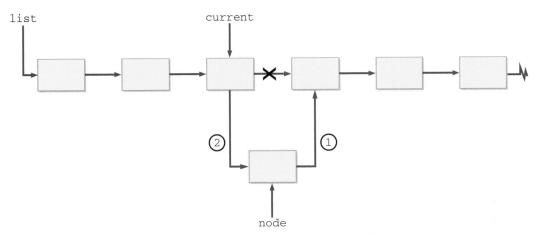

figure 9.3   Inserting a node in the middle of a linked list

First, the `next` pointer of the new node is set to point to the node *following* the current one. Then the next pointer of the current node is reset to point to the new node. Once again, the order of these steps is important.

This process will work wherever the node is to be inserted along the list, including making it the new second node in the list or making it the last node in the list. If the new node is inserted right after the first node in the list, then `current` and `list` will refer to the same (first) node. If the new node is inserted at the end of the list, the next reference of the new node is set to `null`. The only special case occurs when the new node is inserted as the first node in the list.

deleting nodes

Any node in the list can be deleted. We must maintain the integrity of the list no matter which node is deleted. So dealing with the first node in the list is again a special case.

> **key concept**
> The first node in a linked list often requires special handling.

To delete the first node in a linked list, we reset the reference to the front of the list so that it points to the current second node in the list. This is shown in Figure 9.4. If we need the deleted node elsewhere, we set up a separate reference to it before resetting the `list` reference.

To delete a node from anywhere else in the list, we must first find the node *in front of* the node we're deleting. This often means we need two pointers, one to find the node we want to delete and another to keep track of the node before that one. We call these nodes `current` and `previous`, as shown in Figure 9.5.

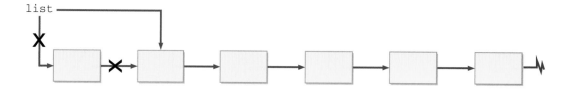

figure 9.4   Deleting the first node in a linked list

Once these nodes have been found, the next reference of the previous node is reset to point to the node pointed to by the next reference of the current node. The deleted node can then be used as needed.

a dynamically linked list example

The program in Listing 9.2 sets up a list of `Magazine` objects and then prints the list. The list of magazines is encapsulated inside the `MagazineList` class shown in Listing 9.3 and is a dynamically linked list.

The `MagazineList` class represents the list of magazines. From outside of the class (an external view), we don't care how the list is implemented. We don't know, for instance, whether the list of magazines is stored in an array or in a linked list. The `MagazineList` class has a set of methods that lets the user maintain the list. That set of methods—add and `toString`—defines the operations to the `MagazineList` ADT.

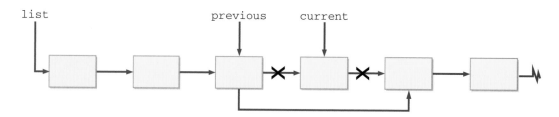

figure 9.5   Deleting an interior node from a linked list

```
listing
   9.2
```

```java
//****************************************************************
//  MagazineRack.java        Author: Lewis/Loftus/Cocking
//
//  Driver to exercise the MagazineList collection.
//****************************************************************

public class MagazineRack
{
   //--------------------------------------------------------------
   //  Creates a MagazineList object, adds several magazines to the
   //  list, then prints it.
   //--------------------------------------------------------------
   public static void main (String[] args)
   {
      MagazineList rack = new MagazineList();

      rack.add (new Magazine("Time"));
      rack.add (new Magazine("Woodworking Today"));
      rack.add (new Magazine("Communications of the ACM"));
      rack.add (new Magazine("House and Garden"));
      rack.add (new Magazine("GQ"));

      System.out.println (rack);
   }
}
```

output

```
Time
Woodworking Today
Communications of the ACM
House and Garden
GQ
```

The `MagazineList` class uses the `ListNode` class to represent a node in the linked list.

The `Magazine` class shown in Listing 9.4 has all data declared as `private` and provides methods to do updates. Note that, because we use a separate class to represent a node in the list, the `Magazine` class itself does not need to have a link to the next `Magazine` in the list. This means the `Magazine` class is free of any issues regarding its containment in a list.

listing
    9.3

```java
//********************************************************************
//  MagazineList.java        Author: Lewis/Loftus/Cocking
//
//  Represents a collection of magazines.
//********************************************************************

public class MagazineList
{
   private ListNode list;

   //-----------------------------------------------------------------
   //  Sets up an empty list of magazines.
   //-----------------------------------------------------------------
   public MagazineList()
   {
      list = null;
   }

   //-----------------------------------------------------------------
   //  Creates a new MagazineNode object and adds it to the end of
   //  the linked list.
   //-----------------------------------------------------------------
   public void add (Magazine mag)
   {

      ListNode node = new ListNode (mag, null);
      ListNode current;

      if (list == null)
         list = node;
      else
      {
         current = list;
         while (current.getNext() != null)
            current = current.getNext();
         current.setNext(node);
      }
   }

   //-----------------------------------------------------------------
   //  Returns this list of magazines as a string.
   //-----------------------------------------------------------------
   public String toString ()
   {
      String result = "";

      ListNode current = list;
```

listing
9.3   continued

```
      while (current != null)
      {
         result += current.getValue().toString() + "\n";
         current = current.getNext();
      }

      return result;
   }
}
```

listing
9.4

```
//************************************************************
//  Magazine.java       Author: Lewis/Loftus/Cocking
//
//  Represents a single magazine.
//************************************************************

public class Magazine
{
   private String title;

   //------------------------------------------------------------
   //  Sets up the new magazine with its title.
   //------------------------------------------------------------
   public Magazine (String newTitle)
   {
      title = newTitle;
   }

   //------------------------------------------------------------
   //  Returns this magazine as a string.
   //------------------------------------------------------------
   public String toString ()
   {
      return title;
   }
}
```

Other methods could be included in the `MagazineList` ADT. For example, in addition to the `add` method provided, which always adds a new magazine to the end of the list, another method called `insert` could add a node anywhere in the list (to keep it sorted, for instance). A parameter to `insert` could indicate the value of the node after which the new node should be inserted. Another operation that would be helpful in the list ADT would be a `delete` method to remove a node.

other dynamic list representations

You can use different types of dynamic lists. For example, in some situations it may make processing easier to implement a *doubly linked list*. In a doubly linked list each node has not only a reference to the next node in the list, but also another reference to the previous node in the list. Our `Node` class might be declared as follows:

```
class ListNode
{
    Object value;
    ListNode next, prev;
}
```

Figure 9.6 shows a doubly linked list. Note that, like a singly linked list, the `next` reference of the last node is `null`. The previous node of the first node is also `null` because there is no node that comes before the first one. This makes it easy to move back and forth between nodes in the list, but it is more work to set up and change.

Another kind of linked list could include a *header node* that has a reference to the front of the list and another reference to the rear of the list. A rear reference makes it easier to add new nodes to the end of the list. The header node could have other information, too, such as the number of nodes currently in the list. The declaration of the header node would look like this:

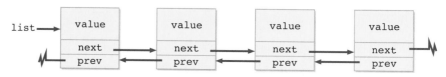

figure 9.6   A doubly linked list

```
class ListHeader
{
    int count;
    ListNode front, rear;
}
```

Note that the header node is the same class as the `ListNode` class to which it refers. Figure 9.7 shows a linked list that has a header node.

You could also combine a header with a doubly linked list, or keep a list in sorted order, depending on the type of processing that you need. The extra work is worth it if it makes the structure more efficient.

LinkedList

The `java.util` package of the standard class library has a `LinkedList` class. The `LinkedList` class implements the `List` interface, including the `iterator`, `listIterator`, `size`, and `add` methods. It also includes other methods, as shown in Figure 9.8. As the class name indicates, the underlying implementation of the `LinkedList` class is a linked list.

Like `ArrayList` and other collection classes, `LinkedList` can store objects of any type. Unlike an `ArrayList`, special methods can be used to access the first and last elements in the list: `addFirst`, `addLast`, `getFirst`, `getLast`, `removeFirst`, and `removeLast`. This works like a doubly linked list, because it is easiest to access elements at the beginning and end of the list.

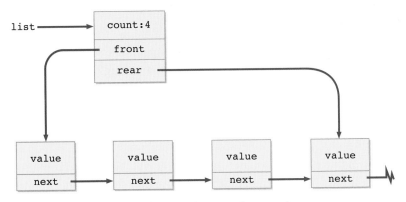

figure 9.7   A list with front and rear references

```
int size()
   Returns the number of elements in this list.

Iterator iterator()
   Returns an iterator of the elements in this list.

LinkedList()
   Constructor: creates a list that starts out empty.

ListIterator listIterator()
   Returns a list iterator of the elements in this list.

Object getFirst()
   Returns the first element in this list.

Object getLast()
   Returns the last element in this list.

Object removeFirst()
   Removes and returns the first element from this list.

Object removeLast()
   Removes and returns the last element from this list.

void add(Object obj)
   Adds the specified element at the end of this list.

void addFirst(Object obj)
   Adds the element to the beginning of this list.

void addLast(Object obj)
   Adds the element to the end of this list.
```

AP→

(AB only)

figure 9.8   Some methods of the `LinkedList` class

9.2 queues and stacks

Some data structures represent important situations that commonly occur in computing. We examine two of these data structures in this section: queues and stacks.

queues

A *queue* is like a list except that you put items in and take items out in a particular way. A traditional queue uses *first-in, first-out* (FIFO) processing. That means the first item put in the list is the first item that comes out of the list. Figure 9.9 shows the FIFO processing of a queue.

> **key concept**
> A queue manages data in a first-in, first-out manner.

Any waiting line is a queue. Think about a line of people waiting to buy movie tickets. A person enters the line at the back and moves forward as ear-

Items go on the queue
at the rear

Items come off the queue
at the front

figure 9.9 A queue data structure

lier movie goers buy tickets. Eventually, each person gets to the front of the line.

Another way to think of queue processing is that the earliest arrival is the first to leave the queue. Imagine a bakery where each customer takes a number, and the baker serves the customers in order according to the numbers they hold. The customer who arrived the earliest and thus has been waiting the longest will be served next. The customers don't need to stand in a line because their number indicates their position in the queue.

A queue data structure typically has operations for adding and removing elements (called *enqueue* and *dequeue* respectively), checking to see if the queue is empty, and peeking at the front element without removing it. Listing 9.5 shows an interface for a queue data structure. This interface was written by the AP committee and will be provided on the AP exam.

A queue can be implemented using a list data structure in which the items are stored in order, like the line of people waiting to buy movie tickets. Items are added to one end of the list and removed from the other.

Another kind of queue is the *priority queue*. In a priority queue, some elements get to "cut in line." The operations on a priority queue are the same as those for a FIFO queue: enqueue, dequeue, and empty. The difference is in the dequeue operation. In a priority queue, the element removed from the queue is the one with the highest priority.

If you've ever been to the emergency room at a hospital, you've probably seen a priority queue. The next patient to be treated is the one with the most serious emergency: a heart attack victim will be treated before a person with a sprained ankle, for example. A traditional FIFO queue can even be thought of as a version of a priority queue in which the priority is the element's arrival time in the queue. Earlier arrival times have higher priority.

Listing 9.6 shows an interface for a priority queue. This interface was written by the AP committee and will be provided on the AP exam.

listing
9.5

```
//****************************************************************
//  Queue.java         Author: AP Committee, comments by
//                             Lewis/Loftus/Cocking
//
//  An interface defining a queue ADT.
//****************************************************************

public interface Queue
{
    //----------------------------------------------------------
    //  Return true if the queue has no elements, false otherwise.
    //----------------------------------------------------------
    boolean isEmpty ();

    //----------------------------------------------------------
    //  Add an element to the end of the queue.
    //----------------------------------------------------------
    void enqueue (Object obj);

    //----------------------------------------------------------
    //  Remove and return the element at the front of the queue.
    //----------------------------------------------------------
    Object dequeue ();

    //----------------------------------------------------------
    //  Return the element at the front of the queue without removing
    //  it.
    //----------------------------------------------------------
    Object peekFront();
}
```

stacks

> **key concept**
> A stack manages data in a last-in, first-out manner.

A *stack* is like a queue except that its elements go on and come off at the same end. The last item to go on a stack is the first item to come off, like a stack of trays in a cafeteria. A stack processes information in a *last-in, first-out* (LIFO) manner, as shown in Figure 9.10.

A typical stack ADT has operations for pushing an item on to the stack, popping an item off the top of the stack, peeking at the top item without removing it, and checking to see if the stack is empty. Listing 9.7 shows an interface for a stack. This interface was written by the AP committee and will be provided on the AP exam.

listing
   9.6

```java
//********************************************************************
//  PriorityQueue.java       Author: AP Committee, comments by
//                                    Lewis/Loftus/Cocking
//
//  An interface defining a priority queue ADT.
//********************************************************************

public interface PriorityQueue
{
   //------------------------------------------------------------------
   //  Return true if the queue has no elements, false otherwise.
   //------------------------------------------------------------------
   boolean isEmpty ();

   //------------------------------------------------------------------
   //  Add an element to the priority queue.
   //------------------------------------------------------------------
   void add (Object obj);

   //------------------------------------------------------------------
   //  Remove and return the smallest (i.e., highest priority)
   //  element in the queue.
   //------------------------------------------------------------------
   Object removeMin ();

   //------------------------------------------------------------------
   //  Return the smallest element in the queue without removing
   //  it.
   //------------------------------------------------------------------
   Object peekMin();
}
```

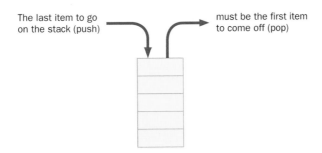

figure 9.10   A stack data structure

listing
    9.7

```
//****************************************************************
//   Stack.java        Author: AP Committee, comments by
//                             Lewis/Loftus/Cocking
//
//   An interface defining a stack ADT.
//****************************************************************

public interface Stack
{
    //----------------------------------------------------------
    //   Return true if the stack has no elements, false otherwise.
    //----------------------------------------------------------
    boolean isEmpty ();

    //----------------------------------------------------------
    //   Push an element onto the stack.
    //----------------------------------------------------------
    void push (Object obj);

    //----------------------------------------------------------
    //   Pop an element off the stack and return it.
    //----------------------------------------------------------
    Object pop ();

    //----------------------------------------------------------
    //   Return the element on top of the stack without removing it.
    //----------------------------------------------------------
    Object peekTop();
}
```

Let's look at an example that uses a stack to solve a problem. The program in Listing 9.8 accepts a string of characters that represents a secret message. The program decodes and prints the message.

The encoded message has each word backward. Words in the message are separated by a single space. The program uses the `ArrayStack` class, shown in Listing 9.9, to push the characters of each word on the stack. When a word has been read, each character appears in reverse order as it is popped off the stack and printed.

```java
//********************************************************************
//   Decode.java        Author: Lewis/Loftus/Cocking
//
//   Demonstrates the use of the Stack class.
//********************************************************************

import cs1.Keyboard;

public class Decode
{
   //----------------------------------------------------------------
   //   Decodes a message by reversing each word in a string.
   //----------------------------------------------------------------
   public static void main (String[] args)
   {
      Stack word = new ArrayStack();
      String message;
      int index = 0;

      System.out.println ("Enter the coded message:");
      message = Keyboard.readString();
      System.out.println ("The decoded message is:");

      while (index < message.length())
      {
         // Push word onto stack
         while (index < message.length() && message.charAt(index) != ' ')
         {
            word.push (new Character(message.charAt(index)));
            index++;
         }

         // Print word in reverse
         while (!word.isEmpty())
            System.out.print (((Character)word.pop()).charValue());
         System.out.print (" ");
         index++;
      }

      System.out.println();
   }
}
```

output

```
Enter the coded message:
artxE eseehc esaelp
The decoded message is:
Extra cheese please
```

The `ArrayStack` class implements the `Stack` interface and uses an `ArrayList` object to store elements in the stack. The push method adds an element to the end of the list and the pop and `peek` methods deal with the element at the end of the list. Note the use of exceptions in the pop and `peek` methods: if the stack is empty there is no element to return, so a `NoSuchElementException` is thrown. By the interface definition, the `ArrayStack` operations operate on the `Object` class so any object can be pushed onto a stack.

listing
9.9

```java
//****************************************************************
//  ArrayStack.java       Author: Lewis/Loftus/Cocking
//
//  Implements a stack data structure.
//****************************************************************

import java.util.ArrayList;
import java.util.NoSuchElementException;

public class ArrayStack implements Stack
{
    private ArrayList elements;

    //---------------------------------------------------------------
    //  Sets up an initially empty stack.
    //---------------------------------------------------------------
    public ArrayStack ()
    {
        elements = new ArrayList();
    }

    //---------------------------------------------------------------
    //  Pushes an element onto the stack.
    //---------------------------------------------------------------
    public void push(Object obj)
    {
        elements.add(obj);
    }

    //---------------------------------------------------------------
    //  Removes the top element from the stack and returns it.
    //---------------------------------------------------------------
    public Object pop()
    {
        if (isEmpty())
            throw new NoSuchElementException();
```

```
listing
   9.9    continued

      return elements.remove(elements.size()-1);
   }

   //------------------------------------------------------------------
   //  Returns the top element on the stack without removing it.
   //------------------------------------------------------------------
   public Object peekTop()
   {
      if (isEmpty())
         throw new NoSuchElementException();

      return elements.get(elements.size()-1);
   }

   //------------------------------------------------------------------
   //  Returns true if the stack has no elements, false otherwise.
   //------------------------------------------------------------------
   public boolean isEmpty()
   {
      return (elements.size() == 0);
   }
}
```

▸ An abstract data type (ADT) hides the data structure behind a well-defined interface. This makes objects a perfect way to define ADTs.

▸ A fixed data structure has a specific size, but a dynamic data structure grows and shrinks as needed.

▸ A dynamically linked list is managed by storing and updating references to objects.

▸ A list ADT has insert and delete operations, which use object references.

▸ There are many types of dynamic linked lists.

▸ A queue manages data in a first-in, first-out manner.

▸ A stack manages data in a last-in, first-out manner.

self-review questions

9.1   What is a collection?

9.2   Why are objects particularly well suited for implementing abstract data types?

9.3   What is a dynamic data structure?

9.4   What is a doubly linked list?

9.5   What is a header node for a linked list?

9.6   How is a queue different from a list?

9.7   What is a priority queue?

9.8   What is a stack?

multiple choice

Questions 9.1 through 9.5 refer to the `ListNode` class in Listing 9.1.

9.1   Suppose `ele` is a reference to a `ListNode` object. Which expression gives the *value* of ele's successor?

a. `ele.getValue()`

b. `ele.getNext()`

c. `ele.getNext().getValue()`

d. `ele.getValue().getNext()`

e. `ele.getNext().getNext()`

Questions 9.2 and 9.3 refer to the following method `printList`, which prints the values in a linked list using recursion.

```
void printList (ListNode node)
{
    System.out.println(_____1_____);
    if (node.getNext() != null)
        printList(_____2_____);
}
```

9.2 Which expressions should be used to fill in blanks 1 and 2?

1	2
a. node	node.getNext()
b. node	node.getValue()
c. node.getValue()	node
d. node.getNext()	node
e. node.getValue()	node.getNext()

9.3 In order to print an entire linked list, the parameter passed to `printList` should be

a. the first node in the list

b. the last node in the list

c. `null`

d. the node returned by a `getNext` call on the first node in the list

e. the value of the first node in the list

9.4 Suppose `head` is a reference to the first `ListNode` in a linked list of at least length 2. Which code segment will remove the second element in the list?

a. `head = head.getNext();`

b. `head.setNext(head.getNext());`

c. `head.setNext(null);`

d. `head.getNext().setNext(null);`

e. `head.setNext(head.getNext().getNext())`

9.5 Suppose head is a reference to the first ListNode in a linked list, and newNode is a reference to a ListNode that should be added at the front of the list. Which code segment will add newNode at the beginning of the list?

a. ```
head = newNode;
newNode.setNext(head);
```

b. ```
newNode.setNext(head);
head = newNode;
```

c. ```
newNode = head;
head = newNode.getNext();
```

d. ```
newNode.setNext(head.getNext());
head = newNode;
```

e. ```
newNode.setNext(head.getNext());
newNode = head;
```

9.6 Which operation would be more efficient with a doubly linked list than with a singly linked list?

a. following a list from front to back

b. following a list from back to front

c. adding an element to the beginning of the list

d. removing the first element in the list

e. printing the elements in the list

9.7 Suppose the numbers 1, 2, 3, 4, and 5 are pushed onto a stack in that order, then three elements are popped off the stack. Those three elements, in the order they were popped off, are

a. 1, 2, 3

b. 3, 2, 1

c. 3, 4, 5

d. 5, 4, 3

e. 2, 3, 4
```

9.8 Suppose a stack is implemented using a singly linked list. Where in the list would it be best to have the push and pop operations take place?

push	pop
a. head of list	head of list
b. head of list	tail of list
c. tail of list	head of list
d. tail of list	tail of list

e. All choices would be equally correct and efficient.

9.9 Suppose a queue contains the numbers 1, 2, 3, 4, and 5, in that order. The next operations on the queue include dequeueing three numbers and enqueueing the numbers 6 and 7, but we don't know in what order. Which of the following shows what the queue might look like after the operations are performed?

a. 1, 2, 3, 4

b. 2, 3, 4, 5

c. 4, 5, 6, 7

d. 6, 7, 1, 2

e. 7, 6, 5, 4

9.10 Suppose we have a priority queue that contains the elements 1, 2, 3, 4, and 5. We do not know the priorities of the elements. If two elements are dequeued, which of the following shows what the queue might look like?

a. 1, 2, 3

b. 2, 3, 4

c. 3, 4, 5

d. 1, 3, 5

e. All of the above.

true/false

9.1 Abstract data types are implemented as objects in Java.

9.2 The next field in the last node in a linked list contains the value null.

9.3   In a linked list, it is possible to jump directly to an element in the middle of the list.

9.4   In a doubly linked list, each node has a reference to the next node and to the previous node in the list.

9.5   A stack uses first-in, first-out (FIFO) processing.

9.6   The enqueue operation adds an element to a queue.

9.7   The push operation adds an element to a stack.

9.8   In a priority queue, the first element removed is the one that was added first.

9.9   A linked list can change size while a program is running.

9.10 A queue cannot be implemented using a linked list.

short answer

9.1   Suppose `current` is a reference to a `ListNode` object and that it currently refers to a specific node in a linked list. Show, in pseudocode, the steps that would delete the node following `current`. Keep in mind `current` can refer to the first and last nodes in the list.

9.2   Assume that the list in Exercise 9.1 was set up as a doubly linked list, with both `next` and `prev` references. Show, in pseudocode, the steps that would delete the node following `current`.

9.3   Suppose `current` and `newNode` are references to `ListNode` objects. Assume `current` currently refers to a node in a linked list and `newNode` refers to an unattached `ListNode` object. Show, in pseudocode, the steps that would insert `newNode` behind `current` in the list. Keep in mind that `current` can refer to the first and last nodes in the list.

9.4   Assume that the list in Exercise 9.3 was set up as a doubly linked list, with both `next` and `prev` references. Show, in pseudocode, the steps that would insert `newNode` behind `current` in the list.

9.5   Would the front and rear references in the header node of a linked list ever refer to the same node? Would they ever both be `null`? Would one ever be `null` if the other was not? Explain your answers using examples.

9.6 Show the contents of a queue after the following operations are performed. Assume the queue is empty to start with.

- ▸ enqueue (45);
- ▸ enqueue (12);
- ▸ enqueue (28);
- ▸ dequeue();
- ▸ dequeue();
- ▸ enqueue (69);
- ▸ enqueue (27);
- ▸ enqueue (99);
- ▸ dequeue();
- ▸ enqueue (24);
- ▸ enqueue (85);
- ▸ enqueue (16);
- ▸ dequeue();

9.7 Does it make any difference to the final queue how dequeue operations and enqueue operations are mixed together? Does it matter how the enqueue operations are ordered among themselves? Explain using examples.

9.8 Show the contents of a priority queue after the following operations. Assume the queue starts out empty. For the enqueue operation, the first parameter is the element and the second parameter is its priority so that (45, 5) means element 45 has a priority of 5. Assume that the smaller the number the higher the priority.

- ▸ enqueue(45, 5);
- ▸ enqueue (12, 8);
- ▸ enqueue (28, 2);
- ▸ dequeue();
- ▸ dequeue();
- ▸ enqueue (69, 0);
- ▸ enqueue (27, 6);
- ▸ enqueue (99, 9);
- ▸ dequeue();
- ▸ enqueue (24, 4);

> ‣ enqueue (85, 2);
> ‣ enqueue (16, 3);
> ‣ dequeue();

9.9   Show the contents of a stack after the following operations. Assume the stack starts out empty.

> ‣ push (45);
> ‣ push (12);
> ‣ push (28);
> ‣ pop();
> ‣ pop();
> ‣ push (69);
> ‣ push (27);
> ‣ push (99);
> ‣ pop();
> ‣ push (24);
> ‣ push (85);
> ‣ push (16);
> ‣ pop();

9.10   Does it make any difference to the final stack how the pop operations are mixed with the push operations? Does it matter how the push operations are ordered among themselves? Explain using examples.

9.11   Two methods of searching were presented in Chapter 6: sequential search and binary search. If we have sorted data stored in a linked list, which searching method would be most efficient? Explain.

programming projects

9.1   Following the example in Chapter 6, design and implement an application that keeps track of a collection of compact discs using a linked list. In the main method of the driver class, add CDs to the collection and print the list.

9.2   Change the MagazineRack program (Listings 9.2, 9.3, and 9.4) by adding delete and insert operations into the MagazineList class. Have the Magazine class implement the Comparable interface, and have the `insert` method call the `compareTo` method in the `Magazine` class, which decides whether one `Magazine` title comes before another alphabetically. In the `driver`, use insertion and deletion operations. Print the list of magazines.

9.3   Design and implement a selection sort (from Chapter 6) that operates on a linked list of nodes that each contain an integer.

9.4   Design and implement an insertion sort (from Chapter 6) that operates on a linked list of nodes that each contain an integer.

9.5   Design and implement an application that simulates the customers waiting in line to buy movie tickets. Use a queue. As customers arrive at the theater, customer objects are put in the rear of the queue with an enqueue operation. When the ticket seller is ready for another customer, the customer object is removed from the front of the queue with a dequeue operation. Randomly determine when new customers arrive at the theater and when current customers are finished at the ticket window. Print a message each time an operation occurs during the simulation. Your queue data structure should implement the queue interface.

9.6   Change the solution to the Programming Project 9.5 so that it represents four ticket windows and therefore four customer queues. Have new customers go to the shortest queue. Show which queue had the shortest waiting time per customer on average.

9.7   Design and implement an application that evaluates a postfix expression that operates on integer operands using the arithmetic operators +, −, *, /, and %. We are already familiar with *infix expressions,* in which an operator is positioned between its two operands. A *postfix expression* puts the operators after its operands. Keep in mind that an operand could be the result of another operation. Postfix notation eliminates the need for parentheses to force precedence. For example, the following infix expression:

(5 + 2) * (8 − 5)

is equivalent to the following postfix expression.

5 2 + 8 5 − *

The evaluation of a postfix expression is facilitated by using a stack. As you process a postfix expression from left to right, you encounter operands and operators. If you encounter an operand, push it on the stack. If you encounter an operator, pop two operands off the stack, perform the operation, and push the result back on the stack. When you have processed the entire expression, there will be one value on the stack, which is the result of the entire expression.

You may want to use a `StringTokenizer` object to assist in the parsing of the expression. You can assume the expression will be in valid postfix form.

answers to self-review questions

9.1   A collection is an object that stores and organizes primitive data or other objects. Some collections are classic data structures.

9.2   An abstract data type (ADT) is a collection of data and the operations that can be performed on that data. An object is essentially the same thing because we encapsulate related variables and methods in an object. The object hides data and operations of the ADT, by separating it from the interface, so we can change the implementation without affecting the interface.

9.3   A dynamic data structure uses references to link objects together. It can grow and shrink as needed. Objects can be added and removed from the structure at runtime by adjusting references between objects in the structure.

9.4   Each node in a doubly linked list has references to both the node that comes before it in the list and the node that comes after it in the list. This makes moving forward and backward in the list easier, and makes some operations simpler.

9.5   A header node for a linked list holds information about the list, such as references to the front and rear of the list and how many nodes are in the list.

9.6   A queue is like a list, except that a queue only adds nodes to one end (enqueue) and takes them off of the other (dequeue). A queue uses a first-in, first-out (FIFO) approach.

9.7   In a priority queue elements can "cut in line." The next element to be removed in a dequeue operation is the one with the highest priority.

9.8   A stack adds (pushes) and removes (pops) nodes from only one end of a list. It manages information using a last-in, first-out (LIFO) approach.

There are many kinds of data structures
used for organizing information.
This chapter examines trees, reviews
hashtables, and introduces
sets and maps, which are part
of the Java standard class
library. Trees have many uses;
we will see how they can be
used in sorting. The material
in this chapter is AB-only.

chapter
objectives

- ▶ Introduce sets and maps.

- ▶ Define the binary tree data
  structure.

- ▶ Show how binary search trees are
  used.

- ▶ Define the heap data structure.

- ▶ Examine the heapsort algorithm.

- ▶ Review hashtables.

10.0 sets and maps

In the Java standard class library, the Set interface defines the operations on an object that represents a set of elements. The Set interface is like a mathematical set. A set is a collection of elements with no duplicates. So for example {1, 2, 3} is a set, but {1, 2, 2} is not. In Java a Set object may only have one null element and it may not have two elements that are equal using the equals method.

We can add an element to a set, remove an element, retrieve the elements in the set, and check to see whether the set contains a particular element. Figure 10.1 lists the methods of the Set interface that are a part of the AP subset. Because the elements in a set do not have to be in order, the Set interface does not require that the elements in the iterator returned by the iterator method be in any particular order.

Since the elements of a Set are Objects any object in Java can be an element of a Set. Because a set may not have duplicates, the elements of a Set should be immutable (unchangeable) objects. Think about it: if a Set contained changeable objects, an object could be changed to become equal to another object in the Set.

There are several classes in the Java standard class library that implement the Set interface. We look at two of them, TreeSet and HashSet, in later sections.

The Map interface in the Java standard class library matches—or maps—keys to values. An example of a map is a dictionary: the keys

AP→

(AB only)

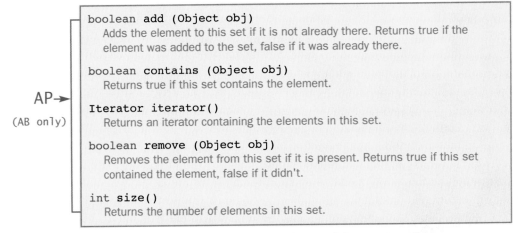

```
boolean add (Object obj)
    Adds the element to this set if it is not already there. Returns true if the
    element was added to the set, false if it was already there.

boolean contains (Object obj)
    Returns true if this set contains the element.

Iterator iterator()
    Returns an iterator containing the elements in this set.

boolean remove (Object obj)
    Removes the element from this set if it is present. Returns true if this set
    contained the element, false if it didn't.

int size()
    Returns the number of elements in this set.
```

figure 10.1   Some methods of the Set interface

in the map are words and the values are definitions. Each word in the dictionary maps to its definition. Duplicate keys are not allowed (dictionaries are long enough as it is without repeating words!), so the keys in a map form a set. Note that this does not preclude two different keys mapping to the same value, just as two words in a dictionary can have the same definition. Like the elements of a `Set`, the keys in a `Map` should be immutable.

Some methods in the `Map` interface are shown in Figure 10.2. The `put` method adds an element to the map. The `get` method retrieves an element: it takes a key as a parameter and returns the value. The `keySet` method can be used to get all the keys in the map. In later sections we will look at `TreeMap` and `HashMap`, two classes that implement the `Map` interface.

10.1 trees

A *tree* is a data structure that organizes information like an upside-down tree. Figure 10.3 shows a tree. A tree consists of zero or more *nodes*. Each node contains data and has a particular position in the tree. Each oval in the figure is a node and the text inside an oval is that node's data.

Trees are a good way to organize hierarchical information, such as the collection of topics in the sciences shown in Figure 10.3. Trees are also an efficient way to store and retrieve sorted data.

> **key concept**
>
> A tree is a data structure that organizes information in a hierarchical structure that looks like an upside-down tree. A tree has zero or more nodes that contain the data in the tree.

AP→
(AB only)

```
boolean containsKey (Object key)
    Returns true if this map contains the key.

Object get (Object key)
    Returns the value that makes the key, or null if this map does not contain that
    key.

Set keySet()
    Returns a Set of all the keys in this map.

Object put (Object key, Object value)
    Adds the key-value pair to this map. The value that used to go with the key is
    returned, or null if there was no mapping for the key before.
```

figure 10.2   Some methods of the `Map` interface

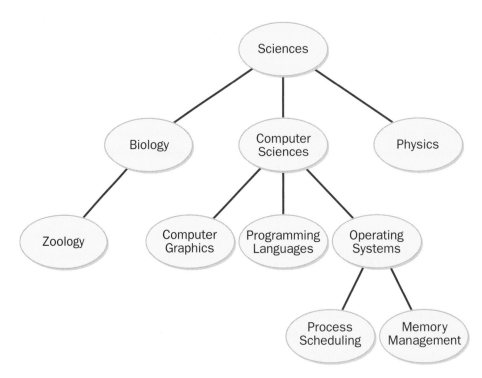

figure 10.3   A tree

A lot of terminology related to trees comes from real trees and from genealogy. A tree (if it has any nodes at all) has one node called the *root*. When we draw a tree, the root is at the top. In Figure 10.3, the "Sciences" node is the root. Each node may have zero or more *children*. A node without any children is called a *leaf*. Figure 10.4 shows a tree with a root and leaves. In the tree, the root node, A, has two children, B and C. We may also say that B's (and C's) *parent* is A, and that B and C are *siblings*.

If we break off the child node from its parent, we can make the child node the root of a *subtree*. Figure 10.5 shows a subtree of the tree in Figure 10.4. Sometimes, instead of talking about the children of a node, we may talk about its subtrees, meaning the subtrees formed by each of its children. The empty tree and the whole tree are also considered subtrees.

> **key concept**
>
> Each child node in a tree forms a subtree. We can break off the child node from its parent so the child node becomes the root of a subtree.

> **key concept**
>
> The height of a tree is equal to the levels of the tree. The root is level 1, and every other node is a level one greater than its parent.

When we need to describe how "tall" or "deep" a tree is, we talk about its *height*. A tree with no nodes has height 0; a tree with a single node (the root) has height 1; the tree in Figure 10.5 has height 2; and the tree in Figure 10.4 has height 3. In general, the height of a tree is equal to the maximum *level* of the tree. The root is level 1 in a tree,

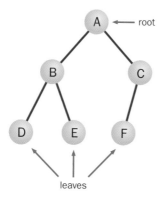

figure 10.4 A tree

figure 10.5 A subtree of the tree in Figure 10.4

and every other node is one greater than its parent. In Figure 10.4, node A is at level 1, nodes B and C are at level 2, and nodes D, E, and F are at level 3. Since the maximum level in the tree is 3, its height is 3.

In this book we are concerned with a kind of tree called a *binary tree*. In a binary tree, each node has at most two children, and they are called the left child and the right child. The tree in Figure 10.4 is a binary tree. The left child of A is B and the right child of A is C. The node C has only a left child, F. We can think of C as having an empty right subtree.

> **key concept**
>
> In a binary tree, each node has at most two children, called the left child and the right child.

Figure 10.6 shows two binary trees representing arithmetic expressions. Binary trees are a nice way to show arithmetic expressions because we don't need to use parentheses to tell us the order of operations. The order in which the operations should be carried out is part of the structure of the tree. The first tree in Figure 10.6 is the expression 7 + (3 * 2), while the second tree is (7 + 3) * 2.

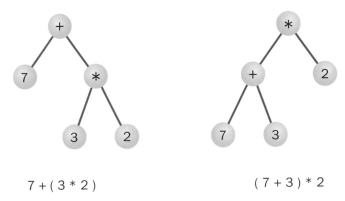

$$7 + (3 * 2)$$ $$(7 + 3) * 2$$

figure 10.6   Binary trees representing arithmetic expressions

Binary trees are usually implemented as a dynamic structure using nodes that look like this:

```
class TreeNode
{
    Object value;
    TreeNode left;
    TreeNode right;
}
```

Like the nodes in a linked list, tree nodes have references to other nodes of the same type. The `left` and `right` references refer to the node's left and right children. A value of `null` means there is no child. The root node of the tree is referenced using a separate variable. This situation is pictured in Figure 10.7.

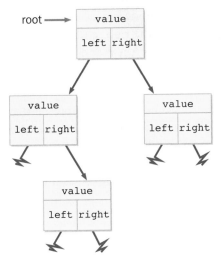

figure 10.7   A binary tree

Listing 10.1 shows the class `TreeNode`, which is an implementation of a node in a binary tree. This was written by the AP committee and will be provided on the AP exam.

listing
    10.1

```java
//********************************************************************
//  TreeNode.java        Author: AP Committee, comments added by
//                                Lewis/Loftus/Cocking
//
//  A node in a binary tree.
//********************************************************************


public class TreeNode
{
   private Object value;
   private TreeNode left;
   private TreeNode right;

   //-----------------------------------------------------------------
   //  Initializes this node.
   //-----------------------------------------------------------------
   public TreeNode (Object initValue, TreeNode initLeft, TreeNode initRight)
   {
      value = initValue;
      left = initLeft;
      right = initRight;
   }

   //-----------------------------------------------------------------
   //  Returns the value of this node.
   //-----------------------------------------------------------------
   public Object getValue()
   {
      return value;
   }

   //-----------------------------------------------------------------
   //  Returns the left child of this node.
   //-----------------------------------------------------------------
   public TreeNode getLeft()
   {
      return left;
   }

   //-----------------------------------------------------------------
   //  Returns the right child of this node.
   //-----------------------------------------------------------------
```

listing
10.1   continued

```java
   public TreeNode getRight()
   {
      return right;
   }

   //-------------------------------------------------------------------
   //  Sets the value of this node.
   //-------------------------------------------------------------------
   public void setValue(Object theNewValue)
   {
      value = theNewValue;
   }

   //-------------------------------------------------------------------
   //  Sets the left child of this node.
   //-------------------------------------------------------------------
   public void setLeft(TreeNode theNewLeft)
   {
      left = theNewLeft;
   }

   //-------------------------------------------------------------------
   //  Sets the right child of this node.
   //-------------------------------------------------------------------
   public void setRight(TreeNode theNewRight)
   {
      right = theNewRight;
   }
}
```

tree traversal

If we want to process every element in a list, we start with the first element, then move on to the next, then the next, and so on until we reach the last element. This is called *traversing the list*. Because trees are not linear data structures like lists, traversing a tree is not so straightforward. There are three different tree-traversal algorithms: preorder, inorder, and postorder.

When we traverse a binary tree we process every node in the left subtree, and every node in the right subtree. We may choose to process the node itself before processing any subtrees, in between processing subtrees, or after processing both subtrees. In a *preorder traversal* we process a node before processing its subtrees. In an *inorder traversal* we process a node's left subtree, then the node itself, then its right subtree. In a *postorder traversal* we process both of a node's subtrees (left, then right) and then we process the node itself.

Imagine following a path around a tree, as indicated by the arrow in Figure 10.8. Notice that we pass by each node three times as numbered in the figure for the node B. In a preorder traversal we process a node the first time we get to it. In an inorder traversal we process a node the second time we get to it. In a postorder traversal, we process a node the third (and last) time we get to it. The nodes in Figure 10.8 would be processed like this:

▸ preorder: A, B, D, E, C, F

▸ inorder: D, B, E, A, F, C

▸ postorder: D, E, B, F, C, A

Suppose the procedure `process` does the processing on a `TreeNode`. Then the following procedure does an inorder traversal, processing every node in the subtree rooted at the node given as the initial parameter.

```
void inorder (TreeNode node)
{
    if (node != null)
    {
        inorder (node.left);
        process (node);
        inorder (node.right);
    }
}
```

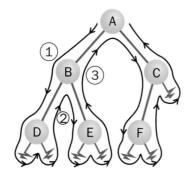

figure 10.8   Traversing a binary tree

To process the whole tree, we call the procedure with the root as the parameter:

```
inorder (root);
```

Now let's look at an application of binary trees that does searching and sorting.

binary search trees

Suppose we want to find an element in a binary tree. Unless the elements are organized in some way, we must examine every node—not an efficient way to operate. A better way to do this is to use a *binary search tree*. In a binary search tree, for any node N, every node in N's left subtree is less in value than N and every node in N's right subtree is greater than or equal to N in value. This means that an inorder traversal of a binary search tree will process the nodes in order from least to greatest.

The tree in Figure 10.9 is a binary search tree whose elements are integers. Notice that an inorder traversal produces the elements in sorted order: 8, 12, 15, 17, 18, 20, 26, 31, 35, 43, 45, 47, 48, 50. If we are searching for the integer 15 in the tree, we first look at the root. Because15 is less than 20, we go down the left subtree. Next we encounter 12. Because 15 is greater than 12, we go down 12's right subtree. The next node we see is 15, and we have found the node we were looking for in three tries. Suppose we had been

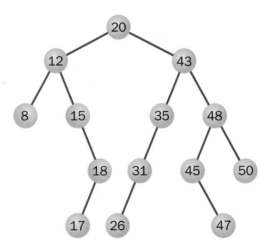

figure 10.9   A binary search tree

looking for 14. At 15 we would go down the left subtree, because 14 is less than 15. But the node storing 15 has no left subtree. So we have already gone as far as we can go and we know that this binary search tree does not contain the integer 14.

When we want to add a node to a binary search tree we use the same approach to find the spot where the new node should go. If we were to add the integer 14 to the tree in Figure 10.9, it would be added as the left child of the node storing 15.

Listing 10.2 shows a program that sorts a list of grades using a binary search tree. It starts by creating an empty tree. Then the grades are added to the tree one by one, and finally the tree is printed.

The class BSTree in Listing 10.3 implements the binary search tree. The constructor creates an empty tree and the method add is used to add elements. The parameter to add is a Comparable object. This lets the tree store any objects that implement the Comparable interface. The first thing the add method does is create a node object whose data is the object given. If this is the first element to be added, its node becomes the root. Otherwise, the recursive procedure addNode is called. The addNode procedure finds the spot in the tree where the new node should be added and adds it. It finds the right spot by recursively going down the left or right subtree, depending on whether the element to be added is less than or greater than the current element. The compareTo method from the Comparable interface is used to compare the elements.

The BSTNode class, Listing 10.4, is the class used to represent a node in the binary search tree. It extends the TreeNode class and provides a constructor that takes a Comparable object as a parameter. This constructor calls the superclass constructor to initialize the node.

BSTree's toString method does an inorder traversal, starting from the root of the tree. At each node it adds the string representation of that element to the string it finally returns. This way the string that gets returned is a list of all the elements in the tree, from least to greatest.

A more general binary search tree class would have other methods, that might delete a node, search for a node, and count how many nodes are in a tree. Deleting nodes is a little bit tricky because the node might have children. Clearly, if a node has no children (e.g., it is a leaf), we can simply delete it, changing its parent's pointer to null. If a node has only one child, we can replace the node with its child. For example, suppose we want to delete the node containing the integer 15 from the tree in Figure 10.9. We simply replace 15 with 18 as 12's right child, producing the tree in Figure 10.10.

```
listing
    10.2
```

```
//***************************************************************
//  SortGrades.java        Author: Lewis/Loftus/Cocking
//
//  Driver for testing the use of binary search trees in sorting.
//***************************************************************

public class SortGrades
{
    //----------------------------------------------------------
    //  Creates a binary search tree, adds grades to it, then prints
    //  the tree.
    //----------------------------------------------------------
    public static void main (String[] args)
    {
        BSTree tree = new BSTree();

        tree.add(new Integer(89));
        tree.add(new Integer(94));
        tree.add(new Integer(69));
        tree.add(new Integer(80));
        tree.add(new Integer(97));
        tree.add(new Integer(85));
        tree.add(new Integer(73));
        tree.add(new Integer(91));
        tree.add(new Integer(77));
        tree.add(new Integer(93));

        System.out.println (tree);
    }
}
```

If the node we want to delete has two children, we replace it with its inorder successor, that is, with the smallest node in its right subtree. The rest of the tree remains the way it is. For example, suppose we want to delete the root, the node containing the integer 20, from the tree in Figure 10.9. The smallest integer in 20's right subtree is 26. So, we replace 20 with 26 and get the tree in Figure 10.11. The nodes of the binary search tree stay in order: because we picked the smallest node in 20's right subtree, 26, to replace it, every node in 26's new right subtree is greater than 26.

listing
  10.3

```java
//************************************************************************
//   BSTree.java        Author: Lewis/Loftus/Cocking
//
//   Implements a binary search tree.
//************************************************************************

public class BSTree
{
   private BSTNode root;

   //--------------------------------------------------------------------
   //  Sets up an empty binary search tree.
   //--------------------------------------------------------------------
   public BSTree ()
   {
      root = null;
   }

   //--------------------------------------------------------------------
   //  Adds an element to the tree in its proper place.
   //--------------------------------------------------------------------
   public void add (Comparable obj)
   {
      BSTNode newNode = new BSTNode(obj);

      // If this is the first node to be added, make it the root.
      if (root == null)
         root = newNode;
      else
         addNode (root, newNode);
   }

   //--------------------------------------------------------------------
   //  Recursive procedure that adds a node to the binary search
   //  tree.
   //--------------------------------------------------------------------
   private void addNode (BSTNode current, BSTNode newNode)
   {
      if ( ((Comparable)(newNode.getValue())).compareTo (
            current.getValue()) < 0 )
      {
         if (current.getLeft() == null)
            current.setLeft(newNode);
         else
            addNode ((BSTNode)current.getLeft(), newNode);
      }
```

listing
   10.3   continued

```java
      else
      {
         if (current.getRight() == null)
            current.setRight(newNode);
         else
            addNode ((BSTNode)current.getRight(), newNode);
      }
   }

   //-----------------------------------------------------------------
   //  Returns a string representing this tree. The info contained
   //  in each node is listed in order, separated by newlines.
   //-----------------------------------------------------------------
   public String toString ()
   {
      return toString(root);
   }

   //-----------------------------------------------------------------
   //  Returns a string representing the subtree rooted at the
   //  given node. Recursively performs an inorder traversal.
   //-----------------------------------------------------------------
   private String toString (TreeNode current)
   {
      String str = "";

      if (current.getLeft() != null)
         str += toString(current.getLeft()) + "\n";

      str += current.getValue();

      if (current.getRight() != null)
         str += "\n" + toString(current.getRight());

      return str;
   }
}
```

The smallest node in a node's right subtree will never have a left child, because if it did, it wouldn't be the smallest node in the subtree. It might, however, have a right child. For example, suppose we want to delete the node containing 43 from the tree in Figure 10.9. Its inorder successor is 45, so we

```
listing
   10.4

//************************************************************
//  BSTNode.java         Author: Lewis/Loftus/Cocking
//
//  A node in a binary search tree.
//************************************************************


public class BSTNode extends TreeNode
{
    //----------------------------------------------------------
    //  Initializes this node.
    //----------------------------------------------------------
    public BSTNode (Comparable data)
    {
        super (data, null, null);
    }
}
```

should replace 43 with 45. The node 45 has a right subtree, which we use to fill in the hole that 45 leaves behind, using the same technique used when deleting a node with only one child. The resulting tree is shown in Figure 10.12.

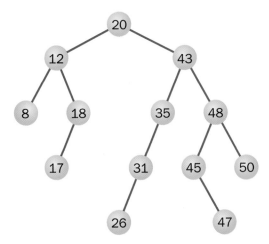

figure 10.10   The tree resulting from deleting 15 from the tree in Figure 10.9

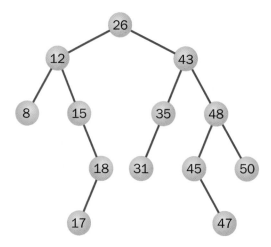

figure 10.11   The tree resulting from deleting the root
from the tree in Figure 10.9

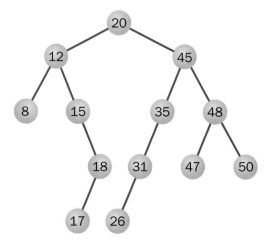

figure 10.12   The tree resulting from deleting 43
from the tree in Figure 10.9

TreeSet and TreeMap

The TreeSet and TreeMap classes in the Java standard class library are
implementations of the Set and Map interfaces using trees. These classes use
a tree to keep the elements (or the keys in the case of a map) in sorted order.
When the iterator method on a TreeSet is called, it returns the elements
ordered from least to greatest. The elements in a TreeSet and the keys in a

`TreeMap` are expected to implement the `Comparable` interface so that they can be ordered using the `compareTo` method.

Because of the tree implementation, the `TreeSet` and `TreeMap` classes can guarantee a time complexity of $O(\log n)$ for the basic operations (because a binary tree has on average $\log_2 n$ levels). Basic operations include adding and removing keys or elements and checking to see whether the map or set contains a particular key or element.

Figures 10.13 and 10.14 show the methods from the `TreeSet` and `TreeMap` classes that are a part of the AP subset.

AP→

(AB only)

> `boolean add (Object obj)`
> Adds the element to this set if it is not already there. Returns true if the element was added to the set, false if it was not already there.
>
> `boolean contains (Object obj)`
> Returns true if this set has the element.
>
> `Iterator iterator()`
> Returns an iterator containing the elements in this set.
>
> `boolean remove (Object obj)`
> Removes the element from this set if it is there. Returns true if this set had the element, false if it did not.
>
> `int size ()`
> Returns the number of elements in this set.

figure 10.13   Some methods of the `TreeSet` class

AP→

(AB only)

> `boolean containsKey (Object key)`
> Returns true if this map has the key.
>
> `Object get (Object key)`
> Returns the value for the key, or null if this map does not have the key.
>
> `Set keySet()`
> Returns a Set of the keys in this map.
>
> `Object put (Object key, Object value)`
> Adds the key-value pair to this map. The value that used to go with the key is returned, or null is returned if there was no map for the key before.
>
> `int size ()`
> Returns the number of key-value pairs in this map.

figure 10.14   Some methods of the `TreeMap` class

10.2 heaps

A *heap* is a kind of binary tree. Before we get into the details, let's define what it means for a tree to be complete. Imagine placing nodes into a binary tree level by level starting with the root and moving from left to right within a level, not skipping any spots. A tree like this is complete. That is, a *complete binary tree* is one in which every level, except perhaps the bottom, has the maximum number of nodes and the nodes on the bottom level are in the leftmost positions. Figure 10.15 shows three binary trees. The first is complete and the other two are not. The middle tree in Figure 10.15 is not complete because the nodes in the bottom level aren't in the leftmost positions. The rightmost tree in Figure 10.15 is not complete because the level above the bottom level does not have the maximum number of nodes.

Now that we know what a complete tree is, we can define a heap. A *heap* is a complete binary tree in which each parent has a value less than both its children. This also means that each node has a value greater than its parent, except of course the root, which has no parent. The tree in Figure 10.16 is a heap. In a heap the smallest element will always be at the root. For this reason, heaps are often used to implement priority queues. The heap is ordered so that the highest priority item is at the top.

When we add and remove nodes from a heap, we have to end up with a heap—a complete binary tree ordered the way we just described. Let us first

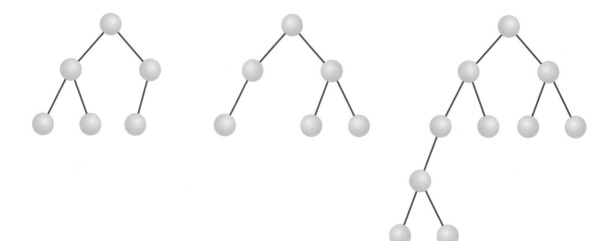

figure 10.15   A complete binary tree and two that are not complete

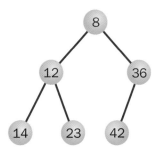

figure 10.16   A heap

consider the case of adding a node. Since the resulting tree must be complete, there is only one choice as to where the extra node can go. Usually it will go immediately to the right of the rightmost node on the bottom level (see Figure 10.17). If the bottom level is full, the new node is added as the left child of the leftmost node on the bottom level. That is, it starts a new row and goes in the leftmost position (see Figure 10.18). This way the heap stays complete. But each parent must have a value less than both its children, too. If the added node is less than its parent, we swap it with its parent. Figure 10.17 shows the addition of 18 to the heap from Figure 10.16. Since 18 is not greater than its parent, 36, the nodes are swapped. We keep doing this until the added node reaches a spot where it is greater than its parent. In Figure 10.17, after 18 is swapped with 36, 18's new parent is 8, which is less than 18, so we are finished, and the ordering of the heap is preserved. We don't have to worry about the other child (42) of the parent (36), because that child was already greater than the parent, so it will be greater than its new parent.

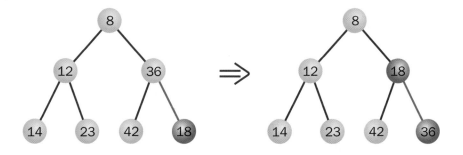

figure 10.17   Adding the node 18 to the heap

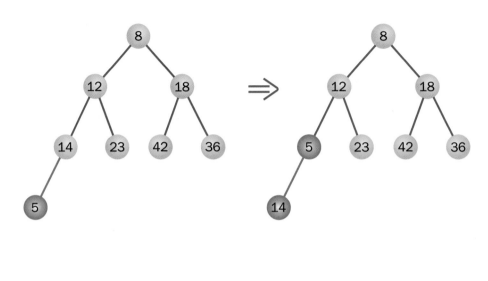

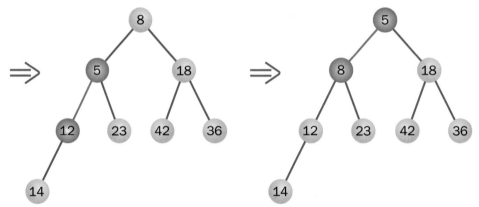

figure 10.18   Adding the node 5 to the heap

The process of swapping a node up into its proper position is sometimes called *bubbling up*. If the new node that is added is smaller than all the other nodes in the heap, it will bubble up to the root position, as shown in Figure 10.18.

Here are the steps to add a node to a heap:

1. Add the new node just to the right of the rightmost node on the bottom level, or, if the bottom level is full, add it as the left child of the leftmost node on the bottom level.

2. If the new node is less than its parent, bubble it up by swapping, until it is greater than its parent or it becomes the root.

When we delete a node from a heap, we must replace it with another node in order to keep the tree complete, unless that node is the rightmost node on the bottom level. The logical node to replace it is the rightmost node on the bottom level. This keeps the heap complete but once again we need to make sure that each node is not less than its parent. If the node that replaces the deleted node is less than its parent, then we must bubble it up as before. See Figure 10.19, which shows an example of this.

If the node that replaces the deleted node is greater than one of its children, then it must be *bubbled down*. When bubbling a node down, we always swap it with its smaller child. This makes sure the new parent is no bigger than either child. Figure 10.20 shows the deletion of the root in a heap. The node that replaces the deleted root is bubbled down until it is no greater than its children.

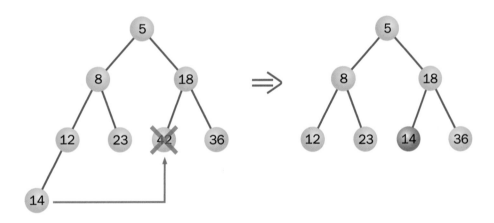

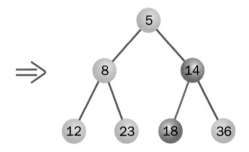

figure 10.19   Deleting the node 42

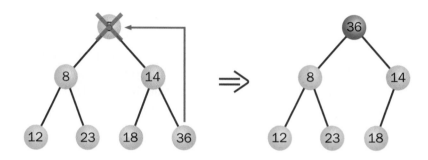

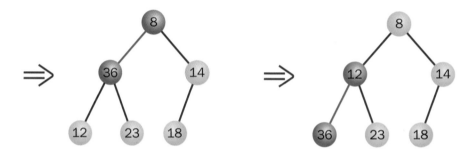

figure 10.20   Deleting the smallest node and bubbling down

Here are the steps taken to delete a node from a heap:

1. Let x be the rightmost node of the bottom level.

2. Replace the deleted node with x.

3. If x is less than its parent, bubble it up until it is not.

4. If x is greater than one of its children, bubble it down until it is not, by swapping with its smaller child.

heapsort

We can use a heap to perform a sort like the way we used a binary search tree to perform a sort. We create an empty heap and add to it, one by one, the items to be sorted. Now the smallest element is at the root. When we remove the root the heap reorganizes itself and the new root node is the second smallest element. We keep removing the root until there are no nodes left in the heap. We now have the elements in sorted order. This is called a *heapsort*.

Inserting or removing an element from a heap takes O(log*n*) time. There are two reasons for this. First, an element will bubble, at the most, from the bottom to the root or from the root to the bottom of the heap. Second, the height of a complete binary tree is O(log*n*). During a heapsort, we add and remove *n* elements from the heap, so heapsort has a time complexity of O(*n*log*n*).

> **key concept**
>
> The heapsort algorithm uses a heap to sort a collection of elements, and has time complexity O(*n*log*n*).

implementing heaps

We have described heaps as a kind of tree, and they may be implemented that way, but more often they are implemented as lists. A list can be created from a heap in tree form by putting the root in the first spot of the list and filling in the list with elements from the second level moving left to right, then the third level, down to the bottom level. It turns out that the ith element's children are the $2i^{th}$ and $2i + 1^{th}$ elements in the list. Figure 10.21 shows the same heap in both tree and list forms.

Lists are used with heaps because a list can be a more convenient for adding and deleting items from a heap. When we add an element we simply

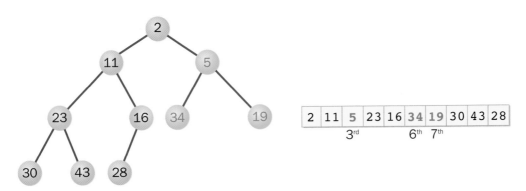

figure 10.21   A heap shown in tree and list forms. The children of the third element in the list are the 2(3)=6th and 2(3)+1=7th elements in the list.

put it at the end of the list, then bubble it up if we need to (using the reverse of the formulas given in order to find parents). In a binary tree, it takes more work to find where a node must be added.

Likewise, when deleting a node, we replace it with the rightmost node in the bottom level of the heap. Using a tree data structure, it takes some work to get to this node, but in a list, it is always the last element in the list.

10.3 more on hashtables

In Chapter 6 we introduced hashtables, a data structure in which data values are mapped to array cells by a hash function. Now we need to look at what happens when two different data values have the same hash code. This is called a *collision*. In this section we'll also look at Java classes that use hashtables to implement the Set and Map interfaces.

handling collisions

There are several methods we can use to handle collisions in a hashtable. One simple method is to let each cell in the hashtable hold more than one element. We can do this by making each cell a pointer to the start of a list. This technique is called *chaining*, and usually we use a linked list. With chaining, each time a new element is added to the hashtable, it is placed at one end of the list at the cell it hashes to. Figure 10.22 shows a hashtable storing integers using the hash function $f(k) = k \% 7$ and handling collisions using chaining. Since 36 % 7 = 1 and 15 % 7 = 1, both 36 and 15 are stored at cell 1. Cell 1 has a reference to a linked list containing the values 36 and 15.

When searching for an element in a hashtable, we compute the hashcode of the element we're looking for and examine that array cell. If the cell contains a null value, then it is empty; otherwise the cell contains a reference to the first element in a linked list. We must then traverse the list until either we find the element or we reach the end of the list. This lessens the hashtable advantage of being able to jump directly to an element. However, if the elements in the hashtable are spread out well (because of a good hash function), we can still get better performance with the hashtable than if we were using a list to store all the elements.

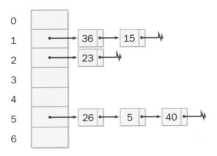

figure 10.22   A hashtable that uses chaining to handle collisions

Listing 10.5 shows a program that creates a hashtable, adds some numbers to it, and then prints it out. The `Hashtable` class, shown in Listing 10.6, uses an array of `ListNode` objects to implement the hashtable. The `ListNode` class was introduced in Chapter 9 but is repeated in Listing 10.7 for your convenience. The `add` method on `Hashtable` adds an object to the hashtable. It uses the `hashCode` method found on every `Object` to generate a hashcode. It then takes the remainder of that code, divided by the size of the hashtable to make sure the object hashes into a valid array cell. If the array cell already has an element in it, the while loop traverses the list and adds the new element at the end of the linked list. On the other hand, the code could have added the new element at the beginning of the list. The `toString` method creates a string showing each entry in the hashtable and the chain of elements stored at that entry. The `HashTest` program uses the same numbers shown in Figure 10.22. Since the `Integer` class returns the `int` value of the integer it represents as its hash code, running the `HashTest` program produces output showing each integer stored in the same array cell as shown in Figure 10.22.

With chaining we can store more than one element in each cell; there is another group of methods for handling collisions that still allow only one element per cell. In these *open addressing techniques*, when a collision occurs, a new hash code is calculated; this is called *rehashing*. If another collision occurs with the new hash code, rehashing is performed again; this continues until an empty cell is found.

The simplest way to rehash is called *linear probing*. In linear probing, if the first hash code is `i`, but cell `i` already contains an element, then cell `(i + 1) % n` is checked, where `n` is the size of the hashtable. This lets us probe down the array and wrap back to the beginning

listing
  10.5

```
//********************************************************************
//  HashTest.java          Author: Lewis/Loftus/Cocking
//
//  Driver for testing a hashtable.
//********************************************************************

public class HashTest
{
   //-----------------------------------------------------------------
   //  Creates a hashtable of size 7, adds numbers to it, then
   //  prints it out.
   //-----------------------------------------------------------------
   public static void main (String[] args)
   {
      Hashtable table = new Hashtable(7);

      table.add(new Integer(36));
      table.add(new Integer(15));
      table.add(new Integer(23));
      table.add(new Integer(26));
      table.add(new Integer(5));
      table.add(new Integer(40));

      System.out.println (table);
   }
}
```

output

```
0:
1:   36   15
2:   23
3:
4:
5:   26   5   40
6:
```

when the end of the array is reached (hence the % n). This continues until either a free cell is found or the search ends up back at i again, which would mean the hashtable is full. Figure 10.23 shows a hashtable in which the elements 36, 15, 23, 26, 5, and 40 have been inserted, in that order. The hashtable uses the same hash function as the one shown in Figure 10.22, but uses linear probing to handle collisions. More complicated rehashing schemes can also be used.

listing
10.6

```
//***********************************************************************
//   Hashtable.java        Author: Lewis/Loftus/Cocking
//
//   Implements a hashtable using chaining to handle collisions.
//***********************************************************************


public class Hashtable
{
   private int size;
   private ListNode[] table;

   //-------------------------------------------------------------------
   //   Sets up an empty hashtable with the given size.
   //-------------------------------------------------------------------
   public Hashtable (int numSlots)
   {
      size = numSlots;
      table = new ListNode[size];
   }


   //-------------------------------------------------------------------
   //   Adds an element to the hashtable.
   //-------------------------------------------------------------------
   public void add (Object obj)
   {
      // Create a node for the given element
      ListNode element = new ListNode(obj, null);

      // Calculate the hash code
      int index = obj.hashCode() % size;

      // Add the element to the appropriate cell, using chaining
      if (table[index] == null)
         table[index] = element;
      else
      {
         ListNode current = table[index];
         while (current.getNext() != null)
            current = current.getNext();
         current.setNext(element);
      }
   }


   //-------------------------------------------------------------------
   //   Returns a string representation of this hashtable.
   //-------------------------------------------------------------------
```

listing
    10.6   continued

```java
    public String toString ()
    {
        String str = "";

        for (int i=0; i < size; i++)
        {
            str += i + ":   ";
            ListNode current = table[i];
            while (current != null)
            {
                str += current.getValue() + "   ";
                current = current.getNext();
            }
            str += "\n";
        }

        return str;
    }

}
```

listing
    10.7

```java
//************************************************************************
//   ListNode.java        Author: AP Committee, comments added by
//                              Lewis/Loftus/Cocking
//
//   A node in a linked list.
//************************************************************************

public class ListNode
{
    private Object value;
    private ListNode next;

    //-----------------------------------------------------------------
    //   Initializes this node.
    //-----------------------------------------------------------------
    public ListNode (Object initValue, ListNode initNext)
    {
        value = initValue;
        next = initNext;
    }
```

listing
  10.7   continued

```
//----------------------------------------------------------------
//  Returns the value of this node.
//----------------------------------------------------------------
public Object getValue ()
{
   return value;
}

//----------------------------------------------------------------
//  Returns the next reference in this node.
//----------------------------------------------------------------
public ListNode getNext ()
{
   return next;
}

//----------------------------------------------------------------
//  Sets the value of this node.
//----------------------------------------------------------------
public void setValue (Object theNewValue)
{
   value = theNewValue;
}

//----------------------------------------------------------------
//  Sets the next reference in this node.
//----------------------------------------------------------------
public void setNext (ListNode theNewNext)
{
   next = theNewNext;
}
}
```

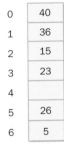

figure 10.23   A hashtable that uses linear probing to handle collisions

HashSet and HashMap

The `HashSet` and `HashMap` classes are implementations of the `Set` and `Map` interfaces from the Java standard class library. They use a hashtable to store their elements. Figures 10.24 and 10.25 show the methods from the `HashSet` and `HashMap` classes that are included in the AP subset. In the `HashSet` class, we hash the element itself to find the cell it belongs in. In the `HashMap` class, we hash the key. The `hashCode` method, which exists on all objects, calculates the hash codes.

Because of the hashtable implementation, the basic operations on `HashSet` and `HashMap` objects run in constant time, O(1), (assuming the hash function evenly distributes the elements in the hashtable). Unlike `TreeSet`, the iterator that is returned by the `iterator` method of `HashSet` does not order the objects returned.

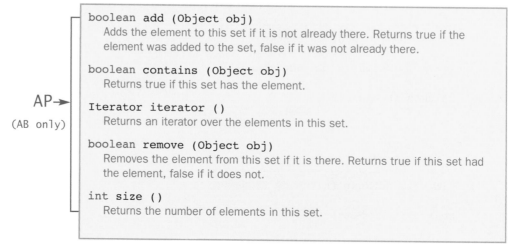

figure 10.24   Some methods of the `HashSet` class

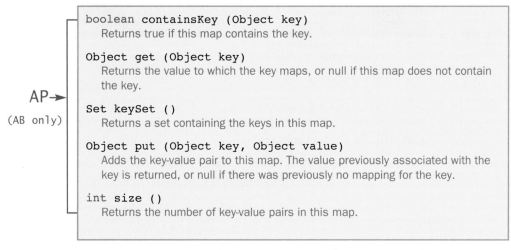

AP→

(AB only)

boolean containsKey (Object key)
    Returns true if this map contains the key.

Object get (Object key)
    Returns the value to which the key maps, or null if this map does not contain
    the key.

Set keySet ()
    Returns a set containing the keys in this map.

Object put (Object key, Object value)
    Adds the key-value pair to this map. The value previously associated with the
    key is returned, or null if there was previously no mapping for the key.

int size ()
    Returns the number of key-value pairs in this map.

figure 10.25   Some methods of the HashMap class

summary of
key concepts

▸ A `Set` object is a collection of elements with no duplicates.

▸ A `Map` object matches keys to values.

▸ A tree is a data structure that organizes information in a hierarchical structure that looks like an upside-down tree. A tree has zero or more nodes that contain the data in the tree.

▸ Each child node in a tree forms a subtree. We can break off the child node from its parent so the child node becomes the root of a subtree.

▸ The height of a tree is equal to the levels of the tree. The root is level 1, and every other node is a level one greater than its parent.

▸ In a binary tree, each node has at most two children, called the left child and the right child.

▸ In a preorder traversal we process a node before processing its subtrees. In an inorder traversal we process a node's left subtree, then the node itself, then its right subtree. In a postorder traversal we process both of a node's subtrees before we process the node itself.

▸ In a binary search tree, for any node N, every node in N's left subtree is less than N and every node in N's right subtree is greater than or equal to N. An inorder traversal of a binary search tree produces the elements in order.

▸ A heap is a complete binary tree in which each parent has a value less than both its children.

▸ The heapsort algorithm uses a heap to sort a collection of elements, and has time complexity $O(n\log n)$.

▸ When chaining is used to handle hashtable collisions, we can store more than one element in each cell, in the form of a list. Methods that deal with collisions while only allowing one element per cell are called open addressing techniques. In one of these, linear probing, when a collision occurs we linearly probe through the table until an empty cell is found.

self-review questions

10.1 What is a set?

10.2 What is a map?

10.3 What is a binary tree?

10.4 What are the three methods for traversing a binary tree?

10.5 What is a binary search tree?

10.6 What is a heap?

10.7 How does heapsort work?

10.8 List and briefly explain two techniques for handling collisions in hashtables.

multiple choice

10.1. Which of the following is not a set?

    a. {0, 3, 1, 2}

    b. {2, 5, –5}

    c. {19}

    d. {–9, –4, –7}

    e. {1, 46, 1}

10.2 Suppose a node in a tree has two children. Then the node must be a

    a. leaf

    b. parent

    c. child

    d. root

    e. sibling

10.3 The height of the tree in Figure 10.26 is

    a. 3

    b. 4

    c. 5

    d. 6

    e. 10

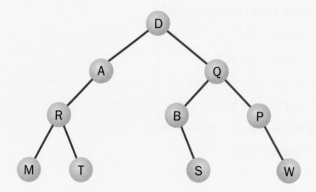

figure 10.26

10.4   Which of the following trees is a complete binary tree?

a. The tree in Figure 10.26

b. The tree in Figure 10.27

c. The tree in Figure 10.28

d. The tree in Figure 10.29

e. None of the above are complete.

10.5   The root node will always be the last one processed in which kind(s) of traversal?

a. preorder only

b. inorder only

c. postorder only

d. both preorder and postorder

e. both inorder and postorder

10.6   Suppose the integers 1 through 5 are inserted into an empty binary search tree. Which ordering will produce a tree with only right children?

a. 1, 2, 3, 4, 5

b. 5, 4, 3, 2, 1

c. 3, 2, 4, 1, 5

d. 1, 2, 3, 5, 4

e. 3, 5, 1, 4, 2

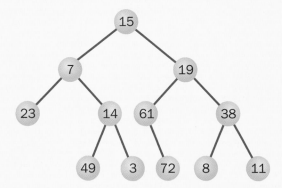

figure 10.27

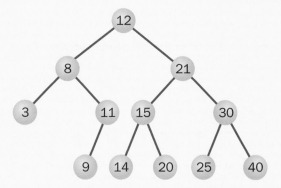

figure 10.28

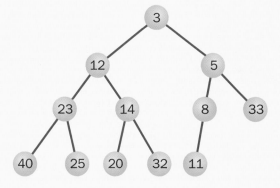

figure 10.29

10.7   When a node with two children is deleted from a binary search tree, it is replaced with

   a. `null`

   b. its child

   c. its inorder successor

   d. a leaf

   e. the root

10.8   The smallest element in a heap resides in which node?

   a. the root

   b. the leftmost leaf in the tree

   c. the rightmost leaf on the bottom level

   d. any leaf

   e. any node in the tree

10.9   The largest element in a heap resides in which node?

   a. the root

   b. the leftmost leaf in the tree

   c. the rightmost leaf on the bottom level

   d. any leaf

   e. any node in the tree

10.10 Suppose x is a value to be inserted into a hash table of size n, and y is the hashcode produced for x. A collision occurs and it will be handled using linear probing. Which expression represents the next cell that will be examined?

   a. x + 1

   b. y + 1

   c. (x + 1) % n

   d. (y + 1) % n

   e. y − 1

true/false

10.1   A set may have duplicate elements.

10.2   Two keys in a map may map to the same value.

10.3   A node in a tree may have both a parent and children.

10.4   A binary tree is a tree used to store binary data.

10.5   A node in a binary tree must have either no children, or both a left and right child; it may not have only one child.

10.6   A binary tree may be traversed in more than one way.

10.7   A tree node can be both the root and a leaf.

10.8   Both a binary search tree and a heap can be used to sort data.

10.9   Each node in a heap must have a value less than its siblings.

10.10 One method for handling a collision in a hashtable is chaining, in which each cell stores a linked list.

short answer

10.1   In Figure 10.26, list the parent, children, and siblings, if any, of the following nodes:

   a. A

   b. B

   c. D

   d. R

   e. S

10.2   Identify the root and the leaves in the tree in Figure 10.26.

10.3   List the nodes in Figure 10.26 using a preorder, an inorder, and a postorder traversal.

10.4   List the nodes in Figure 10.27 using a preorder, an inorder, and a postorder traversal.

10.5   Draw an expression tree for each of the following expressions.

   a. 3 + (2 * 14) − 5

   b. 20 * (10 − 5)

   c. 20 * 10 − 5

   d. (17 % 5) * 11 + 3

   e. (5 + 3 + 2) / 4

10.6   Draw a binary tree where each node contains a letter and

   a. an inorder traversal spells "hello"

   b. a preorder traversal spells "computer"

   c. a postorder traversal spells "binary"

10.7   In the binary search tree in Figure 10.28, list in order the nodes that would be visited when searching for these numbers.

a. 12

b. 15

c. 40

d. 3

d. 9

e. 11

10.8   In Figure 10.28, show where the following elements would be inserted in the tree.

a. 10

b. 1

c. 50

d. 31

e. 16

f. 17

10.9   Show what the tree in Figure 10.28 would look like if each of these six elements were deleted.

a. 9

b. 11

c. 15

d. 21

e. 30

f. 12

10.10 Numbers are added to a binary search tree in the order given. Draw the resulting tree.

a. 3, 14, 5, 26, 17

b. 50, 60, 30, 80, 70, 10, 40

c. 1, 2, 3, 4, 5, 6

d. 10, 9, 8, 7, 6, 5

10.11 When a node in a binary search tree is deleted, we replace it with its inorder successor. Instead, could we replace the deleted node with its inorder predecessor, that is, the largest element in its left subtree? If so, repeat Exercise 10.9 using this method. If not, explain why not.

10.12 Draw a five-node binary tree that is a heap. Draw one that is not a heap because it is not complete. Draw one that is complete but is still not a heap.

10.13 Show what the heap in Figure 10.29 will look like after each of the following elements is added to it.

   a. 15

   b. 41

   c. 7

   d. 4

   e. 22

   f. 1

10.14 Show what the heap in Figure 10.29 will look like after each of the following elements is deleted.

   a. 11

   b. 33

   c. 14

   d. 25

   e. 12

   f. 3

10.15 Perform a heapsort on each of the following lists of numbers. Draw the heap for each step in the process.

   a. 8, 14, 15, 3, 7

   b. 1, 2, 3, 4, 5

   c. 5, 4, 3, 2, 1

10.16 Show how the heap in Figure 10.29 would look if it were stored in an array.

10.17 Suppose we have a hashtable of size 7 that stores integers using the hash function $f(n) = n \% 7$. The hashtable handles collisions using chaining. For each sequence of integers, show what the hashtable will look like after the elements have been added.

   a. 19, 8, 59, 40, 71

   b. 28, 13, 9, 7, 5, 16, 55

   c. 78, 12, 65, 45, 23, 7

10.18 Repeat Exercise 10.17 with a hashtable that uses linear probing to handle collisions.

10.19 Repeat Exercise 10.17 with a hashtable of size 9 using the hash function f(n) = n % 9 and chaining to handle collisions.

10.20 Repeat Exercise 10.17 with a hashtable of size 9 using the hash function f(n) = n % 9 and linear probing to handle collisions.

programming projects

10.1   Write a class that implements the `Set` interface using an `ArrayList` object. Write a driver program to test your new class.

10.2   Design and implement an application that builds a binary tree storing letters at each node, and then prints the letters in the tree using a postorder traversal. Use `TreeNode` (Listing 10.1) objects for each node.

10.3   Design and implement an application that stores your own family tree in a binary tree and then prints the tree. Put yourself at the root, and your parents as your "children" in the tree, with their parents being their children, and so on.

10.4   Design and implement an application that evaluates an arithmetic expression using a binary tree. Include support for integer operands and the operators +, –, *, /, and %. First build an expression tree from the given expression. In order to evaluate the expression, use the following recursive algorithm:

a. Start at the root of the tree.

b. Let `current` be the current node.

c. If `current` is an integer, return its value.

d. Otherwise,

    i. Recurse on `current`'s left child to get the left operand and recurse on `current`'s right child to get the right operand.

    ii. Perform the operation indicated by the node `current` on the left and right operands and return the result.

10.5   Change the `Hashtable` class in Listing 10.6 so that when an element is added to the hashtable, it goes on the beginning of the list for the cell it hashes to, rather than the end. Write a simple driver program or use the one in Listing 10.5 to test your class.

10.6   Write a class that represents a book. Include instance variables
       that store properties of the book and methods that can be used
       to set the property values. Override the `hashCode` method in
       your class to generate a hashcode from the book's properties.
       Write a driver program that creates some book objects, stores
       them in a hashtable using the class from the previous exercise,
       and then prints the hashtable.

answers to self-review questions

10.1   A set is a collection of elements with no duplicates. The `Set`
       interface in the Java standard class library defines a set of oper-
       ations on a set.

10.2   A map is a collection of key-value pairs. The keys in a map
       form a set. The `Map` interface in the Java standard class library
       defines a set of operations on a map.

10.3   A tree is a data structure that organizes information in nodes in
       a hierarchical structure like an upside-down tree. In a binary
       tree, each node has at most two children, called the left child
       and the right child.

10.4   A binary tree may be traversed using a preorder, inorder, or
       postorder traversal. A preorder traversal processes a node
       before either of its subtrees; an inorder traversal processes a
       node after its left subtree and before its right subtree; a post-
       order traversal processes a node after both its subtrees.

10.5   In a binary search tree, for any node N, every node in N's left
       subtree is less than N and every node in N's right subtree is
       greater than or equal to N. An inorder traversal of a binary
       search tree processes the nodes in order from least to greatest.

10.6   A heap is a complete binary tree in which each parent has a
       value less than both its children. The smallest value in a heap is
       always at the root.

10.7   The heapsort algorithm adds all the elements to be sorted to a
       heap. It then removes the elements one by one, always taking
       the root element, so the elements removed are in sorted order.
       Heapsort has a time complexity of $O(n\log n)$.

10.8 Chaining can be used to handle collisions in a hashtable. In this
method, several elements can be stored in a single cell. Each
cell in the hashtable is a reference to the start of a linked list of
all the elements. Linear probing is an open addressing technique that handles collisions by going through the table cell by
cell until an empty cell is found.

abstract—A Java reserved word for classes, interfaces, and methods. An `abstract` class cannot be instantiated and is used to specify abstract methods that are given definitions by derived classes. Interfaces are `abstract`.

abstract class—*See* abstract.

abstract data type (ADT)—A collection of data and the operations that are defined on that data. An abstract data type might be implemented in many ways, but its interface operations are always the same.

abstract method—*See* abstract.

abstraction—The idea of hiding details. If the right details are hidden at the right times, abstraction can make programming simpler and better focused.

access—Referencing a variable or invoking a method from outside its class. Controlled by the visibility modifier used to declare the variable or method. Also called the level of encapsulation. *See also* visibility modifier.

access modifier—*See* visibility modifier.

actual parameter—The value passed to a method as a parameter. *See also* formal parameter.

adaptor class—*See* listener adaptor class.

address—(1) A numeric value that identifies a memory location in a computer's main memory. (2) A name that identifies a computer among all others on a network.

ADT—*See* abstract data type.

aggregate object—An object that contains variables that are references to other objects. *See also* has-a relationship.

aggregation—Something that is made up, at least in part, of other things. *See also* aggregate object.

algorithm—A step-by-step process for solving a problem. A program is based on one or more algorithms.

alias—A reference to an object that is also referred to by another reference. Each reference is an alias of the other.

analog—A measurement that is in direct proportion to the source of the information. *See also* digital.

animation—A series of images or drawings that give the appearance of movement when displayed in order at a particular speed.

API—*See* Application Programming Interface.

applet—A Java program that is linked into an HTML document, then retrieved and executed using a Web browser, as opposed to a stand-alone Java application.

appletviewer—A software tool that interprets and displays Java applets through links in HTML documents. Part of the Java Development Kit.

application—(1) A general term for any program. (2) A Java program that can be run without a Web browser, as opposed to a Java applet.

Application Programming Interface (API)—A set of classes that defines services for a programmer. Not part of the language itself, but often used for basic tasks. *See also* class library.

arc angle—The distance that defines an arc's length. *See also* start angle.

architecture—*See* computer architecture.

architecture neutral—Not specific to any particular hardware platform. Java code is architecture neutral because it is compiled into bytecode and then interpreted on any machine with a Java interpreter.

arithmetic operator—An operator that performs a basic arithmetic computation, such as addition or multiplication.

arithmetic promotion—The act of promoting the type of a numeric operand to be consistent with the other operand.

array—Used to store an ordered list of primitive values or objects. Each element in the array is referenced using an index from 0 to $N - 1$, where N is the size of the array.

array element—A value or object that is stored in an array.

array element type—The type of the values or objects that are stored in an array.

ASCII—A popular character set used by many programming languages. ASCII stands for American Standard Code for Information Interchange. It is a subset of the Unicode character set, which is used by Java.

assembly language—A low-level language.

assignment conversion—Changing one data type into another data type with an assignment. *See* widening conversion.

assignment operator—An operator that results in an assignment to a variable. The = operator performs basic assignment. Many other assignment operators perform additional operations prior to the assignment, such as the *= operator.

association—A relationship between two classes. *See also* operator association, use relationship.

background color—(1) The color of the background of a graphical user interface component. (2) The color of the background of an HTML page. *See also* foreground color.

base case—The situation that ends recursive processing, letting the active recursive methods return.

base class—*See* superclass.

behavior—What an object does, defined by its methods. *See also* identity, state.

big-oh notation—A notation used to compare the efficiency of algorithms. For example, selection sort is $O(n^2)$, while merge sort is $O(n\log n)$.

binary—The base-2 number system. Modern computer systems store information as strings of binary digits (bits).

binary operator—An operator that uses two operands.

binary search—A searching algorithm that needs a sorted list. It compares the "middle" element of the list to the target value, narrowing the scope of the search each time. *See also* linear search.

binary search tree—A binary tree in which, for any node N, every node in N's left subtree is less than N and every node in N's right subtree is greater than or equal to N.

binary string—A series of binary digits (bits).

binary tree—A tree data structure in which each node can have no more than two child nodes.

binding—The process of matching an identifier with the construct that it represents. For example, the process of binding a method name to the definition that it invokes.

bit—A binary digit, either 0 or 1.

bits per second (bps)—A measurement for data transfer devices.

block—A group of programming statements and declarations, which appears in braces (`{}`).

boolean—A Java reserved word for a logical primitive data type that can only take the values `true` or `false`.

boolean expression—An expression that gives a true or false result, mostly used in selection and repetition statements.

border—An edge around a graphical component to make it look better or to group components visually. An empty border creates space around a component.

bounding rectangle—A rectangle in which an oval or arc is defined.

bounds checking—The process of checking whether an array index is in bounds, given the size of the array. Java performs automatic bounds checking.

bps—*See* bits per second.

browser—Software that gets HTML documents across network connections and formats them for viewing. Used to access the World Wide Web. *See also* Netscape Navigator.

bug—Slang for a defect or error in a computer program.

bus—A group of wires in the computer that carry data between components such as the CPU and main memory.

button—A graphical user interface component that lets the user initiate an action, set a condition, or choose an option with a mouse click. There are several kinds of GUI buttons. *See also* check box, push button, radio button.

byte—(1) A unit of binary storage equal to eight bits. (2) A Java reserved word for a primitive integer type, stored using eight bits in two's complement format.

bytecode—The low-level format for Java source code. The bytecodes are interpreted and executed by the Java interpreter, perhaps after coming over the Internet.

capacity—*See* storage capacity.

case sensitive—Differentiating between the uppercase and lowercase versions of an alphabetic letter. Java is case sensitive; so the identifier `total` and the identifier `Total` are different identifiers.

cast—A Java operation that uses a type or class name in parentheses to convert and return a value of one data type into another.

CD-Recordable (CD-R)—A compact disc on which information can be stored once. *See also* CD-Rewritable, CD-ROM.

CD-Rewritable (CD-RW)—A compact disc on which information can be stored and rewritten multiple times. *See also* CD-Recordable, CD-ROM.

CD-ROM—A compact disc that can only be read, not written to.

central processing unit (CPU)—The hardware that controls the main activity of a computer.

chaining—A way of handling collisions in a hash table. Each cell in the hashtable is a pointer to a list of all the elements that hashed to that value.

char—A Java reserved word for the primitive character type. All Java characters are members of the Unicode character set and are stored using 16 bits.

character font—The distinct look of a character when it is printed or drawn.

character set—An ordered list of characters, such as ASCII or Unicode. Each character has a specific, unique numeric value within a given character set. A programming language uses a particular character set.

character string—A series of ordered characters. Represented in Java using the `String` class and string literals such as `"hello"`.

check box—A graphical user interface component that lets the user set a boolean condition with a mouse click. A check box can be used alone or independently among other check boxes. *See also* radio button.

child class—*See* subclass.

child node—A node in a tree that has a parent.

class—(1) A Java reserved word used to define a class. (2) The blueprint of an object—the model that defines the variables and methods an object will contain when instantiated.

class diagram—A diagram that shows the relationships between classes, including inheritance and use relationships.

class hierarchy—A tree-like structure created when classes inherit from other classes.

class library—A set of classes that define useful services for a programmer. *See also* Application Programming Interface.

class method—A method that can be invoked using only the class name. An instantiated object is not needed, as it is with instance methods. Defined in a Java program by using the `static` reserved word.

CLASSPATH—An operating system setting that determines where the Java interpreter searches for class files.

class variable—A variable that is shared among all objects of a class. It can also be referenced through the class name, without instantiating any object of that class. Defined in a Java program by using the `static` reserved word.

client-server model—A software design based on objects (clients) making use of the services provided by other objects (servers).

coding guidelines—Guidelines for creating programs that are easier to read, exchange, and integrate. Sometimes called coding standards, especially when they are enforced.

coding standard—*See* coding guidelines.

collision—What happens when two hash values produce the same hash code. *See also* hash code, hashing.

combo box—A graphical user interface component that lets the user select one of several options. A combo box shows the most recent selection. *See also* list.

command-line arguments—The values that follow the program name on the command line. Accessed in a Java program through the `String` array parameter to the `main` method.

comment—The part of a program where the programmer can write notes and explanations for future reference. *See also* documentation.

compiler—A program that translates code from one language to another. The Java compiler translates Java source code into Java bytecode. *See also* interpreter.

compile-time error—Any error during compilation, often indicating problems with language syntax or data types. *See also* logical error, runtime error, syntax error.

complete binary tree—A binary tree in which every level, except perhaps the bottom, has the maximum number of nodes and in which the nodes on the bottom level occupy the leftmost positions.

component—Any part of a software system that turns input into output. *See also* GUI component.

computer architecture—The structure and interaction of the computer hardware.

concatenation—*See* string concatenation.

condition—A `boolean` expression used to decide whether a selection or repetition statement should be executed.

conditional operator—A Java operator that evaluates one of two expressions based on a condition.

conditional statement—*See* selection statement.

constant—A value that cannot be changed. Used to make code more readable and to make changes easier. Defined in Java using the `final` modifier.

constructor—A special method in a class that is invoked when an object is instantiated from the class. Used to initialize the object.

container—A Java graphical user interface component that can hold other components. *See also* containment hierarchy.

containment hierarchy—The relationships among graphical components of a user interface. *See also* container.

content pane—The part of a top-level container where components are added.

control characters—*See* nonprintable characters.

controller—Hardware devices that control the interaction between a computer system and a peripheral, such as a modem or printer.

CPU—*See* central processing unit.

data structure—Any part of a program, either defined in the language or by a programmer, used to organize data. Arrays, linked lists, and stacks are data structures.

data type—A description of a set of values (which may be infinite). For example, each variable has a data type that defines the kinds of values that can be stored in it.

data transfer device—Hardware that lets information be sent between computers, such as a modem.

debugger—A software tool that lets a programmer step through an executing program looking for problems.

decimal—The base-10 number system, which people use in everyday life. *See also* binary.

defined—Existing for use in a derived class, even if it can only be accessed indirectly. *See also* inheritance.

delimiter—Any symbol or word used to enclose part of a program, such as the braces (`{}`) around a Java block.

deprecated—Something, such as a particular method, that is considered old-fashioned and should not be used.

derived class—*See* subclass.

design—(1) The plan for implementing a program, including the classes and objects used and the important program algorithms. (2) The process of creating a program design.

detailed design—(1) The low-level algorithmic steps of a method. (2) The development stage at which low-level algorithmic steps are chosen.

development stage—The stage in which a software system is first created.

dialog box—A window that pops up to allow brief user interaction.

digital—A representation that breaks information down into pieces, represented as numbers. All modern computer systems are digital.

digitize—The act of changing analog into digital.

dimension—The number of index levels of an array.

direct recursion—The process of a method invoking itself. *See also* indirect recursion.

disable—Make a graphical user interface inactive so that it cannot be used. A disabled component is grayed. *See also* enable.

DNS—*See* Domain Name System.

documentation—Information about a program, including comments in a program's source code and printed reports such as a user's guide.

domain name—The part of an Internet address that specifies the organization to which the computer belongs.

Domain Name System (DNS)—Software that translates an Internet address into an IP address using a domain server.

domain server—A file server that keeps a list of Internet addresses and their IP addresses.

double—A Java reserved word that represents a primitive floating point numeric type, stored using 64 bits in IEEE 754 format.

doubly linked list—A linked list with two references in each node: one that refers to the next node in the list and one that refers to the previous node in the list.

dynamic binding—The process of matching an identifier with its definition during runtime. *See also* binding.

dynamic data structure—A set of objects that are linked using references, which can be changed as needed during program execution.

editor—A software tool that lets the user and store a file of characters on a computer. Often used by programmers to enter the source code of a program.

efficiency—*See* time efficiency, space efficiency.

element—A value or object stored in another object such as an array.

element type—*See* array element type.

else—A Java reserved word that designates the part of code in an `if` statement that will be executed if the condition is false.

enable—Make a graphical user interface component active so that it can be used. *See also* disable.

encapsulation—The characteristic of an object that limits access to its variables and methods. All interaction with the object occurs through an interface.

equality operator—One of two Java operators that returns a boolean result based on whether two values are equal (==) or not equal (!=).

error—Any defect in a design or program. *See also* compile-time error, exception, logical error, runtime error, syntax error.

escape sequence—In Java, characters beginning with the backslash character (\), used to indicate a special situation when printing values. For example, the escape sequence \t means that a horizontal tab should be printed.

exception—(1) A situation during program execution that is an error or out of the ordinary. *See also* error.

exponent—The part of a floating point value that specifies how far the decimal point is shifted. *See also* mantissa.

expression—A combination of operators and operands that produce a result, such as a math equation.

extends—A Java reserved word used to specify the parent class in the definition of a child class.

event—(1) A user action, such as a mouse click or key press. (2) An object that represents a user action, to which the program can respond. *See also* event-driven programming.

event-driven programming—Software development in which the program recognizes and acts on an event, such as a mouse click. *See also* event.

false—A Java reserved word that is one of the two boolean literals (`true` and `false`).

fetch-decode-execute—The cycle through which the CPU continually gets instructions from main memory and executes them.

FIFO—*See* first-in, first-out.

file—A named collection of data stored on a secondary storage device such as a disk. *See also* text file.

file chooser—A graphical user interface component, usually a dialog box, that lets the user select a file.

file server—A computer in a network, usually with a large secondary storage capacity, that stores software needed by many network users.

final—A Java reserved word that is a modifier for classes, methods, and variables. A `final` variable is a constant.

first-in, first-out (FIFO)—A data management technique in which the first value stored in a data structure is the first value processed. *See also* last-in, first-out; queue.

float—A Java reserved word for a primitive floating point numeric type, stored using 32 bits in IEEE 754 format.

font—*See* character font.

for—A Java reserved word for a repetition construct. A `for` statement is executed zero or more times and is usually used when the number of times it will execute is known.

foreground color—The color of any current drawing. *See also* background color.

formal parameter—A parameter name in a method. It receives its value from the actual parameter passed to it. *See also* actual parameter.

fourth-generation language—A high-level language that can do more things, such as automatic report generation or database management, than traditional high-level languages.

function—A named group of declarations and programming statements that can be invoked (executed) when needed. A function that is part of a class is called a method. Java has no functions because all code is part of a class.

garbage—(1) An unspecified or uninitialized value in a memory location. (2) An object that cannot be accessed anymore because all references to it have been lost.

gigabyte (GB)—A unit of binary storage, equal to 2^{30} (approximately 1 billion) bytes.

grammar—Language syntax that defines how reserved words, symbols, and identifiers can be combined into valid programs.

graphical user interface (GUI)—Software that lets the user interact with a program or operating system through images and point-and-click mechanisms such as buttons and text fields.

graphics context—The drawing surface and related coordinate system for a drawing or graphical user interface.

GUI component—A visual element, such as a button or text field, that is part of a graphical user interface (GUI).

hardware—The physical parts of a computer system, such as the keyboard, monitor, and circuit boards.

has-a relationship—The relationship between two objects in which one is made up, at least in part, of one or more of the other. *See also* aggregate object, is-a relationship.

hash code—An integer value calculated from any given data value or object, used to determine where a value should be stored in a hashtable. Also called a hash value. *See also* hashing.

hash function—A method that calculates a hash code. The same data value or object will always produce the same hash code. *See also* hashing.

hashtable—A data structure where values are stored. *See also* hashing.

hashing—A way of storing items so that they can be found efficiently. Items are stored in a hashtable at a position specified by a hash code. *See also* hash function.

heap—A complete binary tree in which each parent has a value less than both its children.

heap sort—A sorting algorithm that adds the elements to be sorted to a heap and then removes the elements, one-by-one, in sorted order.

height of a tree—A measure of how "tall" or "deep" a tree is. The height is equal to the maximum level in the tree. *See also* level of a node.

hierarchy—An organizational technique in which items are layered or grouped to make them easier to deal with.

high-level language—A programming language in which each statement represents many machine-level instructions.

HTML—*See* HyperText Markup Language.

hypermedia—Media types such as graphics, audio, video, and programs that use hypertext.

hypertext—A document that lets a user easily navigate through links to other parts of the document. *See also* hypermedia.

HyperText Markup Language (HTML)—The notation used for Web pages. *See also* browser, World Wide Web.

icon—A small picture used in a graphical interface. *See also* image.

identifier—Any name that a programmer makes up to use in a program, such as a class name or variable name.

identity—In Java, an object's reference name. *See also* state, behavior.

if—A Java reserved word for a simple conditional construct. *See also* else.

image—A picture, often in a GIF or JPEG format. *See also* icon.

immutable—Not changeable. For example, the contents of a Java character string are immutable once the string has been defined.

implementation—(1) The process of translating a design into source code. (2) The source code that defines a method, class, abstract data type, or other programming entity.

implements—A Java reserved word that is used in a class declaration to mean that the class implements the methods in a particular interface.

import—A Java reserved word for the packages and classes that are used in a Java source code file.

index—The integer value that selects a particular element in an array.

index operator—The brackets ([ ]) around an array index.

indirect recursion—The process of a method invoking another method, which eventually results in the original method being invoked again. *See also* direct recursion.

infinite loop—A loop that does not end because the condition controlling the loop never becomes false.

infinite recursion—A recursion that does not end because the base case is never reached.

infix expression—An expression in which the operators are positioned between the operands on which they work. *See also* postfix expression.

inheritance—The ability to create a new class from an existing one. Inherited variables and methods of the original (parent) class are available in the new (child) class as if they were declared locally.

initialize—To give a starting value to a variable.

initializer list—A list of values, separated by commas and enclosed in braces ({}), used to initialize and specify the size of an array.

inline documentation—Comments that are included in the source code of a program.

inner class—A nonstatic, nested class.

inorder traversal—A traversal of the nodes in a tree in which the left subtree is examined first, then the current node, then the right subtree.

input/output devices—Hardware that lets the user interact with the computer, such as a keyboard, mouse, and monitor.

insertion sort—A sorting algorithm in which each value is inserted, one at a time, into a sorted subset of the entire list. *See also* selection sort.

instance—An object created from a class. Several objects can be instantiated from a single class.

instance method—A method that must be invoked through an instance of a class, as opposed to a class method.

instance variable—A variable that must be referenced through an instance of a class, as opposed to a class variable.

instantiation—The act of creating an object from a class.

int—A Java reserved word for a primitive integer type, stored using 32 bits in two's complement format.

interface—(1) A Java reserved word that is used to define a set of abstract methods that will be implemented by particular classes. (2) The set of messages an object responds to, defined by the methods that can be invoked from outside of the object. (3) The way a user interacts with a program, often graphically. *See also* graphical user interface.

interpreter—A program that translates and executes code on a particular machine. The Java interpreter translates and executes Java bytecode. *See also* compiler.

Internet—A worldwide computer network.

Internet address—A name that identifies a particular computer or device on the Internet.

Internet Naming Authority—The governing body that approves all Internet addresses.

invisible component—A graphical user interface component that simply provides space between other components.

invocation—*See* method invocation.

I/O devices—*See* input/output devices.

IP address—A series of numbers, separated by periods (.), that identifies a particular computer or device on the Internet.

is-a relationship—The relationship of a subclass to a superclass. *See also* has-a relationship.

iteration—One execution of a repetition statement.

iterative development process—A step-by-step approach for creating software.

Java Virtual Machine (JVM)—The software device on which Java bytecode is executed. Bytecode does not run on a particular hardware platform; instead, it runs on the JVM.

java—The Java command-line interpreter, which translates and executes Java bytecode. Part of the Java Development Kit.

Java—The object oriented programming language used throughout this text to demonstrate software development concepts.

Java API—*See* Application Programming Interface.

Java Development Kit (JDK)—A collection of software tools available free from Sun Microsystems, the creators of the Java programming language. *See also* Software Development Kit.

javac—The Java command-line compiler, which translates Java source code into Java bytecode. Part of the Java Development Kit.

javadoc—A software tool that creates external documentation in HTML format about a Java software system. Part of the Java Development Kit.

JDK—*See* Java Development Kit.

JVM—*See* Java Virtual Machine.

kilobit (Kb)—A unit of binary storage, equal to 2^{10}, or 1024 bits.

kilobyte (K or KB)—A unit of binary storage, equal to 2^{10}, or 1024 bytes.

label—(1) A graphical user interface component that displays text, an image, or both.

LAN—*See* local-area network.

last-in, first-out (LIFO)—A data management technique in which the last value stored is the first value processed. *See also* first-in, first-out; stack.

layout manager—An object that controls where the parts of a GUI will go. Each container is governed by a layout manager.

level of a node—The level in a tree where a node is. The root is at level one, and every other node is at a level one greater than its parent.

lexicographic ordering—The ordering of characters and strings based on a character set such as Unicode.

life cycle—The stages through which a software product is developed and used.

LIFO—*See* last-in, first-out.

linear probing—A rehashing technique that probes through a hashtable cell by cell, in order, until an empty cell is found.

linear search—A search algorithm in which each item in the list is compared to the target value until the target is found or the list is done. Also known as sequential search. *See also* binary search.

link—(1) Part of a hypertext document that lets the user "jump" to a new document (or to a new part of the same document). (2) A connection between two items in a dynamically linked structure, represented as an object reference.

linked list—A dynamic data structure in which objects are linked using references.

list—A graphical user interface component that presents a list of items from which the user can choose. The current selection is highlighted in the list. *See also* combo box.

listener—An object that responds to an event.

listener adaptor class—A class defined with empty methods which match the methods invoked when particular events occur. A listener object can be derived from an adaptor class. *See also* listener interface.

listener interface—A Java interface that defines the methods invoked when particular events occur. A listener object can be created by implementing a listener interface. *See also* listener adaptor class.

literal—A primitive value used in a program, such as the numeric literal `147` or the string literal `"hello"`.

local-area network (LAN)—A computer network that spans short distances and connects a small number of computers. *See also* wide-area network.

local variable—A variable that does not exist except during the execution of a method.

logical error—A problem caused by inappropriate code processing. It does not cause the program to crash, but it produces incorrect results. *See also* compile-time error, runtime error, syntax error.

logical line of code—A logical programming statement in a source code program. *See also* physical line of code.

logical operator—One of the operators that perform a logical NOT (`!`), AND (`&&`), or OR (`||`), returning a boolean result. The logical operators are short-circuited, meaning that if their left operand can determine the result, the right operand is not evaluated.

long—A Java reserved word for a primitive integer type, stored using 64 bits in two's complement format.

loop—*See* repetition statement.

loop control variable—A variable that determines how many times a loop is executed.

low-level language—Machine language or assembly language.

machine language—The language of a particular CPU. Any software that runs on that CPU must be translated into its machine language.

main memory—The hardware where programs and data are stored when they are needed by the CPU. *See also* secondary memory.

maintenance—(1) The process of fixing errors in or making changes to a released software product. (2) The software life-cycle phase in which the software is in use and changes are made to it as needed.

mantissa—The part of a floating point that specifies the magnitude of the number. *See also* exponent.

map—A collection of key-value pairs. The keys in a map must be unique, but two keys may map to the same value.

megabyte (MB)—A unit of binary storage, equal to 2^{20} (approximately 1 million) bytes.

member—A variable or method in an object or class.

memory—Hardware that stores programs and data. *See also* main memory, secondary memory.

memory location—Where data is stored in main memory.

memory management—The process of controlling portions of main memory, returning memory when it is no longer required.

merge sort—A recursive sorting algorithm that works by dividing a list in half, sorting each half, and then merging the halves together.

method—A named group of declarations and programming statements that can be invoked (executed) when needed. A method is part of a class.

method call conversion—The automatic conversion that happens when a value of one type is passed to a formal parameter of another type.

method definition—The part of the code that gets executed when the method is invoked. The definition includes declarations of local variables and formal parameters.

method invocation—A line of code that causes a method to be executed. It specifies any values that are passed to the method as parameters.

method overloading—*See* overloading.

mnemonic—(1) A keyboard character used as another way to activate a graphical user interface component such as a button. (2) A command word or data value in an assembly language.

modem—A data transfer device that lets information be sent along a telephone line.

modifier—Used in a Java declaration to add particular characteristics to the construct being declared.

monitor—The computer screen.

multidimensional array—An array that uses more than one index to specify a stored value.

multiple inheritance—Creating a class from more than one parent, so that it inherits methods and variables from each. Multiple inheritance is not supported in Java.

narrowing conversion—A conversion from one data type into another in which information could be lost. Converting from `double` to an `int` is a narrowing conversion. *See also* widening conversion.

natural language—A language that people use, such as English or French.

nested class—A class declared within another class.

nested if statement—An `if` statement inside another `if` statement.

Netscape Navigator—A popular Web browser.

network—Two or more computers connected so that they can exchange data and share resources.

network address—*See* address.

new—A Java reserved word that is also an operator, used to instantiate an object from a class.

newline character—A nonprintable character that indicates the end of a line.

node—A single element in a dynamic data structure, such as a node in a linked list or a node in a tree.

nonprintable characters—Any character, such as escape or newline, that is not printed on a monitor or a printer. *See also* printable characters.

nonvolatile memory—Memory that is not damaged or lost even after a power failure. Secondary memory devices are nonvolatile. *See also* volatile.

null—A Java reserved word that means a reference does not refer to any object.

number system—A set of values and operations defined by a particular base value that determines the number of digits available and the place value of each digit.

object—(1) The basic software part in an object-oriented program. (2) An encapsulated collection of data variables and methods. (3) An instance of a class.

object-oriented programming—An approach to software design and implementation that is centered around objects and classes. *See also* procedural programming.

off-by-one error—An error caused by a calculation or condition being off by one, such as when a loop is set up to access one too many array elements.

operand—A value on which an operator performs its function. For example, in $5 + 2$, the values 5 and 2 are operands.

operating system—The collection of programs that includes the user interface as well as software that manages resources, such as memory and the CPU.

operator—A symbol that represents an operation in a programming language, such as the addition operator (+).

operator association—The order in which operators within the same precedence level are evaluated, either right to left or left to right. *See also* operator precedence.

operator overloading—Assigning extra meaning to an operator. Operator overloading is not supported in Java, though method overloading is.

operator precedence—The order in which operators are evaluated in an expression.

order—The term in an equation that tells us how efficient an algorithm is. For example, selection sort is of order n^2. *See also* big-oh notation.

overflow—When a data value grows too large for its storage size, which can result in inaccurate arithmetic processing. *See also* underflow.

overloading—Assigning additional meaning to a method or operator. Method overloading is supported by Java but operator overloading is not.

overriding—Changing the definition of an inherited method to suit the subclass.

package—A Java reserved word for a group of related classes.

panel—A graphical user interface (GUI) container that holds and organizes other GUI components.

parameter—(1) A value passed to a method when it is invoked. *See also* actual parameter, formal parameter.

parent class—*See* superclass.

parent node—A node in a tree that has a child.

pass by reference—The process of passing a reference to a value into a method. All Java objects are passed by reference, so an object's formal parameter is an alias to the original. *See also* pass by value.

pass by value—The process of making a copy of a value and passing the copy into a method. Any change made to the value inside the method does not affect the original value. All Java primitive types are passed by value.

peripheral—Any hardware device other than the CPU or main memory.

physical line of code—A line in a source code file, ended by a newline or similar character. *See also* logical line of code.

pixel—A picture element. A digitized picture is made up of many pixels.

pointer—A variable that can hold a memory address. Instead of pointers, Java uses references, which do the same thing as pointers but without the complications.

point-to-point connection—The link between two networked devices that are connected directly by a wire.

polyline—A shape made up of connected lines. A polyline is like a polygon, but the shape is not closed.

polymorphism—A technique for involving different methods at different times. All Java method invocations can be polymorphic because they invoke the method of the object type, not the reference type.

portability—The ability of a program to be moved from one hardware platform to another without having to change it. Because Java bytecode can work in any hardware environment, Java programs are considered portable. *See also* architecture neutral.

positive infinity—A special floating point value that represents the "highest possible" value.

postfix expression—An expression in which an operator is positioned after the operands on which it works. *See also* infix expression.

postfix operator—An operator that follows an operand. Both the increment (++) and decrement (−−) operators can be applied postfix. *See also* prefix operator.

postorder traversal—A traversal of the nodes in a tree in which the left and right subtrees are examined before the current node is examined.

precedence—*See* operator precedence.

prefix operator—An operator that precedes an operand. Both the increment (++) and decrement (−−) operators can be applied prefix. *See also* postfix operator.

preorder traversal—A traversal of the nodes in a tree in which the current node is examined before any of its subtrees are examined.

primitive data type—A data type that comes with a definition supplied by a programming language.

printable characters—Any character that can be displayed on a monitor or printed by a printer. *See also* nonprintable characters.

priority queue—A queue in which elements are dealt with in the order of their importance.

private—A Java reserved word for a visibility modifier. Private methods and variables are not inherited by subclasses, and can only be accessed in the class in which they are declared.

procedural programming—An approach to software design and implementation that is centered around procedures. *See also* object-oriented programming.

program—A series of instructions executed by hardware, one after another.

programming language—The syntax and semantics of the statements used to create a program.

programming language statement—An instruction in a given programming language.

prompt—A message that asks the user for information.

prototype—A program used to explore an idea or approach.

pseudocode—Natural language used to write out or describe the algorithmic steps of a program.

pseudo–random number—A number that a program seems to create at random but that really comes from a seed value. It is random enough for most purposes.

public—A Java reserved word for a visibility modifier. A public class or interface can be used anywhere. A public method or variable is inherited by all subclasses and is accessible anywhere.

pure object-oriented language—An object-oriented programming language that enforces software development using an object-oriented approach.

push button—A graphical user interface component that lets the user initiate an action with a mouse click. *See also* check box, radio button.

queue—An abstract data type that manages information in a first-in, first-out manner.

quick sort—A sorting algorithm that divides a list into two sublists and sorts each sublist.

radio button—A graphical user interface component that lets the user choose one of a set of options with a mouse click. A radio button is useful only as part of a group of other radio buttons. *See also* check box.

RAM—*See* random access memory.

random access device—A memory device whose information can be directly accessed. *See also* random access memory.

random access memory (RAM)—Basically the same as main memory. Should probably be called read-write memory, to distinguish it from read-only memory.

random number generator—Software that produces a pseudo–random number, using calculations based on a seed value.

read-only memory (ROM)—Any memory device whose stored information is stored permanently when the device is created. It can be read from, but not written to.

recursion—A method invoking itself. Recursive algorithms sometimes provide elegant, though perhaps inefficient, solutions to a problem.

reference—A variable that holds the address of an object. In Java, a reference can be used to interact with an object, but its address cannot be accessed, set, or operated on directly.

refinement—The development stage at which one part of the system, such as the user interface or a particular algorithm, is addressed.

register—A small storage area in the CPU.

rehashing—A way of handling collisions in a hashtable. When a collision occurs, a new hash code is calculated.

relational operator—One of several operators: less than (<), less than or equal to (<=), greater than (>), and greater than or equal to (>=). *See also* equality operator.

release—A version of a software product that is made available ("released") to the customer.

repetition statement—A statement that is executed over and over as long as a particular condition is true. The body of the repetition statement should eventually make the condition false. Also called an iteration statement or loop. *See also* for, while.

requirements—(1) What a program must and must not do. (2) An early phase of the software development process in which the program requirements are established.

reserved word—A word that has special meaning in a programming language and that cannot be used for any other purpose.

return—A Java reserved word that causes the flow of program execution to return from a method to the point where it was called.

return type—The type of value returned from a method. The return type appears before the method name in the method declaration. If the return type is void, no value is returned.

reuse—Using software components to create new ones.

review—Looking at a design or program for errors. There are many types of reviews.

RGB values—Three values that define a color: red, green, and blue.

ROM—*See* read-only memory.

root node—The root of a tree. The root is the only node without a parent.

runtime error—A problem during program execution that causes the program to crash. *See also* compile-time error, logical error, syntax error.

scope—The areas in a program where an identifier, such as a variable, can be referenced. *See also* access.

scroll pane—A graphical user interface container that lets the user "scroll" up and down or from side to side, to see more of partly hidden text or graphics.

SDK—*See* Software Development Kit.

searching—Looking for a target value or a list of values. *See also* binary search, linear search.

secondary memory—Hardware storage devices, such as magnetic disks or tapes, which store information more or less permanently. *See also* main memory.

seed value—A value used by a random number generator to calculate a pseudo-random number.

selection sort—A sorting algorithm in which each value, one at a time, is placed in its final, sorted position. *See also* insertion sort.

selection statement—A statement that is executed if a particular condition is true. *See also* if.

semantics—The interpretation of a program or programming construct.

sentinel value—A value used to indicate a special condition, such as the end of input.

sequential search—*See* linear search.

service methods—Methods in an object that are declared with public visibility and define a service that the object's client can invoke.

set—A collection of elements with no duplicates.

short—A Java reserved word for a primitive integer type, stored using 16 bits in two's complement format.

sibling—Two items in a tree or hierarchy that have the same parent.

sign bit—A bit in a numeric value that represents the sign (positive or negative) of that value.

signed numeric value—A value that stores a sign (positive or negative). All Java numeric values are signed. A Java character is stored as an unsigned value.

signature—The number, types, and order of the parameters of a method. Overloaded methods must each have a unique signature.

software—Programs and data.

software component—*See* component.

Software Development Kit (SDK)—A collection of software development tools. The Java Software Development Kit is another name for the Java Development Kit.

software engineering—Developing and writing software.

sorting—Putting a list of values in order. *See also* insertion sort, selection sort, merge sort, quick sort.

space efficiency—A measure of the amount of memory an algorithm uses.

split pane—A graphical user interface container that displays two components, separated by a moveable divider bar.

stack—An abstract data type that manages data in a last-in, first-out manner.

stack trace—The methods called to reach a certain point in a program. The programmer can use the stack trace to find the cause of errors.

standard I/O stream—One of three common I/O streams: standard input (usually the keyboard), standard output (usually the monitor screen), and standard error (also usually the monitor). *See also* stream.

start angle—The angle at which an arc begins. *See also* arc angle.

state—The state of being of an object, defined by the values of its data. *See also* behavior, identity.

statement—*See* programming language statement.

static—A Java reserved word that describes methods and variables. A static method is also called a class method and can be referenced without an instance of the class. A static variable is also called a class variable and is common to all instances of the class.

static data structure—A data structure that can't grow and shrink as needed. *See also* dynamic data structure.

storage capacity—The total number of bytes that can be stored in a memory device.

stream—A source of input or a destination for output.

string—*See* character string.

string concatenation—The process of attaching the beginning of one character string to the end of another, resulting in one longer string.

strongly typed language—A programming language in which each variable is always matched with a particular data type. Variables are not allowed to take on values or be used in operations besides their type.

structured programming—A kind of programming where each software component has one entry and exit point.

subclass—A class created from another class by inheritance. Also called a derived class or child class. *See also* superclass.

subscript—*See* index.

super—A Java reserved word for the parent class of the object making the reference. Often used to invoke a parent's constructor.

super reference—*See* super.

superclass—The class from which another class is created by inheritance. Also called a base class or parent class. *See also* subclass.

support methods—Methods in an object that are not for use outside the class. They support service methods and are usually not declared with public visibility.

swapping—Exchanging the values of two variables.

swing—The package in the Java API (`javax.swing`) that contains graphical user interface classes. Swing provides components that are not included in the Abstract Windowing Toolkit package, but does not replace it.

syntax rules—Rules for writing valid statements.

syntax error—An error caused by breaking the syntax rules. Syntax errors are a subset of compile-time errors. *See also* compile-time error, logical error, runtime error, syntax rules.

target value—What a search is looking for.

TCP/IP—Software that controls messages crossing the Internet. Stands for Transmission Control Protocol/Internet Protocol.

terabyte (TB)—A unit of binary storage, equal to 2^{40} (approximately 1 trillion) bytes.

termination—Where a program stops executing.

test case—A set of values and user actions used to find problems in a system.

testing—(1) Running a program with test cases in order to discover problems. (2) Evaluating a design or program.

text area—The GUI area that displays, or lets the user enter, several lines of text.

text field—The GUI area that displays, or lets the user enter, a single line of text.

text file—A file that contains data as ASCII or Unicode characters.

this—A Java reserved word for the object executing the code making the reference.

throw—A Java reserved word used to start an exception propagation.

time efficiency—How quickly an algorithm works, based on the number of operations it needs to do. For example, the efficiency of a sort can be measured by the number of comparisons required to sort a list. *See also* order.

timer—An object that generates an event at regular intervals.

token—Part of a string defined by a set of delimiters.

tool tip—A short line of text that appears when the mouse pointer rests on a component. Usually, tool tips tell the user what the component is for.

top-level domain—The last part of a network domain name, such as edu or com.

tree—A data structure hierarchy that "grows" from a single root node.

true—A Java reserved word that is one of the two boolean literals (`true` and `false`).

truth table—A complete list of all of values in a boolean expression, as well as the computed result.

two-dimensional array—An array that uses two indices for the location of one element. The two are usually the rows and columns of a table. *See also* multidimensional array.

two's complement—A way of representing numeric binary data. Used by all Java integer primitive types (`byte`, `short`, `int`, `long`).

type—*See* data type.

unary operator—An operator that uses only one operand.

underflow—When a floating point value is too small for its storage size, which can result in inaccurate arithmetic processing. *See also* overflow.

Unicode—The international character set of valid Java characters. Each character is represented using a 16-bit unsigned numeric value.

uniform resource locator (URL)—A name for a resource, used by a Web browser.

unsigned numeric value—A value that does not store a sign (positive or negative). Java characters are stored as unsigned numeric values, but all primitive numeric types are signed.

URL—*See* uniform resource locator.

use relationship—A relationship between two classes, often shown in a class diagram, in which one class uses another in some way.

user interface—The way the user interacts with a software system, which is often graphical. *See also* graphical user interface.

variable—An identifier in a program that represents a memory location in which a data value is stored.

visibility modifier—A Java modifier that defines how a construct can be accessed.

void—A Java reserved word that indicates no value is returned.

volatile—Describes a memory device that loses stored information when the power supply is interrupted. Main memory is a volatile storage device. *See also* nonvolatile.

von Neumann architecture—The computer architecture named after John von Neumann, in which programs and data are stored together in the same memory devices.

WAN—*See* wide-area network.

waterfall model—One of the earliest software development process models, which moves directly from requirements to design to implementation to testing.

Web—*See* World Wide Web.

while—A Java reserved word for a repetition construct. A `while` statement is executed zero or more times. *See also* for.

white space—Spaces, tabs, and blank lines that are used to set off sections of source code to make programs more readable.

wide-area network (WAN)—A computer network that connects two or more local area networks, usually across long distances. *See also* local-area network.

widening conversion—A conversion between two values of different but compatible data types. Widening conversions usually leave the data value intact. *See also* narrowing conversion.

word—A unit of binary storage. The size of a word is usually two, four, or eight bytes.

World Wide Web (WWW or Web)—Software that makes the exchange of information across a network easier by providing a common user interface for many types of information. Web browsers are used to retrieve and format HTML documents.

wrapper class—A class designed to store a primitive type in an object. Usually used when an object reference is needed and a primitive type would not be enough.

WWW—*See* World Wide Web.

The Java programming language uses the Unicode character set. A *character set* is simply a list of characters, each with a numeric value. Unicode is an international character set that contains letters, symbols, and ideograms for languages all over the world. Each character is represented as a 16-bit unsigned numeric value. Unicode, therefore, can support over 65,000 unique characters. Only about half of those values have characters assigned to them at this point. Characters from various languages are added from time to time.

Many programming languages still use the ASCII character set. ASCII stands for the American Standard Code for Information Interchange. The 8-bit extended ASCII set is quite small, so the developers of Java decided to use Unicode so they could include characters from more languages, such as letters with umlauts (German) and inverted question marks (Spanish). However, ASCII is essentially a subset of Unicode, including corresponding numeric values, so programmers used to ASCII should have no problems with Unicode.

Figure B.1 lists commonly used characters and their Unicode numeric values. These characters also happen to be ASCII characters. All of the characters in Figure B.1 are called *printable characters* because they can be displayed on a monitor or printed by a printer. Other characters are called *nonprintable characters* because they can't normally be seen. Note that the space character (numeric value 32) is considered a printable character, even though no symbol is printed when it is displayed. Nonprintable characters are sometimes called *control characters* because many of them can be generated by holding down the control key on a keyboard and pressing another key.

The Unicode characters with numeric values 0 through 31 are nonprintable characters. Also, the delete character, with numeric value 127, is a nonprintable character. All of these characters are ASCII characters as well. Many of them have fairly common and well-defined uses, while others are more general. The table in Figure B.2 lists a small sample of the nonprintable characters.

Nonprintable characters are used in many situations to represent special conditions. For example, certain nonprintable characters can be stored in a text document to indicate, among other things, the beginning of a new line. An editor will process these characters by starting the text that follows it on a new line, instead of printing a symbol to the screen. Various types of computer systems use different nonprintable characters to represent particular conditions.

Value	Char	Value	Char	Value	Char	Value	Char	Value	Char
32	*space*	51	3	70	F	89	Y	108	l
33	!	52	4	71	G	90	Z	109	m
34	"	53	5	72	H	91	[	110	n
35	#	54	6	73	I	92	\	111	o
36	$	55	7	74	J	93	]	112	p
37	%	56	8	75	K	94	^	113	q
38	&	57	9	76	L	95	_	114	r
39	'	58	:	77	M	96	`	115	s
40	(	59	;	78	N	97	a	116	t
41	)	60	<	79	O	98	b	117	u
42	*	61	=	80	P	99	c	118	v
43	+	62	>	81	Q	100	d	119	w
44	'	63	?	82	R	101	e	120	x
45	–	64	@	83	S	102	f	121	y
46	.	65	A	84	T	103	g	122	z
47	/	66	B	85	U	104	h	123	{
48	0	67	C	86	V	105	i	124		
49	1	68	D	87	W	106	j	125	}
50	2	69	E	88	X	107	k	126	~

figure B.1   A small portion of the Unicode character set

Except for having no visible representation, nonprintable characters are the same as printable characters. They can be stored in a Java character variable and be part of a character string. They are stored using 16 bits, can be converted to their numeric value, and can be compared using relational operators.

The first 128 characters of the Unicode character set are the same as the common ASCII character set. The first 256 characters are the same as the ISO-Latin-1 extended ASCII character set. Many operating systems and Web browsers will handle these characters, but they may not be able to print the other Unicode characters.

Value	Character
0	null
7	bell
8	backspace
9	tab
10	line feed
12	form feed
13	carriage return
27	escape
127	delete

figure B.2   Some nonprintable characters in the Unicode character set

Java operators are evaluated according to the precedence levels shown in Figure C.1. Operators at low precedence levels are evaluated before operators at higher levels. Operators in the same precedence level are evaluated according to the association (fourth column), either right to left (R to L) or left to right (L to R). Operators in the same precedence level are not listed in any particular order.

Precedence Level	Operator	Operation	Associates
1	[ ]	array indexing	L to R
	•	object member reference	
	(parameters)	parameter evaluation and method invocation	
	++	postfix increment	
	− −	postfix decrement	
2	++	prefix increment	R to L
	− −	prefix decrement	
	+	unary plus	
	−	unary minus	
	!	logical NOT	
3	new	object instantiation	R to L
	(type)	cast	
4	*	multiplication	L to R
	/	division	
	%	remainder	
5	+	addition	L to R
	+	string concatenation	
	−	subtraction	
6	<	less than	L to R
	<=	less than or equal	
	>	greater than	
	>=	greater than or equal	
7	==	equal	L to R
	!=	not equal	

figure C.1   Java operator precedence

Precedence Level	Operator	Operation	Associates
8	=	assignment	R to L
	+=	addition, then assignment	
	+=	string concatenation, then assignment	
	_=	subtraction, then assignment	
	*=	multiplication, then assignment	
	/=	division, then assignment	
	%=	remainder, then assignment	

figure C.1   Java operator precedence, continued

You can always override the order of operator evaluation by using parentheses. It's a good idea to use parentheses even when you don't need them to make it clear to a human reader how an expression is evaluated.

For some operators, the operand types decide which operation is carried out. For instance, if the + operator is used on two strings, string concatenation is performed, but if it is applied to two numeric types, they are added in the arithmetic sense. If only one of the operands is a string, the other is converted to a string, and string concatenation is performed.

This appendix is a reference for all of the classes and interfaces (and their methods) from the Java standard class library that are part of the AP subset. The classes are listed in alphabetical order. The package each class is contained in is given in parentheses after the class name.

ArrayList (java.util) implements List

A class that represents a resizable array implementation of a list.

constructors

`public ArrayList()`
   Creates an empty list.

methods

`public void add(int index, Object element)`
   Inserts the element into this list at the index.

`public boolean add(Object obj)`
   Appends the element to the end of this list.

`public Object get(int index)`
   Returns the element at the index. Throws `IndexOutOfBoundsException` if the index is out of range.

`public Iterator iterator()`
   Returns an `Iterator` containing the elements in this list.

`public ListIterator listIterator()`
   Returns a `ListIterator` containing the elements in this list.

`public Object remove(int index)`
   Removes and returns the object at the index in this list. Throws `IndexOutOfBoundsException` if the index is out of range.

`public Object set(int index, Object obj)`
   Replaces the element at the index with the object.

`public int size()`
   Returns the number of elements in this list.

Comparable (java.lang)

An interface for comparing one object to another.

methods

`public int compareTo (Object other)`

Compares this object to `other`. If they are equal, returns zero. If this object is less than `other`, returns an int less than zero. If this object is greater than `other`, returns an `int` greater than zero.

Double (java.lang) implements Comparable

A class that represents the double primitive type.

constructors

`public Double(double arg)`

Creates an instance of the `Double` class from the parameter `arg`.

methods

`public double doubleValue()`

Returns the value of the current object as a double.

`public int compareTo()(Object param)`

Compares this `Double` to `param`. Returns zero if they are equal, less than zero if this `Double` is less than `param`, or greater than zero if this `Double` is greater than `param`.

`public boolean equals(Object param)`

Returns a true value if this `Double` is equal to the specified parameter (`param`).

`public String toString()`

Returns the string representation of the current object.

HashMap (java.util) implements Map

A class representing a map containing key-value pairs, using a hashtable for storage.

constructors

```
public HashMap ()
```
Creates an empty map.

methods

```
public boolean containsKey (Object key)
```
Returns true if this map contains the key.

```
public Object get (Object key)
```
Returns the value to which the key maps, or null if this map does not contain the key.

```
public Set keySet ()
```
Returns a Set containing the keys in this map.

```
public Object put (Object key, Object value)
```
Adds the key-value pair to this map. The value previously associated with the key is returned, or null if there was previously no mapping for the key.

```
public int size ()
```
Returns the number of key-value pairs in this map.

HashSet (java.util) implements Set

A class representing a set of elements, using a hashtable for storage of the elements.

constructors

```
public HashSet ()
```
Creates an empty set.

methods

```
public boolean add (Object obj)
```
Adds the element to this set if it is not already present. Returns true if the element was added to the set, false if it was already there.

```
public boolean contains (Object obj)
```
Returns true if this set contains the specified element.

```
public Iterator iterator ()
```
Returns an iterator over the elements in this set.

```
public boolean remove (Object obj)
```
Removes the specified element from this set if it is present. Returns true if this set contained the specified element, false otherwise.

```
public int size ()
```
Returns the number of elements in this set.

Integer (java.lang) implements Comparable

A class that represents the int primitive type.

constructors

```
public Integer(int num)
```
Creates an instance of the Integer class from the parameter num.

methods

```
public int compareTo(Object num)
```
Compares this integer to num. Returns zero if they are equal, less than zero if this integer is less than num, or greater than zero if this integer is greater than num.

```
public int intValue()
```
Returns the value of this integer as an int.

```
public boolean equals(Object num)
```
Returns the result of an equality comparison against num.

```
public String toString()
```
Returns the string representation of this integer.

Iterator (java.util)

An interface for a group of objects and a way move through the objects one at a time.

methods

```
public boolean hasNext ()
```
Returns true if the executing object contains one or more objects that have not been returned by the next method.

`public Object next ()`
   Returns a reference to the next object in the iterator.

`public void remove ()`
   Removes the item most recently returned by the `next` method from the collection.

LinkedList (java.util) implements List

A class that represents a list using a linked list implementation.

constructors

`public LinkedList ()`
   Creates an empty list.

methods

`public Iterator iterator ()`
   Returns an iterator of the elements in the list.

`public ListIterator listIterator ()`
   Returns a `ListIterator` of the elements in this list.

`public int size ()`
   Returns the number of elements in this list.

`public void add (Object obj)`
   Adds the element to the end of this list.

`public void addFirst (Object obj)`
   Adds the element to the beginning of this list.

`public void addLast (Object obj)`
   Adds the element to the end of this list.

`public Object getFirst ()`
   Returns the first element in this list.

`public Object getLast ()`
   Returns the last element in this list.

`public Object removeFirst ()`
   Removes and returns the first element from this list.

`public Object removeLast ()`
   Removes and returns the last element from this list.

List (java.util)

An interface that represents a list of elements.

methods

`public boolean add (Object obj)`
  Adds an element to the end of the list.

`public int size ()`
  Returns the number of elements in the list.

`public Iterator iterator ()`
  Returns an iterator of the elements in the list.

`public ListIterator listIterator ()`
  Returns a `ListIterator` of the elements in the list.

ListIterator (java.util) extends Iterator

An interface for a list of objects and a way to move through the list elements one at a time.

methods

`public boolean hasNext ()`
  Returns true if the executing object contains one or more objects that have not been returned by the `next` method.

`public Object next ()`
  Returns a reference to the next object in the iterator.

`public void remove ()`
  Removes the item most recently returned by the `next` method from the collection.

`public void add (Object obj)`
  Inserts the element `obj` into the list immediately after the last element that was returned by `next`.

`public void set (Object obj)`
  Replaces the last element returned by `next` with the element `obj`.

Map (`java.util`)

An interface for key-value pairs.

methods

`public boolean containsKey (Object key)`
Returns true if this map contains the key.

`public Object get (Object key)`
Returns the value to which the key maps, or `null` if this map does not contain the key.

`public Set keySet ()`
Returns a `Set` containing the keys in this map.

`public Object put (Object key, Object value)`
Adds the key-value pair to this map. The old value of the key is returned, or `null` if there was no old value for the key.

`public int size ()`
Returns the number of key-value pairs in this map.

Math (`java.lang`)

A class that contains methods to perform various math operations.

methods

`public static double abs(double num)`
`public static int abs(int num)`
Returns the absolute value of the parameter.

`public static double pow(double base, double exponent)`
Returns the result of base to exponent.

`public static double sqrt(double num)`
Returns the square root of parameter num.

Object (`java.lang`)

A class that is the root of the hierarchy tree for all classes in Java.

constructors

`public Object()`
Creates a new instance of the object class.

methods

```
public boolean equals(Object arg)
```
Returns a true value if the current object is equal to `arg`.

```
public int hashCode()
```
Returns a hash code for the current object.

```
public String toString()
```
Returns a string representation of the current object.

Random (java.util)

A class that produces sequences of pseudo-random numbers.

constructors

```
public Random()
```

methods

```
public double nextDouble()
```
Returns a random number between 0.0 and 1.0.

```
public int nextInt(int num)
```
Returns a random number in the range 0 to num $- 1$.

Set (java.util)

An interface representing a set of elements.

methods

```
public boolean add (Object obj)
```
Adds the element to this set if it is not already there. Returns true if the element was added to the set, false if it was already there.

```
public boolean contains (Object obj)
```
Returns true if this set contains the element.

```
public Iterator iterator ()
```
Returns an iterator over the elements in this set.

```
public boolean remove (Object obj)
```
Removes the element from this set if it is there. Returns true if this set contained the element, false otherwise.

```
public int size ()
```
Returns the number of elements in this set.

String (java.lang)

A class that contains methods for creating and parsing strings. Because the contents of a string cannot be modified, many of the methods return a new string.

constructors

`public String()`

Creates a new string of no characters.

`public String(String str)`

Creates an instance of the `String` class from the parameter `str`.

methods

`public int compareTo(String str)`

Compares the current object to `str`. If both strings are equal, 0 (zero) is returned. If the current string is less than the argument, an `int` less than zero is returned. If the current string is greater than the argument, an `int` greater than zero is returned.

`public boolean equals(Object arg)`

Returns true if the current object is equal to `arg`. `arg` must not be null and must be exactly as long as and with exactly the same content as the current object.

`public int indexOf(String str)`

Returns the index of the first occurrence of the string `str` in the current object. Returns a −1 if there is no such occurrence.

`public int length()`

Returns the integer length of the current object.

`public String substring(int startindex)`

`public String substring(int startindex, int lastindex)`

Returns the substring of the current object starting with `startindex` and ending with `lastindex-1` (or the last index of the string in the case of the first method).

TreeMap (java.util) implements Map

A class representing a map containing key-value pairs, using a tree for storage.

constructors

```
public TreeMap ()
```
Creates an empty map.

methods

```
public boolean containsKey (Object key)
```
Returns true if this map contains the key.
```
public Object get (Object key)
```
Returns the value to which the key maps, or null if this map does not contain the key.
```
public Set keySet ()
```
Returns a Set containing the keys in this map.
```
public Object put (Object key, Object value)
```
Adds the key-value pair to this map. The old value of the key is returned, or null if there was no old value for the key.
```
public int size ()
```
Returns the number of key-value pairs in this map.

TreeSet (java.util) implements Set

A class representing a set of elements, using a tree for storage of the elements.

constructors

```
public TreeSet ()
```
Creates an empty set.

methods

```
public boolean add (Object obj)
```
Adds the element to this set if it is not already there. Returns true if the element was added to the set, false if it was already there.
```
public boolean contains (Object obj)
```
Returns true if this set contains the element.

`public Iterator iterator ()`
 Returns an iterator over the elements in this set.

`public boolean remove (Object obj)`
 Removes the element from this set if it is there. Returns true if this set contained the element, false if it did not.

`public int size ()`
 Returns the number of elements in this set.